From Tsar to Soviets

the Russian people and their revolution, 1917–21

Christopher Read
University of Warwick

New York
Oxford University Press
1996

First published in 1996 by UCL Press

UCL Press Limited
University College London
Gower Street
London WC1E 6BT

The name of University College London (UCL) is a registered
trade mark used by UCL Press with the consent of the owner.

First published in the United States in 1996 by
Oxford University Press, Inc.
198 Madison Avenue
New York, NY 10016

ISBNs: Cloth: 0-19-521242-8
         Paper: 0-19-521241-X

Printed and bound in Great Britain.

Library of Congress Cataloging-in-Publication Data are available

Typeset in Classical Garamond.
Printed and bound by
Biddles Ltd, Guildford & King's Lynn, England.

Contents

To my mother and the memory of my father
as well as to
Françoise, Alexandra and Natalia

Quand on n'est pas les plus riches, on doit être les plus sages.
If you are not the wealthiest you have to be the most prudent.

Zola, *Germinal*

Preface

Non-academic friends who hear one is writing a book on the Russian revolution tend to think it rather specialized. Academic friends ask: "What aspect are you looking at?" Today the Russian revolution is considered a broad topic and as such anyone who ventures to write about it is extremely indebted to a wide range of scholars who have produced the specialized work on which a broader appraisal must rely. I am no exception. The present book would not have been possible without the help and inspiration of many friends and colleagues. At the risk of being over-selective I would like to record my thanks to a whole range of stimulating teachers who helped nurture my interest in Russia, in particular: Donald Nichol, Evgenii Lampert, James White, Jacob Miller, Jack Gray, Martin Dewhirst, Peter Reddaway and the late Leonard Schapiro and Alec Nove. My colleagues old and new in the history department at Warwick have been an endless source of information and ideas as have several generations of full-time and part-time students of the department. Particular thanks are due to Edward Countryman with whom I had many conversations comparing the American and Russian revolutions as we ran round our regular circuit. I am, as ever, indebted to many Russian and ex-Soviet friends, notably Anne Kurepalu, Lucy Lezhneva and Slava Nemodruk. The Study Group on the Russian Revolution has provided, for more than 20 years now, an ideal collaborative rather than competitive scholarly environment for testing theories, finding out new facts and keeping up with current scholarship. I am particularly indebted to those who have read drafts or answered queries relating to the present volume, in particular, John Channon, Martin Lowry, Roger Magraw, Mark Levene, Evan Mawdsley, Howard White and Geoff Swain who also kindly allowed me to see the final draft of his book on the origins of the Russian civil war. I would especially like to thank Edward Acton and Dan Orlovsky for reading the entire manuscript. Their suggestions were extremely useful and have helped to make vast improvements. Steve Kerensky's stimulating views have given a new dimension to the later stages of preparing this volume. I would like to thank Sarah Richardson for valuable help on the IT side and Steven Gerrard and UCL Press for their support. Finally, I would like to record my thanks to Françoise and my mother, Joan. I am especially sorry that my father did not live to see the completion of a book he was looking forward to reading. As usual, Alexandra and Natalia have been a hindrance to the completion of my work but without them life would be monochrome.

Note on conventions and transliteration

A minor consequence of the collapse of the Soviet Union has been an increase in problems of nomenclature and transliteration. In the present study, cities are called by the names they had at the time. "Russia" is usually shorthand for the mainly Orthodox Slavic heartland including Byelorussia and Ukraine, though it sometimes, as the context hopefully makes clear, refers to the whole entity of the Russian Empire or Russian Federation (the official name during most of the revolutionary period). Familiar Russian transliterations have been preferred (Kiev rather than Kiyiv, Vatsetis rather than Vacietis) but less well known names have been given in more national forms (Hulyai Pole, Donbas). Dates given are those in use in Russia at the time (that is old style until 1 February 1918) unless otherwise stated. The terms *volost'* (parish), *uezd* (county) and *guberniia* (province) have been preferred to their English equivalents, as have a number of terms of measurement: *desiatina* (1.09 hectares), *sazhen'* (2.13m), *arshin* (0.71m) and *pud* (16.3 kilos). In most cases the plurals have been anglicized.

The term "ordinary people" (or, occasionally, "the people") carries considerable explanatory weight in the text and needs clarifying from the outset. It is intended to be an equivalent to the Russian term *narod*. It includes the mass of uneducated mainly manual labourers and their families from town and countryside and excludes the better educated, professional, gentry and aristocratic classes, – that is the elite – although there are cases where individuals, particularly from the intelligentsia, identified with the former. Intermediate groups, like clerks, civil servants and those in the armed forces, were split with lower levels tending to identify with the *narod*, higher levels with the elite. Artisans tended to be part of the *narod*, while entrepreneurs often aspired to the elite. Precise delimitations are not possible, not least because self-identification is a key element in the definition.

Finally, the bibliography and sources have been produced with the English-speaking reader in mind so that, for example, the works of Lenin are quoted from English editions. I have also tried to keep footnoting to a minimum hoping that specialists will be aware of items that are being alluded to. Of course, any direct borrowings are referenced in the conventional way.

Introduction

A new way of looking at the Russian revolution is emerging. Twenty years ago, Petrograd was seen as the pacemaker of revolution, each stage beginning in the capital and spreading to the country, putting considerable emphasis on national politics conducted in the capital. The almost exclusive actors in the drama were the Provisional Government, the Petrograd Soviet and the leaders of the main parties within them. In particular, the conspiratorial role of the Bolsheviks was often stressed. Such a view, in simple form, can no longer be sustained. For some two decades now revisionist historians have paid more attention to social and, though still to a surprisingly small extent, economic history. The grass roots began to be understood better, though workers and the major cities of Petrograd and Moscow were still the centre of attention. Peasants and the provinces remained largely unexamined. Even more surprising, there were relatively few studies of soldiers and sailors who were deemed to be peasants (or, in some cases, workers) in uniform. Even so, the revisionists made it clear that without taking account of pressures *from* the provinces and the grass roots, the evolution of high politics could not be understood. Today there is more emphasis on the multitude of conflicting pressures and aspirations released by the collapse of the autocracy. There is a greater awareness of the activity of ordinary people as rational participants in the revolution in their own right. The various regional Russian and non-Russian populations of the Empire experienced revolutions different from one another in origin, aspiration, evolution and outcome, depending on local conditions such as proximity to the war front, the number of landowners, the density of population or the fertility of the soil. As a result, events in the Russian Empire do not constitute a single revolution but a multitude of sometimes conflicting revolutions. Every social group, every nationality, every region, every town, every village, had its own revolution.

The building block of each revolution was the individual, and, although there are no "typical" examples since every person is unique, one must bear in mind that people – their hopes, their achievements, their sufferings, their failures – lie beneath the abstractions with which one is forced to deal. Consider two contrasting cases. Karl Ranni, was born in Estonia to a family of farm labourers who moved to the town of Narva, on the edge of the St. Petersburg region, in search of work. When the revolution broke out he was a telegraphist in his early twenties. The war had brought a great demand for his services, modern communications being essential to military endeavour. The revolution of 1917 found him in Kronstadt. He had already been in contact with revolutionaries in Narva and he was one of 200 Kronstadt sailors selected to greet Lenin on his arrival at the Finland Station on 3 April. "I joined the guard of honour. We stood in a circle around the legendary armoured car from which Lenin spoke – so I was lucky, I heard every word of it." He also took part in the October revolution, travelling with thousands of other Kronstadters, to Petrograd. "We naval telegraphists were ordered to guard the central telegraph and telephone exchange to cut off the Provisional Government from its loyal military units. This done, we had only the Winter Palace government residence to take, and I was among those who stormed it." Ranni remembers climbing over a high, spiked gate but also recalls, more in accordance with other accounts, that "there was a tiny side gate with a flimsy lock . . . .The friendly side gate let us all in: soldiers, sailors and insurgent workers." Soon after, Ranni's life and career, as many others, became "like a dream – many things were in those days." It might be truer to say that it was more like one of the wilder fairground rides with its unpredictable precipitous climbs, dark moments of fear and rapid falls. Several days after power was taken he volunteered to work as Lenin's telegraphist becoming Commissar of the Central Telegraph Office, a "spectacular promotion." After personally organizing Ranni's lodgings and canteen pass, Lenin returned and "told me that the higher post and telegraph officials were engaged in sabotage and it was his idea to have them replaced by 'smaller' experts – I, now Commissar – was to head them. My duties included reports to Dzerzhinsky [future head of the Cheka] about all acts of sabotage." Interestingly, he appears to have joined the party only in 1919. When the capital moved to Moscow, Ranni returned to Kronstadt. He was still there during the uprising in 1921 when he was imprisoned by the insurgents "sentenced to death and . . . kept in the Totleben Fort for twenty days, every minute expecting the firing squad." When the mutiny was suppressed it was his captors who suffered that fate. In 1930 he was transferred to Moscow only to be dismissed as "politically unreliable", despite his services for Lenin, possibly because he was an Estonian. Two of his brothers were shot and one sister was exiled in these terrible years. The Second World War found him back in Estonia as a part of the Soviet Army that now occupied that formerly independent country. He moved forward with the Soviet advance, eventually becoming one of many Soviet soldiers who, literally, "left their signatures on the walls of the fallen Reichstag". He eventually retired, with the rank of colonel, to Abramtsevo, near Moscow, building his own house and furniture from wood. Well into his nineties, Colonel Ranni made forays into Moscow to talk to young people and bear witness to his past, a living icon of the twists and turns of Soviet history.[1]

For Alexei Bashkirev the path of revolution ran in the opposite direction, from Gentleman of the Chamber of His Imperial Majesty Nicholas II to peasant and wanderer. It would have been hard to get much higher in tsarist society than he before the war. A family estate with a mansion; marriage into one of Russia's leading families, the Sumarokov-Elston's; a fashionable apartment in St. Petersburg and holidays on his wife's family's estates in the Caucasus and the Crimea testified to his wealth and status. In peacetime his duties in royal service had been in the relatively undemanding administration of the Imperial Forest in Poland, followed by "a long-desired" transfer to St. Petersburg to an equally untaxing "coveted position"[2] on the staff of the Imperial Theatres. The war brought him back to his 1st Fusilier Guards Regiment. He fought – briefly, because he was captured at Tannenberg and remained a prisoner of war until the end of 1918 – to defend the sacred soil of Russia, the tsar and social order. When it became clear by 1916 that all three were even more in danger than ever, his wife's first cousin, Prince Felix Yusupov, assassinated the supposed source of the rot, Grigorii Rasputin, a murder that brought Yusupov the short-lived punishment of exile to his estates. The shocks of the revolution began to burst very early on the Bashkirev family and its property. The Petrograd apartment was invaded during the February revolution by insurgent sailors who claimed a sniper had fired on them from one of the windows. A prominently displayed photograph of Uncle Felix who, "since the killing of Rasputin . . . had become a popular hero", "changed their attitude completely."[3] This was, however, only a foretaste. Hope in General Kornilov as a potential saviour of propertied Russia collapsed when Kerensky "to maintain his own popularity . . . had chased (him) out".[4] The clouds of defeat in the war – "how I loathed those revolutionaries who had brought this about" his daughter wrote[5] – brought deepening disaster. The Bashkirev family began to concentrate around their modest estate at Kurbatika, near the town of Ostrovsky in the Nizhnii-Novgorod region. The revolution continually encroached on the estate despite a robust defence of it in the face of the new authorities by Bashkirev's redoubtable mother, the Princess Chegodaev-Zakonsky. At the same time, Bashkirev's personal life was also changing. His marriage had fallen apart while he was a prisoner, his wife having taken up with another Guards officer and, on his return, he, the third of the brothers to do so, formed an irregular family with an attractive and strong-minded peasant girl named Mania, whose father was himself the illegitimate result of a Chegodaev liaison with another peasant girl in an earlier generation. After the revolution, his former wife moved to Berlin and, in December 1922, the two daughters of their marriage – Xenia and Zinaida – went to join her under the still extensive patronage of Count Sumarokov, now settled in Nice. Bashkirev refused, until the end, to leave Rus-

3

sia and remained behind with Mania and his other family, making a living for them from his ever-diminishing official land allotment. He spent the 1920s searching for and occasionally finding jobs to make ends meet between harvests. He chopped wood and carried boxes in Moscow, spent nearly a year, from 1923–4, as an Inspector of Finance in the Orenburg region, saving enough money to last six months, and then continued wandering. He was officially divorced from Mania and the land allotment was handed over to her, though he still continued to support her and her four children as best he could. He returned to Kurbatika from time to time, living in one of the huts formerly occupied by peasants. The low point was reached in 1928 when, as a result of a fire, 34 houses in Kurbatika, including his, were burned down. He was left with no possessions and, after purchasing a new hut out of the insurance money, had only 25 roubles to his name. He continued to look for employment, often walking the 100 kilometres to Nizhnii-Novgorod in two days in his quest. He found a job in 1928 and moved into very simple lodgings "with an old crone". By 1932 he had been diagnosed as having angina, "most of the teeth are gone from scurvy" and he was letting his beard grow "so as not to bother with shaving".[6] In the mid-1930s he was still eking out a living from private farming, despite crippling taxes, and supplementing it with odd bits of income from here and there. Only subventions from his daughter Zinaida, by then married to Sean Burke who became an Irish government minister, enabled him and his family to survive. In 1937 they had 11 *desiatina*s of land and were one of six households in Kurbatika who still refused to join the collective farm. The last news of him was a letter from Mania to Zinaida of 23 December 1937 reporting that Alexei, then 62 years old, and his brother had "left home some five months ago". No more was heard of either. One does not have to hesitate too long before assuming their likely fate. From opposite directions, the Bashkirev and Ranni families had found a point of contact in Stalin's camps.

A common theme in the lives of Ranni and Bashkirev is that there were few happy endings. Russian history, from 1900 to 1953 especially, was a long series of traumas reflected in the harshness of the lives of the people who lived through them. The years at the centre of our present attention, 1917–21, have a good claim to be the worst of all, with the exception of the Nazi occupation from 1941–44 which outdid in horror even the depths of the purges. As Mao Tse-tung said, a revolution is not a tea party. It is a raw, brutal, violent upheaval often bringing out the worst, most elemental side of the human character. As such, revolution is the first cousin to war. Neither should be idealized. But, as few historians dwell solely on the awfulness of war (perhaps the fault here is not to dwell on it enough) so one should not fail, as recent historians have done in the analysis of French and contemporary revolutions, to get beyond saying no more than that they are bloody and violent. Historians of war have become adept at analyzing the causes, apportioning the responsibility, weighing up the consequences in a relatively balanced fashion. One can rarely say that a war is caused solely by one side. Similarly, to see only the ineptitude of the Tsar, the political stupidity of his generals, the self-interested obsessions of the business and commercial classes or the crude violence of ordinary people would be to present a caricature. Like war, revolution can be subjected to balanced, rational analysis.

Without romanticizing one can distinguish reasons for the involvement of the various actors. In particular, the main focus of the present volume is to restore the autonomous revolutionary activity of the ordinary population to its rightful place in the overall interpretation of the revolution. The history of the French revolution has gone in the direction of trying to show that the revolution was not "popular" throughout France and did not reflect the political will of the mass of the population. However true or false this picture may be, one cannot deny that, by contrast, in the Russian Empire, the revolution was constantly driven forward by the often spontaneous impulse given to it from the grass roots. In the course of their struggle peasants, workers and, perhaps most important in the short term, soldiers and sailors thought out their programmes and developed tactics to achieve them locally and regionally. Their failure to round this off successfully at national level is one of the key questions dealt with later in the book. Even so, this book could have been called *Citizens* since that is what it is about – an episode in the continuing struggle of ordinary people in the Russian Empire to become conscious actors contributing to decisions affecting their lives.

It should be stressed, however, that, despite the emphasis on the provinces and the grass roots, it would be a mistake to revise Petrograd out of the equation and, as has happened in some interpretations of the French revolution, write high politics out altogether, replacing it with a neo-positivist determinism based on geography, economics or culture. Events at the centre – the February and October revolutions to take the most obvious – do have a great impact. The point, however, is that they should be seen against the background of grass roots and peripheral events. For instance, it was only the profoundly revolutionary situation that made the October takeover possible. *Coup de grâce* it certainly was but it was too deeply linked with the broader situation to be considered a coup d'état in the true sense of the word.

While only by restoring the popular movement to its full role can the richness and complexity of the revolution be brought out, it is, unfortunately, the case that our present state of knowledge does not provide all the information necessary to complete the picture, far from it. Traditionally, historical scholarship concentrated on Petrograd and on high politics. Both western and Soviet historians favoured such an approach because, for better or worse, it gave pride of place to the Bolsheviks and Lenin permitting simplified, ideologically driven, "pro-Soviet" and "anti-Soviet" answers to be given to complex questions. But even within its own range of focus, traditional scholarship left surprising gaps. Only recently have scholars, mostly in the Soviet Union in this case, subjected the Provisional Government to serious scrutiny. The forces of the right are poorly understood. Bearing in mind that these are two key themes in the more thoroughly covered area of high politics, one begins to appreciate the difficulties of looking into the more obscure corners of the revolution.

For the past 20 years "revisionist" scholarship has given less prominence to national politics and opened up the social history of the revolution but the revisionist school has also left gaps. As far as social groups are concerned there is relatively little on artisans, less material than one would like on peasants, next to nothing on religious reactions to the revolution, few studies of gender questions and hardly anything on the intelligentsia, the bourgeoisie and white-collar workers. In the end, only the workers of Moscow and Petrograd have been thoroughly studied, though even within that category skilled, unionized, male, factory workers have attracted much of the attention at the expense of unskilled workers, the service and communications sectors and women workers. Workers in provincial industrial centres – such as the textile mills of Ivanovo-Voznesensk, the mines of the Donbas, the docks of Odessa or the oilfields of the Caspian – are only just beginning to be studied in detail.

Recently, scholarship has turned increasingly to cultural questions, not just those affecting the intelligentsia but popular culture as well. Volumes on the culture of workers, on popular festivals in the revolutionary years and on schools and teachers have taken their place alongside works on Bolshevik culture, cultural policy and the reactions of the scientific, artistic and literary intelligentsia. While the intelligentsia is not central to our concerns in the present study this new body of work will be referred to from time to time. Related areas, such as religion and gender, are germane to the present topic but their impact is, as yet, indeterminate. Clearly issues of gender became more important as the revolution evolved but, in the social polarization of the revolution characteristic of the early years, there can be no doubt that class issues were of greater importance and gender was a subtheme within class boundaries. In other words, there was no significant appeal on gender grounds which overrode the class loyalties, as discussed below, of women and men. Similarly, religion played a less central role than one might have imagined, given the prominence of religion in the lives of Russian peasants and workers, particularly women. Although, as we shall see, Bolshevik activists often needlessly attacked the religious feelings of the people by removing icons, restricting the clergy and church services and sometimes carrying out atrocities against priests and bishops, there is no evidence that such acts caused many people to rethink their position and soften their attitude to the counter-revolutionaries who often tried to play the religious card to win popular sympathy. Given the present state of knowledge, one has to assume that religion and gender were not major driving forces of the revolution though they did have important subsidiary roles to play.

Any observer of recent events in the ex-Soviet Union will also be surprised at the relative lack of attention given to nationality issues. There are several reasons for this. First, the focus of this volume is on Russia and the Ukraine. The fascinating, intertwined histories of the Baltic States, Poland, the Caucasus and Central Asia would require much more space to deal with in a fair and adequate manner. Secondly, for the ordinary population of the Slavic heartland, the question of nationality was of secondary importance. Russian and Ukrainian peasants, for instance, knew that they had more in common with each other than they did with landowners of the same nationality. There is no reason to disagree with Stephen Jones' comment that among the non-Russian peoples "the majority of rural native strata would not qualify as nationally conscious."[7] Nationality issues will be dealt with where appropriate, for instance the anti-semitism and Russian chauvinism of the Whites drove many Jews and national minorities into the Red camp for protection during the civil war. However, as far as the broader canvas of the revolution is concerned, manipulation of national feeling seems, from current evidence, to have been largely an elite affair designed, with very limited success, to break up revolutionary solidarity through intervention from above, although, for the time being, the final word has not been spoken and future scholarship may bring about new emphases.

Such a litany of ignorance brings the whole concept of a book like the present one into question. Yet it seemed worth making the effort for several reasons. Most important, while the gaps remain they are being filled and it is now possible to share impressions with the general reader who does not have the time and inclination to read the, increasingly, hefty primary research works, many of which are in Russian. It is also an appropriate moment to alert the non-specialist to the contours of an emerging "post-revisionist" and "post-Communist" interpretation that goes beyond the limitations of the traditional and revisionist schools in gathering together the social, cultural, political and economic histories of Russia and its regions as well as of the minority nationalities. Of course, no new "definitive" view of the revolution can be put forward. In any case, the present study has a much less ambitious aim – to outline the experiences of the ordinary Russian population and stress their role in the revolution. As a consequence the central focus of the interpretation here offered moves away from the struggle between the Bolsheviks and the counter-revolutionary right, a focus common to both traditional and revisionist schools. Instead it is a central contention of the present volume that, although it has to be taken into account, the threat from the right has been overestimated and the key dynamic of the revolution lay in the relationship between an energetic popular revolution and the Bolsheviks. From this perspective, the tragedy of the revolution lies in the Bolsheviks' failure to recognize the real revolution of the time and instead to pursue their own highly structured presuppositions about what the revolution *should* have been like and what the chief actors *should* have been doing. While they certainly incorporated an important part of the popular revolution they were also blind to other aspects and violently repressed parts of it that they neither liked nor understood.

It follows that the approach to the revolution offered here is important in understanding subsequent Soviet history down to the present (even though 1917 has not been interpreted in the light of what came after but has been seen in its own right). The very complex relationship between the people as a whole and the Bolsheviks dates from 1917. It cannot be reduced to the simple polarities of either an overwhelmingly pro-party nation as presented by Stalinists nor as a totally hostile population pinned down solely by terror as presented by the more bilious of anti-communists. Unless we understand something about the fatal knot between party and people that was tied in 1917, it is difficult to understand the rise of Stalinism (or its decline), to attribute full significance to the Second World War in the evolution of Soviet social and political history (since it was this experience that brought party and people closer than anything preceding it) or to understand the events of the present since the explosion of free expression in the last years of the Soviet Union shows how wrong the simple views of the situation were. Underneath "official" life, traditional ideas and complexity continued to seethe, rushing to the surface once the opportunity presented itself in the second half of the 1980s.

PART ONE

Collapse of a society

CHAPTER ONE

Why was Russia revolutionary?

Revolutions are not caused by revolutionaries. In 1876, Petr Tkachev wrote that:

> The *preparation* of a revolution is not the work of revolutionaries. That is the work of exploiters, capitalists, landowners, priests, police, officials, liberals, progressives and the like. Revolutionaries do not *prepare*, they *make* a revolution.[1]

Russia in the late nineteenth century provides a perfect example. The root causes of the revolution lay in the everyday working of Russian society, particularly its harsh and growing level of exploitation of peasants and workers and the rigid barriers erected against political change. The main losers from tsarism's political immobility were a burgeoning and increasingly restless middle class and a more and more unsettled landed elite, which feared for its own security because tsarism appeared to be less and less capable of ensuring social stability. An examination of Russian society shows how assiduously tsarism was preparing its own downfall, not only because of what it did but, even more important, because of what it failed to do.

Rural crisis

The Russian Empire was overwhelmingly agricultural. The livelihood of the vast majority of its population was based on direct exploitation of the fruits of the land, the forests, the rivers and the coast. But that is about the only generalization one can make about it. The ways in which farming and husbandry were conducted varied enormously. In the Baltic region, German Protestant landowners ran modern capitalist estates. In the heartland of Russia, Orthodox peasants tried to maintain an increasing population on ever more divided plots. In the east there were nomadic Buddhist tent-dwellers. There were tribes of animist hunters in the Siberian forests. In the Caucasus, mountain shepherds maintained traditional customs, including fierce, deep-rooted, feuds. Communities tracing themselves back to the ancient Greeks were still to be found on the shores of the Black Sea, site of Colchis, home of Jason and the Argonauts. There were extremely poor Jewish shtetls in Poland, relatively prosperous Hutterite German farmers on the Volga. Independent-minded cossacks of Russian origin defended their borderland villages in the area north of the Caucasus and the Black Sea against all-comers, particularly Turks. There were Islamic emirates in Central Asia, reindeer-breeding Lapps in northern Finland, Inuit eskimos in the Bering Straits region who crossed to and fro between Russia and its neighbour, the United States. The Russian Empire was a museum of human cultures, an anthropologists' paradise. It had the cultural variety of the British Empire all wrapped into one, vast land mass which covered one-sixth of the land area of the globe and stretched through 180 degrees of longitude. St. Petersburg was as close to New York as it was to Vladivostok, and, until the early twentieth century, it took much less time to get to New York. East to west it stretched further than the distance between San Francisco and London or Paris and Tokyo.

Even within the relatively homogeneous Russian- and Ukrainian-speaking areas (where some 66 per cent of the population lived), fortunes varied enormously. In the southern provinces of New Russia, north of the Black Sea, the grain trade was booming, largely as a result of more efficient landowner production, though, by the early twentieth century, the peasant sector was also marketing a sizeable amount. Moving north, into the Black Earth zone, which stretched in a great crescent from the Rumanian border, through the Ukraine and Central Russia (passing south of Moscow) and on to the middle Volga and the Urals, the contrast was considerable. It was this area which was Russia's arc of rural crisis. The fertility of the land had encouraged landowners to take as much of it as they could in the land settlement following the emancipation of the serfs in 1861. The basic principle of the settlement was that peasants should continue to farm land that had usually been theirs, though, to the disgust of the peasants, they were expected to pay the state for it. But in addition to the heavy mortgage repayment burden incurred, the arbitration of the land went against them. Peasants lost about 25 per cent of their land, a loss that was still keenly felt in 1917. In other areas, for instance in the western borderlands, they gained about the same amount. The explanation for this is that the government was hostile to Polish landowners and was happy to see them deprived of land as a punishment for their anti-Russian sympathies in the 1863 Polish rebellion. In the less fertile north, landowners could not make anything of the land without peasant labour and the settlement went more or less according to its proclaimed principles. Nonetheless, the realities remind us that behind countrywide averages, which suggest that peasants lost about 4 per cent of their land, lie enormous local differences.

In areas less affected by emancipation, such as the Baltic provinces where serfs were few, conditions were different again. Here there were large capitalist estates frequently owned and run by Germans or Swedes, with the local population employed as low-paid agricultural labourers, so there were relatively few peasants. In Siberia, the opposite was true, there were many peasant landholders, mostly migrants from European Russia, and very few noble landowners. This alarmed conservatives such as the Prime Minister, Stolypin, who commented on a trip to Siberia in 1910, that it was "an enormous, rudely democratic country which will soon throttle European Russia."[2]

It was not, however, in Siberia that the revolution was brewing but in European Russia, especially the Black Earth zone. Between 1861 and 1905 the situation grew progressively worse for the peasants here. The main engine-room of the crisis was rising population which put increasing pressure on already inadequate plots. Between 1880 and the 1897 census the population of the Empire rose from 100 million to 130 million. By the time of the 1917 revolution it had risen further to 182 million.[3]

The consequences were severe. Russian agriculture, particularly among peasants, was practically untouched by modern methods. Traditional strip farming and three-field rotation were predominant. Horses and wooden ploughs were universal. Peasant livestock breeding and dairy farming were equally traditional. As a result, productivity barely kept pace with the increase in population. Migration could not counteract the full effects. The number of mouths to feed per hectare of land rose inexorably, particularly in the Central Black Earth region. When one also takes into account the rising tax burden and the fact that, despite increasing internal demand, grain prices were falling in response to international market conditions, the plight of the peasantry in the worst affected areas was visibly deteriorating on all fronts. In 1891–2 the fragile subsistence economy broke down in the middle Volga region and there was a great famine which claimed 400,000 victims.

The fact that, even during the famine, grain was plentiful in other parts of Russia, reminds us, yet again, not to generalize too readily about a country of such contrasts and vastness. Even though some sectors were very badly off, there was economic growth and real incomes for many increased. Over the whole period 1861–1913 the overall economic growth rate is put at around 2.5 per cent. A recent meticulous study by Paul Gregory has made a slight upward revision of the figure for the period 1885–1913 to 3.3 per cent instead of the previously accepted 2.5–3 per cent. Given a population increase of about 1.6 per cent per year, there was a slow growth in per capita incomes. Gregory's picture has been forcefully backed up by Steven Hoch who has argued that the crisis of "overpopulation" has been exaggerated.[4] However, one still has to account for two peasant revolutions.

Less is known about exactly how the growing wealth was distributed, a key factor from the point of view of explaining the revolution. Clearly, the most

The Russian Soviet Federated Socialist Republic (RSFSR) in 1921.

prominent feature of distribution in rural areas was extreme inequality. The landowners were a race apart from the peasants. Social mixing was infrequent, intermarriage almost unknown. Apparently mitigating factors like paternalism might often be seen simply as intrusion by the master into the peasants' own lives. Sexual relations between landowners such as Bashkirev and attractive peasant women can also hardly be seen as a factor diminishing the social barriers. Indeed, the resentments aroused by such relations no doubt fuelled antagonisms, particularly on the part of rival peasant suitors, the women's husbands or their families whose powerlessness would be emphasized in the face of such a situation. There is no evidence of comparable relations between peasant men and women of the landowning class.

Though overwhelmingly traditional the Russian countryside was not unchanging. As the nineteenth century gave way to the twentieth the pressures of modernization began to make themselves felt. Industrial recruiters came round more frequently looking for labourers for the factories. They often returned to the places they knew and particular districts became noted for particular trades – Kaluga produced brickmakers, Vladimir produced carpenters – and they tended to recruit by groups so local links between individuals often persisted into the city. An increasing number of girls left the rural areas to take up domestic positions in towns and cities in the households of the new bourgeoisie, others found a place in the service industries working in the expanding retail services trade. Some migrants would drift down into the world of petty criminals and prostitutes focused on, in Moscow for example, the notorious Khitrov market, near the Kremlin, where the visitor could expect to witness brawls and scuffles and was well advised to keep a tight hold on her or his purse.

Change did not come solely through those who left the village. In the 1860s local councils known as *zemstva* had been set up in many areas. Among other things they provided rudimentary health care and education, agricultural advice for the peasants and oversaw the development of an elementary infrastructure – maintaining roads, constructing bridges, damming rivers and the like. Such activities brought a leaven of intellectuals into rural areas as engineers, doctors and teachers and attracted, in particular, idealistic young men and women who were smitten with the intelligentsia yearning to "serve the people", in this case by what were known as "small deeds" rather than total revolutionary transformation. By 1905, a substantial group of rural intellectuals, particularly schoolteachers, had become increasingly trusted by the peasants and, conversely, mistrusted by the landowners.[5] Literacy began to trickle down into the countryside, widening access to broader cultural horizons.[6] Not all areas were equally affected, some remaining hardly changed at all, but in some areas new ideas and new challenges were coming to the fore. Migration turned hundreds of thousands of peasants into Siberian settlers. Young people with independent sources of income began to challenge the authority of parents and village. Tolstoyan tracts encouraged many to denounce the state, especially after Bloody Sunday in 1905.[7] In a few cases, more common in town than country, scientific ideas, particularly Darwinism, began to filter down to the *narod* and challenge traditional religious beliefs. While these were, as yet, very limited processes, they were signs of the direction in which the peasant community was slowly evolving.[8]

Although landowners constituted a privileged minority they did, none the less, have problems of their own. In the first place, there was considerable inequality among landowners themselves. The landowning class itself formed a miniature stratified pyramid at the top of the national one. The apex was a small group of super-rich and super-privileged families. The Romanovs, the royal family, were at the very top. Their personal holdings were immeasurable. The tiny group of dominant families were a group apart. They were highly westernized in dress and customs and the court followed western European royal protocol adapted from French and German models by the leading force in westernizing the elite, Peter the Great, and his successors. They tended to speak western languages in preference to Russian. French was the most frequently used though Nicholas II wrote to his German-born wife Alexandra in English.

The dynasty and the families grouped around it were the rulers of Russia in every respect. They had oceans of wealth and immense institutional power and privileges. In a real sense, right to the very end, governing Russia was the Romanov family business. All their advisers at court came from within the charmed circle of family members and the tiny elite of leading families. The top army leadership came largely from their ranks, their dominance being particularly overwhelming in the politically vital guards regiments that were the prop of dynastic power. Even the February revolution had aspects of a traditional army-based coup d'état, intended to change one Romanov tsar for another.

The broad domination of society by a tiny traditional caste was completely inappropriate to modern conditions. This began to change slowly in the nineteenth century. Competence, rather than high birth, became an increasingly important prerequisite for government or military office but foot dragging meant that the elite continued to dominate key decision-making right to the end. This added enormously to the frustrations and tensions in Russian society and politics. Here, as much as anywhere, Tkachev's analysis of the roots of revolution was being borne out.

The dominance of the major aristocratic families was untouched by the processes going on beneath them. They resisted social mingling and intermarriage with Russia's growing office-holding nobility and were as remote from most of them as they were from the innumerable country squires and small-scale local gentry who populate many nineteenth-century Russian novels and stories. However, noble rank did not, in itself, guarantee elite status. Some impoverished noble landowners with small plots lived alongside and indistinguishably from their peasants. The flop-houses of Moscow had their share of fallen noblemen. Only nobility combined with substantial landownership or important office holding qualified a person for the elite.

It should also be remembered that the gentry class was itself undergoing something of a decline after the emancipation of the serfs. The number of landowners was falling. In 1861 there had been around 128,000 families who held land. In 1877 there were 115,000. By 1905 the number had fallen to 107,000.[9] The reasons for this seem to lie in the difficulties that many land-owners were experiencing in adapting to post-emancipation conditions. Now that their relations with peasants involved money rather than labour service the gentry were having to sink or swim in an increasingly market-oriented society. Many were finding it difficult. They were often underfinanced and, in any case, if money came their way they might well fall victim to the Russian vice of squandering it either at the card table or on spending sprees. Even attempts by the state to prop up the gentry by establishing a Nobles' Land Bank in 1885, which, until 1894, loaned them money at lower rates than those offered by the Peasants' Land Bank set up in 1883, could not arrest the decline. More and more of their land was mortgaged and the class as a whole was in ever deepening difficulties.

Important structural changes should not, however, blind us to the fact that not all the landowners were losers. As is normal with the type of capitalist, market processes that were developing in Russia after emancipation, the mis-ery of many was the gain of a few and the gentry was no exception. Some, usu-ally larger, landowners were able to consolidate and expand as many smaller ones were forced into selling the last of their property, offering rich pickings for local entrepreneurs, sometimes of peasant background, who were able to buy them out.

Industrial innovation

In many cases, the profits that the more successful landowners and entrepre-neurs were investing in land had come from the expanding, modern, industrial sectors of the Russian economy. The leading sector in Russian industrialization was, as in the United States, the development of a railway network. Between the Crimean war and 1885 the network grew from 1360 to 27,000 km. By 1900 there were 48,000 km and by 1914 77,000 km of track. Growth on such a scale opened up demand for iron, steel, wood, coal and oil to provide rails, locomotives, rolling stock and other equipment. In addition, many new skills were required from engine driving and signalling to timetabling and financial management. Peasants and sons of clerks had to be turned into skilled manual and intellectual workers by tens of thousands. There were also very important economic, political and cultural effects. The existence of a rail network broke down local economic isolation and drew larger and larger areas of the country into the national and, ultimately, the international economy. It also increased personal mobility and made migration and resettlement easier.

Alongside railways, the next most important sources of demand for industrial products were agriculture and the military. They needed machines (such as steam tractors for the former, artillery and warships for the latter) and chemicals (for instance, fertilisers and explosives respectively). By comparison, consumer goods showed less strong growth though there was a large textile industry based in Moscow and the Central Industrial Region and here, too, military orders were important. Much consumer demand was met by imports, particularly of luxury goods for the elite, and, sometimes, by foreign investment.

Though there is some argument about whether direct intervention was as important as had once been thought, no one seriously doubts that the state played a major role in Russian industrialization. Given the fact that the state attempted to dominate all aspects of Russian life it considered to be important, it is not surprising that it should have intervened here, too. There is, however, considerable dispute about its impact. Critics of state intervention have focused on the "inefficiency" factor. For the most dogmatic of them, all state intervention is harmful to the maximization of economic growth. However, real life is about more than high growth indices. Policies reflect dominant political interests not academic calculations of maximum benefit. In the real world it is hard to see what alternative there was. A key aspect of the whole process was the state's desire to keep afloat nationally and internationally, which required more military power. This, in turn, required better communications and a higher level of science and technology. It also required funds. The fact that it was successive ministers of finance who were most actively involved points to the issue of raising revenue. Given the deprived and potentially unstable state of much of the peasantry, particularly in 1891–2 when Sergei Witte came to office as Minister of Finance, and the political unacceptability of taxing those who really had the money, the finance ministry had a problem. How could money be raised least painfully? The promotion of healthier new sectors of the economy offered a solution. Economic growth would provide much needed new funds.

A number of important features of industrialization, some obvious, some less so, help us to understand why Russia was pregnant with revolution. First of all, although Witte was an enthusiastic promoter of industrialization he did not speak for all the powerful groups in the Russian state. There was considerable opposition to his policy from those whose interests were damaged by it. Particularly important in this respect were some landowners whose imported goods, whether agricultural machinery or French wine, cost more as a result of tariffs. In fact, protection meant that high prices had to be paid for a whole range of goods, even those of Russian manufacture. In addition conservatives and reactionaries, who were legion in the corridors of aristocratic power, were fearful of the impact that industrialization might have on the social and spiritual fabric of Russia.

They were not the only ones to be concerned. A deep debate was conducted from the 1850s about what Russia's future should be. Industrialization, which had simply "happened" in Britain and, to a lesser extent France, Germany and the United States, was a much more consciously chosen direction in Russia. Opinion was divided about it – initially, between the Slavophiles and westerners. The former looked at what they considered to be the godless horror of the modern industrial city and concluded that Russia should do its utmost to avoid such a fate. They believed that Russia, with its supposedly faithful Orthodox Christian peasants and its "harmonious" paternalistic institutions, represented a higher morality than the "decadent" west. Their view was energetically opposed by the "westerners" who were contemptuous of Russia's contribution to the culture and well-being of mankind and argued that only wholesale adoption of western culture, values and, for some, economic principles, could drag Russia out of its medieval slough.

As the century progressed the westerners divided into three groupings, liberals, populists and Marxists. Of the three, only the last to emerge, the liberals, whole heartedly supported imitation of the west. In their view Russia's future was to be one of parliamentary democracy, constitutional monarchy and capitalism. The other two were socialist in orientation and shared the left-wing critique that argued that the western European political and economic system was simply bourgeois democracy based on the exploitation of labour. This gave them some common ground with the Slavophiles who were equally opposed to the hypocrisy of liberalism.

There was also some common ground between the Slavophiles and populists over the peasantry, which both idealized, though for diametrically opposed reasons. For the Slavophiles the peasants were essentially conservative, while populists argued that they were potentially revolutionary. The debate was particularly fierce when it came to the peasant commune, seen by the Slavophiles as an ideal element in a hierarchy of paternalistic institutions leading up to the autocrat himself. For them, Russia was one big family. For the populists, the commune was a fundamentally socialist institution in that it, rather than individual peasant households, controlled the peasants' land and decided crucial questions for the community by collective argument and often unanimous agreement. Many communes even redistributed the land between peasant families according to changing needs as one family would grow, through the birth of children, and another become smaller as married members left to form new households.

It was over the potentially revolutionary role of the peasants that the Marxists differed most fundamentally from the populists. For them, the peasants were not very promising revolutionary material because they were too scattered to organize effectively and, in any case, the Marxists argued, their aspirations were to own their property, not to socialize it. Rather it was the workers, the proletariat, the wage labourers, who would lead the revolution. Despite this vital difference it would be wrong to draw too clear a distinction between them. On the one hand, the populists themselves were very interested in Marx's ideas. It was a populist professor of economics, N. Danielson, whose Russian edition was the first translation of Marx's *Das Kapital* into any language. Some populist leaders visited Marx and wrote to him. Marx himself also became interested in populism, though he did not live to complete his investigations into the Russian peasantry. He did, however, appear to give some support to one major populist position, namely that Russia might, under certain conditions, go from feudalism to socialism without having to endure all the miseries of capitalism. For their part, Marxists also retained some populist features, in particular the twin beliefs that it was the duty of the revolutionary intellectual to "serve the people" (a phrase that was, interestingly, made famous by a much later peasant Marxist, Mao Tse-tung) and that they should do this by leading the people, or at least, its revolutionary elements. Even as forthright a castigator of populist principles as Lenin shared some of these features. His theory of the party owed a great deal to populist theory and practice.

Industrialization also had social consequences of which three, in particular, are important for our purposes. The first is that, unlike in other countries, Russian industrialization did not lead to the clear emergence before 1917 of a powerful and confident entrepreneurial middle class. There were a number of reasons for this. In the first place, Russian society was very polarized and, traditionally, there was little middle ground. In a world of serfs and serfowners there was no sizeable halfway house. With emancipation coming only in 1861, there was insufficient time for the legacy of serfdom to be overcome. Secondly, the prominence of the state in industrialization compromised the potential independence of any burgeoning middle class. Even where it did not invest directly the state was important to industrialists through its good offices over securing foreign loans, its promotion of railway building and its placing of orders for armaments – offices that were vital to many of the largest companies. In any case, the state had no intention of allowing a free, independent middle class to emerge. None the less, it was not entirely successful in smothering the growth of such a class and, although the bourgeoisie remained weak, it did show important signs of life in the early twentieth century.

Secondly, industrialization led to the emergence of a class that was, in many crucial respects, peculiar to Russia – the intelligentsia. Its emergence is one of the best examples of Tkachev's analysis. To modernize, tsarism needed more educated people. The larger the educated class the more extensive, conscious and powerful the critics of tsarism became. While most members of the intelligentsia were careerists rather than radicals an active minority grew and formed the nucleus of the emerging political groupings of the centre and left – liberal, populist and Marxist. As a result, the intelligentsia evolved from being members of aristocratic discussion clubs in the mid-century to become a powerful, vocal core of organized political groups by 1905. Even the careerists – teachers, artists, writers, managers, engineers, administrators and some army officers – were prone to radicalization at key moments. Thus, tsarism, that desperately needed their skills, was forced to nurture its own critics.

Thirdly, industrialization did, of course, imply the emergence of another class alongside the bourgeoisie and the intelligentsia – the proletariat. In the decades from 1875 to 1905 millions of peasant men and women flooded into the cities and towns to work in the metal and textile factories, in local and national transport and in domestic and retail services. From the village they brought their tradition of egalitarianism and, sometimes rebellion. In the city, traditional and superstitious elements of their beliefs tended to drop away, to be replaced by material and, sometimes, political ones. Most migrants stayed only for five to ten years at the most, although there was a hard core of workers who had been born in the city. Women workers, who usually worked in textiles, domestic service or shops, stayed the shortest amount of time, leaving the village in their mid- or late teens and returning after marriage in order to bear children. Men tended to predominate in heavier, more highly skilled and better paid occupations like metalworking. They were also more likely to be long-term urban residents. For this reason they also tended to be more highly organized into political parties (although that was very rare) and unions (which, until 1905, were illegal). None the less, many less skilled and less unionized workers were prominent in strikes, notably the women workers of St. Petersburg in the 1896–7 strike wave.

There were many reasons for worker unrest, not least the carrying over into urban conditions of the rebellious attitudes of the village, particularly the instinctive refusal to accept inequality and the stubborn resistance to the adoption of the values of the property owners. But the potentially unstable mixture was made far worse by the harsh conditions of exploitation most workers found in the factories. Throughout the period the situation remained almost unbearable for most workers. Wages were low, hours long, factories dangerous, living conditions squalid, discipline brutal, employment insecure and insurance non-existent. The large number of potential recruits to industry, particularly from the overcrowded villages of the Black Earth zone, meant that employers could hire and fire at will. Apart from some skilled workers, who had been trained to do particular tasks, the bulk of workers could be replaced at the drop of a hat. Employment was usually on a yearly basis, which made it easy for firms to reduce their labour force at the beginning of the new working year in September if business was bad. They simply did not re-hire their labourers. While better paid, longer term and more highly skilled workers, such as printers, had the means to live a relatively decent life, the majority were simply short-term factory fodder who would be sacked at the first sign of insubordination, lack of discipline or unfavourable economic conditions. They would then, if they could not find another job, return to the villages from which they had come.

Consequently, the life of workers was very harsh. Above all, the pace of labour was unremitting, even more so than in the countryside where festivals, the weather and inclination towards vodka could punctuate the work cycle. In the city, the relentless pace of the machine demanded conformity. Most factory workers would work 12, and sometimes 16, hours per day for six, or even seven, days per week. Not that vodka did not exert its effects here too, most notably in various Monday rituals that could result in the collective post-Sunday hangover being drunk off by the whole group in a workshop in a renewed binge. Wages were low and workers lived from one payday to the next, having little or no resources to fall back on in the event of a strike, illness, injury or dismissal from work. Working conditions, particularly in "frontier" industries like mining and oil, were very dangerous, accidents frequent, inspection rare, insurance unknown before 1905 and redress totally inadequate. A serious injury could lead to the end of a person's employability without compensation. At this point the "welfare system" of the urban worker would often come into operation – the individual would return to the village and rejoin the family and commune. Those without such, or similar, recourse would be reduced to the flophouse, beggary, criminality.

The pace of work clearly left little time for leisure, especially as summer closure (to enable workers to return home to help with the village harvest) was rapidly giving way to year-round working particularly in the most modern industrial sectors such as St. Petersburg metalworking. None the less, workers did have some time to themselves, much of which was spent in the tavern. The minority who moved away from it attended workers' schools, some of which specialized in Sunday courses to meet their needs; took part in "social" activities such as dances or out-of-town walks that might involve illicit political discussion; involved themselves in trade union or political activities in the semi-legal conditions of post-1905; attended literary, political or scientific meetings; visited the theatre or read books borrowed from union or worker-educational libraries. Tolstoy, whose death in 1910 was the occasion of widespread commemorative meetings many of which were attended by workers, and Maxim Gorky were the most popular authors. Political tracts seem to have been of interest only to a minority. Many workers attended religious services on Sunday and, for some, it was a condition of employment. Workplaces would normally have an icon attended to by one of the older members of the work collective.

Urban living conditions were usually rudimentary. Workers recruited in groups through the *artel'* might share a house and even employ a housekeeper but for most young, single workers accommodation would be shared. In smaller workshops it was not unusual for them to live together on the premises. Larger factories often built barracks to house their workers who would live in dormitories. Where shift work was the norm, the workers might only have a bed while they were off-shift, it being used by someone else while they were at work. Working-class families often shared large basement and apartment rooms with other families, the various "corners" simply being curtained off from one another. In such overcrowded circumstances, the prospect of living a "cultured" life was very restricted. Exposure to illness, poor food and damp housing added to the everyday problems faced by workers.

The proletariat was not so much a stable class as a railway station with a constant stream of people coming into it from the village and returning to the village during bad times or, in the case of women, to have families. One can only really understand the particular nature of the Russian working class by taking note of its migrant nature and its rural links which remained very constant. Many workers still had land or a wife and children in the village. Many sent money home to their families to support them on their inadequate landholdings. Such obligations might be a burden to them but they existed, none the less. In addition, aspects of the cultural influence of the village remained important. The traditions of local democracy, exercised through the commune, and alienation from the "masters", added to the revolutionary potential of the working class in that they were a rudimentary school of self-government and class struggle. As we shall see, important popular initiatives, like the adoption of soviets and the emergence of ideas of workers' control of factories in 1917, had a good deal in common with aspects of rural life that were transferred to the urban environment.

Many analysts, particularly Bolsheviks, played down rural links and pointed instead to the growing number of second and third generation workers – that is, those whose fathers or even grandfathers, had worked in the city – and claimed that these hard-core workers were the backbone of urban political and social unrest. The argument is far from being universally accepted and we shall return to it, and many other aspects of the working class, in later chapters. For the moment, suffice it to say that, despite appalling conditions, worker protest was fairly limited before 1900 because of government repression, the impossibility of organizing and the relatively small number of workers. By 1905 several of these factors had ceased to operate and working-class protest swelled into a flood.

Industrialization was changing the physical face of Russia and altering its social structure at a rapid pace. A number of industrial regions, with differing types of industry, enterprises, and degree of geographical concentration – and distinct from the countryside that surrounded them – were coming into existence. The main ones were around the two major cities of the empire, St. Petersburg and Moscow. In the Moscow region the main industry was textiles, which were produced in some of Russia's oldest factories by its oldest industrial companies. The industry retained its more traditional emphasis well into the Soviet period. St. Petersburg was at the other extreme. It had numerous, very large heavy industrial companies, many of which were state-owned, many others backed by foreign capital. Their main production was armaments. Some of these companies were very up to date and run by the latest methods. Other manufacturing centres included Warsaw and Riga in the Baltic region and the western Ukraine where there were many factories for processing food and the growing number of cash crops, especially sugar. Mining for metal ores in the Urals and coal in the Don basin grew in scale. An oil industry, based on Baku in the Caspian, came into existence. Transport of goods between far-flung regions also meant the growth of towns at railway junctions where maintenance and repair shops were often located as well as the expansion of river ports on the still-important Volga and sea ports, such as Odessa, which was a major shipping point for grain exports to the Mediterranean market. St. Petersburg, besides being a major port for imports and exports, was an important military centre as well. In many towns and cities, military and naval modernization and re-equipment were bringing about the construction of barracks and repair and maintenance shops.

However, it should not be thought that the whole of the country was affected. Each of the industrial centres was surrounded by a vast peasant hinterland. In addition, many of the factories and mines were small and sometimes were scattered deep in rural areas. In many ways, the industrial regions were an archipelago of modernization, consisting of islands of greatly differing size, scattered in a traditional peasant ocean.

Political immobility

While the everyday functioning of Russian society and economy were generating revolutionary tensions in accordance with Tkachev's formula, it was not just what was being done that caused the problems. Perhaps even more important were the things that were not done. After all, revolution was not inevitable in Russia. Appropriate action to alleviate the effects of the problems might well have succeeded in changing the course of Russian history. However, the autocracy, in the last half century or so of its existence, was not prepared to take any such action. In fact, it took the reverse position and tried to change as little as possible.

This was particularly true in the political sphere. The only attempt in the nineteenth century to restructure the country, in the shape of Alexander II's "Great Reforms" of the 1860s – which brought about the end of serfdom, reformed military service and established a system of courts and local government – did not include any complementary power-sharing initiative. Genuine political reform was not on the agenda. Limited attempts to lobby for it were rebuffed.

The change of tsar, occasioned by the assassination of Alexander in March 1881, brought fateful consequences. Instead of interpreting the assassination as a sign that political reform had not gone far enough Alexander's successors were obsessed with the opposite conclusion – reform had gone too far. As a result a number of fateful policies were undertaken. The *zemstvo* system was restricted and dominated even more by the supposedly trustworthy propertied class. It was decided that political loyalty would be best preserved by engaging in a Slavophile type policy of Russification, based on making the Russian language and religion the dominant focus of the cultural life of the whole patch-work empire. This official chauvinism brought protests from nationalities as far apart as Latvians and Georgians and gave a great boost to local nationalist and separatist movements. Minority nationalities were represented well beyond their proportion of the population in all branches of radical, revolutionary and anarchist movements all over the empire. Stalin, the Georgian and Trotsky, the Jew became the best known but they were part of a sizeable cohort. What compensatory benefit Russification brought to the government is unclear. It also entangled the church in politics, associating it closely with the regime as its spiritual policeman. The resentment and violence shown by many revolutionaries towards the church in 1905 and after 1917 can only be understood in the light of its growing involvement with the state.

The situation was made worse by a drift into semi-official anti-semitism. In the aftermath of the assassination crisis of 1881, when the autocracy was suffering from insubstantial paranoid fears of insecurity, pogroms were encouraged to divert opposition away from the real source of the trouble. Though it never became official government policy – and was bitterly opposed by the more moderate individuals within the autocracy as well as by pragmatists who pointed out that encouraging riots could turn out to be disadvantageous by causing danger to property and public order – this fateful example was followed with increasing frequency in moments of local and national crisis. Anti-semitic attitudes were widespread in the elite but not all those who held them advocated sickening violence. There was a tendency, none the less, to associate all revolutionary activity with Jewish plotting. Anti-semitism became a deeply entrenched stock-in-trade of the Russian right, even after the revolution when exiled Russian monarchists were among Hitler's earliest supporters.

There were hopes, when Alexander III died in 1894 that his son, Tsar Nicholas II, would modify the direction of policy. Nicholas took no time in asserting his lack of respect for any such aspirations. In a speech to representatives of the gentry gathered in 1896, he declared that hopes for change were "senseless dreams". The main influence on his outlook was the *éminence grise* of the autocracy, Konstantin Pobedonostsev (1827–1907), an intellectually accomplished reactionary with extraordinary, if baleful, talent. He put the case for Russia's separateness from Europe with lugubrious skill. The Slavophile position never had a more forceful exponent. While Pobedonostsev made out an eloquent case against change, it was proceeding, none the less. In effect, the impact of his principles was to increase tension between the government and established institutions on the one hand and society on the other. Whatever view one takes of change, it cannot be stopped. But that is what the autocracy tried to do.

Russia and the world economy

While its deeds and lack of deeds were vital in explaining the autocracy's growing crisis, there were factors beyond its control that also have to be taken into account. In the forefront is Russia's geography. The Russian land gave, and still gives, the impression of having been the victim of a malevolent curse. Nature, like the wicked fairy in the ballets and folk tales that were so popular in the late nineteenth century, had arranged things in such a way that each benefit endowed was counterbalanced, even outweighed, by a corresponding drawback. The land was extensive, but the vast majority of it was uninhabitable permafrost or baking desert. Where the land was fertile, as in the Black Earth zone, gross overpopulation created poverty. The emptier lands of the steppe harboured abundant game and were also fertile, but the balance was dependent on uncertain rainfall, punctuating periods of plenty with unpredictable, disastrous shortages. Hardly anywhere was there a favourable overall balance, matching fertility, labour and climate in a harmonious relationship. In this respect Russia was totally the opposite of the other superpower gestating at this time, the United States, that had relatively empty spaces teeming with infinitely more easily exploitable resources. In Russian conditions, the overwhelming preoccupation of the population was to ensure subsistence, survival. Beyond that there was very little left to provide a surplus, to provide savings, to provide an accumulation of capital. The fabulously wealthy elite, like aristocracies elsewhere, were more interested in consumption on a massive scale than they were in production.

Without industry and investment the accursed conditions could not be mastered. Some populist economists of the 1880s had even argued that the harsh conditions meant that Russia could never become capitalist, because production was so handicapped by them that it could never be competitive. While their argument retains much force, even to the present day, they had overlooked one vital factor – imperialism and the world market.

While it might be true that Russia, because of her disadvantages, was doomed to remain uncompetitive in most areas in comparison with Germany, France, Britain and the United States, this did not mean that those who had accumulated capital in already developed economies would not seek whatever profitable investment outlets they might find, even limited ones, in Russia's harsh environment. The inflow of investment, welcomed and encouraged by Witte, might result in the distortion and imbalance of Russia's economy since the investors were looking to their own benefit rather than Russia's. Optimists might argue, along with Witte, that this could be turned to Russia's advantage in the long run. For instance, foreign capital helped build up the railway system, the extractive industries and some manufacturing capacity that otherwise would have been much harder to develop. But there were others who argued that the effects were, in the main, harmful. Foreign capital, it was argued, made the situation worse for indigenous development. The creaming off of the most profitable opportunities by foreign capital stifled the growth of native capitalists and shaped Russia's already battered economy on the rack of the world market and the growing international division of labour. From this point of view, the growth of the railway network had harmful effects. It not only broke down Russia's regional markets but facilitated the penetration of foreign goods and also made the international grain market more significant even for Russian peasant producers. The grain price within Russia became linked to that of the international competition as Russia sought to hang on to her European export markets in the face of competition from North and South America and from Australasia. The downward trend in international grain prices, that accelerated after 1881, made life even harder for the peasants and other agricultural producers of Russia. The railways meant that the well-being of the peasants of Saratov was now influenced by the opening up of the American grain fields. The good fortune of Kansas increased the misery of Kharkov. The populists had not foreseen the emergence of capitalist imperialism and its increasing global reach.

Neither the populists nor the autocracy (nor, for that matter, the Soviet and post-Soviet governments) evolved a satisfactory way of integrating Russia into the world market. From the 1880s to the present, policies have swung between complete exclusion and highly supervised, tentative linkages. Full integration was never on the cards. International relations – in the fullest sense, including economic, intellectual and commercial contacts, as well as diplomacy – had an unsettling effect on Russia. The impact of the outside world, serving to underline the difficulty of conditions within Russia, was a factor beyond the control of any Russian government. Even setting aside frequent invasions – by Tartars, Teutonic Knights, Napoleon and the Kaiser – the Russians might feel that the outside world existed only to do them harm. It interfered with Russia's development and highlighted all her shortcomings. It appeared to offer little of benefit.

Overall, it is clear that Russia's problems were deeply rooted in its economy and society. The revolution was not the result of a chance squall that blew an otherwise sound society off course. It was, when it came, the culmination of decades of neglect and maladministration. It was the outcome of a whole epoch in Russia's history. It must, none the less, be emphasized that the picture varied from one part of the Empire to another. Russian society maintained a striking diversity within the web created by the shaping influences of climate, geography, demography, dynastic and landowner power and international economic competition. Economic diversity was even broadened, in the late nineteenth century. While prosperity came to some areas, others sank and became the chief reservoirs of popular revolution. The diversity has even led one recent scholar to say that "Siberia looked to pre-war observers as if it was on the verge of becoming a second Canada; but the central black earth provinces seemed destined to become the equivalent of Bengal."[10]

However, there was perhaps one underlying factor of pre-eminent importance when it came to explaining the problems. The survival of serfdom to 1861 was, in many important respects, a fundamental source of many of the other difficulties. Reliance on unlimited cheap labour had inhibited the development of a productive labour force, distorted the distribution of the population and removed incentives to modernize and mechanize agriculture. It had inculcated deep-seated attitudes on the part of peasants that included in-built hostility to the masters and a disastrously inefficient attitude to work. Only work on one's own plot (or, in Soviet times, the black economy) brought out the best. Work for the master – whether landowner, employer or, in Soviet times, the state – was a resented extortion and diversion. Such attitudes survived abolition and, like the mentalities of slavery in the United States, have to be taken into full account in understanding the problems of modern Russia. It was also the case that state institutions, and the reliance on police, army and brute force in order to govern the peasants, had been built up under serfdom. The Russian state remained, until 1917, essentially a serfowners' state with corresponding powers and attitudes. In the early twentieth century the cultural and institutional survivals of serfdom in Russia were to be found everywhere and their impact has been much underrated in interpretations of the revolution, partly because, for conservatives, it made the autocracy look even more antiquated than it was, while for revolutionaries it undermined their claim to be conducting a Marxist worker-led revolution in an increasingly capitalist society. None the less, this vital factor must be given its full weight. At the deepest level the failure to overcome the cultural, political, economic and social legacy of serfdom was the prime cause of the revolution.

CHAPTER TWO

The revolution of 1905 and after

The warning

The complacency of the autocracy in the face of mounting opposition is all the more breathtaking since Russia was afforded that rarest of historical experiences, an unmistakeable warning of the depth and seriousness of its situation in the form of the so-called 1905 revolution. This is something of a misnomer in that it actually lasted from 1904 to 1907 and was not a revolution. None the less, it was a brilliant illumination of Russian reality and a clear demonstration of its fundamental problems.

As in 1917, the events of 1905 were essentially a series of separate incidents sparked off by a common stimulus, the perceived weakness of the authorities and the manifest need for change. Troops mutinied, workers went on strike, peasants rioted, terrorists blew up important government ministers, the middle class attended protest banquets. From 1902 the disturbances had built up. The initiating cause was the economic downturn that had hit Russia badly after 1900, dried up its foreign investment and brought the Witte system, with its high growth rates, grinding to a halt. Secondly, in 1904 Russia became embroiled in the first of its two major twentieth-century clashes with Japan in Manchuria. While this war began mainly because of Japanese expansion and a Pearl Harbor style attack on the Russian Pacific fleet before any war was declared, there were some in the tsarist government who saw it as a welcome diversion from the tense internal situation. In the well-known words of one minister, Russia needed a "short, victorious war". It turned out to be long and disastrous.

The wave of disturbances, that had hitherto been contained, took a serious turn for the worse on Sunday 9 January 1905. A great demonstration had been called on that day in St. Petersburg in order to present a petition to the tsar. The columns marched towards the city centre. Attempts to halt them on the edge of the city inevitably led to clashes. The troops opened fire. Demonstrators were killed, the march broke up in confusion. Later, a second, even more senseless and avoidable, round of firing began. More unarmed citizens were shot down. Altogether, around 150 were killed and 800–1000 injured. The chief victim, however, was the autocracy. The spectacle of troops massacring peaceful, loyal protestors – some of whom, as all accounts testify, were carrying pictures of the tsar and religious icons and were singing hymns and patriotic songs – was too much. The event quickly became known as Bloody Sunday and, among the educated classes and the workers of St. Petersburg and elsewhere, the prestige of the monarchy fell to its lowest point. However, there were no immediate repercussions.

None the less, over the next few weeks and months the number of disturbances rose steadily. In the provinces, among the subject nationalities, in the villages and in the armed forces a wave of strikes, riots, mutinies and miniature revolutions swept the Empire. In early October the most serious conjuncture of the year occurred. There was an extensive national rail strike that, apart from its economic effects, seriously hampered the movement of troops around the country. A general strike was called in St. Petersburg and a council (soviet) of workers' representatives was set up to co-ordinate it and articulate labourers' protests. The autocracy was faced with a challenge it barely survived. Two options were open to it. Military repression or concession. Nicholas's advisers eliminated repression because, they argued, it would have one of two possible outcomes. First, the troops might conduct the operation as ordered but the cost in human lives and lost monarchical prestige would be so great that the political ground lost might never be recovered. Secondly, the troops might disobey and the power of the autocracy would be at an end. In either event, so the advisers said, repression might well be suicidal for the monarchy. There was no option, they argued, but concession. Nicholas, however, remaining loyal to the principle instilled in him by Pobedonostsev of preserving intact the powers of the autocracy, wanted to choose repression. It was only a threat by his uncle, the Grand Duke Nicholas, to shoot himself if the tsar did not agree, that finally persuaded him to heed the almost unanimous advice of his military, police and political chiefs. A document, known as the October Manifesto, was issued that made unspecific promises of democratic reform. It made three main promises. First, it granted "the unshakeable foundations of civil liberty" without specifying what that meant or how it could be achieved. Secondly, it promised a limited extension of the franchise "insofar as this is feasible in the brief period of time left before the Duma convenes" and left the whole issue of universal suffrage to the new Duma, which, of course, would not be keen to change the electoral base on which its own power rested. The third provision said "no law can be put into effect without the consent of the Duma" – perhaps the most forthright of the provisions even though it implicitly excluded the great mass of existing law from Duma perusal. In a grand flourish of verbal camouflage it concluded by saying that "the elected representatives of the people should be guaranteed the opportunity of real participation in control over the legality of actions of the authorities appointed by us" which appeared to suggest that ministers might be partially responsible to the Duma but stated unequivocally that they would be appointed by "us", that is, the tsar.

Vague though it was, the document did its job. It split the opposition and provided a rallying point for the less radical elements in the opposition. It helped to create a climate in which the next threat, the Moscow uprising of December, was able to be ruthlessly crushed by elite regiments that even went so far as to shell parts of the city. The new balance also allowed the authorities to arrest the leaders of the St. Petersburg Soviet on 3 December and send them into exile. Such acts by the government became more frequent in 1906 and 1907 as harsh military repression, also facilitated by the changed atmosphere brought about by the October Manifesto, spread throughout the country. Militants within the population fought back and, in 1906, some 2,000 government officials are thought to have been killed. There was a suppressed civil war going on that could only have one outcome – the autocracy, backed by the army, reimposed its authority. The government even felt strong enough to begin retracting some of the apparent promises of the October Manifesto when it came to implementing them in the Fundamental Laws that were promulgated on 23 April 1906. They included a number of Catch 22s, the most important being the retention by the tsar of the right to legislate when the Duma was not in session and a clause permitting the suspension of rights when martial law was declared. Before 1914 most of the provinces of European Russia were under martial law. The only area in which the laws were more democratic than the Manifesto was in the franchise, which was much broader than expected.

Naturally enough, from our point of view of trying to understand why Russia was revolutionary, the key question to ask about these events is why did the autocracy survive? At its crudest the answer is that, despite scattered mutinies, the armed forces as a whole remained loyal. But important though the question of the armed forces, and the mentality of the peasant soldiers is, we cannot stop solely at that. We need to look at other aspects, above all the political initiatives of the government. The first saviour of the monarchy was Sergei Witte, who was the architect of the October Manifesto and the system of the Fundamental Laws and the Duma that evolved from it. Witte argued that more genuinely democratic institutions would not be as harmful to autocratic interests as the reactionaries like Pobedonostsev had presumed. In Witte's opinion, it was the revolutionaries, not the monarchy who lacked mass support. Allowing the peasants to vote would simply show up the chronic isolation of the intelligentsia radicals and bring about the triumph of conservative candidates. Like right-wingers in other places at other times, Witte assumed that the right spoke for the silent majority. Allow it to speak and the revolution would be crushed. The elections, however, proved beyond doubt that the peasants were not the tools of the autocracy that the right (and parts of the left) had thought them to be. They voted for radical candidates and the ensuing Duma, despite various boycotts by left-wing groups, had a centre-left majority.

From the government's point of view this was a disaster of the first magnitude. The saviour was now the potential destroyer. Witte's place was taken by the governor of Saratov province Peter Stolypin (1862–1911) and a new, more directly repressive policy was undertaken. This had two main elements, punitive repression of popular uprisings and circumscription of the Duma. In pursuit of the former, armed detachments toured the more troublesome areas. This had begun even under Witte as government authority was restored, but under Stolypin it was stepped up. Rebellious towns, such as Kronstadt and parts of Moscow, were shelled. Villages were burned down. Officially hundreds, but, in reality, probably thousands, of peasants and workers were executed after summary field courts-martial. "Pacification" was felt particularly strongly among the national minorities. While it, inevitably, restored "order" the repressions were a vivid example of Tkachev's formula in action. Resentment and hostility were being nurtured. Expression of such feelings inside the Empire was suppressed, but that does not mean they did not exist. Outside the country, foreign liberal and socialist groups organized massive protests. Russia's international image sank even lower. Although *realpolitik* considerations led to rapid official *rapprochement* between governments, in the popular European and American mind Russia was even more of a pariah state than it had been hitherto. Tsarism was a byword for repression and brutality.

The second string to Stolypin's bow was the limitation of the Duma. The repression had softened the country up sufficiently for him to take decisive steps in June 1907. The Second Duma, which had been elected in the vain hope that it would be less radical than the first, was dissolved. To ensure a more malleable majority, the electoral law was changed so that the preponderance of votes lay with the propertied classes. The principle of equal, universal suffrage was abandoned in favour of a wide, but indirect voting system as a result of which, according to a contemporary calculation by the German historian Otto Hoetzsch, it took 230 landowners, 1,000 rich businessmen, 15,000 lower middle class, 60,000 peasants and 125,000 urban workers to elect one official elector.[1] The success of Stolypin's "coup d'état" showed how deeply the repression had penetrated. It was accepted by a cowed and sullen population. The revolution was over, for the time being at least.

Had the rulers of Russia learned from such a painful, and foreboding set of experiences? Astonishingly, they had not. They did not believe that any fundamental problems had been shown up. The main reason for the upset was, they said, subversion of honest Russian people by Jews and students. In a secret memorandum of 3 January 1906 the Foreign Minister, Count Lamsdorf, argued that the events of 1905 had been promoted "by the Jews of all countries" and "the revolutionary movement [was] being actively supported and partly directed by the forces of universal Jewry" in the form of the "Alliance

Israélite Universelle" actively backed up by masonic lodges.[2] To this nonsense Nicholas added the comment "I share entirely the opinions herein expressed."[3]

Instead of embracing measures to deal with the problems, the spirit of the tsar and his immediate entourage was one of restoring the full panoply of traditional thinking and retracting as many of the political concessions they had been forced to make as they could get away with. From this point of view, even pragmatic conservatives, of impeccable right-wing credentials such as Stolypin and, to an even greater extent Sergei Witte, were considered to be dangerous radicals. The obstinacy of the tsar explains why the possibility most feared by the real radicals, the emergence of a Russian equivalent of Bismarck who would consolidate traditional political and social relations on a more up-to-date footing, never happened. The two most likely candidates for the role did not have the full confidence of the court and were quickly undermined once they had accomplished their short-term function of getting the monarchy out of its immediate crisis. Real initiatives for long-term restructuring were lost in the hazy, mystical, Slavophile populism of the tsar and the tsarina. Serious analysis of the crisis was swamped by oversimplified polemic about Jewish and intellectual "subversion".

Despite these unpromising reflexes, it has become fashionable in recent years for scholars to argue that Russia had the possibility of a fresh start in the post-revolutionary years. According to their point of view, Russia was on the path of peaceful transition to liberalism, democracy and capitalism. They emphasize the growth of democratic institutions and practices; the restrictions beginning to appear on unlimited and arbitrary autocratic power; the beginnings of an independent legal system; the emergence of an active civil society independent of the state; the growth of prosperity and even the emergence of civil rights. Without doubt one can observe such phenomena in these years. Political parties were, for the first time, able to operate legally. Trade unions maintained a difficult but, none the less, legal existence. Courts did throw out some of the more ludicrous prosecutions brought by the authorities, notably the notorious trial in Kiev of the Jew Mendel Beilis for the ritual murder of a Christian child. Censorship was also much less oppressive, although it did still exist. Business, commercial and professional organizations began to give the life of Russia's main cities a more westernized and liberal flavour.

While no one doubts the existence of such new developments (though they might argue about their extent), the meaning of them is much less clear. The assumption that they would have continued to evolve and that the autocracy would have yielded to them and turned itself into a constitutional monarchy is very questionable. In many ways, the growth of liberalism and capitalism simply added one more major dimension to the problems facing Russia. Like all the other phenomena we have been looking at, they made the problems more, not less, acute. In the first place, central foci of the new developments, notably the Duma, were arenas for conflict between the autocracy and the liberals, and even the conservatives. They were not centres of reconciliation. Secondly, they brought a new round of reaction from traditionalists who resented the changes and began to fear that the autocracy was going too far in accommodating them. In other words, the growth of a potential bourgeois revolution in Russia was not necessarily something to bring comfort to the autocracy. Attitudes of the liberals to the regime and vice versa were by no means conciliatory. Most liberals roundly detested the regime and those within the movement, like the former Marxist Peter Struve, who argued that the liberals should work with the regime to achieve their goals, were exiled to the periphery. Even conservative capitalist and business interests saw tsarism, with its baggage of anti-semitism and tendency to arbitrary, crude and brutal repression, as an obsolescent obstacle to progress rather than as an ally. Similarly, the tsarist attitude to reform was, to say the least, insincere. The concessions to liberalism were only extorted from it under conditions of extreme duress for short-term political reasons and were retracted at the first possible opportunity.

Consequently, no one at the time seriously believed that the autocracy was liberalizing. In any case, the liberalization process, even if it were proceeding at the highest level, would still have had to face up to the underlying economic and social problems and it is doubtful if they had any solution for them. If the brief period of liberal control, admittedly in the extraordinarily difficult conditions of 1917, is anything to go by, then the problems of peasants and workers might have become more, rather than less, acute.

For its part, tsarism, in the last years before the First World War, showed how little had changed from its point of view when labour protest began to re-emerge. In 1912, government troops massacred some 200 striking miners in the British-owned Lena goldfields. This brought a massive international outcry. No liberal could stomach such arbitrary, not to mention counter-productive and short-sighted, responses to labour unrest. The autocracy continued in this vein by banning the more militant unions and driving them back underground. The period of supposedly blossoming liberalism in Russia was very short. At most, it lasted from 1907 until the Lena shootings of 1912 that put the clock back to pre-1905 conditions.

There can be little doubt that the tsar and his immediate entourage were happier trying to reimpose traditional authority than they were in experimenting with reform. Rather than converting to liberalism, they showed signs of moving further towards military dictatorship based on authoritarianism, Russian nationalism and anti-semitism. In 1905, Nicholas left no one in any doubt about his support for proto-fascist groups such as the Union of Russian People, rather than for liberals, let alone socialists. Up to the very last, his fundamental ideas had changed but little. When the British Ambassador warned him, in late 1916, that perhaps he was in danger of losing the confidence of his people and it might be in his interests to win it back, he replied that it was not up to him to regain the people's confidence but up to the people to show themselves worthy of his confidence. This is, perhaps, a suitable epitaph for tsarist "liberalization".

From war to collapse

The situation we have been examining so far could have continued indefinitely. In order to understand why it actually came to a head we need to look at the immediate causes of the collapse of tsarism, the particular conjuncture that brought about the emergence of the Provisional Government and the abdication of Nicholas II. There can be no doubt that, in the short term, it was Russia's disastrous performance in the First World War that brought about the final destruction of tsarism.

The initial impact of the war was favourable to the regime. Internal conflicts were put to one side as the whole country took up the national cause of fighting the enemy. Militarily, too, the tsarist army scored some limited successes that may even have been decisive in preventing a rapid German victory because the latter had to pull troops out of the battle for Paris in order to defend East Prussia, which had been invaded by Russia. These forces were sorely missed on the western front and their presence there might have ensured German victory. Be that as it may, the moment of success was brief. The new German reinforcements soon pushed the Russians back and even started to advance into Russian Poland.

Worse quickly followed. The 1915 campaigning season was a series of unmitigated catastrophes from which the autocracy never recovered. The Russian army was soon in headlong retreat as the Central Powers marched forward into the Carpathians and through Poland. Austrian Galicia had been invaded by the Russians in August and September 1914 but the main prize, L'vov (Lemberg) was lost on 22 April 1915. Warsaw was evacuated in early and mid-August. In summer, there were even fears for Kiev. Reinforcements going to the front were met by a constant stream of civilian refugees and bedraggled, broken units heading into the interior to regroup.

Clearly, Russia's strategy had to be rethought. The Germans were not the only problem. The entrenched power of the privileged caste that dominated the upper ranks of the army leadership was also an important obstacle. It could only be uprooted at some risk to the political status quo. But without bringing forward leaders who were capable of dealing with the critical military and political situation, total defeat was inevitable. Dependent as it was on the political support of the established elite, there was no way the autocracy could unhesitatingly grasp the nettle of restructuring, not least because Nicholas had no stomach for it. Instead, improvisations were made that staved off immediate collapse but, from 1915 on, the regime was caught in a trap. It could only save itself by undermining its erstwhile closest supporters and abandoning all it held dear. Essentially, this was only an acute form of the problem that it had faced since the mid-nineteenth century, but in the turmoil of total war the old tactics of evading the real issues and diverting or repressing opposition were even more ineffective than usual.

The final scene of the autocracy's long-drawn-out demise was played out within the limits of the situation that emerged in the high summer of 1915. The crisis of August 1915 brought all the conflicting pressures into focus. The military commanders thought the only solution was that they should have more power. The civilian government were afraid that, given the military's incompetence, such a development would hasten disaster. A third force, the liberals and pragmatic members of the business, professional and gentry classes, began to argue that only their own inclusion in real government could provide a basis for solving the problems.

Exceptionally, detailed accounts of the government's deliberations in this crisis have been published. Among other things, they show that the more competent members of the administration were horrified by the continuing encroachment of the military on their preserve. As the front fell back, the army chiefs demanded that more and more of the rear territory should be put under military rule. The government was determined to resist this process, not only because of its natural inclination to preserve its own power, but also because of the total incompetence of some of the army commanders when it came to politics and the administration of civilians.

The one aspect of the crisis always brought to the forefront of discussion, the tsar's decision right in the middle of it to assume personally the role of Commander-in-Chief in place of his uncle the Grand Duke Nicholas, has to be seen against this background. The most frequently quoted and widely expressed reason for the government's opposition to the move – that it directly linked the fate of Nicholas II to the critical situation at the front – is not the whole truth. After all, the formal role of the Commander-in-Chief only made more explicit what everyone already knew, namely that the tsar was the supreme ruler and had ultimate responsibility for all the actions of his government and General Staff. More dangerous was the implication that, if the tsar were to take on the post, the political balance between civilian and military government would be tipped decisively in favour of the latter. Given the manifest incompetence of the military this was a cause of great concern to the elite. But the tsar was, as usual, unshakeable in his resolve, once he had made up his mind. A collective letter of protest by a number of ministers led to almost all of them being replaced over the next few months. Since the tsar was the ultimate authority, his new duties at the General Staff HQ (*Stavka*) in Mogilev, meant that the focus of government was to be found there and that Russia, from this time on, came very close to direct military rule, or at least to government in which the military's wishes were uppermost. The ensuing disintegration of the civilian government led to what has been aptly termed "ministerial leapfrog". Between August 1915 and the February revolution no less than 36 different ministers held the 13 major offices.

In the popular mind, stimulated by inspired rumours, the baleful influence of Rasputin and Alexandra – who was supposed, in the more imaginative versions, to have been his mistress – were thought to have been responsible for the deteriorating situation at home. In fact, the much exaggerated impact of Rasputin was less a cause of collapse than a symptom. The tsar's prolonged absence and the ensuing decline in the importance of decisions taken in Petrograd made the whole phenomenon possible.

At the same time as the military and civilian elements of government were in conflict the third, and very minor, component of government, the Duma and the business, professional and gentry interests that were focused on it, began to fear that they would have to move much more energetically if disaster at home and abroad were to be staved off. In the middle of the August crisis the majority of Duma members, together with some members of the State Council, formed what they called the Progressive Bloc.

The most important demand of this pressure group was, according to the agreement signed by the participating parties, "the formation of a united government consisting of persons who enjoy the confidence of the country and are in agreement with the legislative institutions as to carrying out, at the earliest possible moment, a definite programme." The basis of any such programme was to be "a decisive change in methods of government". In the forefront of the abuses attacked were tsarism's persistent tendency towards arbitrary government and military dictatorship. In their place, new principles were put forward, notably "strict observance of the principle of legality in administration" and "removal of the dual power of military and civil authority in questions that have no immediate relation to the conduct of military operations". Also included were demands for the release of all political prisoners; a purge of local tsarist administrators; the extension of existing institutions to all parts of the Empire; recognition of rights of minorities, especially Poles, Finns and Jews. The essence of the demands was that the Duma politicians should form a government that would be responsible to the Duma. The autocracy showed no sign of agreeing to this. The battle between the two grew more and more acrimonious over the next 18 months but the challenge had been made. The Progressive Bloc represented an alternative government of the elite and, when the moment came in February 1917, it was from here that the Provisional Government was formed and took its programme.

The first months of the war had been marked by an unaccustomed industrial truce, based on a near universal desire to support the national war effort. This, however, soon began to break down and strikes became more and more frequent. The root cause of industrial unrest was the peculiar effect the war was having on Russia's economy. Traditionally, it was argued that Russian industry simply collapsed because it could not produce the goods required. The constant demand of the generals for more shells, not to mention the industrialists' and landowners' complaints that they could not produce because skilled labour was being constantly skimmed from the factories and fields by conscription, certainly gave this impression. More recently, however, Norman Stone has argued that the roots of the problem did not lie in Russia's inadequate production base but in the administrative inefficiency of the old guard combined with a crisis not of collapse but of growth in the war years.

In Stone's view, the effect of administrative inefficiency was that war materials were hopelessly misused. For example, fortresses were still favoured by the military. This led to concentrating men and materials in small areas, making them an easy prey for enemy artillery. Attempts to persuade the authorities to move to a policy of dispersing the troops and materials over a wide area were denounced as near treasonous attempts to denude Russia of its defences. This was a fatuous line to take in the age of trench warfare and the army paid a heavy price for it. Similarly, the transportation crisis, that eventually played a critical role in provoking unrest in the capital as supplies ran short in early 1917 because of falling deliveries, is attributed by Stone not so much to the inadequacy of the network as to the hopelessly inefficient way in which it was used. In particular, he points to inflexibility in rescheduling trains to take account of shifting patterns of grain production that had led, for a variety of reasons, to the major grain surpluses appearing in the Urals rather than in the Ukraine. In any case, he points out, in the occupied areas the Germans were able to use the network more efficiently than the Russians despite the complications caused because the Russian gauge was broader than that used by the Germans.

However, from our point of view of understanding why the revolution broke out, it is Stone's second argument that is more important. According to this, the economy began to overheat through the massive increase in production of war goods, especially armaments. Hundreds of thousands of new workers were drawn in from the countryside. The chief centre for the production of armaments, Petrograd (as St. Petersburg came to be called in the war because its original name sounded unpatriotically German) grew from a population of 2.2 million in 1914 to around 2.5 million in 1917.[4] The massive cost of the war was financed by the almost unlimited printing of paper money. This in turn led to inflation, the impact of which was to send profits soaring and real wages plummeting, that, more than anything, led to the rising tide of strikes.

Thus, by 1916, the basic elements of tsarism's final crisis were in place. There was bitter division within the elite over the form of government and growing discontent among the ordinary people on account of the rapidly deteriorating economic conditions. Had the autocracy been prepared to make a major gesture of reconciliation with the Duma a new start might still have been possible, but nothing illustrates the entrenched obtuseness of Nicholas II and those around him better than the events of the last months of the dynasty. There was a vast distance between the government and any form of "liberalization" such as that advocated by the Progressive Bloc.

As if to mock the rapidly sinking regime, the military situation, which had contributed to its death agony, took a turn for the better in 1916. In a black year for the Entente on the Somme and at Verdun only the Russian army had brought off even a limited victory. Showing what could be done, despite the conditions prevailing in tsarist Russia, General Brusilov mounted an offensive against the Austro-Hungarian army in Galicia in June. The threat of a break-through brought German reinforcements hurrying southwards. They sealed the gap and recovered some of the lost ground but the Russian advance, in the nightmare conditions of the First World War, constituted what passed for a success. There were even analysts in the early weeks of 1917 who argued that the prospects of the Russian army looked brighter than ever.

However, this was not the feeling of the Entente governments. Concern was such that a high level supply conference was held in Petrograd in January at which tempers boiled over and the British and French delegations showed constant exasperation at the hopeless inefficiency of the Russians. The various tsarist ministries had failed to co-ordinate their demands. Nor had they accu-rately calculated the transport requirements. Expecting a relatively straight-forward shopping list, the visitors were faced with open divisions and arguments within the host delegation. British frustration at the spectacle was such that the leader of the delegation, the sizeable Lord Milner, kept throwing himself back in his chair in amazement, breaking a succession of them.

Like a US intelligence conference in a South American country just before a right-wing coup, the existence of such a meeting and the manifest allied con-clusion about the hopelessness of the tsarist government, fuelled persistent rumours that the Allies were involved in the downfall of the regime that took place only a few weeks later. The French and British Ambassadors certainly had extensive contact with members of the Progressive Bloc and showed clearly that they favoured a liberal solution to the growing political problems. In his memoirs the British Ambassador, George Buchanan, gave a dramatic account of one of his last meetings with Nicholas II in which he claims to have warned the tsar that he was like a friend walking through a wood on a dark night along a path that ended in a precipice. "Would it not be my duty, Sire, to warn him of his danger?" In particular, Buchanan told Nicholas that "if Russia was still united as a nation it was in opposition to his present policy". The solution, he said, echoing the formula of the Progressive Bloc, was to "appoint as President of the Council (of Ministers) a man in whom both he and the nation could have confidence" who should be allowed to choose his own col-leagues. "The Emperor", Buchanan recalls, "passed over this suggestion".[5] British concern could hardly have been more bluntly expressed. Whether involvement went any further is not known. There is no direct evidence to make a link, but there is no doubt about what Britain and France wanted to be done. Two months after Buchanan's audience with the tsar, it was done. The United States recognized the new government on 9 March, Britain, France and Italy on 11 March.

There was, however, much more to the final collapse than Allied plotting.

The cost of supplying the front with the materials the military needed had only been achieved by diverting even more resources from the already hard-pressed civilian sector. The Russian economy in 1916 was characterized by falling real wages, rising prices for manufactured goods and a flourishing *demi-monde* of speculators and corrupt arms dealers fishing for commissions on lucrative and ill-supervised arms contracts. While conditions became more and more difficult for workers and peasants, industrial profits soared. According to the vivid and larger-than-life memoirs of Negley Farson, employed at this time by an Anglo-American arms manufacturer to catch crumbs from the Russian arms contract table, Petrograd and Moscow were full of shadowy godfathers of uncertain influence who had to be bribed, retinues of hangers-on who clustered round the most expensive hotels and beautiful women of unknown origin and uncertain loyalty who kept a close eye on the goings on.[6] There is no doubt that a seedy, speculative world did evolve in Russia in the war years. Bohemian cafés and taverns of dubious reputation were frequented by successful war profiteers. Avant-garde artists found new sources of patronage and distraction among the *nouveaux riches*. The whole atmosphere was completely distasteful in a country where suffering from the war was widespread, though it probably had very little political significance.

The same cannot be said for the other aspects of the economic situation. Urban and rural conditions were moving closer and closer to crisis point. In the cities, strikes continued to increase in number, length and bitterness. Secret police reports for 1916, that were published after the revolution, did not mince their words. They pointed to the "movement of acute and profound resentment against the person of the currently reigning emperor" that had "intensified . . . to a terrifying degree". It was not only the lower classes "strongly attracted by the extreme left" who were affected but also "the middle and higher bourgeoisie led by Kadet circles". The mood of opposition in Petrograd and Moscow, compared to 1905–6, was said to have "reached extraordinary dimensions which it never attained among the broad masses in the earlier period". Even greater difficulties were expected because of the multitude of problems such as "the systematically growing disorganization of transport", "the unsystematic and mutually contradictory orders of state and local administrations", "the unconscientiousness of minor and lower agents of government in the provinces", not to mention "the unrestrained orgy of pillaging and swindling of every kind by shady operators in the most diverse branches of the country's commercial, industrial and socio-political life". This last was confirmation that Farson's experiences were far from unique.

The reports were equally clear about "the principal causes of the present sentiments" of the people that were "the current state of the food problem and, linked inseparably with this, the unparalleled, appalling rise in prices which is incomprehensible to the population". Another report talked of "the lack of sources and means of procuring food among the presently starving populations of the capitals and large population centres". Even for those in less desperate straits the situation was getting more and more insupportable. "Despite great increases in wages, the economic condition of the masses is worse than terrible. While the wages of the masses have risen 50 per cent, and only in certain categories 100 to 200 per cent (metalworkers, machinists, electricians), the prices of all products have increased 100 to 500 per cent." It concluded, "Even if we estimate the rise in earnings at 100 per cent, the prices of products have risen, on the average, 300 per cent."

Political volatility was said to have increased in proportion. There were "open and unrestrained complaints against 'venality in the administration', against the enormous burdens of the war and against the intolerable conditions of daily existence". Tensions were such that, it was reported, "the slightest incident is enough to provoke the biggest brawl". The nationalist, rather than pacifist, undercurrent of much of the unrest was captured in the comment that "The outcries of radical and left-wing elements about the need 'first to destroy the German here in our own country, and then to tackle the German abroad', have begun to elicit more and more sympathy". Ominously, it was noted that there was "a feeling of extreme disrespect for the person of her Majesty the empress Aleksandra Fedorovna" and "a widespread feeling of resentment against her as a 'German'". She was said to have been regarded "even in intellectual circles as the inspirer and leader of the campaign for a separate peace with Germany".[7]

Efforts to contain the rising tide of unrest failed to match the scale of the threat. From 1915, when the problems began to emerge, factories had been encouraged to set up canteens and shops to maintain essential provisions for their workers at affordable prices. This, in itself, had dangers because "workers can use the canteens for clandestine meetings and gatherings" as one representative at a Petrograd security conference put it in autumn 1915. The chairman, General Prince Tumanov, suggested solving the problem by shortening the lunch break "so that workers have only just enough time to get their dinner down". When told that this would not work because it would not allow sufficient time for those who went home to have their lunch and return, a gendarme present put forward a suggestion that the owners should "fit [the canteens] up with gramophones. Have them turned up loud so that no one can hear a word". The chairman welcomed this flash of genius and added that they should also stem the tide of revolution by equipping the factories "with paintings on patriotic subjects".[8] Had these last two suggestions been vigorously implemented we might have been able to attribute the birth of the consciousness industry to tsarist policemen. However, these precocious glimmerings of contemporary methods of thought control through the manipulation of the media were secondary to the traditional techniques of fines, arrest, imprisonment and exile for worker militants. None the less, discontent rose inexorably. The only thing that could have contained it – real improvements in living conditions – were completely out of reach.

Compared to the cities, the situation in rural areas appeared to offer some consolation to the authorities. Unlike the run up to 1905, there were no unusual disturbances in the villages. Things were not, however, quite as tranquil as they seemed. While harvests continued to be good the peasants would at least eat and thus not show the same acute symptoms as inhabitants of the cities, but the terms of trade were turning against them and this led them to disengage from the grain market. With industrial prices rising out of sight, the only way peasants could earn enough to buy manufactured goods was by marketing vastly increased amounts of grain. By 1916, many peasants had reached the conclusion that it was not worth trying to catch up and that it would be better to consume the grain within the village. This contributed to the growing breakdown of supplies to the cities and the army. In this way, the economic difficulties of the peasantry were directly linked to the upsurge of unrest in the towns.

The real storm burst in the winter of 1916–17. Everywhere protest reached new high points. This was most dramatic in the Duma – a body, we should recall, elected in 1912 mainly by the votes of conservative-minded property owners – where criticism of the government became unrestrained. The peak was reached in December when Miliukov made a ringing denunciation of the government's inefficiencies, punctuating each accusation with the rhetorical question "Is this treason or stupidity?"

The Duma-based sections of the elite were getting worried because of the grave decline in internal stability. They wanted action to arrest the threat not only to tsarism but to themselves as well. The signs of real crisis were, none the less, there for all to see. Strikes were getting worse, street demonstrations more frequent.

Fears were expressed about the loyalty of the garrison. The secret police reports had warned that, in the event of serious mass demonstrations the authorities could not "rely on their suppression by garrison troops, since the latter consist of recruits, militia and reserves for whom the interests of the civilian population would be closer and more comprehensible than the fulfilment of military duty".[9] The government, however, was immobile and the tsar considered the crisis to consist simply of the disloyal outbursts of liberal windbags. Panic among the threatened elite began to express itself in plots. The first to surface was the assassination of Rasputin by young monarchists who believed that by ridding the autocracy of its damaging parasite the monarchy might regain its popularity. In the event, sensational though it was, the murder had little impact. There were rumours of other plots racing through Petrograd society circles. General Krymov let it be known that news of a coup would be met with rejoicing at the front. Even members of the royal family were whispering against the tsar. The only plot of any apparent substance, however, was one being put together by the conservative industrialist and supporter of the Progressive Bloc, A. I. Guchkov. Even this was a very amateurish affair.

None the less, the plots, and the mood of the elite, were the most important aspects distinguishing February 1917 from 1905. In 1905, particularly after the publication of the October Manifesto, the elite stood more or less united against the revolutionary threat. In early 1917 it was at sixes and sevens, divided over what should be done next, whether the tsar should be overthrown, who, if anyone, should replace him. Some remained monarchists, others were republicans. Some wanted military dictatorship, others a constitution and democratic government. In 1905 the October Manifesto had provided a banner for all the elite to march behind the government. No such instrument of unity was found in the 1917 crisis and disunity among the elite is a major factor in explaining the fall, not only of Nicholas, but also of the dynasty.

A number of features of the February revolution are worth dwelling on. First of all, when the February demonstrations began no one seriously believed the final crisis of the autocracy was at hand. Demonstrations of a similar kind had occurred at the same time the previous year in connection with one of Russia's most widely celebrated socialist festivals, International Women's Day (23 February). It was also the time of year when the long hard winter was taking a heavy toll and the relief brought by the onset of spring still far off. Food shortages were often particularly acute at this time of year and 1917 was no exception. Tens of thousands of working people, men and women, poured into the streets. The members of the main socialist parties were busy printing leaflets, sending out speakers and doing whatever they could to articulate the workers' demands and make known their protests but the numbers on the streets were far beyond their capabilities to organize in the real sense. At most, they were midwives of worker protest. The decisive moments owed little to them directly. On the street, the turning point came on 26–7 February when a group of soldiers fired on police who were trying to control the crowds. Their mutiny, partly because it was not immediately suppressed, spread like wildfire through the garrison and over the next two or three days officers fled. Military discipline had completely broken down, though it should be remembered that, at this moment, the crisis was still confined to Petrograd and there were millions of still loyal soldiers at the front who might have been used to suppress the mutiny and confine it to one city, as had happened with the Paris Commune in 1871.

Characteristically, the autocracy responded ineptly. It neither staked its all on a thorough repression, nor did it make concessions until it was too late. Even in the early moments of the crisis a new initiative might have worked, at least for a time. At the last moment the tsar did give in and promised extensive reforms. But by then it was too late. The Provisional Government had taken over and the tsar's concessions were not even allowed to be published, nor was his farewell address to the Russian people.

But there were also decisive developments in the army and bureaucracy that were hidden from public view. In particular, the elite was ready to dump Nicholas in order, so it was hoped, to stem the tide of revolution. Even his leading generals were in on the act. His final abdication, on 2 March, was precipitated by his receipt of telegrams from the commanders of the military fronts calling on him to abdicate, a manoeuvre set in motion by his aide-de-camp, General Alekseev. So inept were the interventions, however, that no one had tested the ground to see if the tsar's brother Michael might be prepared to take over the throne. He refused. The generals had unwittingly precipitated the emergence of a republic. Needless to say, political leaders of the Progressive Bloc were also taking advantage of the crisis to implement the principles they stood for. Reluctantly, they turned themselves into a Provisional Government and immediately made major reforms. They were only able to do this because, alongside them, the Petrograd Soviet had also emerged, not yet as a direct challenger for power, but certainly as an important political force. The agreement between them laid the basis for government in the first months of the revolution.

The members of the Progressive Bloc who now stood at the helm of the new Russia were unlikely revolutionaries. Their main aim had been to try to get the autocracy to implement their programme and, in the process, transform itself. The obstinacy of the tsar had, right to the very end, prevented any such evolution. Instead, they found themselves pushed into the forefront of the revolution, dangerously reliant on the more radical forces grouped around the Soviet. Their aim was not to conduct a thorough social revolution in Russia but to prevent one from developing. They wanted to restructure the political and economic system to provide more opportunities for enterprise, capital and the market. Their allies in the Soviet had a vision of social revolution in which the people would control production for themselves. While the left was seriously divided over the pace at which this might be attained, they all, none the less, imagined a very different future for Russia from that which inspired the Progressive Bloc. The scene was set for an eventual tussle between them although, for the time being, a common fear of counter-revolution forced them together.

In a classic formulation, W. H. Chamberlin described the February revolution as "one of the most leaderless, spontaneous, anonymous revolutions of all time".[10] Rather more accurately, if somewhat ambiguously, E. H. Carr described it as "the spontaneous outbreak of a multitude exasperated by the privations of war and by manifest inequality in the distribution of burdens" that was "welcomed and utilized by a broad stratum of the bourgeoisie and of the official class, which had lost confidence in the autocratic system of government and especially in the persons of the Tsar and his advisers".[11] It is important to an overall understanding of the Russian revolution to bear in mind that the February revolution was not simply "spontaneous". The elite played a vital role and its divisions, compared to 1905, represent a, probably *the*, crucial difference explaining the contrasting outcomes of the two crises. Secondly, the "spontaneity" was itself created to no small extent by tsarism's incorrigibly self-destructive tendencies. To the very end, through its inflexibility and ineptness, the autocracy had been the principal architect of its own downfall. To this extent Tkachev's principle had worked out in practice. But, if the first half of Tkachev's argument was that revolutionaries do not start revolutions, the second half was that, once the revolution broke out, they would take the lead and become the decisive force. Would the Russian revolution bear this idea out as well?

Finally, it is essential to bear in mind that it was not the social revolution that brought about the collapse of the Russian state, but the collapse of the state that facilitated the social revolution. Once tsarism had finally committed suicide there was only the flimsy barrier of the Provisional Government to restrain the deep pressures that had been building up in Russian society for over half a century. The fruits of tsarist repression and inflexibility were about to be reaped.

CHAPTER THREE

The contours of national politics: Petrograd, the Provisional Government and the Soviet

The national political story of the revolution has been told many times. In most accounts it is usually Petrograd that leads and the country that follows. The deeply symbolic nature of the Russian revolution, its almost theological aspect as the supposed model of Marxist, or at least Marxist-Leninist, revolution, has underlined this. Leninist historians concentrate on Petrograd in order to emphasize the heroic role of the Bolshevik party and its leader. Ironically, historians completely out of sympathy with Lenin, Marxism and Bolshevism have usually put their emphasis on the capital too, but for precisely the opposite reasons – in order to attribute the negative aspects of the revolution to Lenin and the Bolsheviks. So far there has been no sizeable third way, an interpretation in which the Bolsheviks would not be quite so emphatically in control of history but would themselves be, in large part, shaped by the historical forces of the time. The standard, Petrograd-centred interpretation is not false, but it can be misleading since it is only a part of the picture. It is not the whole revolution. None the less, the contours of national politics have to be examined, if only to put them into context.

First steps: the honeymoon that did not last

The February revolution produced a nationwide honeymoon. It was welcomed by all classes and all nationalities. There could be no clearer evidence of the hollowness of the tsarist myth than the complete absence of any serious support for Nicholas in the final crisis. For the only time in its history, the Russian Empire was united. Officers and men; landowners and peasants; employers and workers; intelligentsia and police; Russians and Jews; Protestants, Catholics, Orthodox, Muslims and Buddhists; young and old; women and men all joined in the celebrations. Close observers, however, were aware that different groups were celebrating different things. The subsequent political history of 1917 revolved around the disintegration of this ephemeral moment of superficial unity. The concealed contradictions and conflicts of interest quickly began to make themselves felt.

This was most obvious at the heart of the revolution itself. Not one but two successors to tsarist power emerged in Petrograd. The Provisional Government, based on the Progressive Bloc of the now totally defunct State Duma emerged only in uneasy alliance with the self-appointed Petrograd Soviet led by revolutionary intellectuals and supported, in the first instance at least, mainly by mutinous troops with a leaven of striking workers. Over a brief period of difficult negotiation the Provisional Committee of the Duma and the Soviet set up an agreement that opened the way for the Provisional Government, on 1 March, to announce its programme of amnesty for political and religious prisoners; full civil liberties including freedom of the press, of assembly and the right to strike; immediate preparation for a constituent assembly; establishment of a militia to replace the police and universal, direct, equal and secret suffrage. Two final conditions showed the influence of the Soviet. First, no troops could be disarmed or transferred from the city, thus protecting the revolution from a possible influx of counter-revolutionary troops to replace the mutinous garrison. Secondly, soldiers were granted such civil rights as were consistent with military discipline and duty.[1]

The last two clauses reflected the Soviet's desire to consolidate the revolution in the military. In addition, on 1 March, the Soviet issued Army Order Number One that encouraged the formation of soldiers' and sailors' committees; obedience to the Soviet; retention of arms under the control of committees rather than officers; strict military discipline on duty but full civil rights off duty. It did not include provision for the election of officers. It was, however, followed on 6 March by Army Order Number Two that recognized the right of soldiers to object to and replace their commanders and called for a commission to settle the limits within which the soldiers might choose their own commanders.[2]

The key political question of the early weeks and months of the revolution was what relationship would there be between the Provisional Government and the Soviet? By and large, the consensus has been that there was an unsatisfactory situation of dual power. There were, indeed, frictions between the two institutions from the very beginning. The first conflict arose between the Soviet and the government over what should be done with the ex-tsar. The government wanted to send him into exile. The Soviet, however, objected. They did not want Nicholas to form a possible focus for foreign-based counter-revolutionary plots. They argued that, like any suspected lawbreaker, he should be brought to justice. In the event, the tsar remained in Russia but was not brought to trial but kept under a very mild form of palace arrest. The first conflict, then, had ended in compromise, something of a rarity in Russian political life.

47

More serious rifts were to follow. In the forefront was policy towards the war. Since the war seriously affected almost all other aspects of political – not to mention social, economic and cultural – life in 1917, it is worth pointing out one or two underlying features of the politics of war and peace. While there was a bewildering variety of policies on the war in theory, in practice there were only two. Should one prosecute the war with energy or fight it relatively passively? No one seriously considered the third possibility – surrender, leaving the German and allied forces on Russian soil. Because of this, the various "peace" policies of the left, based, for example, on a call for peace without annexations or reparations, had an air of unreality since they were based on the very unlikely assumption that the enemy could be negotiated out of all its conquests. Since there was no chance that the Germans would accept such unfavourable terms, even the most resolute of the peace parties (including many Bolsheviks when it came to the crunch) had to accept that they would have to prosecute the war. As a result, policies of war and peace had a somewhat symbolic quality. They defined the intentions and aspirations of those who held them, even though they might not be realized in practice. They were exercises in political exhibitionism as much as efforts to influence events in the real world.

The quality that the new government wanted to stress, above all others, was its solidarity with its allies. There were great hopes in Britain and France that the February revolution would release Russia's fighting energy and this was, indeed, a fundamental motive of the elite in co-operating with the removal of Nicholas. The left, however, was not prepared to participate in an imperialist war. As far as they were concerned, it was legitimate to defend the new democratic Russia against foreign invasion by authoritarian monarchies – a policy which came to be known as "revolutionary defensism". To do otherwise, it was argued, could only lead to counter-revolution. In practice, then, both sides were prepared to prosecute the war. But they fought increasingly bitterly over how this was to be done and with what end in view.

An early victim was the Foreign Minister, Pavel Miliukov (1859–1943), the sheet anchor of Russian liberalism since it had become organized in 1903–4. His enthusiasm for the war was too much for the left to stomach. The conflict erupted on 21 and 22 April when the text of a note to the allies, written by Miliukov and approved by the whole Cabinet, was leaked. The note had been appended to the text of a declaration by the Provisional Government which was, in turn, based on an appeal by the Soviet calling for the renunciation of imperialist war aims by all combatants. Under pressure from the Soviet, the government had agreeed to circulate the declaration to the allies but, under counter-pressure from Miliukov in his capacity as Foreign Minister, had agreed to add the secret note. The note reassured the Allies that the government's official position on the war was unchanged, that is, it still stood by its obligations, including the secret treaties by which Russia stood to make major territorial gains, most notably Constantinople and the Straits, once the war was won. When the note was published public opinion on the left was outraged by its tone of unrepentant imperialism. Troops sympathetic to the Soviet came out into the streets fully armed on 18 April. The military governor of Petrograd, General Kornilov, urged strong repression. There was shooting and the demonstration broke up. But, even so, Miliukov was undermined and left the government at the next reshuffle on 2 May, though he remained a power behind the scenes until October. The crisis proved that the revolution was deepening and that the February alliance was showing signs of serious strain. A few weeks later, this became more obvious.

A swing to the left

The main contours of the revolution in Petrograd in the following weeks and months showed a series of undulations. Up to early July the revolution radicalized. From early July until the disastrous Kornilov affair of late August and early September there appeared to be a prospect of stabilization on a centre-right basis. After Kornilov the swing to the left was resumed with even greater energy and it was against this background that the Bolsheviks took power in October. The rural areas, provincial cities and various fronts followed rather different patterns but our present purpose is to focus on Petrograd.

The war was the chief motive force of radicalization in June and July. Far from taking steps to bring about the universally desired, but hopelessly idealistic, just and democratic peace, the Provisional Government was preparing an offensive. This not only heated up the political cauldron but also prolonged and probably worsened the economic crisis of Petrograd which still suffered severe inflation and interruptions of supplies. But perhaps most important of all the preconditions for a successful offensive was the restoration of discipline in the armed forces. This had been declining steadily since February, particularly among politically sensitive units like the Petrograd garrison. Attempts to restore the power of officers brought sharp conflict between the authorities and the rank-and-file who, with the encouragement of left-wing political activists, interpreted the moves as steps towards counter-revolution and an attack on their soviets. They were determined to resist. The ensuing tension encouraged far-left militants, notably the Bolshevik left and the burgeoning, but extremely factious, anarchist movement in Petrograd, to think of an assault on the Provisional Government.

In fact, the party activists were having their hand forced by the seething anger of parts of the garrison. In response the Bolsheviks supported plans for a demonstration to be held on 10 June at which the participating military contingents demanded to be able to carry their arms. More cautious left-wing politicians were opposed to the more militant. The delegates to the First All-Russian Congress of Soviets, which came together on 1 June with a preponderance of Socialist Revolutionary party and Menshevik affiliated delegates, shared the caution and eventually forbade the demonstration. A week later, however, on 18 June, the Soviets called a peaceful demonstration of their own to back up the Soviet parties as a whole and their line of toleration of the Provisional Government. The spirit of the demonstration was, however, radical and slogans of the left – calling for "All power to the soviets" and "Down with the ten capitalist ministers" (though not, it would seem, for an immediate end to the war) – dominated the procession. The political centre of gravity in the capital had shifted further to the left than was comfortable for the Soviet leadership, let alone the Provisional Government.

The critical dénouement (for the time being) came two weeks later. This time it was troops galvanized by rumours of transfer to the front and the sailors of Kronstadt who put on pressure and organized an armed demonstration in Petrograd on 2 July aimed at overthrowing the Provisional Government, itself, probably coincidentally, thrown into crisis on the same day by the resignation of its five Kadet party ministers.

The accounts we have of the crisis of 2–4 July, particularly from left-wing observers, portray a headless popular movement seeking leadership from the various left-wing political parties and institutions. On 4 July, for example, armed demonstrators went to Bolshevik headquarters where they were praised for their resolve but advised to disperse peacefully. Bolshevik activists complained to their leaders about being used as "firemen", charged with damping down revolutionary ardour. The Kronstadters, joined by workers by this time, went to the Soviet and still found no one prepared to back up their attempted uprising. The day degenerated into sporadic violence and shooting.

Politically the July Days were disastrous for the left, at least in the short term. Despite the news which broke at this critical juncture, that the military offensive had been halted, the Provisional Government was able to turn the situation to its own advantage. The Soviet left was accused of being in league with the Germans and organizing the demonstrations in order to betray Russia. Although they had, reluctantly, been instrumental in undermining the attempted coup, the Bolsheviks were, none the less, singled out as the chief villains. Fabricated evidence was published to show that the Bolsheviks were German agents. Given also the commonly known fact that Lenin (like a number of other former political exiles) had returned to Russia from Switzerland under German protection, it was possible for the Provisional Government to pull off its own disinformation-based counter-coup. The Bolsheviks were outlawed and warrants issued for the arrest of the leaders. Lenin went into hiding, initially in a straw hut in a damp and muddy Finnish field, only emerging fully in the midst of the October revolution. Trotsky, showing perhaps excessive self-confidence in his view that the Provisional Government was weak, went about his normal activities and challenged it to arrest him. It was not until 23 July that the authorities worked up enough courage to oblige. In the streets, it was the turn of right-wing gangs to beat up anyone they took to be Bolsheviks. People who looked like Jews or students were first in line. The Bolsheviks' printing press was smashed up by an army detachment. But although things looked bad, the party still continued to function. It was, after all, not unfamiliar with underground politics, from which it had emerged less than six months earlier. It was even able to hold its Sixth Party Congress in semi-clandestine conditions. But, for the moment, the prospects of the left looked bleak. Wholesale radicalization had come to a halt. The counter-revolution showed some signs of beginning to regroup and take a stand.

Power sharing in disarray

The political conjuncture of early July was, then, a far cry from that of February. The honeymoon was not only over, but well and truly forgotten. The political elites were falling apart, the popular movement building up a vast, but uncontrollable force. Many factors explain the multiple evolutions but in the forefront were the return of front-ranking political leaders of the left who had, of course, been in exile in February; the continuing, ever-deepening economic crisis; lack of resolution of the fundamental problems of land and the rights of workers and soldiers; the insoluble problem of the war and the growing fears of the right over the question of social order. The Provisional Government, and its increasingly uneasy relationship with the Soviet, were a major focus of these new forces.

Since the fall of Miliukov the Provisional Government had been forced to rely more on the Soviet. But this process had caused corresponding deep splits in the Soviet itself. The dominant force in the Soviet, the Socialist Revolutionary (SR) and Menshevik party leaders, were still convinced that the alliance with the liberals had to be maintained. Their increasingly restless followers, particularly in Petrograd, were finding this more and more unpalatable and, as we have seen, were prepared to make their feelings known. The problem was particularly acute since six socialists from the Soviet had joined the Provisional Government on 5 May to produce what was known as the First Coalition. The July crisis and the breakdown of the offensive brought about its collapse. It was only replaced after prolonged negotiations. The new government was headed by the moderate socialist and Minister of War, Alexander Kerensky (1881–1970), a forceful orator from the left of the Fourth Duma who had come to prominence as a castigator of tsarism at the time of the Lena massacre.

Kerensky's all-consuming mission was to save Russia from the humiliation of defeat by Germany. In this he represented the desire of the overwhelming majority of the country. Victory had also been the aim of earlier Provisional Government cabinets. However, Kerensky differentiated himself from the right-wing elements and saw himself as a man of the left, a man who believed fully in the democratic revolution of February. Such principles were anathema to the old guard, particularly among the generals. Where Kerensky believed army committees elected by soldiers could help win the war by enlisting their knowledge and enthusiasm, many officers wanted them abolished and the old disciplines, including the death penalty, restored. It was from this quarter that Kerensky met his nemesis. Elsewhere he sympathized with aspects of the popular revolution and wanted to convene a Constituent Assembly but he did not want to engage in delicate political and social engineering while the war was in full spate. The Provisional Government had already begun to take steps towards land reform and to improve working conditions and wages in factories but in neither case had the measures been very energetic. A Main Land Committee and a Supply Committee had been set up to oversee the rural situation. Their first priority, however, was to ensure stability and protect food production to keep the front going. It is true that this gave peasants some leeway in trespassing on landowners' rights over unsown land, for example, but no steps were taken towards serious land redistribution until it was too late. In its last weeks and months the radical SR leader and memoirist of the revolution, Victor Chernov, who was Minister of Agriculture, tried in vain to alert his colleagues to the need for immediate, energetic steps. Kerensky also leaned in this direction. He shared many principles with leaders of the Soviet right and he included them in his government. But the constant postponement of social reforms opened up a gap between the Provisional Government and the peasants and workers that Lenin was able to step into in October, thanks to Kornilov whose revolt had widened it to fatal proportions.

In the meantime, however, Kerensky formed a new coalition on 23 July that had eight socialist ministers and seven non-socialist, though the minority partners, the four Kadet ministers, still had disproportionate influence. The eight socialists, by and large, had only tenuous claims to be so called and were mostly from the right wing of their parties. In the words of Miliukov "with a slight preponderance of socialists, the actual preponderance in the cabinet unquestionably belonged to the convinced partisans of bourgeois democracy". To which Trotsky later added "it would be more accurate to say bourgeois property".

The impact on power relations within the Soviet itself was enormous. Above all the Soviet leadership was losing support and becoming an empty shell. The policy of compromise with the liberal wing of the propertied classes could not easily be sold to the increasingly militant masses. Above all, the slowness of the Provisional Government, including its Soviet-based members, to tackle the key issues for the ordinary population – the economy, the war, democratization, the land question – drove away their popular support in Petrograd and other key areas. The Soviet leadership was in an impossible situation. They believed that any degeneration of the situation into civil war would be disastrous for both the revolution and the country, which would be swallowed up by the Germans. But the cost of avoiding this awful prospect was postponement of the very essence of what they stood for – social revolution. The SRs supported land redistribution but could never persuade their propertied allies in the Provisional Government to do anything about it. The Mensheviks, also inhibited by their opinion that the Russian proletariat was too weak and ill-educated to form a solid foundation for a genuinely socialist society, could not proceed to even limited steps in the direction of socialist transformation. Their professed Marxism served only to mock their actual policies in the eyes of their enemies on the left. Far from turning the Provisional Government into the tool of the Soviet, the coalition policy appeared to be wrecking the cohesion of the Soviet itself and, given time, the development of the divisions might have given an opportunity for the right to strike at the Soviet and suppress it. Premature action, however, would be disastrous and risk forcing the left back into a self-defensive unity. Whatever dreams of this kind the right might have dallied with in these months, the situation turned decisively against any such outcome later in the summer.

Right-wing counter-attack

In the immediate aftermath of the July Days, however, the right might have been forgiven for thinking that their dreams were coming to fruition. The conjuncture in the capital, and even more so in Moscow, appeared to promise some hope for the triumph of a centre-right solution to the political problems. The right began to organize with something resembling vigour.

The financial, commercial and business elites of Russia's main cities had not been idly watching the decay of their power. Shadowy groupings had formed early in the revolution. In Petrograd the Society for the Economic Rehabilitation of Russia was one. Looking back, one of its central figures, the Petrograd industrialist A. I. Putilov, recalled that there had been no problem in quickly raising ten million roubles for political purposes. The difficulty had been in finding effective ways of spending it. Pamphlets and political lobbying had very limited impact. This reminds us that it was not only workers and peasants who were unused to democratic politics and its associated skills of organization and electoral management. The right was also naive and inexperienced in mass politics and suffered from some of the same diseases as the rest of the political spectrum, notably localism, fragmentation, lack of overall leadership and internal rivalry. There was, for instance, a much better organized and semi-conspiratorial group of bankers, industrialists and centre-right politicians called the Republican Centre, set up in Moscow in May, that had links with government, civil service, army, navy and police, giving it the potential to engage in more energetic and more direct action against the revolution. However, the two groups were unaware of each other's existence before the middle of July.[3]

The industrial opponents of popular revolution began to link up with each other and with the Union of Landowners and the military commanders who were taking similar steps. In August an Assembly of Notables met in Moscow as a preliminary to the Provisional Government-sponsored State Conference. The main item on its agenda was the preparation of a more unified, more coherent and distinctive platform from which the privileged classes could fight back against the ever-encroaching tide of popular revolution. While it was relatively easy to decide the central objective – destruction of the soviets in general and the Petrograd Soviet in particular – there were complications. For example, as its name suggests, the Republican Centre opposed monarchism and certainly did not want to restore tsarism and the *ancien régime*. Their aim was a form of bourgeois revolution that would set up appropriate conditions for the emergence of Russian capitalism. Thus they had restorationist old guard opponents on the right as well as their more obvious socialist opponents on the left. In addition, choice of tactics to achieve their aim was also divisive. The Kadet party, for example, remained hesitant and ambiguous about the advisability of using government-authorized force against the left and was still more mistrustful of extra-constitutional measures. Others began to fall in line behind General Kornilov (1870–1918) who had been appointed Commander-in-Chief on 18 July.

The political tensions of the time showed themselves most fully in and around the State Conference, held in Moscow in August.[4] It had no regular constitutional status but was obviously intended to open the way for a more stable political system. It was not a democratic body in that no open, direct elections to it were held. Nor did it have any powers. Rather it was a forum for representatives and delegates from a whole range of social organizations. As such it was the only occasion in 1917 when left and right assembled together en masse to discuss their opinions. The government, the military, industrialists and bankers were present. But, despite a Bolshevik boycott, so were left-wing organizations. Central and provincial soviets sent representatives, as did some unions. The largest delegations seem to have come from peasant and co-operative associations although the official list of delegates contains the names and affiliations of only half the 2,500 people present so we cannot know its full composition with certainty.

The central theme of the conference was the war and, in particular, the need for national unity in the face of the crisis following the collapse of the offensive on the South-Western Front and the disaster of Tarnopol'. But within the framework of fervent patriotism and defensism generated at the conference, the acutely contradictory forces and political tensions of Russian society came to the surface.

Kerensky's speech opening the conference was a *tour de force*. He pulled together all his undoubted histrionic and oratorical ability to emphasize the need for national unity. He argued that there should be no internal conflicts of class, party or nationality in the face of the crisis. Strict discipline was necessary when confronting a deadly foe like Germany. The focus of unity should, he continued, be the new, democratic, revolutionary Russia that was now prepared to take its rightful place in the community of nations. Each of Kerensky's perorations was met with enthusiastic applause. Despite this, the rest of the conference showed that, in the real world, Kerensky's arguments seemed to be built on sand.

On the second day of the conference the spokesmen of the right took the initiative. First to speak was General Kornilov. His speech was relatively muted since, as part of the deal allowing him to address the conference, he had agreed to avoid referring to his most controversial policies. None the less, he concentrated on the need to impose strict discipline to end the situation of disintegration in the army which he depicted graphically. He called, in particular, for severe limitations on the role of army committees. It was left to General Kaledin, the Ataman (Chieftain) of the Don cossacks, to speak more unrestrainedly for the right. The heart of his speech consisted of six proposals: the army should be above politics and meetings and parties should be banned within it; most soviets and committees should be done away with in front and rear and those that were left should be strictly controlled; the declaration of soldiers' rights should be amended and supplemented by a declaration of their duties; army discipline should be strengthened "by the most decisive measures" (a thinly veiled reference to the taboo subject of capital punishment); vaguely but menacingly, he said that, since front and rear were united, measures applied to the front should be extended to the rear and, finally, the disciplinary rights (sic) of command personnel should be restored. Kaledin had brought the programme formulated behind the closed doors of the High Command into the public gaze.

Kaledin was followed immediately by the President of the Petrograd Soviet, the right-wing Georgian Menshevik leader and government minister, Nikolai Chkheidze (1864–1926), who gave a long, but rather uninspiring, statement of the position of the soviet right on key questions. For instance, he opposed individual land seizures but called for more powers for local land committees in the transition period before the convening of the Constituent Assembly. He called for every effort to be made to defend the country and made a distinction between counter-revolutionary officers in the army, who should be dismissed, and moderate officers who would replace them and should be obeyed.

A more determined response to the right came on 15 August, the third and final day of the conference. A speaker named Kuchin, representing the army committees, launched into a vigorous defence of their role. It was not the committees, Kuchin argued, that threatened disunity, rather they had restored discipline and saved the army when it was threatened with collapse. But the final, evening session of the conference saw the stormiest session of all. A junior cossack captain, Nagaev, refuted Kaledin's proposals and denounced his right to speak in the name of the cossacks. Nagaev argued that ordinary cossacks, trapped in the traditional system of military service, had been the most deprived of the peoples of the Empire. He even compared their limited rights of residence to the Pale of Settlement imposed on Jews. Their *obshchina* (traditional community) had been repressed under tsarism and in 1905 they had been forcibly turned against their fellow peasants with whom they had common cause. He attacked the whole military ethos of cossackdom and called for respect for the democratic rights of ordinary cossacks and pledged the support of ordinary cossacks for democracy and the interests of the people as a whole. His words struck at the very heart of the traditional security system. If the cossacks were refusing to follow their officers blindly what hope did the right have of restoring order? Not surprisingly hostile accusations from the right of cowardice and treachery peppered his brave speech. He was even accused of having links with Germans, words that, according to one report, had the impact of a bomb exploding in the hall.

There were no further significant interventions and, late in the night, Kerensky brought the proceedings to an end. It made no decisions, took no votes and set up no institutions. What had the conference shown? Many reports say it was a triumph for the right but closer examination shows that the situation was more complex. The "moderate" left, got considerably more support from the centre than did Kaledin or Kornilov. But above all, it was Kerensky who dominated proceedings. His opening speech was welcomed on all sides. It was clear that he was the only person who could maintain some show of national unity. This was obvious to allied observers who continued to urge caution on Kornilov because it was apparent that his potential power base was much narrower than Kerensky's and his abrasive style threatened to polarize the situation. Despite the adulation of his immediate supporters the conference showed that Kornilov's popularity did not stretch much beyond part of the officer corps and the dwindling band of the traditional right. But it was, perhaps, this very perception of their isolation and ebbing authority that brought the right to the conclusion that, no matter what the risks, some effort should be made to hold on to such power as they could still command before it was too late. During the conference General Kornilov had held court in his railway carriage and was in the thick of all sorts of half-baked, counter-revolutionary intrigues. The right, which had distrusted Kerensky all along, now appeared to have found its leader. A military coup was being urged from many directions. Within a few weeks Kornilov obliged.

The precise details of the Kornilov revolt remain unclear. It is beyond doubt that Kornilov was deploying his most reliable troops with a view to suppressing the Petrograd Soviet, even paying *agents provocateurs* to start disorders in the capital as a pretext for his actions. It was perhaps symbolic of the fiasco to come that they caroused the night away with the money provided rather than get on with their task. What we do not know for certain, however, is the extent to which Kerensky supported Kornilov. He clearly would have been glad to be rid of the Soviet and appears to have backed this part of the general's plan. However, through the comings and goings of a self-appointed mediator, Kerensky learned that Kornilov intended to replace him, too, and make himself head of government. In a panic, Kerensky tried to get in touch with Kornilov to confirm these intentions. At this point the affair descended into farce. Kerensky tapped out his message on the keyboard of a Hughes apparatus (a primitive teleprinter) asking Kornilov if what the emissary had told him was true. Without bothering to ask Kerensky precisely what he had been told, Kornilov confirmed that it was true. Kerensky was outraged and immediately switched sides, ordering Kornilov to halt. He was also forced to mobilize the Petrograd Soviet to assist him. Soviet supporters, including Red Guards, were armed, and as part of the price for its support, the Soviet demanded the release of its members who were in prison, most of whom were Bolsheviks. Trotsky and others were released but Lenin chose to remain in hiding in a safe house in Finland. The Soviet sent out propaganda brigades to turn Kornilov's troops against their officers. Kornilov himself was thrown into confusion by what he and his supporters ever afterwards called Kerensky's "betrayal". As a result of these developments the resolve of the leaders of the revolt was weakened and its troops refused to march on Petrograd. The affair collapsed without a shot being fired and Kornilov was arrested.

Defending the February revolution: the drive for Soviet power

While the inner details of the revolt remain obscure, its political impact is crystal clear. The trend to the right broke down in confusion and mutual recrimination. The radicalization of Petrograd, and the country, proceeded more rapidly than ever before. The chief victim was the fragile alliance that Kerensky had tried to hold together. Both sides now hated him. The army officers and the right were no longer prepared to go along with him since, it appeared, he had jumped to the left at the crucial moment and destroyed their man. He did not pick up corresponding support on the left because it was widely believed that he had been in on the plot, at least in its early stages. Kerensky's switch to the left was interpreted in the Soviet not as a change of heart but as a sign of extreme weakness. As a result the political situation rapidly polarized, leaving the Provisional Government chronically insecure. In effect, the Kornilov revolt opened up a power vacuum at the centre and set the scene for the October revolution. In particular, the overt attempted coup confirmed what the left wing of the Soviet – the Bolsheviks, the Menshevik-Internationalists, the anarchists and the Socialist Revolutionary left – had said all along. Alliance with the right was dangerous because the right would never put the democratic principles it currently professed ahead of its counter-revolutionary interest in defending its property.

The swing to the left was very marked in key Soviets and, for the first time, the radical Bolshevik line was gaining majorities. On 9 September they won the support of the majority in the Petrograd Soviet and on 25 September

Trotsky was elected chairman. From his hiding place in Finland, Lenin sent a series of ever more shrill letters demanding that the Bolshevik Central Committee take advantage of the new situation and actively prepare a seizure of power by the party in the name of the Soviet. He met a lukewarm response and even began to toy with the idea of bypassing the leadership of his own party by starting the revolt in Helsinki or Moscow. He even threatened to resign from the Central Committee. Eventually, his frustration was such that he moved from Finland to Petrograd (though still in hiding in another safe house) in order to meet the Central Committee face to face. This he did on 10 October when he forced them to pass a resolution putting armed uprising "on the agenda". This rather vague form of words appears to have had little immediate impact on the actions of the party leaders. On 16 October, at the next meeting, Lenin again took part and complained that nothing had been done about an uprising. Indeed, the reports from the localities that were represented at this meeting suggested that only half-hearted and scattered support for an armed uprising could be expected. Two days after this meeting the party's two most influential leaders after Lenin – Kamenev and Zinoviev – published their objections to Lenin's line in the left-wing writer and publicist Maxim Gorky's independent left-wing newspaper *Novaia zhizn'* (*The New Life*). Thus, only seven days before they conducted their action, the Bolshevik leadership was openly divided over whether a seizure of power was a good thing.[5]

Lenin, however, had no doubts and, as he had been earlier, was prepared to bypass the party leadership (even though he had a clear majority in it) and rely on more resolute revolutionary forces. These he found in the form of the Petrograd Soviet and, in particular, its Military Revolutionary Committee. At this crucial point, Trotsky, who had only recently reconciled himself with Lenin after 12 years of polemic against him, proved a more staunch ally than Lenin's closest lieutenants from the long years in the political wilderness.

The Military Revolutionary Committee's official purpose had been to prepare the defence of the city by its inhabitants in the event that the Germans might break through and the Provisional Government desert the city. This scenario was less far-fetched than it seems but, in any case, the important thing was that it was widely believed to be a real possibility by many in and around the Soviet. An elaboration of these fears, in the form of a rumour that the government was planning to leave Petrograd for Moscow and then deliberately open the front to the Germans and give them the dubious honour of trying to restore order in Petrograd, was instrumental in guaranteeing that the garrison would be sympathetically neutral towards a Soviet takeover of power. In addition, the relatively legitimate task of preparing the city's defences provided an excellent smokescreen to conceal preparations for the seizure of power.

It is not, however, altogether clear that, even in the Military Revolutionary Committee, bold, resolute action was being taken to seize power. It appeared to be guarding itself against attack at least as much as it was taking the initiative. There were some grounds for such a mentality. The Provisional Government had, after the Kornilov affair, gone through a final mutation. On 25 September a final coalition was formed. At the forefront of its concern was the rising power of the left. This was focused on the approaching Second All-Russian Congress of Soviets, due to meet in Petrograd in the second half of October. The first such congress met, it will be remembered, in June and had actually had a cooling effect on left-wing passion. The post-Kornilov conjuncture, however, promised to produce a much more resolutely revolutionary body. Should such an assembly be allowed to meet, the Provisional Government feared that it might well form a launching pad for a soviet-based government. With this in view, the Provisional Government took steps to maintain control of Petrograd. On 24 October the Bolsheviks' printing press in the city was closed down. Detachments of troops were ordered out to defend the strategic points around the city, notably its main river bridges. The Bolsheviks' plans for an uprising were, by this time, an open secret thanks to Kamenev and Zinoviev's letter in *Novaia zhizn'*. Kerensky appears to have been full of confidence that any precipitate Bolshevik action could be countered, opening up the way to a débâcle, for the left, on the scale of the July Days and a new and more thorough suppression of the left. So confident was he that he supposedly prepared for the critical confrontation by loudly singing arias from his favourite operas.

Events proved that Kerensky's confidence was ill-founded. It had been based on information given to him by his military advisers who had grossly exaggerated the loyalty of the garrison. In the event, a small minority of the garrison came out in active support of the Soviet and, together with members of armed workers' militias and Red Guards, formed more than sufficient force to overthrow the Provisional Government. The majority of the troops sat and watched, reluctant to side with a government that had sponsored attempts to restore the power of its officers and that was, they believed, trying to embroil them in fighting with the Germans. Only a tiny proportion of the garrison actively defended the Provisional Government. In the forefront of these were a number of officer cadets and the famous Women's Battalion.

The critical confrontation in Petrograd took place on 25 and 26 October. It built up over a number of days with the Military Revolutionary Committee taking ad hoc decisions to counter the military dispositions of the government. For instance, if government troops were sent to control a bridge, a Soviet delegation would be sent to replace them, usually by talking them out of their obedience to their officers. The whole affair was curiously free of out-and-out violence. It was like a kind of shadow boxing. More bold measures, to take the initiative and seize strong points – the railway stations, telephone exchange and so on – were taken by the Soviet after midnight on 24–5 October. It has been pointed out, especially by Robert Daniels, that this change of pace coincided with Lenin's dramatic arrival – still in disguise and after narrowly missing being intercepted by a government patrol – at the nerve centre of activity, the Bolshevik and Soviet headquarters in the Smolny Institute. Reliable, direct evidence that Lenin was the source of this new aggression is scanty but, given his resoluteness, it is a strong possibility. Within 36 hours the city was in Soviet hands, though disruption of its life seems to have been minimal. Trams continued to run. Cafés and places of entertainment functioned as normal. Most factories and workshops continued to operate.

Almost as an afterthought, the question was raised of arresting the Provisional Government, that was in session in the Winter Palace, although it was without its prime minister who had slipped out of the city in order to raise loyal troops from outside the Petrograd garrison. On the evening of 25 October the major set-piece confrontation of the revolution took place, the assault on the Winter Palace. Numbers involved in the attack appear to have been fairly low, probably hundreds rather than thousands. The defenders of the palace melted away. There were reports of violence against some members of the Women's Battalion and there was some looting of the wine cellars. The remaining ministers of the Provisional Government were arrested and detained, for a short period in most cases, in the Peter and Paul Fortress. Lenin appeared at the Second All-Russian Congress and urged it to name a new Soviet-based government. Many of the established leaders of the Soviet were outraged at the arrest of the Provisional Government and, with dire warnings of the civil war these actions would precipitate, many of them left the congress. Even the Menshevik left, led by Martov, joined in the boycott. The majority of delegates, however, supported the Bolsheviks and Soviet power was born. But the new government still had a long way to go to secure its power. However, before going into the crucial question of how it did so, let us return to our main theme of finding out why so many millions participated in the revolutionary activities of 1917 and how these events affected the lives of ordinary people. Everywhere, we have seen the influence of the masses in the turning points. Having sketched out the political outline of the first year of revolution, the remainder of Part I is devoted to discussing the role and complexion of the popular movement in 1917.

CHAPTER FOUR

Streets, factories, workshops, mines

The February revolution began in the streets of Petrograd. Witnesses had no doubt of the importance of the masses. Their memoirs capture the drama. Sympathisers like Nikolai Sukhanov, a leading member of the Petrograd Soviet, recalled that, on the critical day of 27 February, when crowds and soldiers fraternized:

> military detachments were going past, no one knew where to, some with banners and some without, mingling and fraternising with the crowd, stopping for conversation and breaking up into argumentative groups. Faces were burning with excitement. The exhortations of countless street orators to stand with the people and not to go against it to the defence of Tsarist absolutism were received as something self-evident and already assimilated. But the excitement on the soldiers' faces reflected chiefly perplexity and uneasiness. What are we doing and what may come of it?[1]

Pavel Miliukov was a little more guarded but was, none the less, impressed by the scenes he witnessed on 27 February. Particularly important, in his view, were the soldiers who poured in. They were, he said, "the last ones to appear, but they were the real masters of the situation".[2] He believed that they were mainly seeking protection against the authorities who might restore order and punish them for mutiny. None the less, their determination is apparent from Miliukov's account which continues:

> By night time the Tauride Palace had turned into a fortified camp. The soldiers brought with themselves boxes of machine-guns, cartridge belts and hand-grenades, and, I think, they also dragged in a cannon. When shots were heard somewhere around the palace, some

of the soldiers began to run, broke the windows in the semi-circular hall, and jumped out of the windows into the courtyard.[3]

Outright opponents of the revolution, like the conservative Duma politician Vitaly Shul'gin, were outraged by the crowd, not least because it had occupied the main hall and forced the Duma members into a smaller one. He described the same scene as Miliukov in the following words:

> The place was hardly large enough to hold us all. Rodzianko and the Council of Elders sat around the table and the rest of us sat or stood, or leaned against each other as best we could. We were excited, alarmed, clinging, as it were, spiritually to one another. Even opponents of long standing felt the presence of a new element, equally dangerous, threatening, repulsive to all. This new element was – the mob. It was approaching, its breath already felt. At that time very few thought about it but, judging from their paleness and beating hearts, a great many undoubtedly felt, unconsciously, that death, surrounded by the mob, was on the march.[4]

Shul'gin's hyperbole leaves no doubt as to his feelings, nor his opinion about what the authorities' response should have been:

> The mob of thirty thousand with which we were threatened . . . was not a myth but a fact. It came like a cloudburst, a flood . . . This constant outpouring of humanity brought in sight new faces but, no matter how many there were, they all had a kind of stupid animal, even devilish, appearance. God, how ugly they looked! So ugly that I gritted my teeth. I felt pained and helpless and bitterly enraged. Machine guns! That's what I wanted. I felt that only the tongues of machine guns could talk to the mob, and that only machine guns and lead could drive back into his lair the frightful beast. The beast was no other than His Majesty the Russian People. That which we feared, tried to avoid at all costs, was before us. The revolution had begun.[5]

Only the tsar seemed unperturbed. A few days before, on 22 February, he had left Petrograd for the General Staff Headquarters at Mogilev, 700 kilometres from Petrograd. His diary from that time records his weariness of Petrograd with its interminable intrigues and incessant pressures. By comparison, running a war seemed to him like relaxation. On arrival at Mogilev he wrote, no doubt missing the boisterousness of his children, "Here in the house it is so still. No noise, no excited shouts . . . I shall take up dominoes again in my spare time". On 24 February he wrote "My brain is resting here, no Ministers, no troublesome questions demanding thought".[6] The tsarina, in Petrograd, was more aware of events but was equally out of touch with the reality they represented. On 25 February she wrote to Nicholas that the crowd in the streets was:

> a hooligan movement, young people run and shout that there is no bread, simply to create excitement, along with workers who prevent others from working. If the weather were very cold they would probably all stay at home.[7]

The average temperature in Petrograd in February 1917 was −14.5°C, one of the coldest of the decade.[8]

The tumult in the streets more than anything else, was the immediate stimulus producing the panicky reactions of the authorities. But it was neither the first nor the last time on which the streets were occupied by the revolutionary crowd. The dynamic of the revolution – its familiar landmarks of the February revolution, the downfall of Miliukov, the July Days, the failure of General Kornilov's attempted coup and the October revolution – was related to the rhythm of the Petrograd crowd. It is only one of many ironies of the revolution that its power began to decline rapidly at the moment of its apparent success when it helped to bring the Bolsheviks to power. None the less, when we think of the events of the Russian revolution we are thinking of those in which the crowd took part. The following chapters are devoted to looking at popular revolution in more detail. The questions at their heart are what brought ordinary people to participate in the revolution in such large numbers? Who were they? What impact did they have? One thing that the sketches of the crowd quoted above have in common is that each writer invested the crowd with her or his own values. For Sukhanov the people in the streets were heroic revolutionaries. For Miliukov they were perhaps necessary but were not to be trusted because they were incited by low motives (avoiding punishment) and showed a tendency to be unreliable, cowardly and disorganized (running away at the first shot). For Shul'gin they were completely repulsive. For the tsar and tsarina they were simply a malcontent minority upsetting the basic loyalty and devotion of the ordinary Russians – isolate the minority and there would be no more problem. Is it possible, now that passions have subsided, to at least be *more* objective about the revolutionary masses even though, no doubt, the temptation to project our own values on to them is still strong? It is a main aim of these chapters to try to achieve this and to give the people their place in events, not simply as a background to the various political leaders but as an independent force in their own right. A second set of problems arising from this is to consider other rhythms, other patterns of events with a view to showing that the various revolutions going on in the Russian Empire in 1917 did not all run precisely to the beat of Petrograd's political clock.

For the ordinary people of the Empire the February revolution unleashed a torrent of political possibilities. Institutions and organizations such as trade unions and soviets spread through the urban and semi-urban areas of the country reaching to some of its more far-flung industrial outposts in deepest Siberia and the Far East. Just as exciting were the new prospects for political expression. Every organization had its own newspaper, or at least newssheet, in addition to the national, regional and local press. The result was an endless chain of arenas in which there was an explosion of long-repressed opinion and relatively little organization. As the successor state to the autocracy proved to be weak, so the self-organization of the masses could evolve.

Of all aspects of the popular movement its institutional and organizational history has attracted most attention. The network of soviets caught the imagination of observers at the time and has continued to have many admirers. They have often been presented as the epitome of direct, participatory democracy, a path-breaking example of what real self-government might be like. The most fully-fledged examples, like the soviet in the naval base of Kronstadt, lived up to such descriptions. Admirers idealized soviets, critics pointed out their limitations, especially their localism and unwieldiness when it came to implementing the policies discussed with such great passion.

But whatever one's opinion, soviets were one of the great, original features of Russian revolutionary practice. They had first appeared in 1905 to co-ordinate strikes and protests in certain towns and cities but had been rather ephemeral. In 1917 their roots were much tougher. Within three months some 400 had been set up, growing to 600 in August and 900 by October.[9] They were often rough-and-ready institutions reflecting local conditions. Some wielded real power, others were little more than talking-shops. They were often set up in a very ad hoc way. Even the Petrograd Soviet was initially composed of more or less anyone who showed up. Its founding executive committee was self-selecting. Despite frequent efforts to regularize its position, delegates tended to come and go as they pleased without any real check on credentials. Political brokers in party caucuses never controlled the flood in 1917. Rather they resembled surfers balancing precariously on their boards, the danger of being engulfed threatening them continuously. Success in soviet politics between February and October meant being able to ride the wave for longer than anyone else.

While it is clear that soviets played a vital role in the revolution, it is less clear what role they played in the lives of ordinary workers. For many, their lives were more directly affected by institutions like trade unions and factory committees that penetrated even deeper into the fabric of everyday working-class life. Figures for membership of unions show rapid growth. From almost nothing in February 1917 union membership in Petrograd reached 390,000 by October. Nationally around two million people, comprising about 10 per cent of all wage-earners, joined unions in 1917.[10] Workers in an increasing number of factories began to set up factory committees. In Petrograd by the end of May all factories with more than 5,000 workers had them.[11] These, in particular, became the engine-room of worker organization and of integration into political parties, which themselves showed enormous growth in 1917.

While the importance of these developments is self-evident, and we will have to return to soviets, unions, factory committees and associated bodies throughout this study, particularly when it comes to examining the evolution of support for Bolshevism in these months, there are major limitations to be borne in mind. For our purposes of looking, especially, at the characteristics of the popular movement, we have to remember that one cannot equate these organizations with the broader movement. There are a number of reasons for this of which two are the most significant.

In the first place, these organizations were, naturally, areas in which an elite of activists played a greater role than the ordinary masses. People with other calls on their time – like those with full-time jobs in factory or field or women looking after families as well as working – had no spare time for political activism. As a result, those with fewer responsibilities – notably younger, single males and above all reserve soldiers many of whom, given the breakdown of traditional discipline, were in a position of being state-subsidized, full-time, political militants – tended to dominate such organizations at lower and intermediate level. At national level, of course, it was the full-time politicians who were in charge. Thus, one can by no means assume that the various levels of leadership shared the same views and values.

Secondly, it is easy to lose sight of the simple fact that only eight months had elapsed between the fall of the autocracy and the establishment of the Soviet government. By no stretch of the imagination could the repressed, semi-legal institutions like unions and political parties have turned the masses into organized, loyal followers of the leadership in that space of time. If anything, the relatively organized institutions, including the Bolshevik party, were swamped by an enthusiastic and energetic but often ignorant, naive and impulsive mass of new members. It would have been even less likely that institutions such as soviets and factory committees, that did not even exist before February, would have had any more success in containing the outburst.

The very rawness of the new recruits could even lead one to argue that, of all the component units of the popular movement, the urban workers were the most disadvantaged when it came to organization. In the first place, they did not have a natural basic unit. For peasants, the village and its traditional commune provided a focus and a simple, local, political culture that was deeply embedded. The organized, hierarchical structure of the armed forces meant that the regiment (or battleship) provided a base with the army and the front (or naval base and fleet) as the next stages up. Thus local peasants' committees were formed at village and/or *volost'* (parish) level and soldiers' committees at regiment, army and front level. What equivalent was there for the industrial worker? Given the migrant nature of much of the labour force, the anonymous nature of urban life and the frequency with which unskilled (and even skilled) workers might move from one employer to another, there was no equivalent, stable unit. The nearest was the factory (or workshop) committee (plus certain local union committees) that kept in regular contact with the workforce. But initially only a small minority of workers were covered by either factory or union committees. This could be compensated for at moments of crisis by the formation of ad hoc committees to organize strikes and protests, but on a day-to-day basis even the soviet of a city district was remote from its constituents.

There were two important traditional forms of grass-roots worker organization that persisted into 1917, the *zemliachestvo* and the *artel'*. The former was made up of members who had come to the city from the same village or district. Given the fact that various areas specialized in providing work in particular trades such institutions tended to be widespread. Although they had a mainly social function, those who were trying to organize and influence the working class were aware of their significance as important points of contact. The other traditional institution, the *artel'*, was a kind of work collective, a work-team who often hired themselves to an employer as a group and divided the income and the labour among themselves. They also tended to share living accommodation and household expenses and tasks like cooking. In addition to providing a soft landing for recent migrants the *artely* and *zemliachestva* reinforced certain aspects of rural collective attitudes and culture in the anonymity of the city. However, neither provided an answer to the problem of mass worker organization.

It should not, however, be forgotten that for more than ten years workers, particularly in major cities, had, where possible, been electing delegates to a variety of rather modest bodies from the commission to investigate Bloody Sunday and local soviets where they emerged in 1905, through unions, the workers' college of the Duma and insurance fund boards between 1906 and 1914, to the labour groups on the War Industries Committees in 1915.[12] Factory committees, soviets and the Petrograd Assembly of Factory Workers in 1917 and 1918 were, thus, not wholly new to many workers though their predecessors had been somewhat ephemeral.

The implications of organizational limitations were not lost on the revolutionary parties. In many respects, the SRs felt most at home in the traditional institutions. After all, their predecessors had tried to organize among migrant workers as far back as the 1870s. But for the main Marxist parties the problem was more acute. For them, proletarian revolution was supposed to come about after a period of developing consciousness and evolving working-class organization. In no way did Russian workers fit the recipe. Bolsheviks and Mensheviks both stressed the importance of overcoming organizational shortcomings before a sustained revolutionary onslaught could be contemplated. For the Mensheviks, this meant years, as it did for most Bolsheviks. Lenin, though, came round to the view (the consequences of which were to dominate Soviet life for seven decades) that one could, in the circumstances of 1917, have the political and institutional revolution first and get on with the necessary social and cultural revolution afterwards. Not surprisingly, hardly anyone, apart from a few more far-sighted employers, really argued that it was the very fact that they were *less* organized and *more* rural and migrant in background than their western European counterparts that made Russian workers more inclined to revolution. However, a closer look at the participation of the broad mass of workers in the revolution, shows that these features are an integral part of the nature of the Russian working class and of the revolution in which they took part.

At first sight, however, this emphasis seems to contradict the fact that, on the streets, workers appeared to be the epitome of organized, aware political activity. This has helped to give substance to the view that the Russian revolution was what many of its supporters claimed – a proletarian revolution, meaning one in which, on account of their superior organization and, above all, their more sophisticated political awareness, workers were the leading force, the battering-ram of the class struggle.

From their publicly visible on-street activities there would appear to be some truth in this view. Workers do participate in mass demonstrations and they do march under highly political slogans calling for changes in government, for an end to the war and so on. But if one follows them off the streets and back in through the factory gates the emphasis changes. The first, and most striking, change of perspective that results from looking at their life in the workplace is the degree to which worker–management tensions often coincided with major political crisis points. Obviously, any major crisis may well be the expression of innumerable minor crises (and this is truer of the Russian revolution than of many comparable events) but in this case it goes far beyond. When examined in this way, the causes of the local crises can be quite different from their ostensible political expression on the streets. Thus workers were not motivated solely, or even mainly, by broad political aims. Their actions were intimately tied up with the immediate circumstances in which they lived and, above all, worked. Thus, by looking at the workplace, we can get important clues about what got workers involved in revolutionary action.

Revolution and the workplace

The Putilov factory

A good place to start is the giant Putilov works in Petrograd. It was, in reality, a complex of loosely interlinked factories, mostly engaged in armaments production, plus a large naval dockyard. The main factory employed some 26,000 workers in February 1917, rising to 31,000 by the end of the summer. It was divided up into 49 different shops, some with only a handful of workers, others, like the artillery shop, with several thousand. Contact between the various shops was kept to a minimum by the management. It was not only the largest factory in Petrograd and the Russian Empire, but also one of the largest in the world. As such, its significance for working-class political activity had been obvious to all, including the police who kept a firm eye on the place, particularly since it had been noticeably turbulent in 1896–7 as well as 1905 and 1906. Whatever theory one had about who workers were, what they did in 1917 and why, it would have to fit the Putilov workers. If Russia did have the politically aware proletariat embodied in Bolshevik theory, it would have to be found in the Putilov factory, or not at all.

Undoubtedly, the *Putilovtsy*, as the workforce was called, were in the forefront of revolutionary activity in the city in 1917. All the major demonstrations – February, April, June, July, the defence against Kornilov and October – saw massive contingents from the factory taking part. Even in January 1917, before things hotted up, police reports say that 26,000 of them took part in a peaceful demonstration to commemorate the anniversary of Bloody Sunday. From June onwards observers noted a tendency for them to carry Bolshevik slogans. Thus, their on-street activities appear to go some way towards confirming the Soviet view. But this is only the tip of the iceberg. Street demonstrations were the culminating point of a whole complex of pressures and relationships, the focus of which was the workplace. The more we look at internal stresses in the factory, the more obvious it becomes that this is where the revolutionary activities of the *Putilovtsy* originated. It is particularly obvious in their case because the main political crises of the city coincided with peaks of tension within the factory itself.

In the first place, it is just possible that the February revolution might not have taken place, at least in the way that it did, were it not for the struggle going on inside the Putilov factory. Apart from participating in the Bloody Sunday anniversary, January and February saw a rash of strikes, large and small, spreading through the separate shops that made up the factory. The main issues at stake here were wages and working conditions. The largest strike took place in the artillery shop on 13 January in protest against the heavy-handedness of its overseer. The increased tension brought closer police activity and, on 8 February, the almost inevitable clashes occurred. Two thousand workers on their way home confronted a squad of about 50 police on duty outside the gates. Lumps of metal and other heavy materials were thrown at the police, injuring eight of them. This did nothing to calm the atmosphere and tension continued to rise. Eventually, on 22 February, the management decided to close the factory for "an indefinite period". The following day the companion naval dockyard was also shut down. This meant that the entire workforce was flung out onto the street in a high state of rage and anxiety just at the moment when a major crisis of the tsarist regime was taking place. The *Putilovtsy* joined up with women protesting at the lack of food supplies and with strikers from other factories to form the nucleus of what was to become the revolutionary crowd. Within nine days of the lockout, tsarism was dead. But their actions had not been consciously revolutionary from the beginning. The main driving force behind their involvement was the situation they experienced in the factory. They were being squeezed to produce more, the value of their wages was falling. This was the motor of their discontent. The *Putilovtsy* were not expecting, nor immediately aiming at, the overthrow of the regime when the crisis exploded. But, as had always been the case with tsarism, and was partially true of any state in wartime, such things smacked of treason. Confrontation with the police, who had a very high profile in the Petrograd factories, ensured that legitimate protest soon took on the dimension of political as well as economic struggle. This final, fatal episode in the annals of tsarist labour relations, showed the same suicidal intransigence that had characterized them for a quarter of a century. Political slogans had appeared, but they are best understood as the outcome of their day-to-day experiences, not as a sophisticated political position. The outlook of the *Putilovtsy* was, in many respects, an extension of populist, peasant attitudes – the illegitimacy of large-scale private ownership and the solidarity of the ordinary people (the *narod*) against the rich and powerful in moments of crisis – which many of them had learned in their early years in the village, where most of the Petrograd workforce had been born. Not surprisingly, the dominant political grouping in the factory in early 1917 was the SRs, with Mensheviks also prominent. There were only some 150 Bolsheviks in the factory before February.

The *Putilovtsy* joined in the revolutionary honeymoon. Noticeable improvements in their conditions, in the form of wage rises and the enactment of the eight-hour day, were extracted from the employers and the new government. Their situation began to change, however, in late spring. In particular, a long-lasting dispute about new wage and bonus rates smouldered on. In mid-June it caught fire when the government rejected the scheme that had been worked out. All reports for this period agree that the workforce was very angry and was straining at the leash for action. Soviet activists, including Bolsheviks, were trying to keep the workers off the streets rather than beckon them out into them. The factory committee, that had been set up in April, urged workers to "await the general call" and not to act in isolation. After furious argument the workers voted against striking. But this flash point coincided with the on/off 10 and 18 June street demonstrations and, for the *Putilovtsy*, the two pressures can barely be separated. Attempted restraint broke down a few days later and some 30,000 of them joined up with Kronstadters and garrison troops to take part in the July Days. Leaders in the factory, including Bolsheviks, were still doing their utmost to stop the demonstrations, but to no effect. The workers' frustration was too intense and whatever influence the political parties had on them completely broke down. There can be no doubt that it was the turn of events in the factory that energized the workers' protests.

Their actions in the crucial period of September and October can also only be understood in the light of their own particular situation. From late summer onwards, government and management had been trying to make major changes at the factory to halt the decline in output and the increase in costs. Their solution, announced on 9 August, was to propose sacking 11,000 of the 31,000 workers and a corresponding number of the white-collar and administrative staff.[13] The implications dominated factory committee and local Soviet activities throughout August and September and was also of importance to the whole of the left wing in the city. On 26 September a government representative, Palchinsky, met the factory committee and drew a picture of the factory's economic and financial plight in the gloomiest possible terms. The Soviet newspaper, *Izvestiia VTsIK*, which was controlled by the Menshevik and SR right who were participating in and supporting the Provisional Government at this time, wrote that the consequences of rising wages and falling output would have to be faced by the workers – the jobs would have to go. Once again, a major crisis within the factory coincided with the broader crisis of the city and the revolution. The *Putilovtsy* faced the October revolution with one-third of their factory facing redundancy thrust upon them by their own supposed representatives in the Soviet and the Provisional Government. Their actions, however, were much less militant than in the earlier crises and their participation rate in the October uprising was much lower than in February or July. Apathy, continuing economic crisis and the long, enervating, apparently hopeless, struggle of the previous months were taking their toll.[14]

The mines of the Donbas

Among the miners working in the brutal conditions of the Donets valley, the Donbas, situated in the eastern Ukraine, north of the Black Sea and the Caucasus mountains, the revolutionary year took on a different complexion, but the fundamental importance of the work experience and the workplace are just the same. Violence appears to have been much more prevalent than in the north, reflecting the rather more "frontier" attitudes that prevailed in this remote region. There are many more reports of beatings of foremen by workers and vice versa than for elsewhere. Shootings, relatively unknown but not entirely absent in Petrograd, were much more common. As early as 28 June the employers were bewailing the situation and calling on the government for help. Coal production was, of course, vital for the national economy as a whole and any interruption in output would damage the whole of industry and, through this, the war effort. Output, the employers said, was seriously threatened because workers were making "extremely varied and groundless demands". Refusal to meet them was met by threats, usually in the form of throwing managers, engineers and other technical and supervisory staff out of the pits. This, not unnaturally, made such staff reluctant to continue work. This in turn threatened production and increased the risk of gas explosions, collapses and flooding in the mines.

By October the situation had reached crisis point. The arrival of cossack troops in the middle of the increasing turbulence pushed the situation close to a showdown, particularly since relations between cossacks and in-migrants, such as many of the miners, had been poor for a long time. The workers united to call for the troops to be withdrawn. The Soviet of Bokovo-Khrustalsk and Shchetovo-Kartushinsk districts passed a resolution condemning the shamefulness of workers and peasants having bayonets and whips held over them and, in conjunction with many other soviets in the region, said a general strike would take place if they were not withdrawn by 10 October. "In the event of violence being used against us", they said, "we will employ all kinds of desperate terror". If newspaper reports are anything to go by, violence did increase once the strike got under way. Managers, engineers and foremen were targets of arrest, shooting and occasionally murder. Equipment was deliberately damaged. Furnaces, that had to be run continuously, were shut down.

It was not so easy for the government to withdraw the troops even if it had wanted to because, according to reports, they had been sent in by the military rather than civilian authorities and the Petrograd government lacked the authority to countermand the orders. Sending a government plenipotentiary to mediate made little difference. It is likely that the local cossack Ataman, Kaledin, was taking the law into his own hands and carrying out his own miniature Kornilov revolt, aimed at restoring what was, from the point of view of a general, order. But despite this, the workers' demands that we have from this area at this time have no specifically political content such as calling for Soviet power. Even though political authority and its abuse was at the heart of this dispute, the resolutions remained local in scope. We can be confident that if there had been broad political demands the Soviet authorities would have published them since they would have backed up their point of view, but there are none in the main published source collections. But, more important than formal declarations, is the fact that a self-generating revolution was occurring that mirrored events in Petrograd but did not directly follow on from them. The miners of this remote region were, through the logic of events rather than as a result of organization and propaganda, moving towards their own, local October revolution.[15]

The textile workers of Ivanovo

In the very different conditions of the textile area of Ivanovo, where women comprised the majority of the workforce in key areas, the workers' movement showed similar characteristics to Putilov and the Donbas. Local, workplace-based issues were of the utmost importance.

For 35,000 workers, from the Ivanovo-Kineshma *oblast'*, the largest confrontation of 1917 also took place in October, beginning on the 22nd. The outlook of those involved is reflected in their extraordinary list of demands. The seven-page document their union produced had a total of 36 general demands over such matters as wages and work conditions that affected all the workers, but is noteworthy for also having a long string of many more specific demands. There were 21 so-called sanitary-hygienic and technical demands; six were related to apartments and family barracks in which the (mostly migrant) workers lived; eight were about conditions in kitchens; 11 about bath-houses and six about laundries. There were no political demands at all even though this took place deep into the revolutionary period. The demands went into the detail of their everyday working lives and called, for instance, for sufficient hot water to be provided at break-time, and for corridors in the living accommodation to be heated. While these might appear to be trivial, as an encyclopaedia of the irksome, everyday problems that dogged workers' lives this humble document is very revealing. The petty humiliations, the loss of dignity, the outraged sense of justice and equality that echoes and re-echoes through its mundane catalogue of complaints tell us more about the ordinary workers' experiences than a dozen political resolutions.[16]

Reactivity and worker radicalism

An important theme running through worker actions is that many of them were reactive – in other words, workers were responding to pressures from outside as much as taking initiatives on their own behalf. The fateful lockout of 22 February, the government's rejection of the wage and bonus scheme in mid-June, and the threat of mass unemployment in the autumn were forcing the *Putilovtsy* into action. The aggression of Kaledin concentrated worker opposition in the Donbas. Throughout the country the twin pressures of a collapsing economy and attempted counter-revolution were forcing workers to take more extreme steps to defend themselves.

Though local differences, especially where there were national minorities involved, meant that no single place precisely mirrored any other, none the less, the basic matrix of economic, work-related, often reactive demands can be found at the heart of the revolutionary involvement of workers throughout the Empire. For example, Diane Koenker in her pioneering study of Moscow workers, showed that 92 per cent of strikes there in 1917 included demands for higher wages and commented that "the overwhelming majority of strikes in Moscow in 1917 centred on economic issues".[17] In Steve Smith's words:

> The revolutionary process of 1917 can only be understood in the context of a growing crisis of the economy. Western historians have been so mesmerized by the astonishing political developments of this *annus mirabilis*, that they have failed to see the extent to which a crisis in the economy underpinned the crisis in politics, or the extent to which the struggle to secure basic material needs provided the motive force behind the radicalization of the workers and peasants.[18]

Reactivity is particularly noticeable in the period after the July Days. As seen from inside the Putilov, and many other, factories, this was a bleak period of encroaching doom. Far from a rising tide of revolutionary enthusiasm taking hold of workers as the revolution unfolded, the atmosphere in which they lived was one of increasing threats to their livelihood. The disruption caused by continuing economic crisis, the political offensive of the right and the continuation of the war combined to make their everyday working and private lives more difficult than they had been in the early days of the revolution. Their actions, as a result, became geared to survival rather than to plans for the long-term future, that were confined to a small, heroic band of militants. Keeping factories running, and thereby preserving their wages and, ultimately, their jobs, was the concern that came to dominate the outlook of Russian workers in 1917, and beyond.

As early as the beginning of May, factory committees in Petrograd were sending out search parties to locate key raw materials like oil and coal and to find out how to ensure supplies for the future. The situation was already becoming so bad that on 20 May a city-wide conference of worker organizations was held on the supply question. Food supplies were also a matter of growing concern. Workers' resolutions called for the evacuation of unnecessary and "parasitic" elements of the population – among whom it numbered nuns and monks, those who lived off capital and what they called the deceived and pressed labourers who had been brought in from Asia – in order to lighten the food supply burden. They also called for the carriage of luxury items by rail and water to be suspended. Petrograd, with its distant northerly location and long supply routes from raw material and food producing areas, had a particularly acute problem in this respect and is not typical of all Russian cities, though many others experienced comparable difficulties.

These, however, were only pale forewarnings of the impending crises. The failure of the July Days pushed the workers, particularly in the capital, onto the defensive on three fronts, against economic pressures, against the initiatives of the government and the Soviet right, and against the growing threat of counter-revolution.

As we have seen, the Provisional Government, and its new head Kerensky, were determined to use the favourable conjuncture presented as a result of the failure of the July Days to reassert their authority over the popular movement. It was in these circumstances that, on 9 August, the authorities broached the question of the mass redundancies at the Putilov and other factories. Worse was to follow. In the last week of August, Kornilov embarked on his troop manoeuvres that, whatever their ultimate aim, presented an unmistakeable threat to the workers. The factories would undoubtedly be a prime destination for any reactionary forces of "order" coming into the city. Local soviets began to recruit volunteers from factories to serve in the irregular Red Guards, to defend the city in the event of military clashes with Kornilov's approaching forces. While the offensive petered out, the memory of it remained, as did the heightened vigilance of the Petrograd workers and the enlarged Red Guards. Also, the soviet left, including the Bolsheviks, who had been suppressed and whose leaders had been imprisoned, were released to provide a new leadership more in tune with the attitude of the workshops and factory floors of the country.

The weakness of Kornilov's drive for power did not, however, mean that the popular movement was now in the ascendant. Less dramatic, but much more deadly, was the steady erosion of the economy and the increasing difficulties in supplying the city. A new anxiety was added at this time. On 20 August the city of Riga, on the Baltic 500 km from Petrograd, fell to the Germans. The fear that they might now be within striking range of the capital gripped the inhabitants. The government, which may have been playing on this fear rather than believing it, began to talk of evacuating the city. Not only was it thought that the government might leave, but plans for evacuating civilian inhabitants, reposting the garrison and closing down factories were put on the agenda. From the government's point of view, this was a heaven-sent opportunity to break up the revolutionary forces in the city and regain control of the garrison.

This was how the left, and the ordinary population read the turn of events. Their response was, that if the government was going to abandon them, and try to take away the machinery by which they produced, they must take more power into their own hands. The period marked a rapid increase in political aspirations by workers. There was also a major attempt to grapple with the complexities of workers' control leading, in extreme cases, to the takeover of factories. The difficulty here did not lie in seizing the factories, which would have been comparatively simple, but in running them once they had been seized. Lacking the necessary skills and knowledge, the danger was that once a factory had been taken over, the workers could only preside over its collapse as banks refused to grant them loans, suppliers refused credit, distributors and sales networks turned to more reliable producers, not to mention difficulties resulting from dealing with innumerable technical problems from accounting to complex maintenance that were in the hands of management and engineers unsympathetic to the workers. It was in the light of all these considerations that the factory committee at the Putilov works, for example, came to the decision, very reluctantly, on 29 September that in view of the threat of evacuation, the supply problem, the threatened redundancies and the possible need for self-defence against the Germans, they should set up a genuine system of workers' control. It was clearly a last-ditch act of desperation in the circumstances, not a bold and enthusiastically welcomed fresh start. It was under pressure from similar motives that calls for a worker–peasant government also became more insistent, although at this point, details were vague. There can be no doubt that attitudes in Petrograd and among workers in other cities in October were dominated by thoughts of self-defence and resistance to constant, draining pressures. It was this that led them increasingly to call, often out of desperation, for soviet power as a last, defensive resort.

Workers, parties, politics, consciousness

The paradox of resistance leading to new activism highlights one of the key problems in looking at workers' participation in the revolution. How do we assess the political dimension? While the work-related experiences we have been concentrating on provide a foundation for their activities, we cannot explain them solely through that. The importance of reactivity, for instance, highlights the vital relationship between the workplace and the outside world. Quite obviously, the general context of collapsing authority and economic crisis also made their mark. The latter made worker action necessary, the former made it possible. But what was the balance between them? Finally, can we talk about the "consciousness" of working people with any degree of certainty? In part, answers to these questions are linked to the central issue of the relationship between the Bolsheviks and workers that is touched on in Chapter 6. None the less, in order to get a clearer idea of worker motivation and outlook in 1917 we must look at the broader aspects at this point.

A great deal of effort has been put into the search to find the most important reasons for working-class political activity in the Russian revolution. This has mainly stemmed from fascination with the link between Marx's predictions about revolution in capitalist society being led by the proletariat and the emergence in Russia of a political party that claimed to be inspired by those predictions. Surely, one would think, there must be some connection? This has made the Russian revolution into a test case for the Marxist view of a worker-led revolution.

Early-twentieth-century Marxists believed that, as the laws of capitalism inexorably ground on, the working class's position of growing impoverishment, unemployment and exclusion would give it no alternative but to rebel against the owners of capital (the bourgeoisie) and their dependants, that is, to engage in class struggle. It would have, in Marx and Engels' words, "nothing to lose but its chains". Over time the proletariat would come to understand its predicament, that is, its consciousness would develop. By 1900 workers with such an awareness were being called "advanced workers". They would, as a result, join together to form the political energy necessary to carry out the revolution. If the events of 1917 are to be understood as a Marxist, proletarian revolution, it has to be shown that the working class was the leading force in this sense. In order to examine this proposition, scholars have concentrated on questions of organization and leadership in the revolution and have engaged in the task of trying to identify a core of proletarians at its heart. In particular, the debate has revolved around the central issue of whether the process of rising consciousness and class struggle was leading to a higher level of political awareness. In short, was there an advanced working class in the Marxist sense? Almost everyone agrees, up to this point, that there was not, if one looks at the working class as a whole. However, there are many arguments to show that while the class as a whole was "backward" it did have "advanced" sectors.

From the very early days Bolshevik accounts have emphasized that, particularly in Petrograd, there was a group of second- and third-generation workers (that is, workers who had been born in the city and whose fathers might even have been born in the city) who provided the leading revolutionary cadres. They were often, it was said, skilled rather than unskilled workers and were slightly better educated, at least to the extent of being genuinely literate, than the rest. Here, it was argued, was the advanced, conscious working class. Metalworkers in particular were conspicuous in this group. Perhaps coincidentally, perhaps not, metalworkers in Petrograd and Moscow were a bastion of Bolshevism. Therefore, it was concluded, the Bolsheviks were the focus of advanced, proletarian consciousness. This, if nothing else, helped to fulfil the "theological" requirement that the Bolsheviks should be the leading representatives of the proletariat.

Clearly, this view makes a number of implicit assumptions about the role and importance of leadership in 1917 that have to be questioned in the light of the fact that the worker masses were often more radical than the leaders. In addition, other scholars, this time largely in the west because it goes against Leninist assumptions, have pointed to the rural links and migrant nature of much of the labour force. As yet, most of this material relates to Moscow, does not go much beyond 1905 and has not been thoroughly tested in the context of 1917. Interestingly, there are signs, however, that some Russian scholars, under the freer conditions now prevailing, are beginning to look more seriously at the importance of the rural connections of many workers.[19]

There are very good reasons for them to do so. As far as the urban workforce as a whole is concerned, there can be no doubt that most workers were born and brought up in the countryside and maintained important, even if not always welcome, links with the village. The fact that Russian industry had expanded rapidly in the short space of time from the 1890s to 1917 meant that only the countryside could supply sufficient recruits to keep it going. Continued, even accelerated, expansion in the early war years reinforced this, particularly in Petrograd where the workforce nearly doubled in the major factories between 1914 and 1917. In any case, if one includes all workers born in the countryside, Petrograd and, to an even greater extent Moscow, had a majority of migrant workers even in the factories without taking into account the hundreds of thousands of young peasant women drawn into domestic service or working in city shops until they were married and began to bear children. Many male city workers had wives and children or land in the village. Surveys in St. Petersburg showed that, in 1908 in some factories, from 29 per cent (in the Baltiskii shipyard) to 87 per cent (in textile factories) of married male workers had wives and children in the countryside, whom they might not see for years in extreme cases. Even in 1918, 20 per cent of all workers still owned land in the village, though many of them had lost touch with its day-to-day management.

But objective links are not, perhaps, the point. What was most resisted by

Bolshevik and many Leninist commentators, was that the village had a cultural hold over the urban workers. The Bolshevik stereotype tended to show a transition from country yokel – useless material for revolution on account of ignorance, drunkenness, illiteracy and tendency to spontaneous, disorganized political explosions that punctuated long periods of deference, often induced by the church – to the skilled, educated, conscious and organized proletarian who belonged to, and accepted the instructions of, the Bolshevik party. Many Bolshevik memoirs back this up, the writer often emphasizing that he (it was almost invariably a man) had personally followed such a path. Usually, other essentials of the party line such as the limited impact of intellectuals in worker movements, intersperse the comments. A closer look, however, shows not only that many of the writers had picked up the first elements of their revolutionary mentality in the village but that some of them were themselves intellectuals or, at least, showed considerable respect for the intellectuals they encountered in the movement. Very few of them were themselves born in the city.

As part of the attempt to find an advanced working class in tsarist Russia the question of consciousness has attracted considerable attention. How did Russian workers think of their social identity? Did they have a special sense of affinity with other workers? Did they have a sense of identity that was broader, or, perhaps, narrower than this? Evidence for giving a sound answer to this question is sparse and controversial. Any reply must be tentative. We can, however, make a number of comments.

First, there were many jealously guarded gradations within the working class itself. Like workers of the same period elsewhere, there was a division, often based on familiarity with the city and the factory, between those who had crept a little way up the social ladder and considered themselves a cut above those feeding in at the bottom, usually recent migrants from the village. This equates in some ways to the division between "rough" and "respectable", for instance, which was important to British workers at this time. It was reinforced by the division of labour in the factories. The older, more skilled and more settled workers did represent a social and cultural milieu different from that of recent migrants. "Respectability" was greatly prized among the more established workers. Photographs of even a group of workers as radical as the Putilov factory committee in 1917 show its members dressed as if on a Sunday outing in their best clothes – dark suits, caps, heavy dark boots – just like their contemporaries in Britain or Germany.

In one of the finest books on the culture and way of life of Russian workers in the late-nineteenth and early-twentieth centuries, Mark Steinberg has shown the drive for respectability in all its complexity. The printers he studied referred to those employed in factories, and those who worked on the presses, as "workers" (*rabochie*) or even "peasants" (*muzhiki*) while considering themselves to be somewhere between workers and intellectuals.[20] However, they still maintained rural-type rituals of rough music and the carting out of people who had offended against community norms by, for instance, strike-breaking.[21] Steinberg stresses that the overwhelming impulse of the printers was simply to be treated like human beings, an aspiration taken up by activists who argued that they must then behave like human beings and spend less time in taverns.[22] He also noted an ethic of love, goodness, truth and justice that they had taken from religion as well as the more widely noted characteristics of suffering in silence and self-abnegation. This culture is very close to that of the peasants. The picture he presents suggests a group of workers suspended between a rural culture they had not fully shaken off and an urban environment to which they were adapting and in which they were demanding a privileged place for themselves, not a revolutionary upheaval for all. Indeed, Steinberg points out that some activists were worried that some of the printers were putting too much effort into their own cultural self-improvement and not enough into the labour movement – too many dance parties, not enough strikes, as the Menshevik V. V. Sher put it.[23]

None the less, arguments about the sense of differentiation within the working class has played a large part in the debate about the "advanced" worker. There are, however, a number of unanswered queries relating to it. First, though it is intended to show "advanced" workers as being more organized and revolutionary than "backward" ones, it is precisely here that one finds workers who do fit the "advanced" stereotype in terms of education, skill and long-term residence in the city but who are not the most active revolutionaries. In fact, while they certainly defended their own skills and position, many older, more skilled workers, like printers, were less involved in revolutionary activities. Secondly, did the carefully built up and meticulously maintained differentials of relatively normal times hold up in the face of the political and economic hurricane of 1917? Here there are serious reasons to doubt whether the divisions are of primary importance. Instead, the need for broad self-defence, plus the awareness of the much more fundamental cleavages in Russian society which was at the heart of the revolution, swept the internal divisions among workers far into the background. Instead, a broader consciousness of the unity of all workers, indeed of all the ordinary, exploited people including peasants, rushed to the surface. Steinberg found something similar in that, in moments of crisis like the first printers' strike of 1903, printworkers at all levels joined together in united opposition to their employers and the government.[24] In other words, there are grounds for thinking that, in the revolution, the prime identifying link was with the *narod*, the people as a whole, with subdivisions taking second place.

Comparing such phenomena on an international basis opens the debate up to the suspicion that, having attained and gone beyond a certain level of adaptation to the city and the factory, an elite of skilled workers, more likely to be unionized than their unskilled brothers and sisters, tended to move away from revolutionary politics altogether and turned instead to reformism, like workers in the British Labour Party and the German Social Democratic Party. Lenin contemptuously dismissed such workers as an "aristocracy of labour" but no one has been able to develop a sociological net so fine that it can distinguish between the profiles of the "advanced worker" and "the aristocracy of labour". Both are said to be urbanized, better educated, more skilled and more organized. In any case, there is an anomaly, in Marxist terms, in equating "advanced" workers with skilled, that is, better-off workers since, in the original ideas of *The Communist manifesto*, it was ever-growing impoverishment that would lead to "advanced" revolutionary consciousness.

Be that as it may, wherever one looks at the working class as a whole, traces of the broader identification with the *narod* can be found. The demand for the transfer of land to the people or to the peasantry was prominent in many of the major worker resolutions from the early days of 1917. Along with clauses on the conduct of the war, the need for democratization, growing demands for workers' control and criticism of the economic situation, it was firmly entrenched in the workers' programme. In more remote areas, workers, like the miners of the Donbas, saw their struggle as being one with that of the peasantry. There is no doubt that all three branches of the soviets – workers, soldiers and peasants – saw their actions as being part of one movement. There was no sectarian hostility between them and party affiliations ran across the boundaries between them. The main populist party, the SRs, was the largest political party in terms of votes throughout 1917, and this can by no means be attributed solely to its support among peasants. As late as the 20 August elections in Petrograd to the central Duma, the SRs outpolled the Bolsheviks by 205,000 votes to 184,000, not to mention the fact that it was only by moving the party closer to the SR programme and strategy, by incorporating the majority of the peasantry into the revolutionary alliance, that the Bolsheviks were able to gain support at SR and Menshevik expense in late summer and autumn.

The vocabulary of the revolution also has populist resonances. Phrases referring to "the labouring masses" were very common in resolutions as was the word *narod* and its derivatives. The word "proletarian" seems to have been largely used by Bolshevik activists rather than by many actual workers. But even the Bolshevik government, when it came to power, took up the populist vocabulary. It called itself the Council of People's Commissars, and of course, retained the terminology down to Stalin's time – for instance in the quintessentially Stalinist phrase "enemy of the people" – and beyond. By comparison, the word proletarian did not have much resonance in the population and it is hard to imagine many people who would have identified themselves as such in 1917. One new piece of terminology that did fit, however, was the word *burzhui*, a corrupt version of the word "bourgeois", that came to be widely applied by the ordinary people to their social enemies. This reminds us that, given the polarization of Russian society and its clear division into elite and masses, the Russian worker and peasant experienced class struggle in a pure form. The *burzhui* were the enemy, the *narod* those who shared the suffering and were natural allies in the joint struggle. Whatever the

79

lesser divisions, the indications are that this larger sense of identity was more important.

All this is not to suggest that the worker and peasant movements were identical, far from it, but they were complementary and mutually compatible. The view that only the factory and urban experience could make peasants into revolutionaries overlooks the contribution that the long radical tradition of the peasantry made to the revolutionary proclivities of the urban workers. The process was one of interchange. While workers undoubtedly abandoned many characteristics of rural life, notably its more superstitious and religious practices that were replaced by a little education and a great thirst for knowledge on the part of many urban workers, some of the fundamental attitudes survived the journey and flourished in the new environment. Above all, the different aspects of egalitarianism, political solidarity and polarization of village society have to be taken into account. In the next chapter we shall examine what these meant in the village, but for the present it has to be pointed out that they were also important in the city. There was an extensive natural egalitarianism about the urban revolutionaries. None of them saw any reason why those who worked less should be wealthier than those who worked more. They had no truck with the pretensions of the upper classes that their privileged position was justified. Their raw hatred of the authorities was entirely analogous to the peasants' centuries' old opposition to the larger landowners. The class barriers, in both cases, were virtually uncrossable. The chronic polarization of rural society was replicated in the city. Not only were the privileged classes remote from the ordinary population, they were heavily outnumbered, comprising only some 10 per cent of the population, if one includes the educated and professional classes as well. At the other extreme was the 80–90 per cent of the population that lived in a totally different world, and knew it, and was only kept in check by increasing application of force. Defence against repression, over time, welded solidarity in the face of the common enemy, despite the fact that rural and urban communities were divided among themselves over much else. The persistence of self-organization institutions such as the commune in the village and the *artel'* and *zemliachestvo* in the town, as well as the spontaneous setting up of soviets in the first moments of the revolution, show how deep-rooted communal solidarity was and how ordinary people, from the beginning, were uniformly suspicious of initiatives emanating from the upper ranks of society.

Such considerations suggest that, far from being an "advanced" working class teetering on the brink of becoming an "aristocracy of labour", even the elite of Russian workers at the time are better thought of as, in the Thompsonian sense, an "unmade" working class, or a working class still in the making. It retained a sharp radical edge of rural origin which had been honed into a more effective weapon through the unenlightened repression meted out by the state, the overall conjuncture of Russia's weak industrial economy passing through the early and dangerous stages of industrialization when its costs bore down heavily on the workers and its benefits still lay some way off in the future, plus the possibilities that workers had in the towns to strengthen their radicalism and raise their level of organization through contact with each other and with revolutionary intellectuals.[25] From the ordinary person's point of view, the revolution was a settling of accounts with a vicious ruling class that should be done away with without regret and replaced by the organized power of the working population, urban and rural. In the words of Aleksandr Blok's brilliant poem *The twelve*, written in January 1918, the purpose of the revolution for its ordinary participants was "to smoke the nobs out of their holes".[26]

Broadening the picture: patriotism, ethnicity, gender and other aspects of worker identity and activity

Events in the workplace, reaction to outside pressures and political consciousness are not the only pieces in the mosaic of worker activity in the revolution, though they are the most important. The pattern as a whole can only be understood if one takes into account a number of other important characteristics, some of which also impinge on the vexed question of identity. In particular, patriotism, ethnicity, gender, the role of artisans, the question of violence and the relationship of the masses to political parties and organizations are all extremely interesting aspects of worker participation. There is no way, however, that one can come to definitive conclusions about any of them because, in the general rush to prove or disprove the Marxist–Leninist view of the revolution, these issues have been put to one side. Only recently have they begun to attract the attention of historians. While one can only make very tentative suggestions about most of them, we do need to take them into account in order to broaden our understanding not only of the urban masses and the industrial labour force and their actions in 1917 and beyond, but also, as we shall see in subsequent chapters, of the peasantry and the armed forces as well. Needless to say, the emphasis varies between these different groups. Patriotism and ethnicity, for instance, probably reached their most acute expression in parts of the army. Gender, limited though it was as an issue in 1917, seems to have been more prominent among workers than elsewhere. By contrast, one feature that was probably equally spread among all groups was indifference to basic tsarist values of chauvinism, official religion and so on. However, we have a lot to learn about such themes and future research may well come up with some surprises.

Patriotism and ethnicity

An important characteristic of workers was patriotism, though the precise connotations of this obviously varied with nationality. Naturally this feature comes out most strongly in the attitudes of workers to the war and more or less equates with hostility to Germany, though not necessarily to Germans. According to the standard view, popular opinion supported the war in early 1917 but moved to a more critical stance in the summer and autumn, reaching a depth of war-weariness and desire for peace at any price by the start of the October revolution. The situation was not, however, so straightforward and the attitudes of workers to the war were, to say the least, ambiguous. Certainly, in the aftermath of the February revolution workers protested vehemently that they were truly patriotic and wanted the invader to be repelled. In the second half of March, one group of Petrograd workers went so far as to condemn shirking and excessive wage claims as "shameful" in view of the situation. Others said they had only one desire "not to give back the freedom we have gained to be ripped to shreds by the bayonets of Wilhelm and the defenders of the autocracy". A mass meeting of 10,000 at the Putilov factory in early April emphasized that workers were not to blame for production difficulties that were said to be holding up supplies to the front.[27] It was obviously in the interests of the counter-revolution that such rumours should circulate and the right-wing press used this card and variants of it, many times in 1917 in an attempt to turn soldiers and workers against one another. The Soviet took action to refute the claims. Soldiers from the front and factory workers went on exchanges to find out the situation for themselves. In a ceremony at the front on 17 April workers from the Old Parviainen Factory in Petrograd took charge of the regimental banner of the 26th Battalion of the Moscow Regiment and promised to keep it until the end of the war. In a joint declaration the workers said they were encouraged by "the robust mood of the troops and their preparedness to defend the renovated motherland" while the soldiers declared their confidence that the Russian people (*narod*), having won the right to freedom, would be able to defend it so that "the inhabitants of the trenches" would not again have to have recourse to rifles within the country, in defence of the people's interests.

While armaments workers were particularly vulnerable to accusations of disrupting the war effort it was by no means confined to them. Any part of the labour movement was fair game. It was, of course, used against Lenin and the Bolsheviks in the aftermath of the July Days. While this is not surprising, the point is that such an accusation was very damaging. There was a large constituency, including many workers, that was totally hostile to anything that might bring comfort and assistance to the German war effort. Anti-German sentiment remained strong among workers, and their support for peace policies, the implications of which contradicted this, have to be understood in this light. On 11 October a mass meeting of workers at the Putilov factory called for the arming of workers "in order to fend off the internal enemies of the revolution and its external enemy – the German Kaiser". The very next clause called for all power to the Soviets.[28] Clearly the two were linked in their minds and, just as the February revolution was supposed to lead to victory, so, in the minds of many workers in October, a Soviet government was to lead a struggle against the Kaiser. The fact that earlier on the same resolution had called for peace-making at the front only goes to show the complexity of the popular attitude and the growing, but not entirely explicit, acceptance by many workers of Lenin's concept of transforming the imperialist war into a civil war. Clearly, despite the supposed war-weariness and manifest desire for peace, surrender, or anything like it, was not in their minds. A just and democratic peace was acceptable (though totally unobtainable). Anything else was not, even *in extremis*.

One might tentatively suggest that, while ordinary people were hostile to enemy (and, for many, even to allied) governments on class grounds, they felt that the ordinary people of the combatant countries had no quarrel with one another. Thus, their patriotism – their assertion of their Russian or Ukrainian identity – was an extension of their in-built sense of class. They tended to be instinctively "internationalist" with respect to the peoples of other countries, whose rights were, they felt, equal to their own. They did not, however, abandon their cultural identity as a result. For much of 1917 this also applied to many members of ethnic minorities who seem to have readily adopted "All-Russian" values on the question of war, peace and the defeat of Germany. Separate ethnic identity, as opposed to nationwide patriotism, was, as yet, fairly limited, though Poles and Finns were significant exceptions. But, by and large, within the working-class movement in 1917, a sense of overall solidarity seems to have been stronger than ethnic differences. A good example of this complexity is provided by Jewish workers and their organizations. At one level Jewish, even Zionist, identity was well-developed. But, at the same time, there was an assumption among many Jewish workers and leaders that they should fight alongside Russian and other workers, not in opposition to them. After all, the remnants of the autocracy, the growing counter-revolution, the employers and so on were as much the enemies of a Jewish worker as of a Ukrainian or Russian one.

This is not to say that there was a non-racist, internationalist idyll in the midst of the turbulence of 1917. While systematic accounts of ethnic clashes are few and far between we do know that there were horrifying episodes of violence between ethnic groups. Jews, in particular, continued to suffer. But these seem to have been attacks manipulated from above, particularly by counter-revolutionaries attempting to split the revolutionary movement. They were not, by and large, spontaneous outbreaks. The same cannot, however, be said for the emergence of deep-rooted hostilities between Christians and Muslims in the Caucasus that were raised to a higher pitch than ever by the Turkish–Russian war being fought in that area, some aspects of which are dealt with in Chapter 5.

Women workers

In the war years, women made up a large, and rapidly increasing, proportion of the Russian factory labour force. In 1900 they constituted about 20 per cent, in 1914 27 per cent and in 1917 43 per cent. In Petrograd in 1917 there were 130,000 women factory workers out of a total of 417,000.[29] The turbulence of 1905 that encouraged employers to hire women as hopefully more docile labourers and the difficulty of finding male labour in competition with military conscription during the war, had combined to reinforce the role of women. Even in the formerly exclusively male area of Petrograd metalworking there was by 1916 a 20 per cent penetration by women. By and large, however, the separate role of women in the labour movement was opposed by the major political parties. The Bolsheviks, for instance, who were among the most active in organizing women's participation in unions and other activities, none the less saw them as part of the working class rather than as women. Clearly this arose from a desire to strengthen the working class's chief weapon, its solidarity. To suggest there might be a division of interest between female and male components of the class would be to weaken it. The Bolsheviks, including leading women activists such as Alexandra Kollontai, had denounced the separating out of women's interests as bourgeois feminism. They argued strongly that class ties bound women more strongly to men of the same class than gender ties bound them to women of other classes. In the revolutionary situation one can readily understand why the priority should have been expressed in this way.

But even so, there was an important element of women's emancipation in the policies of all the radical parties, from Kadet liberals to the anarchists. It was a natural corollary of their egalitarian aims. As a result of the Provisional Government reforms, women achieved full equality of rights before the law, including voting rights, from which they were still excluded in liberal parliamentary democracies such as Britain, France, the United States and even the mini model democracy of Switzerland. This provided a secure foundation for their participation in the revolution, but discrimination based on cultural factors and the division of labour by gender, that resulted in women taking on family tasks of child-rearing and looking after the household without significant labour input by males, persisted, despite vigorous attacks and utopian schemes put forward by radical feminists.

As far as revolutionary involvement is concerned, however, the picture is less clear. What we have said so far about workers applies, by and large, to women and men. Indeed, we have already had cause to mention women in connection with the Ivanovo strike. Women have also entered into the mythology of the revolution via the rebellious bread queues of the February revolution in Petrograd. They also appear in many accounts of similar activities. Even so, their role differed appreciably from that of men. Given the nature of a traditional patriarchal society such as Imperial Russia, it is not surprising that women were more prominent in "household"-related disputes like food shopping and absent from leading party and union committees. Even in the Bolshevik party, leading women activists tended to take notes at Central Committee meetings, like Elena Stasova, rather than participate in discussion and decision-making. Even feminized industries had male-dominated factory committees and unions. Photographic and memoir evidence shows very weak participation by women in the activities of soviets. Men tended to dominate political and economic decision-making, women tended to play the roles of assistants, if they were present in that area at all. Outside this sphere they tended to get drawn into "women's" areas like education (as did Lenin's wife Krupskaia, for instance), health and organizing other women.

However, as events evolved in 1917, there are signs that a growing awareness of women's participation in the labour movement was coming about. Where resolutions had spoken only about "workers" and "the working people" in early 1917, later in the year the formula "workmen and working women" made an appearance. Specific employment-related demands appropriate to women began to appear by late summer and autumn. At the Putilov works, for instance, a supreme bastion of male-dominated worker activity, the major resolution of part of the workforce of 28 September, called for a maternity insurance scheme, although, somewhat unpromisingly, it was categorized alongside sickness and unemployment. However, it was a start. Undoubtedly, though, this was only a side issue and the mainstream of political activity by workers – devoted to combating economic disaster – left little room for separate gender-related activities. The mainstream issues were equally important to men and women workers and their families.

Artisans

Turning from women to another key group, artisans, the record is even more vague. The official Soviet obsession with factory workers has led to a lack of attention to the large number of workers, the majority in many places, who were employed in smaller establishments. In Moscow in 1917 there were 250,000 artisans compared to 165,000 factory workers, the corresponding figures for St. Petersburg being 58,000 and 234,000 respectively in 1910. Over the country as a whole they were much more numerous than factory workers. Given the dilatory nature of tsarist bureaucrats, the gathering of information on this elusive, diverse, scattered and shifting population was rather beyond their resources. Other revolutions, notably the French, have shown artisans to be a major force. In particular, since their livelihoods depended on the market for their particular skills, they were often vociferous in their denunciations of forces corroding their position. The fact that they also had a slightly more secure position in the labour market than many workers, who could be fired and replaced at will, meant that they could show a little more independence. It was the case that, in Russia, some of the earliest and toughest unions had been set up by artisans defending their traditional crafts against encroaching mechanization. It also seems likely that those based in cities were more urbanized than factory workers as a whole. How these factors work out in Russian terms, we can only speculate about but there is little evidence to show that they were a particularly distinctive part of the mass movements of 1917. They seem, rather, to have blended in with factory workers and the rest and artisanal workers can be found in all sections of the labour movement. They are not, however, without their ambiguities. Printworkers were largely artisanal but also fulfilled as well as any other group the characteristics of "advanced" workers such as high skill level, long-term urban residency and well-developed organizations but they remained resolutely Menshevik in 1917 while the sociologically similar tailors, for example, tended to be Bolshevik. As in other areas, correlations between social background and political involvement is extremely hazardous. Until further research proves otherwise they are best considered alongside the mainstream of the urban working class.

Popular violence and lynch law

In the French revolution, the Parisian artisans, the *sans-culottes*, became famed for their violence. There were also many in Russia in 1917, who have had their supporters since, who equated popular participation in the revolution with mob violence, criminality and hooliganism inspired by a spiteful, envious desire simply to achieve a levelling down in society, what, in Russian, is called *uravnilovka*. Naturally enough, such views tended to come from the propertied classes and the intelligentsia. While what we have already seen shows this interpretation to be mistaken in most respects – worker activities being rational and inspired by a genuine desire for a fairer distribution of wealth and power in society – it would be wrong completely to gloss over the problem of violence. All accounts, though there is no systematic study, show that criminality and violence did increase to the extent of being endemic in cities in 1917. In part this was an inevitable corollary of the weakening of police and state authority and partly it was because the jails had been opened in the first flush of revolutionary enthusiasm and many criminals had been released as well as political prisoners. There were also considerable outbreaks of looting. Criminal violence often accompanied major revolutionary actions. During the February revolution the future Red Guard and memoirist Eduard Dune witnessed a crowd, on the banks of the river Iauza in Moscow, battering to death a policeman who had just shot a boy. "In an instant everyone laid into him. The gray overcoat of the policeman was seen flying through the air above the heads of the crowd towards the railings and into the river. His peaked cap was flung after it and stuck on the ice a long way from the body."[30] There were reports of mass rapes at the time of the July Days and some of the Women's Battalion who defended the Winter Palace in October were assaulted. At this time there was a notorious attack on the palace wine cellar that was followed by looting attacks on middle-class and aristocratic homes in Petrograd. Without doubt, even in less fevered times, the city streets of the Empire were much more dangerous in 1917 than they had been before the revolution.

In addition to the pure criminality that accompanied the revolution there are also frequent reports of more politically orientated violence. In February a group burned down a police station in one of the districts of Petrograd, having first made sure that the hated archives, containing informers' records on the local inhabitants, were destroyed. Clearly, this kind of attack on a hated symbol of authority is something quite different from a pogrom or looting attack. Other activities could lead to groups taking the law into their own hands, what's called in Russian *samosudy*, literally, self-judgments, a kind of do-it-yourself justice. This could include the murder of a factory director, as happened at the Putilov works in early March, the type of endemic violence and shooting in the pits of the Donbas, or simply the beating up on the streets of petty thieves and supposed informers. Ritual violence, such as the symbolic carting-out of the factory of unpopular managers and foremen occasionally happened, sometimes followed by a ducking in a nearby canal or river. Food riots and protests against what were seen as unfair price rises also took place.

Clearly worker activity had a militant, stormy, riotous edge that shaded into criminality. It was precisely this kind of blind, instinctive lashing out at authority that the more responsible revolutionary parties, including the Bolsheviks, condemned as ineffective "spontaneity". Such actions, they thought, chronically weakened the necessary "organized" revolutionary activities that were planned with a successful outcome in mind. The violence was often equated with peasant influence and compared to the rural *bunt*, a kind of riot, that was considered antipathetic to real revolution because, in its mindless, disorganized rage, it was not only easy for the authorities to put down but also gave them an excuse for their repressive policies.

Indeed, the more violent elements of the working class were the unskilled labourers, the *chernorabochii* (literally the black workers because they did the dirtiest and least desirable jobs) who were usually the most recent migrants. Resolutions passed by such workers often show great vehemence. Pushed to extremes by their poverty in late July and feeling, more than any other group, the pressure of rising prices and falling supplies, a group of unskilled workers in Petrograd denounced "capitalist pirates" and "all the brigands and marauders plundering the proletariat" and called for urgent attention to be given to the critical position of the "hungry, barefooted and coatless". "The most extreme measures" were necessary, they said, if hunger were not to bring the revolution to destruction.[31] Indeed, at about the same time, a government minister, Riabushinsky, was arguing that what he called "the bony hand of hunger" might strangle the wilder extremes of the revolution. At this stage, the desperation of unskilled workers met up with the extremism of the Bolsheviks, indicated by the tone of their resolution and their self-description as the proletariat. This identification shows that the Bolsheviks' theoretical idealization of the organized, advanced worker often gave way in practice to their appeal being received more readily by the more backward, spontaneous elements of the movement. Be that as it may, it is clear that the most exploited sections of the working class were being pushed to "the most extreme measures" by their desperate situation and violence might well seem the only way out.

It is, perhaps, all the more surprising then to find that, far from encouraging violence, still less participating in it in a systematic way, the majority of workers seem to have been at one with their leaders in seeing the danger it entailed and the threat it posed to the revolution. Rather than take part in spontaneous violence a whole range of worker self-defence organizations were built up to defend workers' interests against the violent element in the revolution that the workers attributed to former Black Hundreds (that is proto-fascist and anti-semitic elements), renegade former policemen and counter-revolutionary desperadoes and adventurers. These organizations often took the form of irregular militias linked with factory committees. They were set up from late spring onwards to defend factories and their raw materials, often, strangely enough, from their owners who were thought to be manipulating supplies in order to have an excuse for plant closures, or who were feared to be planning to shift vital equipment to more docile areas. The extraordinary turnabout meant that workers were often trying desperately to keep plants open while employers were trying to stop production. Far from smashing equipment in Luddite fashion, the workers in large factories, especially in Petrograd, were pathetically keen on keeping the machines running. Without them, they would be unemployed, penniless and in a hopeless situation.

In reality, however, the impact of such organizations was rather small for most of the period, though they made a great leap after the Kornilov blunder when the Red Guards, a derivative of these militias organized by local soviets for police and defence purposes, were expanded and armed. None the less, they constitute incontrovertible evidence that the popular movement was not simply a mob. In a superbly nuanced evocation the poet Aleksandr Blok, in *The twelve* described the unlikely Red Guard heroes in all their ambiguity:

> Caps tilted, fag drooping, every one
> looks like a jailbird on the run.[32]

Even though there were undoubtedly excesses and atrocities, the great majority of workers condemned them, distinguished them from legitimate violence against oppressors and strove to defend themselves, their own families and the community at large from them.

Tsarist values and religion

Despite their poor education and the increasingly intolerable conditions Russian workers throughout 1917 showed an extraordinary solidarity. While there were many relatively passive workers, there were hardly any who were actively counter-revolutionary. While there were innumerable jeremiahs, particularly among older workers, who thought nothing good would come of the upheaval, there were few who actively sympathized with or became apologists for the employers, or even for tsarism to which most of them had expressed some degree of loyalty in their lives.

Equally surprising is the fact that they were almost uniformly secular and even anti-clerical in outlook. The much-vaunted values of Holy Russia had bypassed the working-class districts of Russian cities. Religion was not a major issue for them and only really appeared in the form of anti-clericalism that itself was an extension of the deep loathing of the ordinary people for privileged, non-working social parasites of many kinds. The clergy and religious orders were attacked as non-producers, not on account of their values or, to any great degree, the role they played in attempting to reconcile the workers to tsarism. It was, of course, a traditional feature of peasant society that religiosity and anti-clericalism could exist side by side, and the workers reflected this. But it would be wrong to give the impression that religion, or any other part of the tsarist ideological system, played any significant role, positive or negative, among the workers. The fact that tsarism melted away with little trace is quite remarkable, and is yet another indication of how shallow the tsarist system was despite its immense repressive power. Its hollowness was very significant in that it meant that, unlike in France, the counter-revolution could not use popular attachment to the church or vestigial loyalty to *ancien régime* values such as nationalism and the monarchy as a means of establishing a broader foundation for attacking the revolutionaries. This exacerbated the chronic problem of the counter-revolution, its inability to find a popular base of any kind.

However, workers were not totally irreligious, though this varied with region, nationality, gender and the religion in question. What held true for the Orthodox in Petrograd did not hold true for Islamic workers in Central Asia or Protestant and Catholic workers in the Baltic, but, for most Russian workers, the religious question was not important when it came to politics and economic survival. Factories and workshops in Orthodox areas usually had icons displayed that were tended by one of the senior workers. Religion might, as Steinberg noted, provide a matrix for the worker ethic of the unity of humanity and the need for truth and justice, but organized, institutional religion was not a major factor in their lives. At the same time, there was no concerted attack on the church at this time either, for all its anathematizing of the revolution and its tainted links with tsarism. In political terms, it was simply irrelevant. It was only during the civil war that the religious question came to a head and serious persecution began, but, by then, much else had changed as well.

Conclusion: issues rather than parties

Perhaps the most important conclusion to be drawn is that workers were only weakly identified with political parties. Despite the upsurge of membership in and of voting for political parties and trade unions in 1917, before which they had been more or less illegal, affiliations were volatile. After all, there had only been some 150 Bolsheviks among the 26,000 workers at the Putilov factory in February. The majority supported the SRs. It was only in late summer that the balance changed, despite Putilov being a Bolshevik stronghold. However, it is clear that, while organizational affiliation was volatile, identification with issues was more stable. The fundamental aims of the workers, for better living and working conditions and for more control over their own destinies, remained the same. It was the failure of their leadership to obtain them that caused them to support new leaders. These in turn, increasingly "borrowed" the slogans of the people they were replacing. They did not, so much, change the political agenda as promise to be more energetic in implementing it. In addition, it was the evolving situation rather than the supposedly corrosive influence of propaganda and organization (or "manipulation") which brought ordinary workers to support more and more extreme positions. Employer sabotage and supply shortages brought them to see workers' control as the only solution, and the difficulties that workers' control entailed encouraged them to be more open in espousing unified soviet (not to be confused with Bolshevik) power as a means of achieving their aims.

This is borne out by many resolutions of the period. For instance, it was clearly expressed at the Second Moscow City Conference of Factory Committees in late September. The major resolution rehearsed all the complaints about shortages and the decaying urban economy and concluded that its programme to combat this could only be realized through

> the immediate transfer of power into the hands of the Soviets of Workers', Soldiers' and Peasants' Deputies, that the conference considers necessary in order to avert the All-Russian lockout created by the Smirnov–Konovalov ministry under the pretext of an oil shortage.[33]

Writing in 1926, the Bolshevik editors of the collection of documents in which the above appears were, perhaps, giving away more than they realized when they summarized the October revolution from the workers' point of view, in a nutshell. They argued that "the question of lockouts and sabotage by the industrialists led on to the question of workers' control and finally – to the task of seizing power". While such a formulation does not entirely exclude the Leninist intervention of a party to bring this transition about it does, none the less, put the emphasis on the workers' own experience and the evolution of their political and revolutionary consciousness through the parallel evolution of their everday experiences rather than by the outside agency of a party bringing revolutionary consciousness in from without. In this way, the evidence of the Russian working class in 1917 confirms Marx's own view that workers were capable of emancipating themselves and would achieve their necessary higher consciousness through reflection on their everyday situation. Following the logical chain this would lead them to realize that the only true solution was to take over the means of production for themselves. This is what the Russian workers, and peasants for that matter, believed they were doing in 1917.

CHAPTER FIVE

Fields, forests, villages, estates

The peasantries of the Russian Empire

At the time of the revolution there were more than 100 million peasants in the Russian Empire. As we have already seen, they lived in very diverse circumstances, so much so that it would be a mistake to think of there being a single "peasantry". In reality, there were many different peasantries. Most would fall within the definition of a traditional peasant – that is, an agricultural producer who possesses some land but produces mainly for subsistence and to pay dues rather than for the market – but they achieved this in many different ways. Given the variety of cultures can we make any useful broad observations about the role of peasants in the revolution? Fortunately, there are a number of primary fault lines that enable us to distinguish major groupings within this mass. Far and away the most important is that between areas in which serfdom had existed until 1861 and those that had not been affected by it.

Former serf-owning regions

Serfdom had stretched from the Arctic north to the Black Sea and from the Carpathians in the west to the Volga in the south east and to the Urals in the east. Naturally, the incidence of serfdom was not uniform in such a vast area, nor was every peasant a private or state-owned serf before 1861, but serfdom and the institutions associated with it were the central reality of the lives of Russian and Ukrainian peasants in this region. Some of its most important effects survived abolition. Above all it had accentuated and perpetuated the deep division in rural society between the all-powerful serfowner–landowner and the peasantry. In the harsh polarization between owner and owned no middle class of any size had been able to develop in the countryside. Even after 1861 there was little change in this respect. The need for self-defence encouraged peasants to cling to their traditional communal organization and its associated, outdated agricultural practices of dividing arable land into small plots or strips, that could not be farmed by modern intensive methods.

But defensive conservatism was not the whole story. Certain aspects of traditional life fed into the peasants' revolutionary activity. In the first place the commune helped preserve the collectivist outlook of the peasantry that many took with them to the city when they went to work there. Secondly, though different in other respects, peasants everywhere in this region had refused to accept the legitimacy of serfdom and of the land settlement that had followed its abolition. The land, they believed, was theirs.

Within this broad framework the peasants lived out their lives in a myriad villages. Although living standards were very low, the threat of hunger not too far removed, and labour (up to 16 to 18 hours a day in the height of the season) was central to peasant life, it would be a serious mistake to think that all, or even most, peasants lived completely wretched, impoverished lives. To survive in the difficult conditions villages were as self-sufficient as possible in food production, economy and culture. Most villages consisted of wooden houses built by peasants themselves, often with decorated fretwork and carvings of animals and birds on the roof ends, though, in some areas, wattle and daub homes with straw thatch resembled those of rural Africa and some were no more than simple dug-outs in the ground. Even so, for the vast majority of peasant communities there was a rich traditional culture. At its heart was popular religion, composed in varying proportions of Christianity, superstition and pagan survivals. Every house had its icon in one of the corners towards which everyone bowed on entering. The year was punctuated by innumerable religious festivals, many of which were occasions for a day off when the men would invariably get drunk on home-made spirits. Traditional folk customs were maintained. Folk wisdom was encapsulated in a host of stories, legends, proverbs and songs, often associated with village rituals of courting and matchmaking, childbirth, funerals, departure for the army or the city and so on. Handicrafts were widespread. Carving and the making of farming tools and household implements were a male preserve. Women engaged in sewing and spinning, making elaborate dresses and shirts for women and men to wear on ceremonial occasions as well as everyday utilitarian clothing. Eighty per cent or more of peasant agricultural produce was consumed in the household or village. Peasants contributed relatively little to the marketed surplus, though their share became increasingly vital to the national economy, particularly after the takeover of landowners' land in 1917–18. Before this, in the late nineteenth and early twentieth centuries, peasants had purchased and rented more and more land from the landowners. As a result, on the eve of the revolution, some 80–90 per cent of land was already farmed by peasants. Law was, by and large, based on custom rather than statute and was enforced either by the commune and its elder (*starosta*) or by informal peasants' courts in 90 per cent or more of cases. Scientific medicine was only beginning to challenge herbal remedies and the lore of wise women. Schooling was still unknown or rudimentary. Representatives of the outside world who had come to live in the village – such as the priest, the migrant, the artisan, the trader, the ex-soldier – were not trusted and were often excluded from the commune or given short rations when it came to land distribution. Temporary visitors to the village – tax collectors, policemen, military recruiters and even factory recruiters offering employment – were aliens. The abstraction of the state was very remote from the realities of peasant life and this affected the peasants' political attitudes. In broad terms, in 1917 they aimed to extend their self-sufficiency even further by taking more and more control into their own hands through the action of village and *volost'* (parish) committees that were often communes or groups of communes in disguise.

The non-serf-owning periphery

The areas where serfdom had never prevailed differed in many vital respects from this heartland and from each other. In Siberia, as well as the many ancient tribes and nomadic peoples that still survived in the remotest zones, a strip of European settlement ran beside the track of the Trans-Siberian railway, which was virtually completed in 1904. Here there were fewer traditional gentry landowners. Instead, independent peasants on their own farms attempted to make a living in the harsh climatic conditions. A rough settler, pioneer, frontier mentality prevailed that was thought by many to be a threat to the traditional values of European Russia. In the Far East, the indigenous population lived unaffected by European influence. There and in Central Asia, nomadic tribes survived, the last ones not being settled until the 1930s. Elsewhere in the Islamic regions sheikdoms continued in power through alliances with tsarism that brought a Russian bureaucratic and military layer at the top but left the peasants, who were among the most backward and impoverished in the whole Empire, in the hands of the emirs. To the west of the Caspian Sea and south of the Caucasus were the isolated ancient Christian mountain kingdoms of Georgia and Armenia, each of which had a distinctive culture and alphabet, derived through and preserved by their separate national churches. Fierce tribalism and a profusion of small arms made Transcaucasia a very difficult area for the central government to control. Endemic feuds and bloody clashes with Islamic groups have continued down to the present day. While some of the tribes showed a democratic and revolutionary drive for political autonomy, like the Gurians who engaged in an extensive rebellion in 1905, others, like the tiny Kurdish minority and the poorest Armenians, were just too illiterate, backward and impoverished to take part in any serious political activity. Both Georgia and Armenia were able to maintain a precarious independence for some years after 1917 but, at the same time, Armenians, like Shaumian, and, more particularly, Georgians, like Tsereteli, Chkheidze and Djugashvili-Stalin, played important roles on the national political stage.

Another group whose role in the revolution was significant were the cossacks who lived to the north and west of the Caucasus in the Don and lower Volga regions. Their independence was legendary and was originally derived from the fact that they were the descendants of escapees from serfdom who had fled into the remote forests beyond the reach of the autocracy. Inevitably, the Russian state had expanded in pursuit but it had never subdued them. Instead it had cultivated their military tribalism and frontier mentality to turn them into the most reliable military and police cadres of the tsar. The broad steppes they inhabited were full of game, that they hunted incessantly, and, as part of their military and hunting role, they became fine breeders of horses and magnificent horsemen.

There was, however, more to cossack culture than the rifle, the uniform, the horse and the whip. There were serious internal divisions that came out into the open in 1917 and helped prevent cossack peasants and farmers from becoming the backbone of a counter-revolutionary "hit-squad" as their atamans, officers and the allies had hoped for. The cossack villages had preserved the communal and collective instincts of Russia proper, but had added to them a more aggressive independence resulting from having to fight for their land, not only against the tsarist state but against a series of local Islamic leaders of whom Shamil, active in the mid-nineteenth century, became legendary. They were also hostile to in-migrants.

Between them and the former serf territories of the middle Volga lay a less defined area known as New Russia where cossacks, capitalist farmers and traditional commune peasants rubbed shoulders with one another, but even here, most peasants remained peasants in essential respects rather than turning into small-scale, individual, market-oriented farmers.

Such centres of true capitalist farming as there were in the Russian Empire lay to the west of the serf regions in Poland, Lithuania, Latvia, Estonia and Finland. Here, though there were traditional peasants, there were more large estates and, consequently, more communities of landless agricultural labourers than elsewhere in the Empire. Other than in Poland, social division between landowner and labourer was often accentuated by national divisions. In Finland and Estonia much of the land was held by families of Swedish origin, and German landowners could be found throughout the region, especially in Latvia. Foreign domination was reflected in the use of German derived names for the provinces – Lifland, Kurland and Estland as well as Finland – and in Swedish and German names for major towns such as Helsingfors (Helsinki), Åbo (Turku), Reval (Tallin), Memel (Klaipeda) and Dorpat (Tartu). The indigenous populations tended to be agricultural labourers or, at best, smallholding peasants. It was in these western regions that one could find a sizeable poor artisan, proletarian and small-farming Jewish population hemmed in by anti-Semitic legislation that severely limited their right of residence and occupation. Poverty did not, however, extinguish the community life and popular culture of the Jewish *shtetl* (village). As a result, nationalism

combined with social divisions to add an extra dimension to revolutionary activity in the west, but the absence of a self-sufficient peasantry enjoying the partial independence resulting from possessing a little land weakened the agrarian movement here as did the absence of a deeply rooted common culture of refusing to recognize the illegitimacy of large-scale landholding. The evidence suggests that radical Russian troops in the Baltic front-line area in 1917 had helped the local population to organize attacks on property.

War on two fronts – national and local enemies

National enemies – the state, the market and the agricultural surplus

While historians have given some attention to New Russia and the north-western borderlands in recent years, the bulk of research on the peasantry has concentrated on the former serf regions of the Russian and Ukrainian heartland. But, despite narrowing the focus somewhat, the diversity and remoteness of many villages make it very difficult to generalize even about the peasantry of this region. None the less, there are certain almost universal features of their experience. Above all, the peasants faced a struggle on two fronts, on the one hand with the society beyond their horizon and on the other with more tangible local enemies. With respect to the former, their role as food producers meant that their main connection with broader society was through the market. But also, related to that, was the problem of government intervention in the countryside, motivated traditionally by the attempt to secure social peace among the rural population. In the latter part of the century, as the government had become more involved in stimulating the economy and building up a massive defence capability, intervention had also become economic. Investment was being squeezed out of the village. During the war, the concern of the government was with the even more fundamental problem of feeding the rapidly expanding factory population and, of course, the ten million or so in the army and navy. This new pressure threatened to destabilize the entire relationship between town and country.

The difficulty arose because the peasant could get on better without the town than the town could without the peasant since the majority of peasant output was geared to subsistence, not the market. Peasants could be induced to produce and market a surplus either under duress – in normal times this took the form of taxation that would force them into the market – or through economic incentives, in other words producing goods that the wider market needed and was prepared to pay for. Otherwise, the peasants were inclined to retain the surplus and improve their own standard of living, by, for instance, feeding it to livestock and thereby increasing their own consumption of meat and dairy products or by converting it into illicit vodka. If they decided to do either of these things then the towns would go short. On the face of it, this should not have been so serious since most of the surplus came from the landlord sector rather than from the peasants, but even here peasants were the key since the poorest of them provided the labour. As we shall see, once the revolution got under way poor peasants and landless labourers tried to acquire land of their own rather than work on the landowners' property. This reduced landowners' output and, frequently, converted land from surplus production to subsistence production by the impoverished labourers whose main concern was to improve their own meagre living standard.

The battle for the surplus was a key feature of the politics of the revolution. It had become acute even before the fall of the tsar. Although harvests were adequate in 1916 the amount of grain being delivered to the state was falling to dangerous levels. By the end of the year the government was being forced to consider requisitioning. On 22 February 1917 the situation in Petrograd was so bad that food rationing had to be introduced. As we have already seen, the shortage of bread was a vital factor in stimulating the disorders in that city. The new government inherited this very serious crisis. On 25 March it introduced a grain monopoly, that put the distribution of all grain under state control, in order to try and deal with the problem. This produced some short-term amelioration but in the longer term was so resented by the peasants that it had the opposite effect and depressed supplies even further. The new government also tried to boost production by campaigning for all available land to be put to use, much of it having fallen into disuse through shortage of labour in the countryside after most able-bodied young peasant males had been conscripted. This also had ambiguous results, to say the least, because many peasants took it as official encouragement to seize empty land. This was just what the government wanted to prevent, not only because they represented property but also because they were afraid that the surplus might disappear beneath a wave of peasant land seizures that would turn Russia's agriculture back to the middle ages and eliminate the already limited, but none the less vital, capitalist and surplus-producing sectors. Even the Bolsheviks, who appeared to support the peasants, tried to ensure the preservation of the larger estates for the same reason. When they came to power they had no magic wand to wave to solve this very real problem and it caused them severe difficulties also. In some sense, the breakdown of relations between town and country that had occurred by late 1916 has never been fully repaired to the present day. Forced requisitioning during the civil war, the experiment of the New Economic Policy (NEP) (despite some successes), the encouragement of voluntary co-operation and, the final solution, forced collectivization, all failed to restore a dynamic harmony between them. This fundamental problem left by the war has profoundly affected Russian history ever since. The battle for the surplus has been one of the longest and most arduous faced by successive Soviet and post-Soviet governments.

Why did the relationship break down in 1916? Numerous explanations have been put forward. Obviously, the war was the chief distorting factor but which aspects of it were most crucial? Traditionally, the blame was laid upon conscription policy that denuded the village of vital labour, not to mention horse, power. However, much of this was compensated for by the expansion of the labour of older and younger males, of females of all ages, of males who did not qualify for conscription and prisoners of war who were set to work, usually on large estates. Norman Stone and others have suggested different reasons, notably the breakdown of transport, that meant that while grain was being produced it was not reaching the cities where it was needed. This was exacerbated by the fact that the estates of the south, the traditional surplus producers, had fallen back as a result of labour shortage while new, largely peasant areas of production, in the Urals and western Siberia were making up for it but the railway schedules were still geared to the old pattern. The result was that the grain was in one area, the trains in another. Co-ordinating trains and grain stretched tsarist organizational abilities to the limit. In addition, the changing terms of the market were going against the peasant, because, naturally enough, industrial production had become totally dominated by the war and commodities of interest to the peasants had become scarce and very expensive. Although, in the early months of the war, grain prices had risen and the peasants had become better off, this had been reversed as industrial prices rose even faster. By 1916, the peasants had to market a good deal more grain in order to purchase iron goods, leather products, textiles or anything else they needed than had been the case in 1915. This removed their incentive to market grain and they retained more and more of it in the village.[1] Given the absence of consumer goods, how could the peasants be encouraged or forced onto the market? This question dominated not only the war and revolutionary years but echoed through the rest of the century. State requisitioning and the grain monopoly were acts of desperation, as were the solutions applied after the October revolution. From the point of view of the peasant, the government might change, and some policies were more favourable than others, but there was a continuity between all of them to the extent that they all tried to re-establish the grain funnel, drawing produce out of the village.

Local enemies – landowners, entrepreneurs, separators

But the battle with market forces and government intervention was only one aspect of the peasants' struggle. The traditional, local enemies were still present. These fell into three categories. The most important of them was the local landowner. Resentment against landowners, no matter how paternalistic they were towards their peasants, was endemic in the village. It was based on the simple, but completely corrosive, assumption that the landowner had no more right to the land than the peasant. The basic peasant principle was that the land should belong to whoever worked it. Peasants could see no justification for a class of people who owned tracts of land that were far beyond the capabilities of an individual or family to work while others struggled by with less land than was necessary for their own subsistence and had to supplement their income by hiring themselves out as labourers either on the estates or in industry.

But the peasant sense of grievance was not limited to the landowner. The second group in the rural community that aroused their resentment were the rural entrepreneurs. These might hold large amounts of land, without having noble status, but more often they owned small industrial establishments such as forges, brick-making factories, mills, dairies, timber-yards and so on that often enjoyed local monopoly status in supplying the village and were roundly detested by the population on account of their high prices. They might also engage in moneylending and other activities not geared to increasing their popularity among the peasants. The profits were often invested in land, hence the sometimes extensive holdings of their owners, and they were often large-scale employers of peasants. This embryonic rural capitalist class, that existed primarily on the exploitation of the peasantry, was the core of the so-called kulak layer in the countryside. However, they were not so much part of the peasant class as a breakaway group, since, unlike the peasantry proper, they did not live primarily by their own labour. The nature of this kulak class is one of the most contentious issues in the historiography of the revolution but, for all the discussion surrounding it, precious little evidence has been produced to show that the peasantry was divided within itself into antagonistic rich, middle and poor sections. As we shall see, the peasant movement of 1917 showed remarkable solidarity among peasants of all kinds against outsiders and exploiters such as these rural capitalists.

The third resented group in the countryside was composed of those who had taken advantage of the Stolypin reforms and left the village commune, the so-called separators who had set up independent farmsteads. Allied to them were town-dwellers who had purchased individual smallholdings. They, too, are often equated with the kulaks. It is undoubtedly the case that the conflict between commune peasants and separators is the main example of struggle within the peasant community in these years. But it is far from clear that the separators were a superior and exploiting class, though potentially they might have evolved in this direction. After all, the first separations had taken place only since 1908. They had occurred much more frequently in some regions than in others and the overall figure of about 20 per cent of households withdrawing from the commune by 1916 does not mean that the most prosperous households in every village had become separators. In any case, it was not the exploitative nature of the separators that had aroused the opposition of the commune peasants so much as the fact that they did not accept the legitimacy of what the separators had done. The land the separators had taken out of the commune remained, in the eyes of those still within it, commune land. Like the land added to landowners' estates after the emancipation of the serfs, the loss of land they had themselves worked was felt even more acutely by the peasants than the existence of traditional landowners' land. Separators violated the fundamental peasant principle that the land belonged to all who worked it. Once the opportunity arose, the commune pressured the separators back into conformity with this norm. Though there were exceptions, most of the separators seem to have gone along with this and the struggle was much less acute than that which developed between peasants and landowners and between peasants and rural capitalists. Some of them may even have seen that there were advantages in working with the commune peasantry in taking over landowners' land as the revolution progressed.

Thus the peasants faced a war on two fronts. The economic pressure on them came from the government and market while, in their eyes, the means for responding to this pressure was to take land and resources from their enemies and opponents within rural society. Expropriation of landowners, breaking the power of rural entrepreneurs and reassimilating the separators were the obvious means to meet the larger ends. How did the peasants go about this in 1917?

The early stages of the peasant revolution

In some ways the revolutionary activities of peasants in 1917 arose from similar roots to that of workers. Like workers, the main concerns of peasants were with work-related and local issues. Where the factory and the city in which a worker lived dominated her or his outlook, so for the peasant it was the village and the local landowner who were in the forefront. Many of their revolutionary acts can only be understood in the light of the local conjuncture. But the horizon of peasants was much narrower than that of workers and where workers' consciousness may have been capable of some broadening as 1917 unfolded, this was less true of the peasantry. In addition, there were some ten peasants for every worker, so the scale of the peasant movement was greater and so was the range of local variations. The peasant movement was slower to get under way than the workers' but peasants, from the outset had firmer revolutionary aims in that they had long believed that they were the rightful possessors of the land, an objective that could only be achieved through social revolution.

There was also a difference in their relationship to government. Where employers and government were hard to distinguish for workers, particularly in the public sector and the armaments industry, for the peasant the government and the landowner were not quite so fused together, even though, traditionally, the landowner had not hesitated to call on the repressive apparatus of the state when necessary. The difference arose because, unlike the factory owner, the landowner was not a primary exploiter. Most of the peasant's economic problems arose from the demands of the state and the market. The landowners were, in peasant eyes, the obstacle preventing them from meeting these demands because they occupied the land that the peasants needed. Also, the peasants were more handicapped in their struggle in that, being scattered over the vast landscape of Russia, they were much less amenable to broad, regional and national organization than workers. To some extent, this was compensated for by their vigorous local organizations but these were not replicated at national level.

Finally, there is a long-running discussion, arising from Lenin's views on and strategy towards the peasantry that points to important internal differentiation but in the opposite direction from that applied to workers. Where the more educated, slightly better-off and more skilled and enterprising workers were thought, by Lenin, to be the backbone of urban revolution, he argues

101

precisely the opposite for the countryside. Here, the more prosperous peasants were equated with exploiters and, in Leninist theory, they were the ones referred to as kulaks. It was the poor peasants and landless labourers whom Lenin looked to as the most reliable allies of the working class in the countryside. There is a particular irony here in that it was precisely this supposedly revolutionary class of poor peasants who were likely to migrate to find work in the cities where, of course, they fed in at the bottom of the heap to become, according to Lenin, the raw, ill-educated, unreliable, spontaneous and backward elements of the working class. No one has explained at what stage on the road between village and town the momentous transition from revolutionary asset to burden took place in the lives of these unfortunate, exploited migrants.

There is no agreement about the precise periodization of the peasant movement in 1917. Soviet historians once saw a replication of the phases of the urban revolution, beginning with the so-called period of peaceful evolution, from February to July, followed by a heightening of the counter-revolution in July and August, followed in turn by a burgeoning peasant insurrection in September and October. While one might argue, particularly about the precise nature of the last phase, the schema does have some truth in it. The rural revolution began slowly, but did build up and there were major local uprisings by autumn.

Russia's myriad villages appear to have taken the news of the fall of the tsar very much in their stride. In only a very few areas, such as Mogilev and Chernigov, which were influenced by the patriotic feelings of officers at the nearby front, were there pro-monarchist disorders of any note. The first steps the villages took were organizational. Spontaneously, throughout the Empire, peasant committees sprang up at the grass roots. They were to remain the engine room of peasant activity throughout the revolution. They took slightly different forms in different places but all shared the characteristic of being organs of direct, participatory democracy. The peasant committees were, essentially, an extension of the village commune to parish, that is, *volost'*, level and they co-ordinated peasant activity in the locality. Sometimes they took the name of soviets, but this was relatively rare, only 11 per cent of *volost*s in European Russia having soviets by October. However, in essence, the *volost'* committees were indistinguishable from soviets with respect to their functions. They were already widespread by the time the Provisional Government tried to formalize and control them by fitting them into a hierarchy of land committees stretching right up to government level. This was done on 21 April. They became the lowest level of the official hierarchy of land committees. At the top was the Main Land Committee, that reported to the government on land-related problems. Below this were *guberniia* (province) and *uezd* (county) committees with the *volost'* and village land committees at the bottom.

All accounts agree that there was a major cleavage between the *volost'* and *uezd* levels. Where *volost'* committees were staffed by working peasants and represented a lively, direct, dynamic, local, participatory democracy, the *uezd* committees, because the county town was remote from most of the villages in the area, became a focus for urban-based, rural sympathizers with the peasants rather than for peasants themselves. It was at this level that political parties began to function. This was even more marked at *guberniia* level, where peasants had little direct influence.

The key administrator was the Provisional Government Commissar, who replaced the tsarist governor, in each *guberniia*. Initial attempts by them to seize the initiative from the peasants at local level by recruiting non-peasants such as priests, rural entrepreneurs and even landowners onto the local committees, had broken down within weeks and the *volost'* committees had become truly representative of the peasantry. Incorporating them into the official hierarchy was intended to damp down their activity and draw them into the waiting game that the government was playing over the explosive land question. This ploy utterly failed in many areas, and association with the Land Committees higher up often stimulated and legitimized early anti-landlord activity by the peasantry.

The very existence of the Main Land Committee, the chief task of which was to prepare the way for agrarian reform, raised the expectations of peasants. It encouraged them to look at the land in a new way, to see it as something that would soon be in their possession. While peasant ideas diverged widely on this issue from those of the Provisional Government, the contradiction was not yet apparent. Instead, the peasants began to encroach on the prerogatives of landowners, and government policy appeared to give a degree of legitimacy to peasant ideas of a temporary co-stewardship of landowners' property.

The first issue that brought these pressures into the open was the problem of unsown land. For a country at war, and in the throes of a serious supply crisis, the existence of such land was an affront to common sense. By 1916 some ten million hectares of land had been taken out of production. Only two million had been farmed by the landlords but most of the remainder had been rented from them and farmed by peasants. Less than two million actually belonged to peasants. It had fallen into disuse mainly because of conscription that had called nearly half of all able-bodied males into the armed services by 1916, not to mention the requisitioning of 2.6 million horses, that deprived the countryside of essential draught power for ploughs, carts, hauling trees and so on. Naturally, peasants had ceased to work on rented land, that they had to pay for, and continued to work on their own plots. This was, in itself, damaging to the surplus because this had come mainly from what they produced on the landowners' land. The lack of renters had meant a fall in rents, but, because 60 per cent of private land was mortgaged to banks and they had to continue to pay high interest rates on it, landowners refused to accept lower rents and stood out for the old levels. By the beginning of 1917, the amount rented by them to peasants had fallen to 25 million hectares from 32 million in 1914.

Once the *volost'* committees were organized, the first thing many of them did was to try to reduce rent levels even further. Though, as with most aspects of the peasant movement, systematic figures are hard to find and controversial, there are many examples of peasant communities deciding upon major rent reductions. A fall from 12 roubles per hectare to three roubles was not uncommon. Overall, reductions to about half or a quarter of 1916 levels were decreed by peasants. Only in the most radical *guberniia*s, such as Penza and Samara, did peasants refuse to pay rents on principle. In many cases, they paid the unilaterally decreed rents into *volost'* committee funds, pending the final settlement of the land question by the Constituent Assembly.

In order to squeeze more land into the rented sector at the new low rates, many peasant committees also withdrew labour from landlords in various ways. This might take the form of simply not allowing labourers to work for them or, more frequently, setting high wage rates. In many cases, war prisoners were taken off landowners' estates and set to work for peasants, particularly for those families whose main male worker was away in the army or navy. In fact, the revolutionary habit was beginning to catch on among prisoners themselves. The first strike of prisoner of war labourers took place in April and war prisoners began to stand up for better hours and conditions. In some cases, the idea behind depriving the landowner of cheap prisoner labour was to open up jobs at higher rates for the village poor. *Volost'* committees ensured compliance with their decisions among peasants by implementing sanctions, usually fines or deprivation of property, on those who undercut the new pay rates or paid higher rents than those agreed.

The government was very worried by these developments but, apart from asserting that all rents had to be agreed with landowners and that prisoners should be treated better, it did very little. Its policy of encouraging the renewed cultivation of unsown lands, incorporated in a decree of 11 April, was actually encouraging and helping to legitimize many of these early activities that took on a sense of urgency in these weeks because the spring sowing was due in late April and the land had to be prepared by then. Both the peasant committees and the government wanted to see production maximized, though the government wanted to see the more controllable Food and Supply Committees organize this rather than the peasant-oriented land committees.

The unsown land problem and the issue of labour, though less dramatic than the still extremely rare outright seizure of land, were the first schools in which peasants began to learn about the new relationships coming into force in the countryside. Repression was still relatively weak and, in any case, the army had instructions not to fire, for the time being, on peasants. This, plus the expectation, that was now apparently a certainty, that there would be a land reform, encouraged the peasants to be bolder. In particular, they became very sensitive to actions by landowners that seemed to them to be designed to limit the possible effects of such a reform. Attempts to sell land, livestock or equipment aroused peasant suspicions. In many cases they started to intervene in the management of estates where they saw evidence of such activities. This often began with the task of compiling an inventory of the local estates, something that, it could be argued, was within the committees' legal remit of preparing the ground for the land reform. Be that as it may, peasants began to supervise all aspects of estate management, particularly activities such as tree-felling where an owner could quickly chop down and market whole areas of forest before anything could be done.

One Soviet historian, A. D. Maliavskii, referred to the growth of what he called "peasant control", analogous to workers' control in the factories, and there is a lot of truth in the comparison. Peasants were learning new ways of acting and becoming bolder. *Volost'* committees began to stand up to the highest in the land. Villagers in Novgorod *guberniia* took over a royal estate on 7 May because those in charge of it had oppressed the local population and "in unscrupulously fulfilling the orders of that traitor to the Russian people Tsar Nicholas Romanov, had attacked the people like wild beasts".[2] In Efremov, in Tula *guberniia* Prince Golitsyn was ordered by the local *volost'* executive committee to present it with an inventory of his sown and unsown land, together with his plans for it, by 18 April. They also forbade him to sell livestock without permission. Non-compliance with such orders was met with threats of fines or confiscation. This was not always enough. Vigorous resistance sometimes occurred. In Kostroma a rural entrepreneur named Makarov, who employed many labourers and owned windmills, a creamery and a brick-making factory, as well as a considerable amount of land, fought successfully against the *volost'* committee's attempt to prevent him from renting further land from the local landowner. He apparently achieved his victory by threatening to open fire on the peasants.[3]

The Provisional Government and the landowners respond

Terrorism was rare on either side at this stage of the revolution. Makarov's example, though effective, at least in the short term, was not followed by many property owners. That is not to say that resistance to the peasants was not being organized. The corrosion of their property rights led landowners to concentrate on the problem of halting the process. They turned, naturally, to the government to help them. While successive Provisional Governments were opposed to the dissolution of estates from below, this did not make them unambiguous upholders of landowners' rights. Other considerations had their place. For instance, the surplus had to be preserved and even increased, public order had to be maintained, the prevailing democratic conditions required the authorities to be mindful of mass, i.e. peasant, opinion. Above all, it had to appear that the promises of reform were being kept. Add to this the fact that the coalition partners gave varying priority to each of these issues and it becomes clear that policy towards land could not be straightforward.

The government's deepest hope was to be able to placate landowners and peasants, both of whom were represented within it, and it never came to terms with the fact that this was a completely unattainable dream. In the event, its temporizing antagonized both sides, each of which began to look elsewhere for the unconditional support that the Provisional Government could not afford to give. The outcome was that it could do little but urge that the final solution of the land problem could only be dealt with by the Constituent Assembly.

While this might be the framework in which they acted they, none the less, had to face the day-to-day administrative problems associated with the countryside. Needless to say, these were linked to other key problems, notably the war. Only relatively peaceful villages, particularly in areas close to the front, could provide the recruits, supplies and political environment necessary for the continuation of the war. Given the complications, how did landowners and government respond to the peasant challenge? Is there clear evidence of a toughening of attitudes, particularly after the failure of the July Days had turned the conjuncture in Petrograd and other major cities in favour of the counter-revolution?

Viewed from the capital, the situation after July certainly appeared to offer the hope of exerting greater control over the countryside and a number of measures were taken by the authorities to take advantage of the new turn of events. A public order decree was enacted on 6 July that made it an offence, punishable by up to three years' jail, to incite attacks on part of the population. Although this was ostensibly aimed at preventing pogroms there was nothing to stop it being applied to incitement to attack landowners. On 8 July the government confirmed that land seizures were completely impermissible, pending the decision of the Constituent Assembly that would hand all land to the people. In the middle of the month new instructions detailing the powers of the land committees were issued by Chernov, the SR Minister of Agriculture. It was emphasized that they could only prepare the transfer of land and could only put unsown land into cultivation in conjunction with the supply committees. A procedure was laid down by which landowners would inform the supply committee of any vacant land. The supply committee would then inform the land committee which would offer it to the peasants at a rent agreed with the landowner. In the event of a dispute at *volost'* level the *uezd* and *guberniia* land committees would mediate. These provisions appear to have had little effect in the main trouble spots.

At the same time, certain of the generals were trying to tighten up the situation in areas under their jurisdiction. On 8 July Kornilov forbade peasant demonstrations in the rear area of the South-Western Front which he commanded. On 17 July Denikin followed suit for the Western Front and on 31 July *Stavka* (General Staff Headquarters) enacted it for all fronts. There were reports that, at this time, landowners in front areas could get troops sent in to repress disorders at the drop of a hat. There are some signs that this was being replicated on a wider scale. National figures indicate that 11 military expeditions were mounted against peasants in the first four months of the revolution, while the figure for July and August was 39. Arrests of peasant militants were also significant at this time though the evidence is unsystematic. A study of incomplete figures for 26 *guberniia*s in Central Russia concluded that there were seven arrests of *uezd* land committee members and 104 of *volost'* committee members in the period from July to October. In one county in Smolensk *guberniia* 70 members from 14 of the 17 *volost'* land committees were arrested in July. In the country as a whole, 2,000 land committee members are thought to have been arrested by the Provisional Government in July and August.

Landowners were also organizing to defend their interests. The All-Russian Union of Landed Proprietors, that had been set up originally in 1905 and existed until 1910, had been revived in 1916. In May 1917 it held a conference attended by delegates from 31 *guberniia*s. Among them were not only owners of large estates but smaller proprietors, notably separators who had split from the commune.[4] In the aftermath of the July Days it began to explore ways of using the law to resist the peasant movement. In mid-August, for instance, lawyers were instructed to take individual and collective legal action against land and supply committees. On 7 September the supply and land committees were put under the jurisdiction of the administrative courts.[5]

Given the counter-pressure it is not surprising that, in a few cases, land seizures of the early part of the revolution were being reversed. The 2nd *Guberniia* Peasants' Conference in Kazan heard complaints to this effect at its meeting in mid-September. On 30 July the Main Land Committee reversed decisions by local committees in the Don Cossack Territory after landowners had complained that rents had been fixed at too low a level. The Committee emphasized that arrangements allowing peasants to cultivate empty land were intended to boost the national war effort, not provide a vehicle for peasant rebellion against landowners. Landowners were not always so successful. One landowner in Kazan *guberniia* tried to take advantage of the current situation to return and eject the peasants from his property. However, the peasants got wind of his plans and forced him, at gunpoint, to desist. They also confiscated his carriage and he had to walk back to town.[6]

On the face of it, some of the most conclusive evidence that the post-July conjuncture led to setbacks for the peasant movement come from national figures that show a significant decline in reported incidents in August and September. However, it is important to take into account here that this was the harvest period and peasants were preoccupied with work in the fields and had little spare capacity for political and revolutionary activity. The correlation between peasant activity and the agrarian cycle has often been pointed out. Incidentally, despite the extension of the sown area, the harvest for 1917 was disappointing as a result of poor weather and it only brought in 2.64 thousand million poods instead of the 3.04 thousand million of 1916. This, in itself, held the menace of future shortages even more acute than those of the winter of 1916–17. None the less, once the harvest had been brought in, the peasants could begin to think about their social and political problems once again. The question of sowing winter wheat was uppermost in the minds of many and the pattern of April began to reassert itself. Eyes began to be cast on land that was still, in the peasants' opinion, being occupied by owners who had more than they could handle. In addition, the Kornilov débâcle in late August meant that the national conjuncture in favour of counter-revolution was being replaced by a new revolutionary upsurge. It is not clear how the dramatic events in some rural areas were related to this broader pattern. It is more likely that, as hitherto, local factors were dominant, but there can be no doubt that the rural and urban revolutions were facing new problems and new possibilities in September and October.

Autumn uprising?

The view expressed almost without exception in Soviet accounts of the peasant movement in September and October is that there was an uprising taking place. The root of this suspicious unanimity is that Lenin's assumption that there was a significant upsurge in the countryside was a key foundation for his view that the country as a whole was ripe for Bolshevik revolution. He did not argue that the peasants were turning to the Bolsheviks en masse, but he did believe their actions were ceasing to be compatible with the principles of the Provisional Government and its major components, particularly the SR leaders who were members of it. He wrote to this effect a number of times in these weeks. For example, in "The crisis has matured", written on 29 September, he referred to the existence of a developing peasant revolt.

Was Lenin correct? Is there evidence to back up his assumptions? Do the arguments of Soviet historians stand up to rigorous scrutiny? Overall, the indications are that there were more serious incidents – meaning ones involving larger numbers of peasants with more radical aims and resulting in greater violence – but that such outbreaks remained limited. There was no conflagration involving the entire peasantry.

One of the most dramatic incidents occurred in Kozlov *uezd* of Tambov *guberniia*. On the night of 6–7 September a former schoolmaster, curiously named Romanov, who had leased some land in 1917 and become a *khutorianin* – that is a separator whose dwelling was built on his land rather than in the village – opened fire on a group of peasants from the village of Sychevka who he thought, possibly correctly, were engaged in stealing his property. Two of the peasants were killed. The village *skhod* (gathering) decided immediately to take revenge. That evening Romanov's farm was attacked and he too was killed. These events became a signal for the peasants of Kozlov *uezd* to mount a general attack. Fifty-seven landowners and 13 *khutoriane* in 18 *volost*s of

Kozlov *uezd* were attacked, with varying degrees of severity. At first, the local authorities, based in the city of Tambov, some 75 km from the county town of Kozlov, reacted by using their troops. Three groups, totalling around 450 officers and men, were sent in. Although they did make 170 arrests it was a disastrous error since many of the soldiers were local lads, some of them even coming from Kozlov *uezd*, and there were examples of them allowing peasants through their cordons around estates and even of them joining with the peasants. Reinforcements had to be called in from Moscow. About 550 cossacks and junkers (officer cadets), whose equipment included two armoured cars, were sent and on 14 September they reached Kozlov. On the 15th a squad of 30 cossacks and 150 junkers arrived in Sychevka. The following day another 300 cossacks were dispatched from Moscow. Troops were also brought in from nearby Lipetsk. Fifteen hundred peasants were arrested and held, in grossly overcrowded conditions, in Kozlov jail. The arrests provoked further protests and appeals from the peasants to members of the local garrison whose support for the authorities seems to have continued to waver. On 25 September garrison troops joined with radical members of the Kozlov Soviet and, at a meeting attended also by representatives of officers of the local and Moscow squads, passed a resolution calling for the withdrawal of the repressive expedition. On 27 September they withdrew.

It was not simply military repression that had pacified the area. A political solution was also implemented that backed up the military saturation of the epicentre of the rebellion, that had itself spread, on a smaller scale, to other counties in Tambov and neighbouring Riazan *guberniia*s. On 12 September a crisis meeting in Tambov, attended by the local and provincial authorities plus representatives of the *guberniia* soviets of peasants and of workers and soldiers, agreed to a document which stated that the Constituent Assembly would, when it assembled in November, hand land to the peasants and that, in the meantime, all land should be put under the protection of the land and supply committees that would conduct a full inventory. The *guberniia* procurator and the commissar also signed, thus giving the document some semblance of legality. The landowners protested vigorously and on 23 September when the situation was rapidly becoming more favourable to the authorities, supplementary clauses pointed out that the *volost'* and *uezd* land and supply committees had no right to interfere in the day-to-day management of estates without the permission of the *guberniia* committees. Landowners also protested to the Provisional Government that, being aware of the delicacy of the local situation, they did not repeal the document but did engineer the withdrawal of the signatures of the *guberniia* commissar and procurator, thereby depriving it of legal enforceability.

Events in one *uezd* do not constitute a national uprising. Nowhere else were there quite such extreme conditions as in Kozlov. But there were serious disturbances elsewhere that were causing great anxiety to the *guberniia* commissars in the most troubled regions, and to the Provisional Government. As early as 31 July the commissar for Smolensk had reported that the peasants in his area did not recognize the Provisional Government and only took their lead from the All-Russian Peasant Soviet. In late September the commissar for Podol'ia claimed that, in the popular mind, government power was a fiction. The commissars of Riazan (on 30 September) and Nizhnii Novgorod (16 October) threatened to resign because they were refused troops to quell disorders. Though the requests may have been tactical, that is aimed at getting more forthright support from the Provisional Government, there is no doubt that they were facing increasingly serious problems. The fact that the government could not provide troops also shows what pressure it was under. In any case, the limitations of military solutions were highlighted by one small development. Despite the massive intimidation of mid-September, when their village had been swamped by hundreds of troops, the peasants of Sychevka in Kozlov *uezd* set up a militia on 23 October.

Such considerations, however, did not prevent the Union of Landed Proprietors from screaming for cossacks to defend their property. They called increasingly for martial law and, on 27 September the Provisional Government did step up the availability of repressive squads, allowing the use of firearms against peasants. Compared to the 39 occasions on which troops were used in the escalating troubles of July and August, they were sent in 105 times in September and October. There are calculations which say that they opened fire on peasants on 112 occasions in these months. Repressive squads were built up in Moscow, Kazan, Kharkov, Perm, Saratov and Omsk *guberniias* in October. On 11 October proposals were put in hand for setting up shock squads for repressing peasants composed of soldiers recovering from wounds, who were deemed to be more courageous and reliable on this account. This was intended to sidestep the key danger of using troops, namely the risk that they would not obey (there are reports of this from Podoliia and Ufa at this time) or, even worse, join in the disorders. While Soviet sources sometimes have a tendency to make mountains out of molehills when dealing with such questions, there is no reason to doubt the existence of an unprecedented and serious wave of violence in a minority of *guberniias* that sometimes resulted in the deaths of peasants.

In order to reassert control, there were attempts to provide a new political lead. In many places there were calls by the authorities to apply the "Tambov formula" of promising land via the Constituent Assembly but, in the meantime, limiting the initiative of local land committees to the tasks of guarding rather than administering estates, and then only under the supervision of the land committees higher up. The SR leadership increasingly backed the proposal. The party leader, Chernov, argued for it eloquently in the press on 8 October. The only solution in the face of mounting peasant pressure was, he said, to hand the land to the land committees pending the outcome of the Constituent Assembly. Procrastination would be fatal. "Halt the fire! Don't play with flames!" he urged. Some commissars at *guberniia* and *uezd* level, many of whom were members of the SR party, called on the Provisional Government to do this and, when it refused, enacted the Tambov formula on their own authority, for example in Nizhnii Novgorod and Kursk and parts of Riazan and Samara *guberniias*.

There was also a last attempt to issue a draft law at national level to control the situation. Maslov, who had replaced Chernov as Minister of Agriculture in the August reshuffle, proposed a formula that would hand monastery, state and land normally worked by peasants to the land committees. Rents would be set at pre-war levels and collected by land committees and then, after tax, handed on to landowners.

The provisions were attacked from right and left. They were too radical for the Provisional Government. It was reviewed by the Main Land Committee on 16 October and, after being amended, was put to the Provisional Government on 17 October. It was not approved but sent for further review. Ironically, the revised draft was one of the last items the Provisional Government ever discussed because it came to its final full session on 24 October when it was not approved. This was, of course, irrelevant in the circumstances because the revolution had already begun.

In any case, the reception of the draft law on the left was no more promising. Lenin argued that it simply turned the land committees into rent collectors for the landowners. It also preserved the capitalist sector in Russian agriculture and this had led to charges among Soviet historians that it was simply a charter for the preservation of landowners. While this is true, it is not the whole truth. One of the main reasons for trying to preserve the capitalist sector was the eminently practical one that, if it were abolished at a stroke, there was a danger that the surplus would be extinguished and the country would starve. When, after October, the capitalist sector was rapidly liquidated, this is precisely what happened.

How extensive was the peasant revolution?

Reading many accounts of the peasant movement by Soviet historians such as Maliavskii, on whose work much of the above information perforce relies heavily, and others one gets the impression that the whole peasantry was active. Close observation, however, shows that active rebellion was engaged in only by a minority of peasants and that, even in the most troublesome *guberniias*, most peasants did not get involved. What, then, do we know about the peasantry as a whole in this period?

In the first place, it would be a great error to assume that inactivity implied satisfaction with the status quo. Rather it was a sign that the peasants were prepared to wait a few more months to get the land, since the expectation that it would soon be theirs appears to have been universal among the Russian and Ukrainian commune peasantry. This would suggest two main reasons why those who were more impatient decided to get involved. In the first place they may have had more pressing local problems than the others, suffering greater poverty and land hunger, and secondly, they may have been quicker to come to the conclusion, later in the year, that the promise of land was fading and that they should act with greater rapidity. This would explain the more violent dimension of peasant activity in September and October. Both of these hypotheses have some evidence to support them.

The most striking feature of peasant disturbances, not only in 1917 but in the preceding decades as well, is their prevalence in a continuous belt of 12 or so *guberniia*s running through the Black Earth zone from the Ukraine, then south of Moscow and on to the Volga and the Urals. At first sight it would seem unlikely that these most fertile and potentially prosperous provinces would be the ones worst affected by land hunger and poverty. In fact, they were so affected precisely because they were fertile and this meant that the struggle by landowners to control as much land as possible was especially intense. Because the land was fertile and Russian agriculture tended to be under-mechanized and traditional, a large labour force had been necessary to exploit it. The serf system had come into existence centuries earlier to fix the labour force to this fertile land since without them it was useless. This had meant that they were traditionally areas of greater population. But the unprecedented population rise of the late nineteenth century pushed the number of inhabitants to the threshold of what the land could support. The growing economic problems of the peasantry, catalogued in Chapter 1, pressed particularly hard on parts of the population of this area.

Before going on to ask which sectors of the peasantry were most active, it should be borne in mind that the implication of the concentration of distur-bances in a dozen or so *guberniia*s is, of course, that the remaining 38 *guberniia*s of European Russia were hardly affected by active peasant encroachment on landowners' property. For *guberniia*s near the front line the reason for this seems to have been the frequency of the use of troops to quell disturbances, plus the natural anxiety of the population that the army should not be weakened, thereby risking an extension of the area of German occupa-tion. The different social structure of the Baltic Provinces, where large estates and agricultural labourers were more common than the commune and landholding peasants and vestigial estates that characterized Russia and the Ukraine, also explains the relative lack of disturbances there since, with nota-ble exceptions, the labourers were too weak to assert themselves. Elsewhere, in the Russian and Ukrainian heartland, the peasants seem to have been con-tent to go along with the Provisional Government and SR promises of reform in the near future, insofar as they were aware of them. Their delegates backed this policy at conferences and were active in supporting such a change, but were only slowly taking action to step up the tempo of reform. In this sense they were much less revolutionary and more legitimist than the active minor-ity, but they were no less determined that, in the end, the land should be theirs. Only the belief that the transfer should be orderly and "just" held many of them back, though there may also have been an element of caution – the fear that there might yet be a backlash against those who had stepped out of line.[7]

Apart from its clear geographical distribution, can we say anything more precise about who took part in the peasant movement? At the moment, there are many different theories. While it is fairly well established that younger male peasants were active, there are many examples of older peasants and sometimes of women, taking a major part in disturbances. But the main discussion has revolved around whether the different layers of the peasantry – variously defined as rich, middle and poor or, using the Russian terms, kulaks, *seredniaks* and *bedniaks* – and landless labourers, *batraks* – played noticeably different roles in the revolution. For Soviet historians it was poorer, but not necessarily the poorest, peasants who led the revolution while the kulaks were, it was argued, opposed to it, though there were admissions that information was sparse. Looking comparatively at peasant revolutions in the twentieth century, including Russia, Eric Wolf came to the conclusion that it was middle peasants who were the engine room of revolution because they were less satisfied than the rich peasants, and therefore had an interest in revolution, and were less handicapped by poverty and dependency than the poorest peasants, and therefore had more prospect of fighting to complete their independence. One western survey of the peasant movement in 1917, by Graeme Gill, makes no reference to social differentiation within the peasantry. Shanin's classic works on the Russian peasantry from 1900 to 1914 also argue that the existence of a kulak class has been much exaggerated. Disputes about the 1920s among western historians, have also cast doubt on the existence of a clear distinction between rich, middle and poor peasants and have tended to see the village and particularly the commune, as an entity, pushed together in the difficult and sometimes disastrous conditions of 1917–21 and 1929–34, in mutual defence against the violent intrusions of the city and the outside world. Maureen Perrie, however, points to "the conflicting interests of different groups of peasants in different situations."[8] One can only say, at this stage, that there is no consensus. However, looking at the records of peasant activities, and the thinness of the evidence for the supposed second social war – that between kulaks and the rest of the peasantry – one can only be struck by the solidarity of the peasant community. Where activities were decided upon, it was usually through the *volost'* committee, on which all peasants were represented and whose decisions were accepted by almost everyone, or by means of the traditional village *skhod* or gathering at which all could speak and whose decisions usually represented a consensus also accepted by all.

This is not to deny the existence of divisions within the peasantry. There were some peasants who did have more land and livestock than others and who occasionally hired labour, while there were others who had little or no land and might even be landless labourers. The point, however, is that, compared to the divisions between all peasants on the one hand and landowners, separators, rural entrepreneurs and the state on the other, the internal divisions were of secondary importance. The record of their revolutionary involvement seems to bear out this interpretation.

Two other myths, that rural revolution was dependent on returning soldiers and/or Bolsheviks, have also failed to convince many observers. The documentary record shows that, while there undoubtedly were instances where such influences were important, they were not at all decisive in the overwhelming majority of peasant activities. By and large they were well prepared to understand, promote and defend their own interests without excessive tutelage from without.

The moral economy of the peasant movement

Having looked at the extent and type of activities in which peasants engaged, can we say anything about the characteristic features of such activity, notably the principles on which the peasants acted? Here the record is better established. Throughout the Russian and Ukrainian peasantry certain themes recur. By and large, the peasants showed that they were egalitarian, that the labour principle was important to them, that they were patriotic during the War even though they shed surprisingly few tears at the fall of the dynasty, and that violence against the person was rare. In many cases they also showed that they believed in acting in legitimate and orderly fashion, though according to their own principles rather than those of the landowners.

Certain striking features of peasant activity can be observed over a wide range of examples. In particular, the peasants appear to have acted according to a traditional code of social justice based on a sense of equality and of labour being the main entitlement to land. While this varied in detail from one area to another, the fundamental principles emerge time and time again. Wherever peasants protested, at least in the great majority of actions that were rational and co-ordinated rather than in the minority of reactive, spontaneous and more riotous outbursts, they did so in the name of justice as they perceived it. We have already seen that unilateral rent reductions were a widespread phenomenon while total abolition of rent was rare. In deciding to enforce rent reductions, peasant committees often did so in the name of their own code. They prefaced the decision with phrases like, "we find it just to establish rent at two roubles per *desiatina*", as one village *skhod* in Bessarabia put it. Their justification for reducing the figure to this level from the earlier level of 12 roubles per *desiatina* was that, under the old order, "the landowners burdened us beyond belief with exhorbitant, back-breaking payments".[9] The fundamental drive of the peasants in the early part of the revolution was not to abolish the existing systems – of rent, sharecropping and so on – but to re-establish them on new principles. Another peasant grievance, requisitioning, was dealt with in similar fashion. Rather than refuse requisitioning outright, since they accepted the need for it in wartime, the peasants tried to establish norms that shifted the weight of it on to those with more livestock and other requisition-able produce. The *guberniia* peasant conference in Kostroma proposed in late May that farms with less than three animals should be exempt, those with three to nine should give one-third, those with 10–20 should give one half and those with more than 20 should give three-quarters. The effect of this would, of course, be to restore much greater equality of distribution of livestock. This could even extend to the land question itself. When estates were seized outright or encroached on severely by peasant committees, it was not uncommon for landowners to be left with a share equivalent to that of the peasants. Similarly, when tools and equipment were expropriated and put to common use, the landowner was often either left with some or given the same right to use them as anyone else.

The root of this idea of equality was the peasants concept of labour as the key entitlement to land. Land should belong to whomsoever worked it. This theme runs constantly through the history of all peasant protest. It was embodied in the principles of the land policy of the SR party and the populist movement that preceded it, though not all land was to be subject to it for fear, as we have seen, of wiping out the surplus in the short term at least. The initial attempts to deprive landowners of hired labour, whether it be that of poor peasants or of subsidized war prisoners, had the same objective. The land-owner would have to manage on his own resources. If the landowner could do this, then, in theory at least, it was acceptable to the peasants. Landowners who went along might survive the revolution, at the price of becoming indis-tinguishable from the peasantry itself. Although figures are not totally reliable for the country as a whole, studies by John Channon have shown that, in parts of the Ukraine, some 25 per cent of the landowners were still farming in the mid-1920s. If they could not manage, the peasants' response was direct. As one of them put it "we will leave them to die like cockroaches in a trough".[10]

Do these radical principles apply only to those peasants who took an active part in the rural revolution in 1917? What of the large number, perhaps even a majority, who did not? Even here, similar ideas seem to have been at work. The peasant sense of legitimacy helped to preserve their patience until the appropriate state authority distributed the land in an orderly fashion but their sense of equality and of the labour principle was no less pronounced in that they were fully convinced of their right to the land and would not be prepared to forgo it. These principles had been fundamental in the commune and applied not only in landlord–peasant relations but also in peasant–peasant relations. The redistribution of land, livestock, forests, pasture, equipment, buildings and so on was usually done with an eye to propping up the poorest part of the community first and the wealthiest last. Attempts by rural entre-preneurs to establish new exploitative relationships were resisted vigorously.

Other aspects of peasant activity are also worth remarking on. Like work-ers, they tended to be patriotic. In their eyes the war was necessary and there are few or no examples of peasant opposition to it as such. While they might dispute exactly who should bear the burden there was no major resistance to conscription until the summer of 1917, although how extensive it was then we do not know for certain. In fact, peasant attitudes tended to be hostile to the anti-war movement for longer than the workers. As late as June there are examples of deserters, who, far from being welcomed in the countryside, were beaten up as abettors of the German aggressor. One can, perhaps, speculate that in the peasant mind the war was a simple question of self-defence against a traditional enemy whose evil deeds were entrenched in popular culture. None the less, such conceptions show no sign of serious breakdown in 1917. Clearly, peasants situated closest to the front were the most affected by the war and the best informed, but were also the most determined to continue it because a new German advance would be a disaster for them. Elsewhere, apart from conscription and requisition, the war was rather remote. For many, for instance those among the Siberian settlers, the reinvigorated grain market could even bring relative prosperity. Thus, for peasants, the war issue was not the most important. There was no conception that their desire for land might threaten the war effort through reducing the productivity of agriculture, the problem that obsessed the political elites of left and right in 1917.

Given the broad misconceptions about peasant activity it is worth pointing out one more important characteristic of the peasant movement, namely that it was very rare for violence against the person to be initiated by peasants. Even in the most violent period of 1917, the wave of estate seizures in the most turbulent areas after the harvest, cases of violence against individuals were notable for their infrequency. The murder of Romanov in Sychevka was, as we have seen, a response to his murder of two peasants. The attack on Romanov was considered by the village *skhod* and carried out under its authority. Thus, even in extremes like this, a rough sense of peasant justice was often at work.

It was, however, very rare for peasants to pass "death sentences" of this sort. Apart from that, the procedures adopted seem to have been typical, although balanced, objective judgement is extremely difficult since the great bulk of the evidence we have about peasant activities comes from landowners, either directly or through the militia authorities to whom they complained. Naturally enough, they would not spare the agonizing details in such complaints since their aim was to show that the situation was sufficiently serious for the authorities to intervene. While the concept of the violent peasant rioter can by no means be dismissed as a complete myth, on current evidence at least, one has to make allowances for the fact that the main sources we have are not only totally out of sympathy with the peasants, but often feel personally aggrieved that "their" peasants could be hostile to them and consequently had a vested interest in exaggerating the violence.

This leads to many difficulties of interpretation. For instance, contrary to the usually very utilitarian concepts of the peasants, i.e. that everything that could be used should be preserved, there were increasing numbers of cases of the destruction, usually by burning, of manor houses that could have been put to good, alternative uses. Why did peasants do this? One set of explanations, taken up by those out of sympathy with the peasant movement and shared, not unnaturally, by landowners whose homes were put to the torch in this way, was that the peasants were simply being wantonly destructive. This is the image that prevails in much traditional western historiography. However, scholars, defending the peasant movement, argued that such actions were more rational than they appear.[11] Instead of being mindlessly destructive, in a way uncharacteristic of the peasant movement in general and even of other aspects of the same peasant action that resulted in the burning down of a house, the aim of the peasants was to strengthen the new relationships they were establishing in the countryside by depriving the landowner of his "nest". This made it more difficult for the landowner to organize a counter-revolution in the village since he would lack a base and, in any case, to the peasant mind, the landowner usually had enough houses elsewhere to satisfy his needs. It has also been suggested that some burnings had a symbolic, ritual aspect[12] though this, too, was a way of cementing the new social relationships.

One should not, however, minimize the problem of law and order in the countryside, or romanticize about it. As with the towns and cities, the villages were affected by the decline in authority, the freeing of criminals of all kinds from jails and the falling discipline of the army that was unleashing a torrent of often desperate and dubious armed men who, far from being revolutionary heroes, turned to robbery and violence. Gangs formed that were even capable of robbing trains. Roving deserters and undisciplined troops in and around garrison towns were at the heart of much of the criminality recorded in the militia reports for 1917. While it is by no means true that all deserters behaved in this fashion, a violent, well-armed, criminal element brought chaos and fear to the small towns and villages through which they passed. Though systematic figures are either absent or unreliable, it is likely that a high proportion of crimes of violence against the person and aggravated robberies were carried out by people of this kind.

The peasant contribution to the revolution in 1917

From the point of view of the peasants, the experiences of 1917 were a series of self-generating mini-revolutions. While dramatic events like land seizures remained rare, the whole of the country was affected by a massive change in relations between the landowners and the peasants. Where peasants had been cowed into submission for decades by the certainty of reprisals, they were quick to realize that the power of the major proprietors to defend their wealth and privilege was diminishing by the week. The responses to this were, as we have seen, remarkably similar over the whole of Russia and the Ukraine even though the peasantry were not organized on this scale. Even so, the mini-revolutions occurred simultaneously over a vast area. Why? After all, revolutionaries, particularly those in the Marxist tradition, had argued that the peasants could not be a successful revolutionary force because they were difficult to organize on a large scale. It was a key advantage of the urban workers, so it was thought, that they could be more readily organized and therefore make a greater impact. None the less, the rural revolution of 1917 was a formidable component of the many events that erupted in that tumultuous year. The answer lies in the fact that, at the local level, the same problems had been repressed and the same solutions had been hiding deep in the peasants' hearts. The acquisition of the land by those who worked it was an almost universal principle. The weakening of the state enabled the simultaneous revolts to take place without fear of reprisal. In addition, the promise of acquiring the land was given prominently by the authorities themselves, subject only to the decisions of the Constituent Assembly, which may explain why much of the peasantry was less active in 1917 and this could, therefore, be seen as a short-term gain for the government. But the promise could not be ignored, or even postponed, indefinitely. Any backsliding on the issue would be likely to lead to the more patient peasants following the example of their harder pressed brothers and sisters. Thus, despite the lack of organization of its activities at a national level, the conjuncture of events was ensuring that the peasants would be a formidable revolutionary force. Earlier views of the relative impotence of the peasants had pointed to their inability to undermine or overthrow the state whenever they had challenged it. The Russian revolution, however, was characterized by the overthrow of the state preceding the social revolution. This crucial difference meant that the peasants were in the vanguard of the revolution, against the expectations of many revolutionaries. Others, notably populists and anarchists of the Bakuninist tendency, had predicted that the peasants would be a key revolutionary force in Russia. Even so, such people did not manage to lead the revolution via their links with the peasants. Why not?

The political outcome of 1917 can be seen from the point of view of asking why the Bolsheviks succeeded? and we will deal with this later. But an equally important question is, why did the SRs fail? After all, even in November, they still heavily outpolled the Bolsheviks, though the situation was complicated by the split in the party that eventually led to its left wing joining the Soviet government for some months. The question cannot be answered solely in terms of looking at national politics, the "manipulation" of the situation by the Bolsheviks and so on. Looking at the grass-roots revolution shows an additional important dimension to their failure. When the tsarist authorities fell, and as the year progressed, the SRs were taking over an increasing number of key administrative posts in the provincial administration. Many of the *guberniia* commissars, for instance, were SRs or SR sympathizers. As with the Provisional Government and the workers, the rural administrators were put in a highly contradictory situation. While they claimed to side with the peas-

ants and did, in theory, support the transfer of much of the land to the peasants, they were charged in their day-to-day activities with restoring order in
the villages and, in effect, siding with the landowners and joining with generals and colonels in maintaining order. Their arguments for doing so – that the
war had to continue and that the resolution of the land question had to wait
until the convening of the Constituent Assembly – were hard for the peasants
to accept as the year progressed. The economic situation had deteriorated to
the extent that the goods needed by the peasants were no longer available.
The political situation was also deteriorating and the promised assembly was
continually postponed. The result was that, while local militants in the *uezd*
and *guberniia* peasant committees and soviets were still inclined to stick to the
party line, the patience of the peasants themselves was running out and direct
action coming to the fore. At this point, it was often local SR chiefs who had to
dissuade peasants, sometimes forcibly, from taking the law into their own
hands. The chiefs were allowing themselves to be transformed into the main
prop of authority at local level. The military and police squadrons that were
deployed with increasing frequency in the villages often went in under the
orders or with the backing of, the local and national SR party functionaries.
Naturally enough, this severely undermined their revolutionary credentials.
By the time the new Soviet government appeared to give unconditional support to the peasant movement, the SRs had compromised themselves in the
eyes of many peasants and had made themselves irrelevant. Complicated
arguments about the impact of the new land settlement on the war and the
possibilities of civil war, fell on deaf ears as they had done in the cities.

The peasants, as the workers in 1917, had acted to fulfil desires for self-
management and self-government at the local level. In reality, the remoteness
of the village had meant that, in calmer times, the outside world had not been
especially bothered by events in the village as long as taxes were paid, recruits
were forthcoming, the surplus was marketed and there were no rebellions.
The commune, the *mir* and the *skhod* had protected the traditions of local self-
administration and, in 1917, they were the institutions that came to the fore in
the villages, plus the *volost'* committees as an extension of them. Released
from the repressive power of the state, they flourished and re-established
themselves throughout the Russian and Ukrainian territories of the Empire.
The universality of the peasant revolution and its drive for self-government is
very striking. Nowhere were the old authorities, the old proprietors, able to
exercise influence over the movement and rally peasants to the cause of counter-revolution. Elite patriotism, the church, loyalty to the tsar, all the supposedly internalized values of the old regime were shown to be politically
threadbare. As the provincial commissar for Orel *guberniia* put it as early as
March "the idea that the peasants of Orel might repeat the role of the
Vendéans" (who had created a popular movement against the revolution in
France in 1793) "has no basis in fact".[13] The peasants were, for the time being,
able to resist the outside world. Even the attempts by the new authorities to

control and supervise their institutions after October nearly brought about the collapse of the Bolshevik government and defeat by the counter-revolution, even though the peasants never sympathized with the latter. It was only in 1929, when collectivization began, that they were destroyed. 1917 saw the resurgence of the traditional peasant institutions and the 1920s saw their golden age. The future looked deceptively promising for the peasants as 1917 drew to its close.

CHAPTER SIX

Barracks, battleships, the line

All accounts of the Russian revolution agree that soldiers and sailors played a critical role at crucial moments particularly in Petrograd. One has only to think of the mutiny that turned the February demonstrations from a crisis into an incipient revolution or of the sailors who formed the backbone of the July demonstrations and who had it in their power to overthrow the Provisional Government there and then or, last but not least, of the soldiers and sailors who joined in the October uprising and of the even greater number who sealed its success by refusing to obey orders to resist it.

At the simplest level it is obvious that, in a revolution, people with weapons have the upper hand. In the words of Mao, political power originates in the barrel of a gun. In Petrograd, where civil power was focused, control of the garrison meant control of the city and control of the city meant control of the government. In other words, the Petrograd garrison was the leading arbiter of national politics, a fact recognized from the very beginning of the revolution.

However, when it comes to explaining why troops took part in the revolution, the consensus breaks down. By and large, explanations revolve around the class origins of the soldiers and sailors. Many, many observers think of the army, in particular, as "peasants in uniform" and associate its progressive fragmentation in 1917 with the impact of land seizures. In this view, troops simply left their posts in order to go home and get their share of the spoils. There are a number of objections to this. Deserters were not popular in the villages even as late as July and many formed bands of desperadoes that terrorized the provinces. Thus, it seems that many did not reintegrate into their home communities. In any case, most troops had no cause to fear that they were forgotten back home. Peasants were very conscious of the sacrifices that the soldiers were making and, far from edging them out, peasants were often concerned to give them special help by, for instance, forcibly redeploying prisoner labour from landlords' land to that of absent soldiers and their families. Most important of all, however, is the fact that desertion rates, before October, were much lower than the anecdotal evidence would suggest. The vast majority of troops remained at their posts and the High Command, while they were not overjoyed at the desertion rates that existed, did not see desertion as the most important problem they had to face.[1]

Marxists, particularly Bolsheviks, have tended to play down the peasant aspects of the army and navy. For them, the idea that such crucial actors in the revolution should be seen as peasants first and foremost was anathema. They argued that the most active part of the military was of proletarian rather than peasant origin. In particular, they pointed to the sailors to back up this assertion. The navy tended to recruit people who were skilled in handling machinery, since this was an important part of naval duties, and thus it was that the sailors were disproportionately proletarian compared to the army. It was because of this, the Bolsheviks argued, that the Baltic Fleet sailors were prominent in the revolution. Why the Black Sea fleet remained impervious to Bolshevik penetration in 1917 is not, however, explained in this theory. Since, as we have seen, much of the proletariat was itself of peasant origin, the argument lacks conviction, even though the navy was more proletarian than the army.

While these aspects of class certainly have to be borne in mind, it is even more important in explaining the revolutionary involvement of the military to take into account the special interests they had not as peasants and workers but, quite simply, as soldiers and sailors. In this respect their activities are analogous to, but distinct from, those of other participants in the revolution. It was the oppressive structures of everyday experience in military service that were uppermost in the minds of soldiers and sailors. In the front rank of these were discipline and the question of peace.

Democratization – the army committees

Nothing shows the enormous impact of the February revolution, and the rapidity with which it overflowed the boundaries set for it by its elite participants, better than the rapid spread of democratization in the army. From one end of the country to the other, unpopular commanders were deposed and in a few cases, done to death. The traditional authority of officers was eroded almost instantaneously in that soldiers and sailors no longer assumed that they had no alternative but to knuckle under to brutal discipline. Instead, they began to set up their own, as yet undefined, committees to represent and safeguard their interests. The initial results were spectacular. In Kronstadt, from the very first days the spearhead of radical revolution, the leading officers were arrested. The Commander of the Baltic Fleet, Admiral Viren, was thrown overboard to die in the freezing waters of the Gulf of Finland. Several others shared his fate. In Petrograd, the officers feared for their lives and went into hiding until things had calmed down. Not all officers shunned the revolution. Some, like the Bolshevik trainee naval officer, Fedor Raskolnikov took part. He wrote that, even among officers, there were very few supporters of the monarchy. In both army and navy, officers called up and volunteering during the war were more likely to be radical than the regular officers of the pre-war era.[2]

But the effect was felt far beyond Petrograd which had been the centre of the February revolution. Miniature revolutions took place in military units all over the Empire. For instance, in the distant fortress of Kars, today part of Turkey, a mass movement of soldiers carried through their own version of the February revolution. On 6 March they arrested the senior officers. As the new commander reported in a telegram to the Commander of the Caucasus Front, General N. Yudenich, "In view of the pressing need to prevent the breakdown of order in the city [and] the fortress, delegates from the military sections speedily elected me, Colonel Karamyshev, as temporary commander pending the appointment of a new one or until my confirmation in the post, and set up a special committee to assist me".[3] This illustrates the beginnings of the soldiers' movement very well. The takeover was spontaneous, orderly and responsible. Far from being an anarchic attack on officers, a more acceptable colonel was chosen as the new commander. The need to maintain, rather than to undermine, order was a key motive. The permanence of the new arrangements was underwritten through the appointment of a committee to supervise the actions of the new authorities.

There were many thousands of incidents of this nature in the first few weeks of the revolution. The result was something completely unprecedented. A modern army was undergoing a massive change in the middle of a murderous and exhausting war against a formidable enemy. From one end of the Russian Empire to the other committees of soldiers and officers were set up to represent the formerly powerless members of the armed forces and to supervise the acts of the commanders. What did the new committees want and how did they go about their task?

Their demands revolved around two sets of issues. In the front rank was the question of democratization which meant, first and foremost, an assertion of the committees' right to exist and, secondly, other demands of which one of the most popular, most rapidly spreading and most radical was the call for officers to be elected. Elements of traditional discipline – such as the requirement to salute officers while off duty, the use of the diminutive by officers to soldiers and a whole host of petty, irksome regulations – came under fire and were done away with.

Initially the second set of issues – namely the war and the various means to bring it to an end – were less important, but began to grow steadily as the months went by. There can be no doubt that, in the very first weeks, the revolution and the subsequent changes in the army and navy were seen by all to be means to ensure a more orderly and successful war effort. There was even a widespread belief that victory was now possible. This sentiment was, however, very fragile and was soon replaced by a general feeling among the troops that, while it was legitimate and necesssary to defend Russia, it was out of the question to conduct offensive operations. Instead the troops began to look towards a diplomatic offensive to succeed in removing the Germans where force of arms had failed. Expectations of a peace settlement began to grow rapidly and, in some places, fraternization took place as a means towards expediting this process. It should, however, be made absolutely clear that no-one envisaged peace at any price – that is, surrender – at this stage, though some might have accepted a separate peace. Thus, from the very beginning, the complexity of the peace issue began to emerge. The difficulty arose because the most widespread and deeply rooted attitude to the war was made up of two completely incompatible elements. The first was a desire to free the Empire of German and allied occupiers, the second was the demand that there should be a speedy end to the fighting. At no point in 1917, or even most of 1918, was there any chance of achieving both of these aims.

In the early weeks of the revolution, however, these implications were not obvious. What was much clearer was that the traditional command structures of the army and navy were changing rapidly. Unquestioning obedience, based on the fear of punishment, even execution, had been swept away. Instead, soldiers and sailors demanded the right to participate in the decisions on which, quite literally, their lives depended. How did the authorities react to the sweeping changes?

As early as 15 March General Alekseev, the acting Commander-in-Chief, submitted an alarmist report to the new Minister of War, A. I. Guchkov. Already, he said, the Baltic Fleet was not battleworthy and "the terrible hour" was approaching "when some army units would be completely useless for battle". Supposed concentrations of German forces suggested that they might be preparing a "swift, powerful strike in the direction of Petrograd".[4] Under current conditions the defence of the capital could not be guaranteed. The consequences of its loss, the report continued, would be disastrous. There would be internal strife in Russia and the shedding of "torrents of blood".[5] By and large, though they were less graphic, the commanders shared Alekseev's pessimism. The army, all reports agreed, was on the verge of disintegration. How could it be saved?

Faced with this question, some unexpected answers were produced. For the moment, those like Kornilov, who, in the face of "mutiny", wanted to use the good, old methods of repression and the death penalty, were not listened to. Instead, on 24 March, Alekseev himself instructed the commander of the Romanian Front that officers' and soldiers' committees should be allowed to spread throughout the army.[6] Ironically, the Petrograd Soviet, in Army Order Number Two of 6 March, had tried to limit the role of committees, to take the election of officers off the immediate agenda and to ensure that committees did not interfere in strategic decision-making. Many commanders had been trying to prevent their formation altogether.

Election of officers was considered a particularly inadmissible practice though it was being engaged in on a wide scale, at least in the form of deposing the most hated officers. As we have seen, where this happened the troops were often content to accept a replacement appointed from above. Some commanders, however, preferred to reimpose those who had been thrown out. This practice was supported by the High Command and the War Ministry on 5 April when one of the front commanders, General Denikin, declared that interference by soldiers' committees in the business of appointing and posting command personnel could not be tolerated, "*De facto* establishment of election" would, he said, "be fatal to the army".[7] Although this order said deposed officers should return to their units, it had to take into account that in many cases this was not possible and alternative arrangements were proposed.

Stiffening resistance to the committees was an early sign of the return to tougher methods demanded by many officers. At around this time the commander of the Ninth Army was complaining to his superior on the Romanian Front that "maintaining discipline becomes more difficult every day". Officers "rights" were diminishing and the abolition of the death penalty had taken away "from commanders the necessary means to maintain order" and weakened authority.[8] The next few weeks saw serious steps being taken that were supposed to restore as much of traditional discipline as could be salvaged, but in setting out on this fateful course the army leadership and the Provisional Government began to undermine themselves at an ever increasing rate. The centrepiece of their evolving strategy was the preparation of a new offensive. In the run up to it, a concerted effort was made to regain control of the army.

There were two intertwined reasons for undertaking the offensive. Most obviously it was rooted in military and diplomatic necessity. The military elite had supported the February revolution, up to a point, in order to clear the decks for action against Germany and her allies. In addition, the new government, still dominated by the Kadets at the time, wanted to strengthen its links with the Western Powers. But in addition the preparation for the offensive became a centrepiece in the government's strategy of restoring order. It was argued that only the enemy would benefit if the military prerogatives of the officers were to be eroded any further. With this justification, the most concerted effort was made to roll back what the ordinary soldiers and sailors saw as the gains of February.

As we have seen, even the rapid failure of the offensive in July was turned by the government to its own advantage. It diverted the blame for the disaster from itself and laid it at the door of the enemy within, that is, those who had resisted the preparation for it. The Bolsheviks were turned into the chief scapegoat and were accused of being German agents.

However, the policy as a whole failed because it stirred up deep resentment and led to an increasingly desperate search by the soldiers and sailors themselves for a remedy against the return of repression.

The revolutionary movement at the front

While the details and significance vary from place to place, there can be no doubt that, throughout the armed forces, there was a massive, self-generating revolutionary movement from below characterized by an energetic drive towards self-organization on the part of the masses of ordinary soldiers and sailors, but, before plunging into examples we need to remind ourselves what the main dispositions of the army and navy were. In 1917 the front line stretched from the Baltic to the Black Sea. Distributed along the line were 14 armies or army groups organized into five major fronts. These were, from north to south, the Northern Front (with 1.2 million men in the Twelfth, Fifth and First Armies), the Western Front (1.4 million in the Second, Third and Tenth Armies), the South-Western Front (2.8 million in the Seventh, Eighth, Eleventh and Special Armies), the recently formed Romanian Front (1.6 million in the Fourth, Sixth and Ninth Armies) and, finally, facing the Turks, the Caucasus Front (0.9 million in the Seventh Independent Army Corps and the Independent Cavalry Corps of the Caucasus).

This amounted to eight million troops in the line. There were also 220,000 people working in private support organizations at the front. The most noteworthy feature was that there were more troops in the southern part of the front, defending the Ukraine, than in the northern half defending Petrograd and Moscow. This was partly because of the hasty setting-up of the Romanian Front in late 1916 when the Romanian Army collapsed shortly after joining the war on the Allied side.

In addition, some two million troops were spread through the rear military districts of Russia.[9] They were largely reserves or recuperating wounded who tended to play a major role in the politics of the towns and cities in which they found themselves. In particular, the Moscow and Petrograd garrisons were, of course, crucial to the politics of those cities and, hence, of the country which was governed from them. The two major naval concentrations were the Baltic Fleet with 85,000 sailors and 20,000 soldiers divided between the main bases of Kronstadt, Helsingfors (Helsinki) and Reval (Tallin)[10] and the Black Sea Fleet (40,000 officers and men based mainly at Sevastopol in the Crimea). The insignificant Pacific Fleet based at Vladivostok played little part in the events of 1917.

The precise surroundings in which the millions caught up in the Imperial Russian Army and Navy found themselves varied enormously from one place to another. Sailors in the Baltic Fleet had been almost continuously bottled up in their ships. The infantry and artillery at the front might be fighting in the trenches, like their counterparts in France and Belgium, while many others found themselves in the vast forests and swamps of eastern Poland and western Byelorussia, where the front was less well defined and one might bump into enemy patrols at any time. Further south, mountain warfare was the order of the day in the Carpathians and the isolated valleys of Romania. In the

Black Sea the fleet engaged in active operations, fending off Turkish and German coastal raiders, as well as showing the flag and making raids itself. Troops in the far-flung Caucasus had some of the worst conditions to endure. At one extreme were the high mountains and valleys, at the other the arid desert of northern Persia in the area of Tabriz. To make matters worse, they were at the end of the most tenuous of all the army's fragile supply lines. In the rear, too, there were many differences. Garrisons in the major cities were more active than those dispersed in Siberia. Troops in provincial towns were often closer to the peasants of the area in which they found themselves than they were to those of their home province. Despite the diversity, the general features we have identified – the drive for democratization, the desire for a treaty to end the war, the officers' attempts to restore order – were present in all areas, but there were many variations on the basic themes that reflected the specific features of each locality. An examination of areas remote from Petrograd shows that they were quite capable of taking revolutionary initiatives without any extensive prompting from elsewhere. In fact, the two most consistently turbulent fronts, in Romania and the Caucasus, were furthest away from the capital. It should be stressed once again that neither of these case studies is deemed to be "typical". The point is to show how rapidly revolution would evolve in response to local factors rather than promptings from the centre.

The Romanian Front: the Kagul mutiny

Remoteness did present difficulties. The commanders of the Romanian Front held up the news of the February revolution for fear of its local consequences. On 4 March an NCO who had been overheard discussing the February events with a soldier was arrested and sentenced to death by a court martial.[11] Such desperate measures could not, however, do more than delay the inevitable. By the end of the month, committees had been set up and in early April truly revolutionary events were under way. On 1 April soldiers of the 188th Infantry Division arrested their chief-of-staff, Lieutenant-Colonel Senkevich. On the 7 April, at Kimpolung (Cimpulung Moldovenesc), General Miller, the commander of the 26th Army Corps, was accused of counter-revolutionary activities, namely trying to suppress Army Order Number One and failing to recognize the authority of the soviet. When General Miller tried to order soldiers with red flags out of the inspection parade on that day the troops turned on him, beat him, arrested him and had him sent to Petrograd under armed guard.[12] The report on the incident sent by the commander of the Ninth Army described the meeting of soldiers that had taken this decision as "a wild, undisciplined, mindless crowd", although in fact, its relatively measured action suggests that it was far from being a straightforward mob and was already on the road to taking more mature decisions. The very fact that they sent the arrested commander to Petrograd is eloquent evidence that they believed their actions to be more legitimate than those of the general and that the new authorities would back them. Significantly, the chairman of the meeting was not a soldier but a veterinary doctor, showing that, at crucial moments, officers of intelligentsia background might well come to the fore.[13]

Be that as it may, the scene was set for a long, difficult and bitter set of confrontations in the area throughout the spring and summer. The desire to see a start made on active peace negotiations spread among the soldiers, and arrests of officers grew in late April and May. In the second half of May the growing tensions in the Sixth Army reached a peak as preparations were undertaken for the June offensive. They burst into open revolt at Kagul on the eastern bank of the Prut between Galati and Kishinev. The initial spark was provided by complaints about rotation of forces in the line and the re-forming of supposedly unreliable units. Various corps and regiments refused to obey orders and began to extend their demands into calls for peace and redistribution of land, to which end they formed links with the local peasantry. Livestock was seized from landowners and there were numerous other illegal acts not specified in the reports. Many more units were wavering. According to the report of the front commander to the War Ministry the main issues at the heart of the revolt of the 163rd Infantry Division were the lack of confidence felt by soldiers in their officers, the immediate conclusion of peace, lack of confidence in the Soviet of soldiers' and workers' deputies (presumably the Petrograd Soviet) and in the Provisional Government and finally the holding of weapons and ammunition "which might come in handy in the rear".[14]

Only the formation of a strike force including elite and ethnically non-Russian cavalry, artillery, aviators and armoured units enabled the authorities to regain control, without having to open fire. Four officers who had led the revolt and 222 soldiers were arrested. The most important were sentenced to twelve years hard labour. The incident was a microcosm of the main revolutionary forces of the moment: initially military based complaints spilling over into broader politicization that was only brought under control by playing off ethnic rivalries and using Muslim troops to suppress Russian rebels and Romanian peasants. Above all, the event showed not only that a minority of officers might be an essential part of mutinous forces but that a spontaneously "Bolshevik" programme of peace, land and lack of faith in the Provisional Government and the Soviet right wing, could be generated by troops far away from any serious direct Bolshevik influence and at an early stage of the revolution.[15]

The suppression of the mutiny in Kagul was by no means the end of turbulence on the Romanian Front. The situation became more and more alarming from the point of view of both the authorities and the troops. For the commanders, nominally headed by the King of Romania, and the army's hosts, the presence of rebellious Russian armies, who supported local social-democrats and peasants, played on the Romanian landowning elite's inherent fears of a peasant uprising. In addition, the emergence of increasingly assertive Jews among the troops provoked the strongly anti-semitic reflexes of the Romanian rulers. On 1 May, a speech, made in French to help get the message across to the upper classes at whom it was aimed, by a Jewish Under-Officer named Giller denounced the misdeeds of the Romanian ruling class, called for the deposition of the king and the release of political prisoners. The incensed Romanian authorities called for the withdrawal of all Jews from army units operating within Romanian territory.

Not surprisingly, Romania was already becoming a focus for extreme right-wing Russian forces who began to see it as a possible platform from which counter-revolution could be launched into Russia itself. One of the worst pogroms had taken place in 1903 in Kishinev, Moldova, a slice of ethnically Romanian territory incorporated in the Russian Empire. As 1917 progressed, the Black Hundreds, the reactionary mystic Badmaev and the "Holy Rus'" organization all gravitated to the Romanian monarchy as a focus of support. This polarization, pre-figuring what Kornilov was to do on a national scale, created a corresponding radicalization on the part of the popular movement. The Soviet right, composed of Mensheviks and SRs, which dominated this area, became alarmed at the growth of the counter-revolution and condemned the reactionary policies of the Romanian oligarchy. Such declarations were not, however, enough to satisfy the grass roots and a gap began to open up between the Soviet leaders and the popular revolution. The troops continued to take action themselves. In late June Russian troops surrounded the jails and released political prisoners on their own initiative. They also increasingly encouraged and even joined in with peasant expropriations of great landowners. Where this not infrequently degenerated into simple looting, the elected soldiers' committees strove hard to return the offenders to the path of revolutionary discipline.[16]

Overall, one could almost conclude that the centre followed the periphery as far as the Romanian Front went. It experienced a deep, radical, self-generating revolution that, in many respects, was the precursor of events in Petrograd and which owed little to outside tutelage. This was also the case on the Caucasus Front that also exhibited its own sources of revolutionary energy from the very beginning.

The Caucasus Front

After the revolution in the fortress of Kars, a Special Committee was set up to supervise the actions of the officers and purge the command personnel of its most hated members. Two ordinary soldiers were included in this committee. There was also a Soviet set up, chaired by a Menshevik junior officer named Markarian. By April the front commander and future White Guard leader, General Yudenich, reported that all units had committees. Like their counterparts elsewhere the new organizations defended soldiers newly won rights to be treated more like human beings and threw out officers who were not prepared to adapt to the new situation. There was no question of an attack on all officers. The actions of the committees show that, by and large, they tried to make the punishment fit the crime. The most intransigent officers were expelled from the front, others were merely censured. Those who supported the new order were accepted. There was no wave of violence against officers as a whole.

While the early activities resemble those occurring elsewhere in March and April the further development of the revolution on the Caucasus Front began to be influenced by the specific characteristics of the area, in particular the already very harsh conditions of service in the region and the complexities of nationality issues, not only in the army itself but among the civilian population in its area of operations from the Black Sea coast to the mountains and on into northern Iran and the Caspian area.

The winter of 1916–17 and the spring of 1917 were very tough periods for the troops in the Caucasus. Epidemics, the lack of preparation for mountain warfare, the bitter conditions and the rapidly escalating supply crisis all added up to create a potential for disaster. Fuel was very scarce. The complement of Russian troops fell by 100,000 over the winter. In April the losses in some sectors were colossal. The fighting complement of the Army of the Caucasus fell from 141,000 to about 100,000. The Turkestan Corps fell by a half from 31,000 to 16,000 in the first half of the month alone. Lack of supplies and forage were threatening the complete collapse of the front. The tenuous transport routes in the area were partly to blame for this. The most remote unit, the Persian expeditionary force of 50,000 men, was separated by 400 roadless kilometres from its supply depots. All this meant that the Caucasus was hit particularly badly by the declining national economy. The Chief Quartermaster telegraphed to Petrograd as early as 7 April that the supply situation was one of "extreme danger" and threatened "impending catastrophe". The losses from epidemics, the cold and the fighting put increasing pressure on the fit and the survivors. They had to cover for the losses. This meant longer periods at the front, constant postponement of leave and receding hopes of being replaced.

The already desperate situation became even more explosive. In May and June regiments and whole divisions began to press for return to the rear and the Staff HQ was besieged by delegates from units demanding to be replaced. Not surprisingly, given the lack of action from above, some units began to move without orders. Only constant pressure from the army commanders for a continuation of the war and the massive preponderance of SR and Menshevik defensist sentiments, backed by a stream of delegations to and from Petrograd, kept the front going at all.[17]

The endemic crisis provided a threatening context for the already turbulent politics of the region and of the multiplicity of nationalities in the army itself. Complicated interlocking rivalries between Muslims, Christians, Russians, Ukrainians, Georgians, Armenians, Azeris, Turks, Kurds and Cossacks flared into violence and pogroms. Political differences, between nationalists, federalists and socialists, plus class conflicts between landowners, peasants, workers and capitalists overlay the divisions to make a very complex mosaic. There was even a suggestion from a Zionist officer, Junior Captain Zagorovsky, that an army of 500,000 to 600,000 Jewish troops should be formed and sent to the region to advance south against the Turks and liberate Palestine.[18] While such a proposal remained a fantasy, reality itself was complicated enough as a couple of illustrations will show.

The relatively mobile nature of parts of the front meant that, compared to others, there was a high proportion of cavalry (seven divisions) to infantry (12 divisions). This, in turn, meant a substantial cossack presence in the area, which bordered their home territories. Cossack communities were themselves riven by political and social divisions. The first fracture line was between the traditional atamans (chieftains), and the independent cossack farmers of the villages who made up the rank and file. The second separated the cossacks as a whole from non-cossack in-migrants, known as the *inogorodnye*. As a result, cossack politics could sway from the ultra-democratic, when it came to asserting rights against the old chieftains, to the cautiously conservative when it came to preserving cossack rights, emanating from the fallen tsarist regime, that bolstered their privileges against the increasingly strident claims of the *inogorodnye*.

As a result of the conflicting pressures there was considerable diversity of reactions to the situation among cossacks. Some units expressed mutual confidence between officers and men, but elsewhere relations were more hostile and there were extensive purges of cossack officers in March and April in something like a fifth of cossack units. For instance, as a consequence of the Kars incident the 1st Taman Regiment deposed its commander and replaced him with a junior staff officer. The regimental meeting also drew up a list of untrustworthy officers that included all the senior ones. On 25 March, in the Sal'iany garrison, some officers at a general meeting threatened that within two weeks the old order would be restored. Only the intervention of a lieutenant, who was chairing the meeting, prevented the officers from being subjected to immediate reprisals.

However, when it came to defining relations between cossacks and the ordinary soldiers, the cossacks attempted to hang on to their rights and privileges. They were also wary of the question of land redistribution. While they defended the collective rights of the cossack villages against their own chiefs, they were aware that they were in a better position than the *inogorodnye* and did not want to see their communal and military fund land handed over. There was some risk of this since, in the Kuban, the *inogorodnye* comprised 56 per cent of the population but owned only 8 per cent of the land, while in the Don 49 per cent of the population were cossacks and they held 70 per cent of the land. Only 10 per cent was in the hands of the peasantry. In many cases the antagonisms within the cossack community came second to defence of cossack rights as a whole against outsiders. The outcome of the pressures could be seen at the cossack section of the Caucasus regional and front conference held in May. There was a strong defence of cossack communes, a call for greater autonomy and calls for political equality between cossacks and peasants. However, there were no equivalent calls for equal land rights for peasants.[19]

South of the Caucasus the situation was even more complicated. In a massive war like that of 1914–18 the "sideshows" can be overlooked. A particularly vicious one, with repercussions extending down to the present day, took place in northern Iran and Eastern Turkey around Lake Van and the south shore of the Black Sea. The Russian command sent an expeditionary force of 40,000–50,000 into the area with the rather fantastic objective of linking up in Baghdad, 1,500 km away, with British troops moving up from the Persian Gulf. The advance of a sizeable Russian force predictably stirred up a hornet's nest. Here, deep traditional hostilities, brought to a head by massacres of vast numbers of Armenian Christians by Islamic Turks in 1915, combined with the politics of the war and the upheavals of the revolution to produce a hell on earth for many of those caught up in the tragedy.

For the Russian troops, many of whom were Siberian peasants, the desert terrain was unbearable. Added to this were difficulties caused by the increasing distance of the front from its supply bases that brought about greater shortages. Under such conditions the temptation to loot overwhelmed many parts of the army, especially when the rouble eventually collapsed against the local currency in May–June. As a result, the army on the spot was no longer able to purchase sufficient local supplies as an alternative to shipping everything from Russia. Banditry and pogroms against the local population occurred in a number of places and the army command frequently turned a blind eye.

These events, in turn, sparked off enmities in the whole region. An Armenian battalion attacked Kurdish villages in the Trebizond area in late April and early May while, for their part, Kurds took reprisals against Armenians, even within the borders of the Russian Empire near Echmiadzin. Georgians also joined in the attacks on the Persians. The local Muslim population also feared that the Russian occupation would consolidate the hold of Christian Armenian feudal landowners who exploited the serfs of the area. This was not the end of the chain of enmities. There were also tensions between Armenians and Azeris and between Kurds and Nestorian Christians. The sorry cycle of reprisal and counter-reprisal thus gathered momentum. Attempts were made by organized soldiers committees to bring matters to an end and resolutions were passed supporting the rights of Persian peasants against the great feudal landowners of the region. A giant demonstration of the garrison troops at Tabriz in late March proclaimed that "Russian bayonets will not be directed against Persian democrats".[20] There were cases of troops refusing to attack Kurds out of solidarity, but the harsh conditions brought the good work of the committees to nothing.[21]

The politics of the Russian troops in the area also had its own complexities. In particular there were severe differences between separatist nationalists who wanted to set up distinct Georgian and Ukrainian units and left-wing federalists in the Menshevik, Bolshevik and Socialist Revolutionary parties who opposed it. There were even disturbances between Ukrainians and Russians and between different groups of Georgians over the issue.[22] The examples show vividly that energetic, spontaneous forces were ready to assert themselves among soldiers once the state was seen to be weakening.

From committees to front-wide organizations

A central focus of early spontaneity had been the setting up of a system of local committees to organize revolution at grass-roots level. The next stage was to bring them into a broader regional network. This was done by organizing front-wide conferences of soldiers' deputies that began to meet in late spring. Above all, the front conferences show two things. First, they give an impression of the overall balance of forces in the army and, secondly, they are the point at which grass-roots pressures linked up with politics on a national scale. For the moment, there was little direct conflict between the two levels. Soldiers still retained faith in the Provisional Government and wanted to defend their country against the foreign invader. The elected representatives at the early conferences were overwhelmingly defensist. The SRs were usually the largest grouping and the Mensheviks the second largest. For the time being, Bolshevik representation was minimal. At the South-Western Front Conference of Soldiers' Delegates, held in mid-May, 36 per cent of delegates claimed to belong to a political party, the majority of them being Mensheviks. Among the 64 per cent of non-party delegates the majority supported the SRs, the rest the SDs with only some 2 per cent supporting all other political parties, from anarchists to Kadets. Of the 700 delegates only about 50 claimed to be Bolsheviks.[23] A similar balance existed at most of the military conferences held in the spring of 1917, the major exception being the Romanian Front where the soldiers' organization, that was still dominated by officers, was used to repress the more radical troops. Some of the conferences co-operated with broader revolutionary forces in their area to set up important local organizations like the Romanian, Black Sea and Odessa Soviet, known as Rumcherod, which became an increasingly important local counterweight to Petrograd across the whole of the south-west region.

Acute divisions between troops and the Provisional Government, however, lay in the future. For the time being, the government and military authorities were trying to use the committees to restore discipline and the fighting ability of the troops. Thus, while the slogan of war to a victorious conclusion had been derided by the troops, the resolutions at these conferences tended to be overwhelmingly in favour of defensive warfare. The Conference of the Western Front in mid-May voted by 610–8 in support of defensive operations while the South-Western Front Conference decided against obstructing preparations for the planned offensive by 554 votes to 26. Only one person voted against a resolution of support for the Provisional Government and a Bolshevik resolution to transfer power to the soviets was defeated 570–52. Rumcherod overwhelmingly supported the Provisional Government, a feeling no doubt heightened by the fact that the area was becoming a focus of counterrevolution and the revolutionary forces should not, therefore, be split.[24] The Caucasus Front also voted to support the government's policy of putting off key decisions until the Constituent Assembly.

While all this might seem satisfactory from the point of view of the government, closer observation shows that there were rather more ominous undertones present. The support given to the Provisional Government was clearly not unconditional. The conferences also passed resolutions calling for the carrying out by the government of the basic policies of the popular movement, namely active work for a negotiated peace, the transfer of land to those who worked it and the defence of workers' rights and living standards. The conference of soldiers of the Western Front passed a long resolution defining soldiers' rights that indicates the political balance of the moment very well. The resolution accepted the need for strict discipline while on duty but infractions were to be dealt with by an elected disciplinary tribunal, not by the officers alone. In addition, there were demands for full civil liberties including freedom of speech and freedom of assembly "inside and outside the barracks", full participation in the political process and non-interference by military authorities in off-duty activities. Although the South-Western Front rejected calls for an immediate transfer of power to the soviets, it did support the transfer of land to peasants via the Constituent Assembly. On the Caucasus Front the resolution on soldiers' committees called for them to have the right to challenge the appointment of officers. In some places, radicalism had begun to go further. The Kagul mutiny came out in open opposition to the Provisional Government and, in the Baltic, loyalties were being transferred to the soviets and more active revolution was being promoted so that even in early May soldiers were joining agricultural labourers (there being relatively few peasants in the region) to expropriate landowners as they were doing in Romania.[25] While local conditions were important in the Baltic – notably the memory of the vicious repression carried out by the landowners in association with Stolypin's government in 1906 plus the German names and background of the landowners selected for attack – the signs of impatience were unmistakeable. In May, the Latvian Riflemen voted not to support the Provisional Government, as did the first conference of Baltic sailors. Even so, the Riflemen's resolution still had defensist overtones of opposition to the German–Austrian seizures of territory and called for resistance to them.[26]

In addition, it is worth noting that the majority of delegates to most of these conferences did not belong to a party and were, like workers and peasants, committed more to policies and issues than they were to parties, which remained weak and could not call on much store of loyalty. In other words, the mass of soldiers would offer their support to whomsoever was more likely to carry out the programme they favoured. They would go along with the government insofar as it remained committed to the search for peace, the setting up of army committees, the redistribution of land, the defence of workers' living standards and rights and the democratization of the country by means of the Constituent Assembly. The growing inability, or unwillingness, of the Provisional Government to pursue these aims set the scene for a deepening of the revolution in the army as the months went by.

Radicalization of the revolutionary movement in the army and navy

There were three forces above all that speeded up the radicalization of the troops. In ascending order of importance these were growing nationalist and ethnic tensions; the deepening supply crisis brought about by the progressive collapse of the economy and, thirdly, the clumsy efforts of the authorities to stop these processes by restoring "order" by heavy-handed means. In many respects, the impact of such pressures on the armed forces reflects their impact on Russian society as a whole in these months.

It should, perhaps, be mentioned here that centrally directed political agitation and propaganda was not so much an agent of radicalization in itself. Rather already radicalized troops (and civilians, for that matter) sometimes turned to it to give shape and direction to their discontent. Even so, as the current examples have shown, they were quite capable of organizing themselves, particularly on the periphery since it was beyond the reach of radicals in the centre.

Ethnic tensions

Throughout the first revolutionary year ethnic and nationality issues began to make themselves felt in the armed forces. In particular, various groups attempted to form national units, that is, to concentrate people of shared ethnicity in the same divisions and armies. In the forefront of this were Ukrainian nationalists. From the Caucasus, through the Ukraine and on into Petrograd, Ukrainians began to form Ukrainian units. There was considerable pressure from the floor at the South-Western Front Conference in May to promote separate Ukrainian units as official policy, but it was defeated, not only by political manoeuvring but also because it was seen as a secondary issue by most delegates. This did not prevent the nationalist minority from asserting itself, thereby setting off clashes with non-nationalists. As the Ukrainian Rada (the equivalent of the Petrograd Soviet but with a political and social composition closer to that of the Provisional Government) became more overtly separatist, so it stepped up attempts to form a Ukrainian army to defend Ukrainian interests. Further north, in the early weeks of the revolution, Ukrainian troops in the Petrograd region were reported to be spontaneously congregating around the largest Ukrainian units that were stationed in Tsarskoe Selo. Ukrainian nationalists in the army held many meetings in these months, not just in the Ukraine but as far away as Simbirsk on the middle Volga. Smaller nationalities, particularly Latvians, Georgians, Armenians and Jews, began to organize themselves, in many cases calling for the formation of national units that could fight, if needs be for national rather than Empire-wide interests. By the end of the year there was even a Greek division formed consisting of 170 officers and 1,200 men.[27] Ironically, in the last, desperate months of the Imperial Army, after the Bolshevik takeover, the High Command and the Allies saw the formation of national units and armies as the best means of keeping the Eastern Front going, on the assumption that troops from territories such as the Ukraine, that were occupied by the Central Powers, would continue to fight to liberate them.

Although these are all important developments that were, over the years, deliberately played down in Soviet historiography and overlooked in many western accounts, it does not necessarily follow that one can rehabilitate them to the extent of calling them national-liberation movements, as does Mikhail Frenkin, the former Soviet historian who emigrated to Israel. They fall somewhat short of this on a number of counts. First of all, they were divisive even within the nationalities involved. Many Ukrainians, Georgians, Jews and so on opposed separatism and remained within the Empire-wide political system, at least for the time being. Secondly, the main political elites, of right, centre and left, mistrusted separatism. For the right, it was the negation of everything they stood for, namely Great Russia one and indivisible. The views of the Kadets were little different on this question. For them, nationalist movements were German-inspired. According to them, Crimean Tartar disturbances had coincided with the appearance of German warships off the Black Sea coast.[28] Ukrainian separatism was, they said, ". . . yet another link in the German plan to break Russia [sic] up".[29] The Kadets' partners in the Provisional Government more or less went along with this, diverting serious discussion away from decolonization and emphasizing the need for unity in the struggle against the internal and external enemies of the revolution. While they were not above exploiting it for their own political ends, the Bolsheviks, too, were out of sympathy with separatism and tended to promote their own internationalist, class-based analysis. At the Seventh (April) Conference of the party, Dzerzhinsky said the party was "against the right of self-determination" and a Georgian delegate, Makharadze, said that the nation state "belonged to the past, not the future".[30] Lenin's pronouncements were less clear-cut and the party evolved a half-way house policy that opposed national separatism but encouraged very ambiguous relationships of devolved power within the context of continued, strong centralization. But none of the major parties gave serious support to separatism in 1917.

A third important limiting factor is that there were few, clear-cut ethnic groups. Each had its own minorites. Many national areas were smaller versions of the Empire as a whole. For example, the Ukraine looked fairly homogeneous, but the cossacks wanted to assert their own independence within it. This in turn, was further complicated by relations with other ethnic, tribal and religious groupings in the area such as the Cherkassians, Chechens, Ingush and others. The more one looked into the situation the more complex seemed the interlocking relationships. There were also specific difficulties. The Poles were restrained in fighting against the Germans for fear of coming into conflict with brother Poles fighting on the German side. The Byelorussian separatists found it easier to organize in the chaotic conditions of the Romanian Front than they did on the more disciplined Western Front that ran through their own territories. Finally, and perhaps decisively, there is very little evidence that nationalist and separatist sentiment penetrated very deep among the major nationalities. Such issues rarely figured prominently in the demands of the popular movement. If anything, solidarity against the Germans and even a naive internationalism fitted better with the outlook of ordinary soldiers, not to mention peasants and workers.

Economic crisis

A second important element promoting radicalization of the army was the endemic and deepening economic crisis, that also had a major effect on workers and peasants. As far as the soldiers were concerned the vital question was supplies, not just of arms and equipment but also of food and clothing. Failures of production and, probably more important, of distribution, were getting worse by the week.

Complaints by troops that they were "hungry and ill clothed", as some troops of the First Army put it in May,[31] go back to the early days of the revolution. Supplies of clothing and boots for the soldiers were, in all cases, well down on requirements, sometimes by more than 50 per cent.[32] In early April supplies of food for troops and forage for horses was down to between 60 per cent and 80 per cent of the requirement.[33] Railway deliveries to the European theatre were also down by about a third over the first sixth months, even falling below half at the worst moments.[34] Naturally, demoralization and illness followed. On the Western Front in June and July respectively 181,000 and 177,000 men fell ill, of whom nearly half had to be evacuated to the rear. By comparison, 30,000 and 45,000 were treated for wounds in the same months.[35]

Economic collapse began to feed on itself. Transport difficulties, caused by some 25 per cent of locomotives being out of service by summer, starved factories of fuel and raw materials and the front of food and equipment. As output fell, so a goods famine meant progressive withdrawal of food producers from the market, since there was nothing to buy with the money they received for their produce. This led to more shortages and greater disruption. Hungry and desperate people, civilian and military, began to loot supplies in transit. This made matters even worse. In early September, the fronts, especially the Northern Front, were down to 10–20 per cent of normal supplies of food. This led to stopgap solutions of massive forced requisitioning in the areas immediately behind the fronts. Grain, meat and tobacco were in very short supply. Soldiers in the worst affected Caucasus theatre threatened to quit the front if they were not fed. Elsewhere, there were many minor skirmishes and even some mutinies. Three regiments of the Tenth Army categorically refused to undertake duties in October on account of their physical weakness. Epidemics got worse. The plight of the troops went from the unbearable to the unimaginable.[36]

The political consequences are easy to imagine. In Frenkin's opinion, hunger was a more important source of rebellion in October than propaganda. Certainly, the situation of the Provisional Government among the troops was precarious. The gains of February had been eroded. The war could no longer be fought, though the Government failed to admit this and continued to try to keep the front in existence. Hunger and illness were all that the troops had to show for seven months of revolution. This provided an ominous backdrop for the political events of September and October.

Reactivity: fending off the counter-revolution in the armed forces

While the economic and supply crisis can help to explain the front soldiers' growing impatience with the government, it is not the full explanation by any means. Rather, the main confrontations continued to be political, particularly over the democratization of the army. The attempts of the General Staff and the Provisional Government to restore order provoked a growing backlash among the troops. The conflict was particularly acute since the restoration of order and discipline were seen by the old authorities as a prelude to restoring the war-fighting capacity of the army and navy. The soldiers and sailors did not want this, they wanted a more urgent quest for peace. Thus, the questions of authority in the army and of peace were inextricably locked together. It was in this sphere, above all, that the fate of the government was decided.

As we have seen, the surge of democratization in the army in the early weeks of the revolution had posed an acute problem to the military authorities leading them and the government, in the absence of any other viable policy, to adopt a partially conciliatory attitude to the restless soldiers and sailors. This went as far as the proclamation of a limited Declaration of Soldiers' Rights on 11 May. The spirit of forced compromise was extended to the network of soldiers' committees with the government even encouraging their development and then trying to win them over to government ends, in the front rank of which was the restoration of the war-fighting capacity of the army and navy. In other words, the committees were to become the agents of Provisional Government policies among the troops. General Ruzskii even proposed, on 6 March, that government commissars should be appointed to explain the political situation to the troops, an idea that, like forced grain requisitioning and the practice of sending propaganda trains to the provinces, the Bolshevik government enthusiatically borrowed from its Provisional Government and tsarist predecessors. However, the committees were not so easily tamed. New strategies had to be devised. The first was the June offensive, which we have already looked at, the second the stepping up of counter-revolution after the July days.

Generals who had never accepted the moderate approach to mutiny began to show their hand. On 9 July Kornilov banned soldiers' meetings on his South-Western Front and after Tarnopol', when large parts of his army were turned into desperate, disorganized bands of brigands, marauders and rapists as they sought to flee the collapsing front, he had 14 deserters shot. On 15 July Brusilov called for Rumcherod to be broken up because it had, in his view, "taken broad control" of Odessa and the south-western corner of the Ukraine as far as the Romanian Front.[37] Indeed, some soldiers' committees had begun to call for Soviet power in the run-up to the offensive and many units had refused to take part in preparations for offensive warfare. This had, for the first time, spread to artillery as well as infantry units on the Northern Front.[38]

The Provisional Government was faced with its most severe crisis in the first two weeks of July. The offensive had failed. Preparations for it had, in any case, stirred up a hornets' nest that only military success could, perhaps, have contained. The more disciplinarian generals like Kornilov and Denikin, on whose support the government depended to no small extent, were itching for more vigorous action to restore authority. In the capital, only vacillation by the radical left, including Lenin, had fumbled a spontaneous opportunity generated by Kronstadt sailors and Petrograd workers to overthrow the government. Political forces on left and right were, in other words, polarizing rapidly.

In this atmosphere, restoring order in the army had to be the centrepiece of any realistic strategy by the authorities to save their position. On 8 July military regulations were tightened up and on the 12th the death penalty was reintroduced at the front. A major conference of the government, the General Staff and the front commanders was held on 16 July to work out the details of the new policy direction. Denikin led the demands for a return to what amounted to pre-revolutionary discipline based on a repeal of the Petrograd Soviet's Army Order Number One and the Declaration of the Rights of Soldiers and called for the general reintroduction of the death penalty. According to Brusilov's memoirs, Denikin made it abundantly clear that he blamed not only the Soviet for the chaos but also the Provisional Government itself.

Boris Savinkov, a former SR terrorist and now a close aide of Kerensky, argued that the officer corps itself must take its share of the blame and he called for older and incompetent officers to be replaced by younger ones. Kerensky argued that neither Denikin nor anyone else could turn the clock back and that implementation of his proposals would lead only to chaos. A solution could only be found through the new set of conditions and relationships that had obtained since February. He foresaw a particularly important role for government political commissars in restoring the war-fighting capacity of the army and navy.

The resolution supported by the majority of participants was, however, drafted by the advocates of tougher measures. It called for a restoration of the authority of officers; the extension of military courts and the death penalty to the rear; the expulsion of political activity from the army; censorship of "harmful" literature and the prevention of "harmful" agitation; strict control of the committees whose functions should be limited to routine organizational tasks and strict control of commissars whose relationship to the command staff should be better defined. The government, however, refused to accept this recipe for disaster though some of the measures were implemented. Kerensky was aware that a mechanical return to discipline would not, on its own, solve the problem and the government also embarked on a political strategy to stabilize the situation focused on the convening of the State Conference held in Moscow a month later.[39]

From the ordinary soldiers' and sailors' point of view, however, the new conjuncture was clear. The authorities were on the offensive in the army and navy just as they were in the factories and villages. The period from July to the end of August saw the most concerted effort of the whole revolutionary period to slow down and even control the popular movement. While this strategy did slow things down in many respects it only did so at the expense of building up even deeper resentments that forced the popular movement to burst out with renewed force later on. The catastrophic failure that reversed the momentum the authorities had tried to build up was, of course, the Kornilov affair. In the army and navy in particular this blunder had an electric effect.

Prior to Kornilov's manoeuvres, the authorities had been steadily trying to gain ground. In late July and early August many thousands of troops were arrested for insubordination. Very few were charged although some were tried and a handful were executed. Regiments deemed to be particularly troublesome were broken up and their members posted elsewhere. While this served to spread radical ideas as much as control them, it was none the less the case that the reports from the fronts for the period of mid-August were more optimistic than at any other time since February. The situation was still very poor, from the authorities' point of view, but it did appear to be stable. Desertion rates had fallen to around 200 per week for the major fronts, according to official calculations. In some areas the numbers leaving were being outnumbered by former deserters going back into the line.[40]

It was against this background that Kornilov was engaging in his final preparations and the fate of the government hinged on a couple of garbled exchanges over a primitive teleprinter between himself and Kerensky. Whatever the intricacies of the affair as far as the troops were concerned, it was instantly interpreted by them as an attack on their rights. The need to "defend the gains of the revolution" was brought home to more and more people. The old elites, it was universally believed, were organizing to restore their privileges and defend their property. Only a new wave of self-organization could save the revolution from them. Despite his last-minute conversion to alliance with the Soviet, Kerensky's support within the armed forces was minimal. Hardly anyone at the grass roots trusted the Provisional Government.

In the wake of the Kornilov affair, reports began to come in from all over the front and from some rear areas that relations between soldiers and officers had sunk to an all-time low point. A commissar on the South-Western Front informed Kerensky on 8 September that there had been "a wave of Bolshevism as a natural reaction after the Kornilov adventure".[41] On 10 September, a staff officer on the Romanian front wrote to his superior that "In the final analysis the Kornilov action undoubtedly worsened relations between soldiers and officers" that, beforehand "had changed sharply in a positive direction".[42] Even in the distant Caucasus, where the official view on 11 September was that the Kornilov affair had passed by comparatively harmlessly and that the committees were "with rare exceptions" acting in a useful and constructive fashion, there were signs among the troops of renewed militancy.[43] By 25 September, for example, the soldiers of the Akhaltsikhe garrison were calling for, among other things, a complete break with the bourgeoisie, the arming of workers and revolutionary soldiers, the arrest of leading Kornilovites, the repeal of the death penalty for soldiers, the handing over of power to a renewed Soviet of workers', soldiers' and peasants' deputies and the rapid convening of the Constituent Assembly.[44]

The situation was particularly tense on the Northern Front, especially around Riga, which was lost to the Germans on 21 August, leading many on the left to fear that the government was deliberately opening the front to the enemy in order to restore order in Petrograd. The Twelfth Army, that had been in the forefront of radicalization throughout the revolution, continued to be a thorn in the side of the Provisional Government. The temperature had been raised more than a little by the appearance in the area of one of the government's elite "battalions of death" that, instead of fighting the Germans, began to skirmish with the 2nd Latvian Rifle regiment and the militia on 12 August.[45]

The conjuncture of repressive measures of this kind, foreshadowing the civil war that was already building up, with the opening of the front to the Germans and then the Kornilov affair all seemed to point to the old elite using every means in their power to roll back the revolution. Troops were in the forefront of opposition to Kornilov and they began to take extreme measures of self-defence in the crisis. On 28 August the 17th Siberian Rifle regiment denounced the growing "bourgeois–Black Hundred bacchanalia" that aimed at drowning the revolution in the people's blood. They pledged themselves to defend their army organizations and their rights with all their strength, if needs be with weapons in their hands.[46] As Kornilov's manoeuvres became more open so the resistance became more active. In the Finnish town of Tammerfors the revolutionary committee of the garrison tried to control the border to prevent non-revolutionaries from using it. Officers suspected of counter-revolutionary sympathies were arrested.[47] Local action at Luga and Gatchina by committees undermined Kornilov's advance by persuading the troops whom he had mobilized not to fire on fellow soldiers. In the situation of crisis more and more soldiers turned to their committees for self-defence and looked to them to control the officers, many of whom were arrested.

From this point on, increasingly radical resolutions were passed by soldiers all over the country. Many of them echoed Bolshevik policies. On 10 September the 511th Sychevsk Infantry regiment called for transfer of power to the soviets, so did the Siberian and Latvian rifle regiments of the Twelfth Army. But it was not only in the Petrograd region that such voices began to be heard. On 2 October the Turkestan Army Corps, serving on the South-Western Front, supported a representative from the Provisional Government-oriented pre-parliament. But they made it clear that this was conditional on the government falling into line with the popular movement. In particular, they called for a unified socialist government to be set up that would not compromise with the counter-revolutionary elements in the elite. If the government did not do this then it was agreed that power should be transferred to the Soviet of Workers', Soldiers' and Peasants' Deputies.[48] On 5 October the 507th Rechitsa regiment called for the transfer of power to the soviets and for a democratic peace.

As well as resolutions, there are indications that mass fraternization at the front reached a scale that it had never before attained. When it had first begun, in spring, it was common for fraternizing infantry units to be fired on deliberately by their own artillery. In late September and October, however, it began to cause serious alarm to the military authorities. On 25 September it was reported to have reappeared on the Romanian Front.[49] On 2 October large-scale fraternization was reported from parts of the Eleventh Army serving on the South-Western Front.[50] The report from the Western Front on 24 October, the very eve of the Bolshevik takeover, said there was mass desire for fraternization. Refusal to obey orders, a growing desire for peace and increasing Bolshevik influence were all mentioned. Complaints about poor quality food and exhaustion were said to be widespread. The soldiers' faith in the committees, which were frequently still controlled by elements supporting the army authorities, was declining.[51] Reports from other fronts were equally gloomy. On the Northern Front the situation continued to get worse. In particular there was a growing desire for a speedy peace agreement and increasing numbers of Bolsheviks were being elected to committees.[52] Oddly enough, the officially recorded desertion rate remained low, even on the troubled Northern and Western Fronts.[53] How the growing opposition to the Provisional Government was harnessed by the Bolsheviks will be a main focus of the next chapter.

PART TWO

Constructing a new order

CHAPTER SEVEN

The popular movement and the political parties

The previous chapters have shown, beyond doubt, that in 1917 there was an explosion of independent activity within classes, institutions, organizations, groups and individuals throughout the Russian Empire. We have seen that this activity was often outside the confines of the state and of the struggle to control the state, that is, it went beyond what we normally think of as politics. And yet, in the final analysis, it was the outcome of the battle to control the state that had more influence than any other single factor in arbitrating between the various forces unleashed in 1917. But, to make the picture even more complicated, it would be quite wrong to see the central political struggle as something that existed in isolation from the grass-roots conflicts and pressures. The deep movements in Russian society created the political tide, the Petrograd politicians had to swim in it as best they could. The key political question is why did some groups succeed and others fail in this enterprise?

In particular, the success of the Bolshevik party in coming to power in October 1917 can only be understood in relation to their links with the popular movement. But its importance does not stop there. Even more significantly, the fate of the Bolshevik revolution and the nature of the emerging Soviet state, was shaped at least as much by the relationship of the Bolsheviks to the mass of workers and peasants as it was by the conflict with the Whites.

Political parties in 1917 – leaders and led

The main transmission belt between local and national was the political party. The main, mass parties – the Socialist Revolutionaries and the two wings of the Social Democratic Party, the Mensheviks and Bolsheviks – underwent the dizzying experience of moving from illegality to power within a few months. Many of the leaders went from exile and imprisonment into Provisional Government cabinets or into the Soviet Council of People's Commissars within six months. They remained aware that the reverse transition might be equally rapid. Taking Lenin's disguise from him in the middle of the October uprising, his friend Bonch-Bruevich commented "Give it to me; I'll put it away. It may come in handy again one day, who knows?"

Lower down the parties the February revolution also had dramatic effects. For the first time they could organize without police harassment. There was no threat of arrest for militants. Unions could also be organized without restrictions and strikes could be conducted within the law. As a result the old rules of clandestine or semi-clandestine organization no longer applied but in the whirlwind of events in 1917, new ways of acting had not crystallized. Everything was in flux, including political organizations. The main element of stability was provided by the leaderships, that remained in place throughout the year. There were, however, massive changes lower down, not least because of the volatility of voters in the new conditions. Members flooded into political parties for the first time and maintained only vestigial loyalty to them, being prepared to move to another fairly rapidly if their original one appeared to be selling out its principles. The parties that appeared to be closest to the instinctive programme of the *narod* were the ones that picked up members and voters. Failure to fulfil that programme could result in an equally rapid exodus.

The division between party leaders on the one hand and their mass membership and voters was accentuated by a social cleavage. The main leadership of all the major centre and left political parties was heavily weighted towards the intelligentsia, even though each party claimed to be orientated towards the interests of other groups in society. Given the low level of education in tsarist Russia and the repressive political conditions which had meant that any form of politics had to be conducted under great difficulties and with great risks involved, it is not surprising that the peasants and workers did not produce their own leadership. Instead, politics was a full-time, revolutionary occupation for dedicated intellectuals. Almost all had been university students, though not all had completed their courses. They tended to come from better-off, better-educated families. Lenin's father, for instance was a school inspector in Simbirsk *guberniia*. Ironically, the headmaster of one of the schools under his authority, the school his son Vladimir attended, was the father of Alexander Kerensky. A few came from an artisan background, like Stalin and Trotsky, but they tended to have risen above it via education. Hardly any came directly from the peasantry or the working class with which they identified.

The fact that intelligentsia domination survived in 1917 promotes the question of how firmly the political parties were implanted in the mass of the population. According to the most detailed study of the political linkages of workers, carried out by Diane Koenker as part of her broader study of the working class in Moscow, the evidence is ambiguous. Figures for the objective aspects of political affiliation – party membership, contributions to funds and appeals and newspaper purchase and readership, each of which could be seen as a measure of the varying strength of commitment in descending order with voting for a party as the last significant element – show that, apart from voting, only a small minority of Moscow workers were active participants in political life as measured by these criteria.

For workers outside the two major cities we have even fewer data. For peasants, there is still less systematic information, although there seems to be no need to disagree with the judgement we mentioned earlier that there was a cleavage in terms of direct peasant participation between grass-roots institutions such as village and *volost'* committees and *uezd*, *guberniia*, regional and national bodies where political activists tended to dominate. In fact, this cleavage is probably characteristic of the relationship between local and national politics as a whole.

As a result, as one might expect, people from similar social backgrounds often gave varied political expression to their grievances. One has only to compare the sailors of the Baltic and Black Sea Fleets. In terms of class background, while they were not identical, the two fleets did have a very similar composition. The Black Sea Fleet even had a revolutionary tradition going back to 1905. However, in 1917 it was the Baltic Fleet that was more militant. It also had a higher proportion of Bolsheviks, while the Black Sea fleet remained largely SR. Different traditions had different weight among peasants, workers, bourgeois and aristocrats depending on their local situation. Given the extreme novelty of mass politics, steps to turn this patchwork into relatively coherent, unified political parties was in its infancy. To achieve this had been the work of decades, if not generations, in other countries. It could not be done in Russia in weeks and months.

The growing, and decisive, role of the popular movement is reflected in the evolution of national politics in 1917. Here three main processes were dominant. First of all, the influence of the Kadets and the centre right forces around the Provisional Government tended to decline. Their prestige was at its highest in February and reached its nadir in September–October, when they were overthrown, though they did partially recover in October–November by picking up support from the rest of the right which more or less disappeared in political terms. Secondly, the centre left, the SRs and Mensheviks, rose rapidly in popularity and influence in the first few weeks and months, held steady for a while and then suffered a sharp decline, particularly the Mensheviks. The tensions involved caused deep splits in both parties. Thirdly, the Bolsheviks started out with no real influence or mass support compared to the SRs and Mensheviks but they did become more popular in key areas in late spring and early summer, followed by the July setback from which they recovered rapidly in September.

Beneath the apparent changes, there was a good degree of stability. The fundamental split, between left and right, remained about the same. The political "evolution" was not a swing from one to the other but a series of regroupings within the two camps. The rise of the Bolsheviks did not reflect a swing to the left by the population as a whole but a turning from the left parties that had been sucked into the Provisional Government to those that had not. Referring to the evolution away from the Bolsheviks after October, it has been claimed that what the workers of Petrograd were looking for was "'better' Bolsheviks".[1] By the same token, one could argue that they had turned to the Bolsheviks in the first place because they were looking for better Mensheviks and better SRs. In other words, the popular agenda – a better deal for workers, land redistribution, protection from the economic crisis, greater direct democracy and a just end to the war – remained a relatively stable programme in search of implementors. Equally, the conservative elite who had supported the February revolution as a pre-emptive strike, continued to try to prevent deepening social revolution, but began to see the old right-wing parties as useless tools to accomplish their aim and turned to the Kadets as a potentially more successful stabilizing force within the political system. Important differences remained on both sides. Right and left were split among themselves between those who wanted a degree of democracy and were reluctant to act outside legitimately established institutions and those who were prepared to overthrow parliamentary democracy itself. Supporters of parliamentary democracy from both sides united in the Provisional Government and came under attack from extremists on the left and the right. There was some truth in the view that the situation was bringing to the fore the less scrupulous leaders on both sides, the Bolsheviks of the left and the Bolsheviks of the right, as the politicians of the centre saw it. All this meant that the nightmare that haunted the centre throughout the revolutionary months – the outbreak of civil war alongside continued hostilities by Germany and its allies – was increasingly likely. While the political elites, from Lenin to Kornilov, saw what was happening, did the political consciousness of the ordinary population evolve sufficiently to understand the implications?

As far as the mass of the population is concerned the answer is, quite simply, no. The great majority of people were in a fog when it came to national politics. A Provisional Government enquiry in spring 1917 had identified the low level of culture among the peasants as the greatest obstacle to the democratization of the country. One witness reported that the national revolution was understood in the village as simply a battle between "the tsar and the students". Obviously, the vigorous pursuit of immediate, local interests was not matched, in the countryside, by any comparable engagement with national issues at anything resembling a sophisticated level. There is no sign that this was changing very much as the year progressed. Provincial workers and soldiers and sailors in most areas would also fit this picture. They could defend their immediate interests, and were increasingly aware of their power to do so, but they were less quick at converting their experiences into a broader framework. The state remained remote.

But that is not the whole story. The revolution threw up, from local level, hundreds of thousands of local activists. They led the myriad local activities, joined political parties, participated in *uezd*, *guberniia*, regional and national Soviets and Soviet congresses, joined revolutionary organizations such as the militias, the Red Guard and, eventually, the Red Army. The new Soviet system was to become dependent on them and they on it as many of them eventually took leading positions in it. While intelligentsia leaders were still the General Staff of the revolutionary parties, activists from the grass roots were the officer corps. They transmitted party policy downwards and popular opinion upwards. Their voices rang out at Soviet congresses, articulating the views of the groups from which they had sprung. Their greater contact with higher revolutionary echelons gave them a somewhat broader perspective than that of the people as a whole, but it still remained rough and ready and unsophisticated. Their loyalty was to their programme and principles rather than to any specific organization. They appear to have swung readily to whichever party of the moment seemed closest to implementing their principles. In key Soviets, like Petrograd and Moscow, they made up the body of voters for whose support the political leadership competed. When, as we have mentioned, Bolsheviks began to win majorities in the Soviets, it meant that these militants had moved from supporting the SR–Menshevik executive to supporting the Bolshevik platform. It did not mean that they had become unconditional converts or that they were yet prepared to accept real party discipline. As they saw it, it was a set of policies they were voting for, not a group of people, still less a theory of world revolution. Should policies in which they believed not be implemented, they might well move their support elsewhere once again.

The popular movement, the centre and the right

The relationship of all national parties to the masses is crucial in understanding the reasons for political success and failure in this volatile and immature environment. In the first place, and most obviously, without taking the popular movements into account it would be impossible to understand the fate of the centre and right. At its simplest, their problem was that they stood, in differing degrees, for the defence of large-scale private ownership. The peasants and the workers stood for redistribution of property without compensation. The two positions were totally irreconcilable. The energetic pursuit of the two positions by the parties involved could only result in a civil war. In any such conflict, the propertied class risked being heavily outnumbered. The apparently secure and certainly immobile conditions of tsarism had prevented the propertied class from even seeing the need to cultivate a measure of support in mass society. It is hard to see what basis for rapprochement existed. The polarization of Russian society was increasing, not decreasing as the revolution approached. The elite paid a heavy price for its neglect, at times extreme, of the ordinary population. In 1917, it had no success at all in attracting mass support. The ideological weapons of tsarism – the mystique of monarchy, religiosity, slavophilism – proved to be totally hollow. This, in itself, is one of the most revealing aspects of the popular movement. The traditional ideology, for all its apparent strength, and the supposedly impregnable and imposing edifice of tsarism as it was before the war, proved incapable of rallying mass support. Eighty per cent of the population voted for radical socialist parties – SRs, Bolsheviks and Mensheviks mainly – while most of the rest turned to the Kadets, themselves a party outside the traditional right. Octobrists, Nationalists, monarchists and so on were wiped off the political spectrum. While they were able to build up an armed force, as we shall see, in order to fight the civil war in 1918 and 1919, it was composed largely of officers, plus troops loyal to them who had nowhere else to go. A mass base, even a minority one, never showed any sign of developing. Total inability to attract popular support, together with a chronic tendency to split and split again once the autocracy no longer provided a focus of loyalty, destined the right to oblivion far more effectively than the machinations of its political opponents.

The problem of popular support also came out particularly acutely in the political experiences of the Kadet party and the Provisional Government. Unlike the counter-revolutionary right proper, the Kadets were committed to a parliamentary system based on universal suffrage. It became increasingly obvious, however, that any such system would be dominated by parties further to the left and the political influence of the Kadets would be at an end in the moment of their triumph. While they were able to consolidate their position as the main non-socialist party in Russia and the Ukraine, that was not enough. Where four-fifths of the population supported one or other socialist party – that is, a party that stood for the redistribution of property – a party like the Kadets, based on liberal principles with the defence of private property, as always, in first place, could make no headway. They had only come to the fore in February because, although in the minority, they had been able to dominate the undemocratic Duma, that had been elected on the severely restricted Stolypin franchise in 1912. They had never received a popular mandate and showed no sign of succeeding in rallying sufficient support. Their only hope lay first in the continued belief of the moderate left in the need for unity with the classes that the Kadets represented, mainly the professional middle-class plus some landowners and gentry. Secondly, in the longer term, they hoped that a better conjuncture might be brought about by the distant prospect of a "victory election" after the Germans had been defeated, an election in which, it was thought, a jubilant and patriotic electorate would support the government that had brought about the victory. The trouble here was that Russia had to defeat Germany and her allies. A vicious circle opened up. The resolution that the Kadets showed for the war made it practically impossible for them to build up popular support. A just peace sounded much more realistic to the population than the improbable prospect of victory. The masses remained unimpressed by centrist politicians and turned towards those on the left who promised more resolute action to implement the popular programme.

The popular movement and the left

The rise of the Bolsheviks and the collapse of support for the Mensheviks and SRs are two sides of the same coin. Essentially, most who had supported the Mensheviks in the early months and a substantial number who had supported the SRs, switched to the Bolshevik party in August and September. None the less, the SRs remained the largest party, even though they were unable to exploit their numerical preponderance. The crucial point, however, is to explain the rapid and wide-ranging growth of support for the Bolshevik party. In February the party had had about 10,000 members and was a small minority, even in the soviets. By October–November around 200,000 people belonged to the party and no less than ten million voted for it. Why did they do so?

In order to answer this question adequately we need not only to distinguish the immediate, practical reasons for their rise but also the imagined reasons in the minds of the Bolshevik leadership, and Lenin in particular, since the relationship between the two is vital for understanding the outcome of the revolution.

Lenin's revolutionary practice: the path to October

When he arrived back in Petrograd on 3 April after his journey from Switzerland, Lenin immediately launched himself into taking control of his party. He laid down, following the precedent of Moses, ten principles intended to guide his flock, his so-called April Theses. The one that caused the most shock was his assertion that the party should give "no support to the Provisional Government". This made him the first party leader on the left to break the February honeymoon. For his opponents, Lenin's "anarchist" principles, that included concentrating on the soviets rather than the evolving parliamentary processes, went against their efforts to bolster the centre and left-wing alliance to ensure the triumph of democracy and the defeat of tsarism and its right-wing allies. However, Lenin was quicker to see that what was correct in bringing about the democratic revolution was not necessarily correct once it had occurred. The bedrock of Lenin's view, first formulated in Switzerland but reiterated in the April Theses and throughout the ensuing months, was that:

> the country is passing from the first stage of the revolution – that, owing to the insufficient class-consciousness and organization of the proletariat, placed power in the hands of the bourgeoisie – to its second stage, that must place power in the hands of the proletariat and poorest sections of the peasants.

His entire strategy was based on following this through to its logical conclusion. The party had to be made to fit the new situation. The most important thing (bearing in mind the great importance Lenin gave to the formation of class-consciousness) was to separate proletarian forces from bourgeois ones, to preserve proletarian purity.

The April Theses were not, however, a clarion call for immediate proletarian revolution. The reference to the unpreparedness of the working class suggested some time would have to elapse before it was ready to take on its role. Twice in the theses he talked about the necessity of "patient" explanation of key principles. He also said "It is not our *immediate* task to 'introduce' socialism". In other words, there was no precise timescale attached. Lenin blew hot and cold on the question of seizure of power but, for the time being, his formula that "we preach the necessity of transferring the entire state power to the Soviets of Workers' Deputies" was ambiguous. To preach something is not identical with immediately putting it into practice. Indeed, he defended himself vigorously against accusations that he was in favour of "immediate" revolution.

Rather, the task of the Bolshevik party must be to ensure that nascent workers' power should be immunized against the mass of "petty-bourgeois" influences, in the front rank of which were the defensists of the SR and Menshevik parties who wanted to support the bourgeoisie over the war. This remained fundamental to Lenin's view of what he was doing in 1917. And, incidentally, they show beyond doubt that Lenin, as much as any Menshevik, had a "theory of stages". It was the definition of the boundaries between them that brought about conflict, not the issue of whether or not there were such things as historical stages. Lenin had no doubts on that score.

In addition, the April Theses included a prominent denunciation of the imperialist war; defence of the soviets as "the only possible form of revolutionary government"; "abolition of the police, the army and the bureaucracy"; officials to be elected and displaceable at any time and their salaries to be limited to that of the average wage of a competent worker; a call for "confiscation of all landed estates; . . . the immediate amalgamation of all banks in the country into a single national bank and the institution of control over it by the Soviet of Workers' Deputies" and, finally, the creation of a new revolutionary International to help spread the revolution to other countries. Clearly, Lenin envisaged a deepening of the revolution on all fronts.

Whatever the correctness of Lenin's views, in practical terms the principles enunciated in the April Theses were of immense importance. They turned the Bolshevik party into the main opposition to the February Revolution from the left. Refusal to support the Provisional Government and denunciation of the leaders of the other Soviet parties as petty-bourgeois stooges, bizarre though it seemed at first, meant that, should the masses become disillusioned with their parties, they would know where to go. This was the secret of Lenin's success in 1917. The party's oppositional stance, bereft, for the time being, of any responsibility for putting its principles into practice and for the ensuing consequences, gave the leadership broad scope for forging an alliance with the various parts of the popular movement. It also explains why, once they had to take responsibility after they came to power, their popularity fell just as their predecessors had done. It was beyond any politician's power to fulfil all the expectations of the people.

This, however, was not the impression that the party gave to its growing band of followers. For them, the party represented, quite simply, the deepening of the revolution and the adoption of the programme of the popular movement. The resoundingly revolutionary policies of the Bolshevik leaders contrasted starkly with the tone of the Menshevik and SR right in the Petrograd Soviet and, eventually, the Provisional Government. Their line was that a revolutionary agenda could not yet be implemented because the centre would not stand for it, nor would the western allies. To antagonize them would be to force them into a single bloc with the monarchists and the reactionaries. This would threaten reprisals against the still weak soviets and the ill-organized working class that would jeopardize the gains already made. In addition, the war, and all that it implied in terms of maintaining a war economy that would supply food and munitions to the troops as well as provide for the civilian population, could not simply be sloganed out of existence. In crude terms, the soviet right said that nothing further could be done for the time being and was put in a position of constantly preventing a deepening of the revolution – as we have seen with respect to its efforts to control peasant land seizures, restore discipline in the armed forces and maintain at least a minimum level of organization in the factories in order to keep them producing. This brought them into head-on collision with the popular movement. In these circumstances, the Bolshevik party, allying itself with the popular movement, grew by leaps and bounds. Where the soviet right was constantly warning that things could not be done, Lenin and the Bolshevik leadership claimed everything was possible. Not only could land be seized, officers undermined, factories supervised but if this were done, the economy would grow, the creative revolutionary potential of the country be unleashed, the war question be solved by its transformation into a triumphant revolutionary crusade into Europe and people's power be secured. Such promises could not fail to attract the increasingly frustrated militants of the other parties and the popular movement in general as they saw even the gains of February being eroded by the end of summer. Incidentally, this does not imply that the Bolshevik leaders were being Machiavellian in adopting such policies. It was not conscious deception that drove them, Lenin seems to have really believed that the policies would work.

The alliance between the Bolshevik party and the popular movement did not come about instantaneously. It occurred in phases driven by the unfolding logic of the situation as much as by Bolshevik energy in promoting their cause. The first major congress representing the popular movement was the national

Congress of Soviets of Peasants' Deputies that met in Petrograd in early May. It had 1115 delegates. Fourteen were Bolsheviks. Almost half were SRs. Its main action was to pass overwhelmingly a resolution on land that declared "The right of private property in land is abolished forever . . . Hired labour is not permitted". To cultivate land was deemed to be the right of everyone, including women. Co-operatives were permitted but not individual proprietorship. Judging from this first step into the national political arena the peasants showed not only the ability to organize more rapidly than the workers and soldiers, but also had adopted an instinctively revolutionary programme without having to be goaded into it by the Bolshevik-led proletariat as Lenin constantly claimed they would have to be. In no meaningful sense of the term could this resolution be described as "petty-bourgeois". While the congress and its delegates were very much more representative of SR activists than of working peasants, there can be no doubt that they had formulated a programme that reflected the attitudes of the peasantry.

The first national Congress of Soviets in June was not much more favourable to the Bolsheviks. Seven hundred and seventy-seven of its 1090 delegates declared a party affiliation. One hundred and five were Bolsheviks and 32 Menshevik-Internationalists, compared to 285 SRs and 248 Mensheviks. Clearly, the surge towards the Bolsheviks had barely begun. Significantly, however, the Congress met shortly after the First Coalition Government (that is, one including liberal capitalists and socialists) had been set up and its contradictions were beginning to make themselves felt. The views of the left, that socialists should take over the whole government, began to be heard. It was at this juncture, it will be remembered, that the Bolsheviks planned their demonstration, ultimately forbidden by the Congress, against the "Ten capitalist ministers". This, however, began to make opponents of such actions appear to support "capitalist ministers", a bizarre position for so-called socialists and revolutionaries. The Soviet right was still in control, but the signs were looking more ominous. Their entry into government meant that they were abandoning a large area of the battlefield to the Bolshevik leadership, who were not slow to exploit it.

This conjuncture could, of course, present problems for the Bolshevik leaders. If they relied on being oppositional they could not afford to be seen to compromise. It was precisely this dilemma that hit them in the July Days, when, as we have seen, popular elements were pushing them into even more radical steps than the leadership, or, more precisely, Lenin, was prepared to take.

By July, then, there was little sign of a Bolshevik breakthrough. They had consolidated their position, particularly in Petrograd, but even here, they remained in the minority in the Soviet and the August City Duma elections saw them outpolled by the SRs. Apart from Lenin's bravado at the First Congress of Soviets, when he declared that the Bolshevik party was ready to take power alone, there was nothing to suggest that they were in the driving seat of destiny. The Provisional Government's attack on them after the July Days, when they were accused of being German agents, could, however, be seen, perversely, as the beginning of their rise. After all, one implication of it was that the government took the threat posed by them seriously and this, in itself, was a kind of recognition, an acknowledgement that Lenin's bravado was not as empty as his opponents claimed. As the short-term impact of the accusation that they were German spies wore off, it was the deeper implication that began to assert itself.

Be that as it may, up to the July Days, the party did not appear to have gone much beyond the "patient explanation" referred to in the April Theses. The July catastrophe itself was taken very badly by Lenin. The slogan "All power to the soviets" was, he said, no longer valid because the soviets were under the control of the arch-enemies of the proletariat, the petty-bourgeois traitors from within. He talked about waiting for the formation of a new and different system of soviets and insisted that only armed uprising could now salvage his European revolutionary dream. For the time being, Lenin thought that Bolshevik policies were further than ever from being implemented and that it was even time to go back into the underground.

Ironically, it was after July when they were able to do relatively little, that Bolshevik political strength began to grow. With its leaders imprisoned or in hiding, with a series of court appearances to give them the halo of martyrs, the Bolshevik party was able to convince more and more people that their only crime was that they unambiguously favoured the pursuit of the revolutionary programmme of the overwhelming majority of the population. It was resolutions to this effect that began to gain support in important soviets in August when, for the first time, Bolshevik proposals began to get majorities.

The first Bolshevik proposal to get majority support in any part of the Petrograd Soviet was in its workers' section on 7 August when resolutions condemning the reintroduction of the death penalty and calling for the release of left-wing political prisoners were passed. The real turning point, however, came in late August and early September, when the meetings were dominated by the rise and fall of the Kornilov mutiny. This uprising from the right quite naturally strained the credibility of those in the Soviet, that is, its Menshevik and SR leaders, who had put their faith in collaboration with the Provisional Government. Kornilov had been kept out of Petrograd by the forces of the Soviet and the street, not by the coalition with the Kadets (though the latter had stayed at the margins of Kornilov's movement). In this atmosphere, those who stood for new forms of soviet democracy, appeared to have been proved correct. The successful show of force by the Soviet also increased its self-confidence. The scene was set for a turn towards soviet power and the Bolsheviks.

The emergence of a Bolshevik majority came in two stages, the first, in a dramatic all-night sitting of the Petrograd Soviet. Kamenev was the leading Bolshevik spokesman, since Lenin was still in hiding. The main thrust of the resolution that he put forward at the All-Russian Executive Committee was that there should be a decisive break with the propertied classes and an exclusively left-wing government that would proclaim a democratic republic. This was, in many respects, a compromise in that it seemed to envisage the continuation of the state-building process on the basis of the Constituent Assembly, rather than a transfer of power to the soviets. It also called for the transfer of landowners' land to peasant committees without compensation and without waiting for the Constituent Assembly; workers' control; some measures of nationalization and a just and democratic peace. Discussion was transferred from the All-Russian Executive to the floor of the Petrograd Soviet on the evening of 31 August. No better symbol of the political situation could have been devised. The Kornilovites were in the course of being defeated, but the threat they presented created an unusually tense atmosphere in the Soviet. It also preoccupied many of its regular members, including its large military element, who were still on duty defending the capital against Kornilov, so the meeting was less well-attended than usual. None the less, the confrontation was obvious. Despite the current conjuncture, Tsereteli, the leading figure in the dominant Menshevik–SR block, argued that the bourgeoisie was still necessary to the revolution. Without it, the economy would collapse entirely and this would strengthen the counter-revolution. Not unexpectedly, this clashed violently with the mood of the Soviet and he was extensively heckled, whistled at and jeered. By contrast, affirmations by other speakers of the need for firmness in dealing with the right were greeted with applause. Many non-Bolsheviks supported Kamenev's resolution. At 5.00 a.m. on 1 September it was passed by 279 votes to 115 with 51 abstentions. The conjuncture could not have been clearer. Even in the extreme conditions prevailing, Tsereteli had been forced to argue that the Soviet could not implement its revolutionary programme. Arguments that the left could and should take over power began to attract more and more militants. Given a choice between being told they could or could not achieve their goals, many of them plumped for the former.

This, however, did not prevent the Menshevik–SR caucus from sticking to its line of alliance with the bourgeoisie when the All-Russian Executive Committee resumed its discussion of Kamenev's resolution later the same day. The dominant argument was that Petrograd was not Russia and the country as a whole was not ready for a soviet government. The Bolshevik resolution was defeated. Clearly, this put the Petrograd Soviet and the All-Russian Executive Committee on a collision course. The second, more decisive, stage of the crisis, took place on 9 September when the question of the composition of the Presidium (organizing committee) of the Petrograd Soviet was discussed. The current Menshevik–SR dominated Presidium had raised the issue in an attempt to reverse the swing to the Bolsheviks. Once again adopting what appeared to be a reasonable compromise position, Kamenev argued that the new Presidium should be based on proportional representation. A narrow majority agreed with the Bolshevik line. The old leadership saw this as an issue of confidence and resigned in a costly fit of pique. As a result, a new Presidium, with Trotsky resuming his role from 1905 as its chairman, came into office two weeks later. It was composed of four Bolsheviks, two SRs and one Menshevik.

Bolsheviks thus stood at the head of the institution that was most representative of the popular movement but they still had to cut their cloth to the prevailing mood of the delegates, whose support for them was conditional, not absolute. In the transitional period between the first acceptance of a Bolshevik resolution, on 1 September and the vote on reorganizing the Presidium on 9 September the Bolshevik group faced defeat on a number of occasions. The nature of the proposals they put forward was essential to their getting a majority. There was no party whip system to ensure control by the leadership. Their measures had to be acceptable to the delegates. Ironically, the compromises embodied in their two crucial victories, on the democratic republic and proportional representation, went against Lenin's views and he was critical of what he saw as Kamenev's drift to the right. But, in Lenin's continued absence, the Bolsheviks in the Soviet were putting on their most "liberal" face. When he took over the chairmanship, Trotsky glowed magnanimously:

> We are all party people, and we shall have to cross swords more than once. But we shall guide the work of the Petrograd Soviet in a spirit of justice and complete independence for all fractions; the hand of the Presidium will never oppress the minority.

The story of how the Bolshevik leaders moved from this democratic position to the acquisition of power and the rapid suppression, not only of counter-revolution but also of the rest of the soviet left has been told many times. In most accounts, however, the political dimension has been uppermost. From the point of view of more firmly integrating the revolutionary activities of ordinary people into the overall framework, it is essential to meditate more deeply on the nature of the relationship of the Bolshevik party to the popular movement.

In the first place it would be wrong to attribute the entire change of direction to the impact of the Kornilov affair. In the August elections to the Petrograd City Duma, though the Bolsheviks were outpolled by the SRs, they were, none the less, the second largest party with 33 per cent of the votes. This represented an increase of 14 per cent compared to the last equivalent elections (to the district dumas) in May. The suppression of the Bolsheviks, that had not prevented them from mounting an energetic campaign though they did have to call themselves Social Democratic Internationalists, was clearly working in their favour. The main Menshevik newspaper attributed the Bolshevik success, and the stunning collapse of the Menshevik vote to an insignificant 23,000 or about 4 per cent, to "the inadequacy of creative work on the part of the democracy, which has not given the masses any concrete results".

While the SRs were holding their vote the underlying tendency was for former Mensheviks to switch to the Bolsheviks, looking, as we have already mentioned, for "better Mensheviks". Many Menshevik activists and even whole Menshevik party local branches such as that on Vassilevsky Island, one of the inner suburbs of Petrograd, switched en masse to the Bolsheviks. The Kornilov mutiny certainly hastened the process but the lack of "concrete results" was a much more fundamental element. In addition, it should not be forgotten that the new mood was not only visible in Petrograd. In other cities, soviets were reacting in much the same way as in the capital. In the Moscow Soviet, for example, the Bolsheviks gained a majority on 6 September.

The radical upsurge of September and October is frequently described as an upsurge in "Bolshevization". Indeed, Bolsheviks were its main beneficiaries. But the relationship between the party and its new supporters was not a simple one. Naturally enough, Soviet historians had little hesitation in presenting the development as the Russian people's road to Damascus, their spiritual conversion which, they argue, was the outcome of the determined efforts of Bolshevik propaganda to win them over to party principles or, to put it another way, to "raise" their consciousness. But the evidence enables one to go beyond such a simplistic interpretation. The popular movement did not turn towards Bolshevism because they had become converts to its basic philosophy.

Overemphasis on Bolshevik agency overshadows other vital ingredients in the October revolution. First of all, the upsurge of opposition to the Provisional Government was, as we have seen, largely spontaneous and widespread. Traditional interpretations have emphasized that areas in which Bolsheviks were strong – the Petrograd region, the Baltic and the Northern and Western Fronts – were more "advanced" than other areas. Our examination has shown that it is not so simple. Radicalization was, in some respects, as "advanced" in areas like the Romanian Front, the Caucasus and the Donbas, where there was little or no Bolshevik influence. From this point of view the main cause of the late upsurge was not Bolshevik activism or a conversion experience but the sharpening of confrontation initiated so thoughtlessly and disastrously by General Kornilov. Even after February, Tkachev's analysis held true. The main force deepening the revolution continued to be the old elite. It was still determinedly digging its own grave by ruthlesssly and misguidedly pursuing its own aims in an unenlightened fashion. Behind its policies there lay a foolish confidence that continued to lead them to the conclusion that the revolution was only the work of a handful of outside, German-funded agitators who could easily be swept away. Like many comparable propertied elites, they believed not only that they were born to rule but that they were truly supported and accepted by the ordinary population. The old regime never accepted that there were deep social and political flaws in its fabric.

But, even though the Kornilov affair, and the lesser attempts at restoration that had preceded it, were the main cause of acute radicalization, it was not inevitable that the Bolshevik party would be its beneficiaries. A second major factor has to be added. This was the refusal of the other major soviet parties to go along with their constituents. In the army, the factory and the village, the SR and Menshevik right had become managers, officers, restorers of order indistinguishable in the eyes of many from the old elite with whom they were allied. It is ironic that Kerensky, who presented himself as a martyr for democracy for the rest of his life, was overthrown because he refused to go along with the overwhelming movement of the population and showed no urgency in developing stable, democratic institutions that were at the heart of the popular movement's programme. The Provisional Government did not fall because it was a democracy overthrown by ruthless and unscrupulous manipulators, it fell because it refused to listen to the population. As a result, Bolshevik leadership came about, to a significant extent, by default. No other major Soviet party was prepared to identify itself with the popular movement.

Thirdly, an examination of Bolshevik strength, even in its heartland areas of the Baltic Fleet, Petrograd garrison and Northern and Western Fronts indicates that formal Bolshevik representation was not as strong as one might expect. Even impeccably Bolshevik sources of the period, such as the memoirs of F. Raskolnikov, a leading representative of the party among the soldiers and sailors of the Petrograd region, provide evidence to support this view. Even within ten days of the October revolution he found, on visits to Novgorod, Staraia Rus' and Luga that the situation of the Bolshevik party was not uniformly favourable. There was much support for the Bolsheviks, he says, but little in the way of formal organization. In Luga there were military units that supported the Bolsheviks but insufficient party members for groups to have been formed.[2] In Staraia Rus' the local soviet of 36 members had so few Bolsheviks there was not even an organized party fraction, though it had selected four Bolsheviks to represent it at the local Congress of Soviets which Raskolnikov had been sent to attend.[3] In Novgorod there were only 176 party members, up from 102 ten days before his visit. Interestingly, of these, 150 were soldiers and only 26 were workers.[4] None the less, a number of units were pro-Bolshevik and one, of 300 men, was described as "all Bolsheviks". But the language here has to be interpreted correctly. The distinction between party membership and support for the party was a vital one. The latter category implied opposition to the Provisional Government and a desire for more energetic implementation of the principles of the popular movement. The former suggested a deeper commitment, though this would be much less marked in the case of recent arrivals. Even taking this into account the number of people deeply committed to the party's aims was still small. Most of those prepared to vote for Bolshevik resolutions were doing so for tactical reasons.

Other pieces of information fit the same pattern. In mid-October, even after a "rapid rise", the Bolshevik party organization on the whole Northern Front numbered only 13,000 members, concentrated in the Fifth and Twelfth

Armies and the 42nd Army Corps. Two thousand of these party members were in the Fifth Army.[5] These numbers were not large considering there were over a million men serving on the Northern Front at this time. According to Frenkin, the Bolshevik military organization in Petrograd numbered 500 members in March–April, 1,800 in August and 5,800 in October, at which time there were 271,000 troops in the city and 467,000 in the area as a whole.[6] The same source gives an indication of Bolshevik strength in the Moscow region, where there were 850,000 garrison troops. The Moscow Region Congress of Soviets, held in late September and early October, comprised 390 delegates of whom 130 were Bolsheviks. A Bolshevik resolution urging the seizure of power by the Soviets received 45 per cent of the votes. The Bolsheviks were at their strongest in the soldiers' section where the executive committee, based as was normal on proportional representation, was made up of six SRs and six Bolsheviks and three Mensheviks. They were at their weakest in the peasants' section where the executive committee was made up of 11 SRs and one Bolshevik.[7] It is worth noting that the disparity between Bolshevik support among soldiers and among peasants is striking evidence that soldiers were not just "peasants in uniform" whose politics was limited to the land issue but had a distinct agenda of their own.

All this indicates that the undoubted movement towards Bolshevism among the troops as well as among the wider population was transient. Above all, what the new supporters of Bolshevism were voting for was soviet power as the centrepiece of the popular movement's programme and the means for achieving its other goals. But that does not mean there was a fusion between them. In many crucial areas the popular movement could not be contained within the framework that the Bolsheviks had set out for it. For example, the popular movement was not focused on soviet power alone. Most of the resolutions that mentioned it called also for a rapid convening of the Constituent Assembly. In other words, soviet power was seen at the grass roots as compatible with the Constituent Assembly, while for Lenin they were completely contradictory. The grass roots also wanted a unified socialist government, not a one-party Bolshevik one, though here it was the failure of the leaders of the SRs and Mensheviks to countenance this, not just Bolshevik determination to rule alone, that made a left-wing coalition impossible. It was also the case that, although anti-capitalist and anti-landowner feelings were deeply felt and frequently expressed, there was no real conception of worker hegemony in the revolution. Rather the *narod* was acting in unison. The whole tragic ambiguity of the revolution is to be found precisely here. For the mass of militants the Bolsheviks were a vehicle for achieving the specific aims of the popular movement. For Lenin and the Bolsheviks, the popular movement was a vehicle for achieving their broader and more messianic aims. A clash between the two was unavoidable. It was not slow to materialize.

Bolshevik dreams

Of all political movements, Bolshevism ultimately represented a great deal more than just its most prominent current political line, in this case soviet power. It seems unlikely that those who flooded to support the Bolshevik party were aware of the deeper implications of Bolshevik policy. For most, Bolshevism appeared to be the instrument by which popular power would be achieved. The Bolshevik leadership assiduously cultivated this impression through adopting the slogans of Peace, Bread, Land and All Power to the Soviets. However, leaders and observers from other Soviet parties, unlike their followers, were not won over by the siren song. Having the advantage of knowing the Bolshevik leaders as a result of 15 years of close, abrasive contact and unending insults from them during the long years of exile, they were less easy to convince than the ordinary population who were more prepared to take Lenin and his comrades at face value.

One of the most acute (though by no means infallible) observers of Bolshevism at this critical moment was N. N. Sukhanov, a member of the tiny Menshevik-Internationalist faction and close ally of Martov. His testimony, written during the first five years of the revolution and published in seven volumes in 1922, is particularly interesting because, as a former underground Social-Democratic activist, he knew the Bolshevik leaders well and was close to their position on key issues. As he says in his memoirs, he was himself tempted to join them after the Kornilov revolt because he had long favoured soviet power. "The mass" he readily admitted, "lived and breathed together with the Bolsheviks. It was in the hands of the party of Lenin and Trotsky".[8] Even so, he did not join them. "We were divided not so much by slogans as by a profoundly different conception of their inner meaning. The Bolsheviks reserved that meaning for the use of the leadership and didn't carry it to the masses".[9] For the masses there were "lavish promises and simple fairy tales".[10] "We did not fuse with them", he continued, "because a number of features of the positive creative strength of Bolshevism, as well as its methods of agitation, revealed to us its future hateful countenance".[11]

There is considerable truth in his account. The Bolshevik programme did contain a great deal of small print and wide-ranging dreams that were not obvious to those coming to its support. The most important of the differences was that the Bolshevik leaders did not fully share peasant aims on land. They were opposed to it being parcelled out to, and worked in the traditional way by, peasants. Though they were prepared to put it under peasant control, they wanted to keep the large estates intact because they were more productive. There were other important distinctions. Peace, to Lenin, meant civil war. Soviet power meant proletarian, that is, Bolshevik power. Where the people thought they were taking power for themselves, they were actually handing it over to a new, authoritarian leadership with almost unlimited aims.

Without recognizing the utopian foundation to the Leninist outlook one cannot understand Bolshevism. The movement did not see itself as a means to implement specific policies to improve the conditions under which the masses lived and worked, but as a source of transformation not only of Russia, but of the whole world. It took seriously Marx's view that the task of communism was the liberation of the whole of humanity from the alienated condition in which it found itself, subject to tyrants of its own making – God, economic "laws", the market, the division of labour, the family, gender inequality and so on – which, instead of serving humanity had come to exercise domination over it. In Marx's words, humanity had, up to the present, been living out its "pre-history". Communist revolution would transform human nature and open up a new era in which life would be organized according to reason, ability to give and need to receive.

While many people, not only Marxists, have vast hopes for the future of humanity, few took them as seriously as Lenin. In particular, he devised an instrument, the party, that was to gather together all who shared the vision, the "conscious" elements of the population in the vocabulary of the time. The main theme of his revolutionary career was the forging of an implement, the party, to bring the revolution about. The theme came to the forefront of Lenin's theory and practice around the turn of the century. In 1902 he produced a major work devoted to the issue, entitled *What is to be done?*, and in 1903 he brought the question to the Second Congress of the Russian Social Democratic and Labour party. Even though Lenin was defeated on the vital vote over defining party membership, he was none the less victorious in getting control of the main party institution, its newspaper. He achieved this later in the conference by driving enough of his opponents out, by means of insults or attacks on their credentials, to create a majority for his own platform. The party split into Bolshevik and Menshevik wings as a result. Although both wings continued to share the same political programme down to 1917 and there were many attempts on both sides to reconcile the factions, Lenin always used any means at his disposal, fair or foul, to maintain the division. Why was it so important to him?

If the heart of Lenin's theory was the party then the core of the party was its "consciousness", its shared awareness of why revolution was necessary and how it should be conducted. In particular, the most important component was "class-consciousness". Marx had argued that the various social classes reflected on their experiences and this led them to a better and better understanding of their real interests. The gap between their actual interests and their understanding of those interests narrowed and they became conscious of their true interests, that is their class-consciousness grew. In the jargon, the class ceased to be a "class in itself" and became a "class for itself". The better education and greater power of the bourgeoisie, so the argument continued, gave them considerable advantages, not only in understanding their own real interests but also in undermining the attempts of rival classes, notably the proletariat, to form their own class-consciousness. None the less, Marx thought that proletarian class-consciousness would develop and lead workers to understand their historical role as overthrowers of capitalism and establishers of the highest stage of human existence, communism. In Marx's opinion, only communism, that is shared control over work and production, could fulfil the proletariat's interests and needs. Finally, since the proletariat and associated groups made up the overwhelmingly largest class of human society in terms of numbers, their needs could be equated with the needs of humanity as a whole.

Above all, by means of the party, Lenin was trying to create and preserve an agency to evolve within itself and to pass on to the working class the pure form of class-consciousness, unpolluted by class traitors and compromisers, against whose illusions and machinations his own counter-machinations were a regrettable necessity. The party would bring together the class-conscious. Essentially, this meant two groups. In the first stage, the lead would be taken by revolutionaries who would be full-time activists. Though Lenin did not like to bring out all the implications, it was clear that they would be mainly intellectuals and, indeed, as we have already seen, the founders and leading cadres of the party were revolutionary intellectuals, like Lenin himself. They would educate the proletariat into an understanding of its own interests and the party would draw into its ranks those workers who had achieved this level of consciousness. They would be the key element in transferring class-consciousness to the class as a whole that would, thereby, become a class in itself, recognize its interests and join in the struggle to establish the communist society that corresponded to them.

There were a number of important implications in these ideas but, for the moment, we will look only at the most important, the implication of hierarchy. If the leaders and advanced cadres were at a higher stage of consciousness then there was no question of equating their views with the views of those lower down. The party leadership did not, therefore, see itself as the reflection of the actual opinions and immediate interests of workers but as the representative of the enlightened opinions and higher interests of the workers, of the workers as they would be once they had come to realize their true position in society and their role in history. As far as the popular movement was concerned, Lenin's theories thus assigned the ordinary people a subsidiary role. They were the pupils whom the party had to teach. They were the rank and file who should obey their leaders who knew their interests better than they did themselves. Indeed, following the wishes of the workers was a recognized heresy designated "*khvostizm*" ("tailism"), so-called because it implied hanging on to the tail of the workers. Lenin believed that the party should be holding the reins.

However, the reality of the party was rather different. Far from being a disciplined, organized and increasingly conscious entity, Lenin's party, and the other groupings within the Social-Democratic party, resembled nothing so much as a group of quarrelling sects with Lenin as the Ayatollah and the Leninists as the arch-fundamentalists, fearful of potentially polluting contact between themselves and the infidels. To stretch the spectacle into a model of revolutionary preparation is to strain common sense to the extreme.

Secondly, it is not at all clear that ordinary members of the party were fully aware of the finer points of theory. Thirdly, the war had introduced a new reorientation of left-wing politics between defensists, who supported their national war efforts and internationalists who opposed working-class participation in the war, sometimes on pacifist grounds. Lenin, however, was no pacifist. Rather he dreamed, as he wrote in September 1914, of "the conversion of the present imperialist war into a civil war"[12] – clear evidence of the breadth of Lenin's imagination as well as of the gulf between himself and the popular movement which was barely conscious of such a scheme.

Finally, and most important, the massive explosion in party membership in 1917 was completely incompatible with its supposedly Leninist party structure. For every member it had in January 1917 it had ten by October, rising to a total membership of about 200,000 by then. In other words, it was a mass party with a regular mass membership and, as such, was hardly distinguishable from any other. It was no longer composed of "professional revolutionaries" since the members flooding in had no real schooling in Marxist theory. As was remarked at the time, it had been "de-bolshevized".

However, it is essential to point out that, although this is true for the party as a whole, there was still an all-controlling leadership that dominated the mass of new members. While the leadership continued to show that it was not fully disciplined by falling into warring groups over every major initiative, from Lenin's April Theses, through the July Days, the seizure of power in October, the Brest-Litovsk Treaty, military and trade union policy during the Civil War and the adoption of NEP in 1921, it is essential to note that, despite the divisions, Lenin's line was eventually followed on all of these key questions. In other words, the "bolshevik" structure of the party boiled down to Lenin's domination of it. This is confirmed by the fact that, after his illness and death in 1924, the divisions were no longer able to be healed and the leadership fell into purging and, eventually, bloodletting.

Lenin's party, then, was not so different in terms of its nature. The idea that it was a special, purified repository of class-consciousness is dubious, to say the least. In reality, it was a conspiratorial party with a strong leader while in the underground, that retained its centralized, hierarchical structure when it was transformed into a mass party, mainly because of Lenin's absolutely crucial role in leading it. New members, supporters and voters flocked to it in 1917 because of the line it pursued not the metaphysical dimensions of its inner nature. The leadership, however, and Lenin in particular, were certain that their control over the party and the masses was legitimized by their own higher consciousness. In a sense, there were two parties – the tiny, "conscious" core and the rest.

One other aspect of theory must, however, be taken into account. In order to examine it we need to turn to Lenin's most sustained theoretical work of

1917, *State and revolution*, written during his post-July exile. Two major themes are intertwined in it. First, that existing state structures should not be taken over by revolutionaries but smashed by them and, secondly, that the evolution of modern capitalism made revolutionary transformation of economy and society easier than ever.

The first idea was derived from Marx's writings on the Paris Commune of 1871 and can be found in Lenin's April Theses and other writings. One set of provisions was geared to preventing the build-up of oppressive groups under the control of ruling minorities, especially state bureaucracies and military and police forces. To prevent them from being used to oppress the population Lenin, following Marx, argued that all officials should be elected and subject to recall by their electors and that they should not be paid more than the average wage of a worker. Everyone should participate in administration. The army and police would be replaced by a militia, that is the armed people themselves taking it in turns to guard and defend the revolution. It was these considerations that were at the heart of the statement in the April Theses that talked of "Abolition of police, army and bureaucracy".

The second idea was derived from the writings of the Austrian social democrat Rudolf Hilferding. He had argued that the growth of cartels and large corporations, plus the evolution of finance capital (that is the growth of banks as the main source of investment) had some positive repercussions for socialism. In the first place, the domination of the market by monopolies meant that planning would be easier, particularly as capitalist cartels were themselves forming in order to try to smooth out the vicious and unpredictable forces of the market. The rise of modern banks also brought about a separation between ownership of capital and decisions about investment. The pool of capital controlled by the investment managers did not belong to them, it belonged to the millions of people who made deposits in banks. But this capital pool was anonymous. No one could say where a particular dollar had come from or to whom it belonged, it was simply part of the vast reservoir of money in the bank's hands. The decision about what to do with it was made by a trained official, a manager, not by the money's owner. If the critical investment process was routinized in this way then, so the argument went, socialist transition would be easier because it was much simpler to introduce new criteria and new officials at the management level than to expropriate and replace a multitude of individual investors. The idea of nationalizing banks became something of a socialist panacea. If the supposedly relatively simple operation of bringing the banks under control could be achieved, then investment would be under the control of the people and would be diverted to projects that were appropriate to their interests not to the interests of the minority of private investors. Not surprisingly, then, we find in the April Theses the provision that "All banks in the country should be immediately amalgamated into a single national bank, and control over it should be instituted by the Soviet of Workers' Deputies". In *State and revolution* Lenin elaborated on these themes arguing that management of enterprises was also routinized and could be taken over with relative ease. For example, Lenin wrote that the administrative tasks of "accounting and control" necessary for the first stage of communism had:

> been *simplified* by capitalism to the extreme and reduced to the extraordinarily simple operations – that any literate person can perform – of supervising and recording, knowledge of the four rules of arithmetic and issuing appropriate receipts.[13]

Finally we should look at another surprising aspect of Bolshevik policy at this crucial moment, particularly in consideration of the fact that the Bolsheviks were Marxists. They had no economic programme. There was little or no guidance on how society and economy would function after the Soviet takeover. On the morrow of the revolution would the market continue to function? How would the grain surplus be maintained? Would the stock exchange continue to operate? How would inflation be brought under control? Would Russia's international trade continue? There is not a trace in Lenin's writings of 1917 of any serious approach to any of these issues. There are frequent, almost millenarian, assertions that the revolution would release the required resources. In Lenin's view, only revolution could fend off an economic catastrophe, but his reasons for thinking so are based on political eschatology rather than economic analysis. For instance, on 14 September he had written:

> Only the dictatorship of the proletariat and poor peasants is capable of smashing the resistance of the capitalists . . . *Power to the Soviets – this is the only way to make further progress gradual, peaceful and smooth* . . . Power to the Soviets means the complete transfer of the country's administration and economic control into the hands of workers and peasants, to whom *nobody* would dare offer resistance and who, through practice, through their own experience, *would soon learn* how to distribute land, products and grain properly.[14]

Only Soviet power, he wrote at around the same time, could "make the country secure against military and economic catastrophe". A takeover would get "the support of nine-tenths of the population of Russia" who would manifest "the greatest revolutionary enthusiasm . . . without which victory over famine and war is impossible". Firmness by the soviets would overcome resistance:

> No class will dare start an uprising against the Soviets, and the landowners and capitalists, taught a lesson by the experience of the Kornilov revolt, will give up their power peacefully and yield to the ultimatum of the Soviets . . . [S]uch measures of punishing the recalci-

trants as confiscation of their entire property coupled with a short term of arrest will be sufficient.[15]

The overcoming of shortages was, for Lenin, only a matter of expropriating those who had too much. For instance, in the event that they would have to continue the war:

> we shall conduct it in a truly revolutionary manner. We shall take away all the bread and boots from the capitalists. We shall leave them only crusts and dress them in bast shoes. We shall send all the bread and footwear to the front.[16]

The underlying assumption was that "the resources, both spiritual and material, for a truly revolutionary war in Russia are still immense".[17]

It was not just in September that Lenin was turning to such themes. They go back to the discussion on the April Theses and are rooted even deeper in Lenin's ideas on the war. In April he had argued in very similar terms:

> [T]he workers, soldiers and peasants will deal better than the officials, better than the police, with the difficult *practical* problems of producing more grain, distributing it better and keeping the soldiers better supplied etc. etc.
>
> I am deeply convinced that the Soviets will make the independent activity of the *masses* a reality more quickly than a parliamentary republic . . . They will more effectively, more practically and more correctly decide what *steps* can be taken towards socialism and how these steps should be taken . . . [T]he Soviet will be able to take these steps more effectively for the benefit of the people if the whole state power is in its hands.
>
> What compels such steps? Famine. Economic disorganization. Imminent collapse. The horrors of war. The horrors of the wounds inflicted on mankind by the war.[18]

Lenin's line had been very consistent throughout the year. Revolution would save the population from disaster, not add to the confusion. It would continue a "gradual, peaceful and smooth" process. There was not the slightest hint that the new revolution would divide the country further. Instead it would unite it so that the recalcitrant minority would be so heavily outnumbered that it would not dare to offer serious resistance and would cave in. The vision was deeply rooted in Lenin's mind. It relates closely to his argument about the ease of transition elaborated in *State and revolution*. It was precisely the belief that it was only a dream that led the SR and Menshevik leadership to support continuation of the alliance with the Kadets.

Faced with the complexities of Lenin's thought, many of his critics have

167

accused him of manipulation and deliberate deception. The ease with which one can juxtapose quotes that are sometimes totally contradictory, has no doubt added to this. To preach Soviet, people's power in public and proletarian or Bolshevik power ("which is one and the same thing") in private backs up such views. The urgency with which he fought in practice for Bolshevik power contrasts with statements reflecting a magnanimity similar to that shown by Trotsky when he became chairman of the Petrograd Soviet. In September Lenin had mused over "a peaceful struggle of parties inside the Soviets; they (the people) could test the programmes of the various parties in practice and power could pass peacefully from one party to another". At the Second Congress of Soviets he said:

> And even if the peasants should continue to follow the Socialist Revolutionaries and give that party a majority in the Constituent Assembly, we shall say to them: Good and well! Life is the best teacher; it will show in the long run who is right . . . In the forging of new institutions, we must follow in the footsteps of life, allowing complete creative freedom to the masses.[19]

Ten weeks later he dissolved the Constituent Assembly by force. His ideas on land and the peasantry were ambiguous. In party discussions he insisted on the division between poor peasants and the rest, but in public he usually talked of the peasantry as a whole. The April Theses called for land to be nationalized and held by peasant committees until the Constituent Assembly made a decision, a line repeated in early September. In late September he argued that "If power is in the hands of the Soviets, the *landowners'* estates will immediately be declared the *inalienable property of the whole people*".[20] On peace his definitions were often unusual. On 14 April at the Petrograd City Conference of the party he said "'Down with the war' does not mean throwing down bayonets. It means transferring power to another class". In mid-September he even saw that it might be necessary to be "defensist" under certain conditions: "if our proposal for peace is rejected, if we do not secure even an armistice, then we shall become 'defensist', we shall place ourselves *at the head of the war parties*, we shall be *the war party par excellence*."[21]

For many writers, both favourable and hostile, Lenin has become more than a person. In his own country he was an icon around whose cult prayer-like language was appropriate – "Lenin lived, Lenin lives, Lenin will live forever" was a typical example. For enemies he was "the compulsive revolutionary"[22] or worse. Since the late 1980s, in his own country, the turn against Lenin has been as exaggerated as his former cult. In the fullest biography of him to be published in Russia the violent, conniving, cruel and authoritarian aspects of his personality are as relentlessly dwelt on as his genius, humanitarianism, wisdom, self-sacrifice, determination and sensitivity were in the past.[23] In many respects Lenin is treated in a more hostile fashion than Stalin was in the same author's earlier study.[24] There is, of course, a tendency to personalize blame for a failed system because it avoids having to think about more painful, deeper rooted reasons for things having gone wrong. The classic example is blaming Hitler for the evils of Nazism, a simple answer that gets everyone else off the hook. However, the Lenin problem goes much deeper into Russian history and is much more complex than it appears. Lenin was the product of a tradition of revolutionary extremism going back, in the comparable case of Bakunin, to the first half of the nineteenth century, a tradition best explained by the intransigence of tsarism in the face of even moderate change that tended to deprive radicals of a legal voice and drove them into greater extremism than their equivalents elsewhere. Once again, the shortcomings of the new system were rooted in those of the old. One cannot simply dismiss Lenin as a Machiavellian extremist driven by a desire for personal power or gain.

While no politician is free of manipulation and deliberate deception, looking at Lenin's work as a whole in these months – his writings and his activities – suggests an alternative explanation. Fundamentally, Lenin wanted to bring about revolution, that is obvious. The goal of liberating the poor and the weak from the arrogant power of the rich was all that mattered to him. Everything else, even his Marxism, served that end. But, and perhaps we should not be so surprised at this, given the probability that he might never gain power, he devoted little or no attention to post-revolutionary problems. In analysing the political conjuncture Lenin was always penetrating and trenchant (though not always correct). In his drive to conduct revolution he was unstoppable. But in laying out the future beyond that, his ideas took on a most un-Lenin-like aura of romanticism and naivety. From this point of view, the doctrinal issues of class divisions in the peasantry and so on were of secondary importance compared to the necessity of carrying out the revolution. His contradictions were not Machiavellian manipulation but a sign of his preoccupation with the larger issue. His "liberal" musings over peaceful transition of power and his utopianism over the ease of transforming the economy were, in part, dreams in which Lenin himself believed. If they were deceptions, they were also self-deceptions. While it would be absurd to say that Lenin, of all Russian politicians of the time, was above deceit, it should be remembered that his complexity cannot be fully explained by that alone.

Lenin's campaign for an insurrection

In early September Lenin, increasingly excited by the potential for revolution he sensed from scrutinizing the newspapers brought to him in his Finnish hideout, began, once again, to grasp the situation by the scruff of its neck. At first, he seemed to be toying with the prevailing liberal spirit. In early September he wrote an article suggesting that perhaps a peaceful Soviet takeover might be possible, a startling reversal of his insistence, since the July Days, that only armed uprising was on the cards. This dalliance, induced by the broad anti-Kornilov movement, was short-lived, and, perhaps, only intended for public consumption anyway. It was soon replaced by an urgent series of appeals to the Central Committee to implement the policy of armed uprising. The sequence of increasingly frustrated letters with which Lenin bombarded his colleagues is quite astonishing. At one point he offered to resign in order to take his fight to the membership. At other times he tried to bypass them, arguing that perhaps the revolution might begin in Moscow (where in fact the balance of forces was much less favourable to the Bolsheviks than in Petrograd) or, even more bizarrely, in Helsinki where a regional Congress of Soviets was due to be held. In his increasingly frenzied determination to launch an uprising both dimensions of Lenin's approach – questions of immediate tactics to strengthen the necessary link with the masses and the larger theoretical underpinnings and aspirations – became inextricably intertwined.

The swings in Lenin's advice were unprecedented. The first communication, written on 30 August at the height of the Kornilov crisis, urged that the task of the left was not to take over but to put pressure on Kerensky to "arrest Miliukov", "arrest Rodzianko" and adopt left policies on arming workers, transferring land and establishing workers' control.[25] The next, and equally un-Lenin-like contribution if only because of its title, "On compromises", urged that the Bolsheviks should agree to "a government of SRs and Mensheviks" (who were now suitably redefined as "our nearest adversaries" to distinguish them from "our direct and main class enemy the bourgeoisie") in which the Bolsheviks would make no claim to participate.[26] In "The tasks of the revolution", written in the first half of September, the emphasis again was on "ensur[ing] the peaceful development of the revolution"[27] through transferring power to the soviets, a move that would be supported by such an overwhelming majority of the population that resistance would be impossible. At the same time as this article was written for publication, Lenin began to urge, in secret, something rather different, namely that "The Bolsheviks, having obtained a majority in the Soviets of Workers' and Soldiers' Deputies of both capitals, can and must take state power into their own hands".[28] Clearly Lenin was still driven by his hidden agenda. His colleagues, however, did nothing to act on his suggestion. This made Lenin's tone considerably more shrill in his next letters. To say that insurrection was un-Marxist was, he snapped, one of "the most vicious and probably most widespread distortions of Marxism" and "an opportunist lie".[29] On 23 September he wrote "there is not the slightest doubt that at the 'top' of our party there are noticeable vacillations that may become ruinous because the struggle is developing".[30] On 29 September he again urged a Bolshevik takeover:

> To miss such a moment, to "wait" for the Congress of Soviets, would be *utter idiocy*, or *sheer treachery* . . . To refrain from taking power now . . . is *to doom the revolution to failure*. In view of the fact that

the Central Committee has *even left unanswered* the persistent demands I have been making . . . I am compelled to regard this as a "subtle" hint at the unwillingness of the Central Committee even to consider this question, a subtle hint that I should keep my mouth shut, and as a proposal for me to retire.

I am compelled *to tender my resignation from the Central Committee* . . . [31]

On 1 October "procrastination is becoming positively *criminal* . . . It is not necessary to 'begin' with Petrograd . . . Victory is certain, and the chances are ten to one that it will be a bloodless victory".[32] On 8 October he proclaimed that a pro-Bolshevik world existed:

It is clear that all power must pass to the Soviets. It should be equally indisputable for every Bolshevik that proletarian revolutionary power (or Bolshevik power – which is now one and the same thing) is assured of the utmost sympathy and unreserved support of all the working and exploited people all over the world in general, in the belligerent countries in particular, and among the Russian peasants especially.

There could be no better example of Lenin's confidence in the wider mission of Bolshevism. The letter continued:

Marx summed up the lessons of all revolutions in respect to armed uprising in the words of "Danton, the greatest master of French revolutionary policy yet known: *de l'audace, de l'audace, encore de l'audace*". . . . The success of both the Russian and the world revolution depends on two or three days fighting.[33]

Such ringingly apocalyptic declarations continued to be treated with dismay by the Central Committee. On 8 October yet another revolutionary scenario was urged. "It is in the vicinity of Petrograd and in Petrograd itself that the insurrection must be decided on and effected . . . The fleet – Kronstadt, Vyborg and Reval – can and must advance on Petrograd".[34]

At this point Lenin decided to put in an appearance at the Central Committee. But that was by no means the decisive end of his campaign, which was pursued right into the very night of the October revolution. The centrepieces of this last stage of his campaign were his two appearances at Central Committee meetings held on 10 and 16 October in Petrograd. They were both highly charged occasions. The arrival of Lenin, briefly emerging from hiding, the all-night discussions in smoke-filled rooms, the convening of a new meeting on the 16th to broaden the representativeness of the gathering, the open publication of Kamenev and Zinoviev's arguments against an uprising and the immense consequences of the Bolshevik's ensuing actions all gave the events of this crucial fortnight the atmosphere of theatre rather than reality. After much pressure from Lenin the meeting on the 10th agreed that the party's policy should be guided by the seizure of power and that an armed uprising should be "put on the order of the day".[35] These rather vague formulations cloaked the continuing differences between Lenin and the moderates, who feared that precipitate action would lead only to a repeat of the July Days débâcle. The moderates attempted to rally their forces on the 16th. Central Committee members from Moscow, where the situation called for greater caution than in Petrograd, were able to attend. A roll call of the state of readiness of key districts and military units gave a rather mixed picture of the potential for revolution. Clearly, though there was some potential, there was no sense of the masses straining at the leash for a Bolshevik armed uprising, still less of a world-wide yearning for revolution as Lenin had insisted, and continued to do at the meetings.

Lenin's main intervention on the 16th, however, was to castigate his colleagues for not implementing the "decision" of the 10th. It was, he said, a perfect example of how not to implement a resolution. Nothing had been done. He also became immensely irritated when the discussion turned back to the principle of insurrection and was not, as Lenin wanted, limited to deciding how best to put the principle into practice. The publication, two days later, of Kamenev and Zinoviev's letter showed that the principle was by no means decided even by 18 October, just a week before the insurrection.

From the 16th to the 24th Lenin went back into hiding in Petrograd and his exile of September was repeated in miniature. Once again, his only contact with his leading party colleagues was by letter. Again, the tone of deep frustration emerged. On the night of 24 October he wrote a letter that, compared to the others written earlier, seemed to suggest nothing had changed. "The situation", he wrote, "is critical in the extreme. In fact it is now absolutely clear that to delay the uprising would be fatal . . . Everything now hangs by a thread . . . We must not wait! We may lose everything!". Imprecision over detail was the same: "Who must take power? That is not important at present. Let the Military Revolutionary Committee do it, or 'some other institution' which will declare that it will relinquish power only to the interests of the people". The populism implicit in this last phrase was not accidental. The definition of the "people" in whose interests the revolution was to be conducted, was glossed as "the interests of the army (the immediate proposal of peace), the interests of the peasants (the land to be taken immediately and private property abolished), the interests of the starving". In the excitement of the moment Lenin's Marxist elaborations dissolved into much more traditionally revolutionary concepts. Problems are decided "by peoples, by the masses, by the struggle of the armed people". It is "the people" who "have the right and are in duty bound to decide such questions not by a vote but by force". Lenin justified his position not by an appeal to Marx but to "the history of all revolutions".[36] There is no reference to the proletariat at this critical time. While it would be wrong to read too much into something written in the heat of the moment, it is none the less revealing of Lenin's deepest revolutionary instincts.

Sending a letter was not enough. That same evening Lenin left his safe house and made his way through the darkened streets to the hub of party and soviet activity, the Smolny Institute, (where he took off his disguise, so thoughtfully put away by Bonch-Bruevich just in case) and proceeded to put more energy and spirit into the uprising. It has even been argued, by R. V. Daniels, that his arrival was crucial to the change from a defensive to an offensive posture. While we have no direct evidence to back this up, there can be no doubt that the situation did develop more and more rapidly in the direction he favoured. By 10am the next morning, only some 12 hours after the letter quoted above was written, the Military Revolutionary Committee of the Petrograd Soviet, the spearhead of the insurrection, was able to proclaim "The Provisional Government has been deposed. State power has passed into the hands of the organ of the Petrograd Soviet of Workers' and Soldiers' Deputies – the Military Revolutionary Committee which heads the Petrograd proletariat and garrison". The populist tone remained prominent even in this brief but momentous declaration:

> The cause for which the people have fought, namely the immediate offer of a democratic peace, the abolition of landed proprietorship, workers' control over production, and the establishment of Soviet power – this cause has been secured. Long live the revolution of workers, soldiers and peasants!

One might be forgiven for having thought that it was the popular movement that had triumphed in October, not the Bolshevik party. There was no reference to the special role of either the proletariat or the party, nor was there any subtlety about class divisions within the peasantry. Power, it was strongly implied, had passed to the people.

Many participants, even some Bolshevik party leaders, thought that this was, indeed, what had happened. This was what they had joined in the uprising to secure. There was, of course, more to October than the actions of the Bolsheviks alone. The coalition behind the insurrection was much broader.

In some respects, the October insurrection took the form of a defensive action against the final blunderings of Kerensky's government. After all, it was the Government which had tried to take the initiative. A detachment of loyal soldiers seized the Bolsheviks printing press on 24 October and others began to control the bridges before any Soviet activity had started. Kerensky was apparently confident that he had the forces available to control the situation and break the power of the Petrograd Soviet and, perhaps, even to prevent the Second All-Russian Congress of Soviets from meeting. It was this last eventuality that galvanized the Military Revolutionary Committee into taking coun-ter-measures to ensure that the Congress would be able to meet. Its force dis-positions were geared to countering those of the Provisional Government and usually took the form of loyal Soviet forces from among the garrison troops or the Red Guard militia arguing, rather than shooting, Provisional Govern-ment troops out of their positions. Violence was relatively limited, persua-sion, argument and propaganda all-determining. Only on the night of 24–25 October did energetic positive action to seize the city's strong points emerge from the Soviet. Soviet forces were sent to railway stations, the post office and other key points in the city. Still resistance was verbal rather than physical. Even the General Staff Building was taken on the evening of the 25th simply by swamping it with Soviet supporters. When the overthrow of the govern-ment was proclaimed the next morning it was still actually in place. It was only on the evening and night of the 25th–26th that anyone thought to do anything about it. The arrest of the remaining ministers took place after the only major set piece struggle, the "storming" of the Winter Palace. There were real exchanges of gunfire here and casualties but, even so, the event had an air of tragi-comedy. According to N. N. Sukhanov, while the confrontation was going on in Palace Square, people were entering and leaving the building without hindrance through its other doors. The arresting group could, he maintained, simply have walked in. Indeed, this is more or less what hap-pened. Attackers began to infiltrate, defenders slipped away. Far from being the heroic assault depicted in Eisenstein's film *October*, the attack, in the words of its organizer, Antonov-Ovseenko, had "a totally disorganized char-acter . . . By the time we entered the (military) cadets were not offering any resistance". In a gesture full of portent for the bureaucratic system that was being born that night, the first thing Antonov-Ovseenko did when he arrested the ministers was to write a docket and get all present to sign it. They were then led away to the Peter and Paul Fortress across the river. After questioning, most of them were released. Soviet power was proclaimed at the first session of the Second All-Russian Congress of Soviets. The great aim of the popular movement had, at last, been implemented.

It would, however, be quite wrong to see the outcome as a Bolshevik gift to the popular movement. Rather, it was the popular movement's gift to the Bol-sheviks. The "defensive" action of the Military Revolutionary Committee over controlling the city in order to allow the Congress to meet was, as we have seen, matched by a much broader "defensive" mentality in the villages and factories of Russia. Peasants were trying to defend what would soon be their land and forests from the pre-emptive asset-stripping of the landowners. Workers were trying to defend their jobs and the modest gains in conditions they had enjoyed in the early weeks of the revolution. In addition, the possible evacuation of the city and the opening of the front to the Germans, brought the Petrograd garrison firmly into the defensive picture. Their most important gain, the right not to be transferred to the front, was in danger. This effectively neutralized the garrison and helps to explain the most salient feature of the October revolution in Petrograd, the complete absence of any real resistance. The officers, the most likely source of support for the Provisional Government, did not feel any great loyalty to ministers who had first betrayed Kornilov and then appeared to have fallen further and further into the hands of the left. The troops did not want to defend a goverment that seemed to be on the point of betraying them. As a result, most remained neutral because the soviet cause also appeared rather remote. But neutrality of most of the garrison was enough to ensure the victory of the fairly small soviet forces. Where there was no opposition, minimal mobilization would succeed. It was the popular movement, above all, that had ensured there could be no opposition.

From this perspective, one interpretation of October that has never gained much support, namely, that it might have occurred without the Bolshevik uprising, deserves some consideration. Without plunging into counter-factual history, there can be no doubt that, as we have seen, a great head of steam for soviet power had been building up anyway. It is not impossible that the Second Congress might have proclaimed soviet power regardless. A survey of its 670 delegates representing 402 soviets, conducted on their arrival at the Smolny, shows that 505 of them arrived already committed to supporting the principle of "All power to the soviets". A further 107 supported various forms of people's government without coalition with the bourgeoisie. Only 55 delegates supported continuation of the coalition with the Kadets.[37]

While one interpretation might be that the figures reflect the party affiliation of the delegates and their soviets, it is much more probable – in the prevailing conditions of very loose party structures at the grass roots, the volatility of activists and the commitment to issues rather than parties – that it was the desire for soviet power that led many militants to support the Bolshevik party, rather than a commitment to Bolshevism that led them to support soviet power. When we come to define the relationship between Bolshevism and soviet power we enter into a loop. Bolsheviks were dominant in the seizure of power because more and more of those involved in it identified with the Bolsheviks. But they identified with the Bolsheviks because the Bolsheviks supported soviet power. Therefore, more or less by definition, to be an active supporter of soviet power in October was, for the masses, practically the same as to be a Bolshevik. While we can see from this that the Bolsheviks become the focus of the movement for soviet power (because there was no other, given the continued line of the SR and Menshevik leaders for alliance with the Kadets) this is more the fruit of Lenin's tactical provision in the April Theses that they should give "no support to the Provisional Government" than the logical outcome of deep movements of class-consciousness, proletarian hegemony, poor peasant–kulak splits, party organization or any other part of the paraphernalia of Leninism. As we have seen, to some extent, Lenin himself temporarily jettisoned "Leninism" in the heat of the moment and took a traditional, unqualified populist stand with broad, international, apocalyptic overtones. But being the focus of a movement is not the same as being its main creator. Even if the focus had not been there, the movement would have continued to exist.

The popular movement thrust Lenin and the Bolshevik party leadership into power in October, not surprisingly, since they were the only significant party to identify with it. But the fatal knot between the two was extremely complex. The Bolshevik party did not come to power to implement the programme of the popular movement, except as a necessary preliminary, but to transform not only Russia but the world in accordance with their own underlying assumptions. They believed that those assumptions had brought them into power. Unfortunately, they had not. Lenin resembled the engineers struggling to control the nuclear reactor at Three Mile Island who, though they achieved the major goal of avoiding a meltdown, had done so, according to some reports, despite having misunderstood what had happened and using methods designed to solve a different problem from the one with which they were actually faced. Like them, Lenin had achieved the main goal, in his case that of leading a socialist revolution, but many of his assumptions about it were mistaken or, at least, highly controversial. It was not rising class-consciousness that had brought the popular movement into line with the Bolsheviks. The seizure of power did nothing to avert, and a great deal to deepen, the prevailing economic crisis. International revolution did not occur. The optimistic assumptions about ease of transition and the overcoming of resistance very quickly unravelled.

Even before this became clear the Bolsheviks' opponents were able to spell out the real consequences of the takeover of power. The SR and Menshevik leaders argued that the revolution could not be deepened because the costs in human terms would be too great since it would provoke economic ruin, German conquest and civil war. On the other hand, the Soviet left and the Bolsheviks argued that not deepening the revolution would incur enormous costs. Further revolution would end internal strife and prevent further decline in the living standards of the majority. The world would be won for socialism. Who was right?

In the unique conditions of Petrograd the uprising had gone more smoothly than its organizers had dared to hope. But it was not the end, only the beginning of a long journey. Would it be so easy in the rest of the country? Would the army leadership be able to halt the process and arrest the newly formed government? Would resistance prove tougher than expected? What would the outside world think and do? Although they were to co-exist for some time yet, dreams were beginning to give way to reality.

CHAPTER EIGHT

The contours of national politics 1917–21

The Provisional Soviet Government

While it is conceivable that power might have been seized by the soviets irrespective of the Bolshevik coup, there can be no doubt that the outcome would have been quite different from the revolution that actually occurred. Far from limiting themselves to fulfilling the basic popular programme, which is what most of the grass-roots activists expected, the Bolsheviks saw the acquisition of power as nothing less than a turning point in world history. Though Lenin's principles may have been strained in the process of coming to power, once there they came into full play. The Bolsheviks' main purpose in holding power was to implement their grandiose principles. All subsequent phases of their power have shown an intertwining between long-term dreams and a constantly intruding set of realities.

In the first place, however, power had to be consolidated. The vote for soviet power at the Second All-Russian Congress of Soviets was only a first step. From then on the going began to get tough. The first significant clash with the former authorities was a rather scrappy and confused battle at Pulkovo between hastily assembled Soviet forces – composed of Baltic sailors, garrison troops and civilian militia volunteers – and Krasnov's cossacks, who had been brought in by Kerensky to defend his government. While, this time, there was a real exchange of fire, the decisive work was done by propaganda squads who went among Krasnov's small force of around 700 and persuaded them not to risk their lives in order that the authority of officers could be imposed. They arrested Krasnov and handed him over to the Soviet. For the time being counter-revolution proper was halted and gave way to a brief phoney war.

Another challenge to the October uprising in Petrograd came from a strike of white collar employees in the civil service and the banks. It threatened chaos in government administration and in the economic life of the city. The refusal of the strikers to recognize the legitimacy of the new government was the first sign that the transparent transition from bourgeois administration to soviet supervision was only a dream. It promised, instead, to be very rough indeed. For the time being, however, the lack of any alternative to the Soviet government condemned such actions to failure.

Even closer to home, there was significant opposition to the uprising from within the Soviet itself. No major Soviet leader or group rallied to the Bolsheviks. Even Martov, who had been calling for soviet power for some time, ultimately walked out of the Second Congress in protest. The Menshevik leaders organized forces loyal to themselves to put pressure on the Bolshevik leaders to relinquish their power and to share it more broadly. In particular, through the railwaymen's union, they threatened a paralyzing strike. The new authorities overcame it by a combination that was to become increasingly familiar of partial concession, slander of the opposition leaders as petty-bourgeois counter-revolutionaries and the use of the pro-Bolshevik minority of railway workers to undermine the legitimate union leaders.

In reality, attempts to dislodge the Bolshevik government at this moment were unlikely to be successful. Opposition to Bolshevism from the leading personalities of the Soviet was motivated, as much as anything else, by their knowledge of Lenin and the consequent distrust of his aims. The mass membership of their organizations knew much less about Bolshevism. For them, it was simply the most resolute supporter of the aims of the popular movement. So, once again, the hopelessness of the soviet right was brought out. They could only oppose Bolshevism by highlighting their own powerlessness to achieve their aims. As a rallying cry, "support the bourgeoisie" left a lot to be desired for revolutionaries. How could they rally support within the soviets to roll back soviet power? Their boycott marked the departure of a whole generation of prominent revolutionary leaders into, as Trotsky put it as Martov left the Congress, the "rubbish-bin of history".

Lenin's emergence from the underground at the Second Congress of Soviets was the pinnacle of his career. His revolutionary vision was coming true. He stood at the head of the victorious popular movement in the moment of its triumph. The time had come, he announced, for the construction of the socialist order to begin. He called for the abolition of the old state apparatus, the ending of the war (described as a "routine task"), the annihilation of private landed property, genuine workers' control of industry and the construction of the world's first proletarian state. His opponents on the left continued to be critical of his programme on two counts above all. In the words of Sukhanov, "utterly to destroy all the old state apparatus in the desperate conditions of war and famine meant to consummate the destruction of the productive forces of the country, and not fulfil the most urgent tasks of peaceful construction aimed at the cultural and economic elevation of the labouring masses". In addition, "to construct (not merely a Soviet) but a 'proletarian Socialist State' in a vast, economically shattered peasant country meant taking on oneself tasks known to be utopian". The case against this "not yet digested jumble of Marx and Kropotkin" could not be put at this point in the Congress as it was decided not to debate Lenin's speech, one more pointer to the authoritarian future.[1] The Congress accepted the declaratory decrees on peace, calling for an immediate end to hostilities in Europe, and on land, abolishing the landlord sector and handing the land over to the peasant land committees.

One issue, however, proved to be slightly trickier for Lenin and that was the key question of forming a new, Soviet-based government. The walkout by the established non-Bolshevik party leaders made the Bolsheviks' isolation too obvious for comfort. There was still a strong sentiment that favoured an all-Soviet government and, indeed, many of the participants in the October revolution believed that this was what they had been fighting for. The threatened railwaymen's strike in favour of coalition made negotiations imperative. Lenin's tactical genius again made itself felt. The land decree, taken lock, stock and barrel from the SRs, had not had much effect on the peasants, who conducted their revolution for themselves but it did have an effect on the SR party activists at the Second Congress. It split them. The left decided to support the Bolsheviks because they were implementing SR policy and because they were internationalists. As a result the Bolsheviks had the fig-leaf of a coalition government in the form of the participation of five Left SRs as ministers when the final composition of the Soviet government was announced. The word "provisional" actually appeared in its first official title. Many expected that it would soon give way to the long-awaited Constituent Assembly, due to be elected in November and to convene in December.

The "triumphal march" of soviet power

In the country as a whole soviet power was undertaking what became officially known as its "triumphal march". Even while the Second Congress was in session, exciting news of the spread of the revolution was being brought in, as John Reed recalls in *Ten days that shook the world*. Garrison delegates in particular came to the Smolny. There was a Commissar from nearby Tsarskoe Selo panting and covered with the mud of his ride.

> The garrison of Tsarskoe Selo is on guard at the gates of Petrograd, ready to defend the Soviets and the Military Revolutionary Committee . . . The Cycle Corps sent from the front has arrived at Tsarskoe, and the soldiers are now with us; they recognize the necessity of the immediate transfer of land to the peasants and industrial control to the workers.

A telegram arrived in the early hours of the morning of the 26th:

179

> Comrades! The Twelfth Army sends greetings to the Congress of Soviets, announcing the formation of a Military Revolutionary Committee which has taken over command of the Northern Front!

The telegram was typical in that it was not by means of the party that the new authorities turned their potential power into real control of the country but by means of a series of military revolutionary committees that were set up in association with local soviets. Even in Petrograd it was the Military Revolutionary Committee of the Soviet that had organized the October revolution. It had controlled the movement of troops, Red Guards and workers that had brought about the downfall and arrest of the Provisional Government. It had also helped defend the capital from the half-hearted attempt to recapture it for the old authorities. Throughout the country the example was followed and revolutionary committees of the soviets took over in many major cities and towns, usually dispersing the alternative "bourgeois" foci of local power, the city and town dumas.

While the taking of power in Petrograd had been a formality, Moscow was a foretaste of bitter and bloody struggles to come. In the first place, the situation of the Moscow Bolsheviks was different from Petrograd. Even the party leaders there, like Nogin, were reputed moderates who had not wanted to press for an early uprising. They were aware that in Moscow the Provisional Government and the right were in a stronger position than in Petrograd. Indeed, Kerensky's last cabinet, formed on 25 September, had taken on a distinctly "Muscovite" flavour. No less than eight of the 16 ministers were based in the city. None the less, despite doubts, the Moscow Soviet had dutifully followed Petrograd on 5 September in passing, by 355 votes to 254, a radical, Bolshevik-proposed resolution similar in terms to the Petrograd one. It did not call for the overthrow of the Provisional Government but referred to the possibility of a "resolute struggle for power by the representatives of the proletariat and revolutionary peasantry". The long shadow of Kornilov was cast over the proceedings and the accusation that the government sympathized with Kornilov was duly made, as was the view that the revolution might only be able to achieve its aims "through a break with the politics of compromise and a resolute struggle of the broad masses for power". As yet, these were threats, not realities. In any case, the Bolsheviks' hold on the joint soviet of workers and soldiers in the city was tenuous. They had a majority in the workers' section but the Menshevik–SR block retained a sufficiently large majority in the soldiers' section to give them overall control. As a result of elections held on 18 and 19 September the Bolsheviks had 48 out of 120 joint executive committee seats, the SRs 35 and the Mensheviks 25.[2] Not surprisingly, "preparations" for the seizure of power in Moscow were perfunctory. On 24 October the Soviet, after wrangling for weeks, finally agreed on the regulations for a Red Guard for the city. There was no military revolutionary committee until the last minute. Once news of the coup in Petrograd arrived, the battle had to be joined with improvised forces against a relatively powerful foe with a substantial force of officers and military cadets at its disposal. As a result, there was serious fighting. The Reds held, and then lost the Kremlin to White forces on 28 October. The following day saw perhaps the bitterest fighting. Some measure of its fierceness can be gathered from the casualties. The largest Red Guard unit in the city, from the Zamoskvoretsk district, sustained 225 killed or wounded from its nominal strength of 1500.[3] The estimate of 1000 casualties altogether would seem to be justified. The opponents of the Soviet takeover capitulated on 2 November.

In the next two weeks Bolsheviks took a complete grip on the new revolutionary institutions in the city, helped not a little by the boycott by the soviet right, in support of a broad socialist coalition, that left the field completely open to Bolsheviks and their allies. The re-elected soviets were overwhelmingly Bolshevik. The powerful presidium of 15, set up on 14 November, consisted of 11 Bolsheviks, three Left SRs and one United Social Democrat. It was chaired by the historian, M. N. Pokrovsky.[4] One cannot, however, attribute the outcome solely to Bolshevik manipulation and the mistakes of their opponents. Bolshevik support in the city was, in any case, very high. In the September municipal elections they received 51.5 per cent of the votes on a fairly low turnout. The Kadets obtained 26.3 per cent and the SRs 14.1 per cent. The Mensheviks had a derisory 4.1 per cent. In the city elections to the Constituent Assembly held in mid-November (when twice as many voted) the Bolshevik per centage fell slightly to 47.9 per cent and the Kadets rose to 35.2 per cent. No other party reached double figures.[5] Bolshevik support among the soldiers was particularly high. In the Constituent Assembly election they received 81 per cent of the votes of the 61,000 soldiers in the city who took part.[6] If we compare the results with those of the first municipal election, held on 25 June we can see striking changes. In June the SRs had obtained 58 per cent of the vote, the Kadets 16.8 per cent, the Mensheviks and Bolsheviks 12 per cent each.[7] The volatility of the electorate and the impact of the Kornilov affair in undermining the soviet right could not have been clearer. Nor could the grouping of the anti-Bolshevik vote around the Kadets after October when the city polarized into Bolshevik and Kadet, having been overwhelmingly SR only a few months earlier. The overwhelming redistribution of votes reflected changing moods based on the immediate social, political and economic conjuncture; the fidelity of the popular movement to its own programme; the desertion of the popular movement by the soviet right and the emergence of the Bolshevik party as its champions. It would be naive to think that the 363,000 who voted Bolshevik in November, compared to 75,000 in June, were supporting the long-term Bolshevik programme of world revolution. They were largely former SR and Menshevik voters looking for more resolute implementors of the popular programme. One could not find a better example of the political conjuncture that brought the Bolsheviks to power.

The experience of Moscow fitted well with that of other key areas in which

Bolshevik influence was rocketing at this decisive moment. A look at the Russian Empire's third major city, Kiev, shows how important local differences could be. Here the Bolsheviks and the Soviet left had far more formidable obstacles preventing them from coming to power. In the forefront was the Ukrainian Rada, which was largely composed of nationalists who wanted to weaken, and eventually break, the Ukraine's ties with Petrograd. The confused struggle for power in the city lasted until 3 March 1918. The Bolsheviks did not have a majority in the Kiev Soviet in October 1917 but the Petrograd coup did lead to an increase in their support. Still lacking a majority they put their faith in a Ukrainian Soviet Congress that they hoped would be dominated by urban and military sections, favourable to themselves. However, the nationalists from the Rada saw to it that their own rural supporters were in the majority. When the Congress met on 4 December, in a reversal of later events at the Constituent Assembly, a Ukrainian SR delegation backed by troops ejected the Bolshevik chairman, leaving control of the congress in the hands of the Rada.

The bulk of Bolshevik delegates retreated to the largely Russian-populated eastern Ukrainian industrial centre of Kharkov where they were more secure. They regrouped their forces and, with Petrograd's help, sent a Red force to recapture Kiev. The Bolsheviks left in Kiev staged an uprising in order, it was hoped, to control the city before the arrival of outside forces and lessen the affront to nationalist feeling presented by this apparent "invasion". After extensive fighting from 16–26 January the Bolsheviks gained the upper hand and were still in the process of consolidating their power in the Soviet and suppressing rival organizations when, on 3 March, the German Army arrived to occupy the city and eventually install their favoured candidate, Hetman Skoropadsky, as puppet dictator.

The fighting had been even fiercer than in Moscow and shows that civil war, in the form of armed revolutionary struggle, had already begun. Not all areas, however, saw bitter struggles over the transfer of power. In many places, once news of the Petrograd events had filtered through, formal declarations of the assumption of power were made by local soviets and no resistance was forthcoming. In most cases nothing changed for the time being. In some towns declarations of soviet power had even preceded that in Petrograd. Kronstadt had declared its "independence" on 29 May and, despite agreements patching up the breach, the Provisional Government exercised authority there only insofar as the local soviet allowed it to. As early as April and May central government observers were reporting something similar from Tsaritsyn and in distant Krasnoyarsk, in Siberia, the soviet ruled almost without hindrance. In the midst of its general strike,[8] the soviet at Ivanovo–Kineshma anticipated Petrograd by four days in virtually taking power on 21 October. It should be emphasized that in all these places it was soviets, not the Bolshevik party, that had taken over. In some places Bolsheviks did not dominate the soviets and in any case, as we have seen, to be a Bolshevik meant little more to all but hard-core activists than to favour soviet power as a means of defending the popular programme.

One might have expected the central focus of tsarist and elite power, the front headquarters of the army, to put up some resistance to the Bolsheviks. It did not, however, do so. The bare facts of the case are that, after tentative feelers in both directions, the new Soviet government moved towards a showdown with *Stavka* (GHQ) in November. On 9 November the new government dismissed General Dukhonin, the head of the army. On the 10th his successor, Lieutenant Nikolai Krylenko set out from Petrograd for *Stavka* at Mogilev with an escort of armed Baltic Fleet sailors. He arrived in Mogilev ten days later and took the town without any resistance. The only victim was Dukhonin who had been persuaded to stay behind. He was arrested and beaten to death by an angry mob of soldiers, sailors and peasants despite Krylenko's urgent plea that there should be no lynch law.

Why had it been so easy to capture *Stavka*? The main problem for the old authorities was that they had been unable to raise enough politically reliable troops. On occasions when they thought they had done so, they were able only to sit by and watch their forces melt away under pressure from revolutionary militants. The officers had no cards left to play to win back the support of their soldiers. Disheartened, most potential leaders of the counter-revolution who found themselves in Mogilev fled to areas where they thought conditions would be more favourable than the Northern and Western Fronts that, as we saw, were the most heavily bolshevized of all. In this way, the Soviet Government was able to complete its takeover of the key northern and central parts of European Russia by the end of November.

It had not, however, taken full control of the country. The most threatening centre of resistance beginning to form was in the Don cossack region, controlled, after a fashion, by Ataman Kaledin, who had made the most outspoken attack on the Provisional Government from the right at the Moscow State Conference in August and was thus, along with General Kornilov, the favourite of the counter-revolutionaries. Kornilov himself, after breaking out of prison in Bykhov near Mogilev, fled to the Don and was named Commander of the gathering White forces in the area. They did not, even at this early stage, have everything their own way. There were pockets of Soviet power plus the treacherous sand of Russian and cossack peasant and worker communities of the south who wanted no part of counter-revolutionary adventures. Serious fighting was already under way by the end of the year and a soviet uprising took Rostov, thanks to the indifference of Kaledin's rank-and-file cossack troops. However, more determined White forces drove the insurgents out five days later on 2 December. It was only two months before Kaledin's government collapsed again under insurgent Red threat. This time, Kaledin could see no way out and, after a final speech to his assembly, committed suicide.

By the end of February, Red forces had rooted out opposition in the cossack centres, but the matter did not rest there. The main Russian White force in the area, the Volunteer Army, led by Generals Kornilov, Denikin and Alekseev, and consisting, perhaps appropriately, of around 10,000 men like the Grand Old Duke of York's army, had not been subdued. After its withdrawal from Rostov it had no secure base and fought its way towards areas it hoped might provide one. In early April it made a direct assault on the Kuban cossack capital, Ekaterinodar. The attack failed. What was, perhaps, worse, it cost them the life of their most recognized leader, General Kornilov. From that time on Denikin became leader. Thus, even in the early civil war stage, military struggles and counter-struggles were being conducted on a significant scale. In addition, the fundamental problem of the counter-revolutionaries, their inability to find a way of arousing any sizeable popular support, was already beginning to show itself. A small army in a hostile political environment was not likely to be a serious long-term challenge to the revolution. It was only towards the end of 1918 and in 1919, when significant foreign intervention, in the form of supplies and troops, began to arrive that the attrition of the White forces came to a halt and they were able to go on the offensive in a major way.

None the less, the early battles in the south were noted for their fierceness. Both sides appear to have resorted to terror against their opponents. In the Black Sea Fleet headquarters there are reports that 350 to 400 "*burzhui*" including children were done to death during a three-day sailors' reign of terror in early February. In the Rostov region the Reds also appear to have executed suspected White sympathizers. The Whites themselves conducted a terror against the revolutionary miners of the area, shooting many, leaving others to die down the pits.[9]

During this early period there were many other areas where the writ of the new authorities did not run, most notably the breakaway nationalities of the Baltic region – Poland and Finland in the front rank but also Estonia, Latvia and Lithuania that were "protected" from Moscow by their German occupiers – and the Transcaucasus. Here independent revolutions were being conducted, unleashed by the collapse of the central Russian state but following channels dependent on local circumstances and aspirations.[10] The nationalist movements themselves did not, however, pose any real threat to the centre since, apart from some border squabbles (which, in the case of Poland, grew into full-scale war by 1920), they were self-absorbed and wanted nothing more than to be left in peace by the centre. The new states were, however, used, with varying degrees of willingness, as havens for Russian counter-revolutionaries whose threat to the Soviet government was more serious. Other areas – like the Ukraine, Central Asia and Siberia – were also still confused but, for the moment, key towns and lines of communications were, by and large, under Red control. But there were still pockets of resistance, not to mention indigenous populations that were, to all intents and purposes, outside the struggle.

By and large, where necessary, revolutionary committees had been used to overthrow the political remnants of the old order. This is hardly surprising and was certainly in line with the expressed views of the grass-roots militants and much of the population. Much more controversial was the role of military revolutionary committees in suppressing parts of the left, including representatives and members of the popular movement itself. This was done when criticism of Bolshevik domination of the new government was expressed. Even in the heartland of Bolshevism, the Twelfth Army, the new government had to resort to force to get its way. At the Twelfth Army Congress of Deputies of Soldiers' Soviets, that opened in late October, no party had a majority of the 500 delegates. The Bolsheviks came closest. Two hundred and forty-eight voted for their resolution. The meeting broke up. This only encouraged strong-arm tactics and, on the authority of the military revolutionary committee, the pro-Bolshevik Sixth Latvian Regiment occupied the Twelfth Army HQ and the offices of the electoral commission. Many arrests were made. On 1 November the Fifth Army committee was forced to hand over its duties to a Bolshevik task group that included soldiers.[11] The use of intimidation ensured that, when the first Congress of Soldiers' Deputies of the Northern Front met on 28 November, 80 per cent of its delegates were Bolsheviks, 20 per cent Left SRs. No Mensheviks and Right SRs were allowed to take part.[12]

The same task group seems to have been charged with the ticklish job of establishing control over *Stavka*. Krylenko had at his disposal a substantial force of Baltic sailors, volunteers from the Latvian Regiment and other semi-private "armies" attached to various revolutionary militants loyal to the Soviet Government. It was this force that, ostensibly on the authority of the local revolutionary committee, attacked and killed Dukhonin. Krylenko also called an immediate halt to the Ukrainianization of parts of the army that Dukhonin had been undertaking.

Thus, already, within a month of the October revolution, similar methods were being used to suppress soldiers' committees and parts of the revolutionary movement that did not conform to the Bolshevik recipe, as were being used against real opponents of the revolution like Dukhonin. In this instance, it was probably the same individuals who carried out the acts. While there was an important difference in that, for the time being, left-wing opponents were not being killed, force and violence were, none the less, being used as the chief persuaders.

This is borne out by the fact that these were not isolated instances, nor were such actions confined to a few regions. Everywhere those who expressed support for parts of the popular programme that did not coincide with Bolshevik policy – notably the call for a broader based government and an end to intimidation of the left – met the same response. In the south, Rumcherod, which right-wing generals had targeted for suppression after July, was finally brought to its knees by Bolsheviks. Here, even the local revolutionary committee stood out for a unified socialist government rather than a Bolshevik one. Military units on the Romanian Front were split over support of "bolshevism", by which they meant choosing either immediate peace or a continuation of the war. When, on 20 November, Rumcherod voted not to recognize the Soviet government a high-level delegation was sent from Petrograd to defuse the crisis. This was only achieved by the threat of force.[13]

Throughout the first few months of the revolution the committees were the spearhead of the new government. In hundreds of localities they took over and began to establish the new order, that included suppression of parts of the popular movement – for instance peasant committees and separatist and decentralizing committees set up by national minorities – as well as bourgeois class enemies. There are a number of important features to notice about the use of revolutionary committees and the violent establishment of soviet power at the expense of opponents on the right and on the left. First of all, the committees were made up disproportionately of soldiers together with workers. There were hardly any peasants involved although there was an important leaven of revolutionary intellectuals. It was not unusual for soldiers and sailors to make up 50 per cent of the committees. Since soldiers' soviets, particularly in the north, had been more solidly Bolshevik than many worker and most peasant soviets, it follows that Bolshevik troops were a key, and in many respects, leading, hegemonic force in the October revolution. It is important to note that the "bolshevism" of these soldiers and sailors was based on the assumption that the Bolsheviks were the party most likely to realize their main desires, notably for an end to the war and the establishment of a democratic, soviet system. They do not appear, by and large, to have been aware of the deeper aims of Lenin and the Bolshevik leadership, other than at a sloganistic level.

Some within the party, and some who shared its professed principles, were already, by January 1918, warning that the supposed proletarian revolution had been hi-jacked by soldiers and sailors and was in severe danger of becoming "militarized". In the forefront of the discussion was A. A. Bogdanov who, with a prediction that is perhaps only now coming true, suggested that "future historians will maintain that there took place a peasant revolution in the countryside, and in the cities a worker–soldier revolution that in time became predominantly a soldiers' revolution". The predominance of soldiers had come about through the impact of the war that had also put rationing and other forms of strict, centralized state control high on the agenda. In Bogdanov's view, with striking ease and rapidity, "the Bolsheviks became not a workers' party but a workers'–soldiers' party". The result was what he called "war communism".[14]

A second major feature of the revolutionary committees is that, not surprisingly, they were heavily dominated by Bolsheviks. Left SRs were the only other party to have any substantial representation. Out of the eight to 12 members of a typical committee 60 per cent or more would be Bolsheviks. However, the format did allow for some tactical flexibility in areas where Bolshevism was weak or non-existent so that there are some cases of Right SRs and, very occasionally, of Mensheviks joining local revolutionary committees. In essence, the committees were a reflection of the Soviet Government itself at this time, real one-party control being masked by minority participation in a hollow revolutionary coalition.[15]

All this seems to suggest that the Bolsheviks came to power in an illegitimate, conspiratorial manner, variously described as "Machiavellian" by liberal critics and "Blanquist" by left-wing opponents. However, an important third feature of the committees and the takeover has to be recognized that somewhat modifies this view. While they did manipulate ruthlessly and did not shrink from using violence and coercion of right and left the Bolsheviks did also have substantial levels of support and a formidable ability to mobilize that support far beyond the capacity of any other actors in the political drama of the period.

The best guide to Bolshevik strength is the result of the Constituent Assembly election held in November 1917. The Bolsheviks won about 25 per cent of the votes with some 50 per cent going to the SRs and allies, though how this was distributed between left and right is impossible to determine. The Menshevik vote had slumped disastrously. The Kadets were the only party on the centre-right of the spectrum to get any appreciable support at all. But the overwhelming fact was that 80 per cent of the population had voted for one or other socialist party. Roughly speaking, the Bolsheviks split the military vote fairly evenly with the SRs and their allies. However, the Bolsheviks predominated in military areas nearer to the focus of power, notably the Northern and Western Fronts. They were also strong in the Petrograd and Moscow military districts. They predominated in the Baltic Fleet but were heavily outnumbered in the Black Sea Fleet. The Bolsheviks were outvoted on the South-Western Front and were at their weakest on the Romanian and Caucasus Fronts. Incidentally, the voting patterns tend to indicate that soldiers' and sailors' votes did not mirror those of the social classes from which they came and, to that extent, they were voting for their own, military-based agenda. Bolshevik strength among civilian voters was at its height in the Moscow and Petrograd regions. They had an overall majority in the Moscow region and were the largest party in the city of Moscow and the city and region of Petrograd. In only six of the remaining 50 provinces for which we have results were they the largest party.[16]

The Bolshevik party undoubtedly disposed of considerable support where it mattered. Much of it derived from the growing disillusion with the other parties and a belief that the Bolshevik party was the best representative of the popular movement, a tragic misunderstanding that took decades to unravel as it became clearer that the Bolshevik leaders saw themselves as nobody's representatives, in the accepted sense of the word. It was sufficient, however, to ensure their ability to ride the immediate crisis. Naturally enough, there was a large constituency prepared to support decisive measures to suppress the old elite and its institutions. After all, that is what the revolution was about for most ordinary people. By comparison, once its own weapons of coercion had gone, there was pitifully little support for the old elite. There was nothing around which they could mobilize large numbers of people and it simply crumbled away. The ensuing civil war saw them almost completely reliant on foreign support for their efforts and they failed miserably to find any issues on which they could build a broad base of popular support.

More surprising, in many ways, than the powerlessness of the old elite within the country, was the failure of the other parties of the left to mobilize their support. This was particularly true of the SRs, who still had the largest numerical block of votes in the Constituent Assembly election even taking into account the split in the party between its right-wing majority around Chernov and the left-wing minority around Spiridonova and Steinberg who supported the Soviet Government for some months. This is explained in part by the nature of that support. SR voters were predominantly, though not exclusively, peasant and were scattered throughout the country. In addition, the fact that the Bolsheviks themselves began to implement the centrepiece of SR policy, the transfer of land to the peasants' committees, made it difficult, to say the least, for SRs to oppose the Bolsheviks wholeheartedly. A second important factor is the involvement of these parties, including the Mensheviks, in the alliance with the bourgeoisie that was the bedrock of the Provisional Government. This identified the party leaders, in the minds of many, with the authorities rather than the people. Where, for example, the SR and Menshevik leaders had, out of genuine fear of the terrible consequences, urged the soldiers to continue to fight, the Bolshevik government, soon after coming to power, urged them to go home and to take their weapons with them in order to defend the revolution, if needs be. The Bolsheviks had been the only major party to proclaim "the revolution in danger" and to take energetic steps to save it. The abject failure of the leaders of the other soviet parties to throw themselves on the side of the people in the period of the Kornilov revolt and afterwards had fatal results. Why should the people come out with them against Bolshevism when they had not come out with the people against "Kornilovism" and the attempted restoration of bourgeois order? The Bolshevik leaders had undoubtedly supported the workers, soldiers and peasants at this crucial moment. True, there was little realization as yet about the limitations of the Bolsheviks' association with the people. It was only when the deeper implications of Bolshevism began to be perceived that the Mensheviks and SRs began to make what one historian, Vladimir Brovkin, has described as a "comeback". By then, however, the approach of civil war and continuing economic collapse had fundamentally changed the situation. Only gradually did the population begin to become aware of what their new rulers stood for. It was also the case that many Bolsheviks were themselves unaware of the full implications of the process they had set in motion.

From Constituent Assembly to Brest-Litovsk

With every week that passed the new government was increasingly expected to begin to produce results. If the Bolsheviks' position of irresponsibility had been essential to the growth of their popularity, it followed that, once in power, they had either to fulfil the expectations of their supporters or suffer political reverses. For the first few weeks and months, government activity was dominated by slogans, postures and what Lenin was to refer to as propaganda by decree – that is, continuing the practice begun with the decrees on peace and land, of encapsulating policy in official statements, frequently unenforceable laws and the constitution. Few policies were actually implemented. The Bolsheviks were far from controlling events and had neither the power nor the apparatus to do much else.

In one area, however, the Bolsheviks did act decisively. When the Constituent Assembly finally convened, in January, the non-Bolshevik majority caused problems. It refused simply to rubber stamp the Bolshevik system and, after a day of courageous resistance, it was broken up by a typical task group of soldiers and sailors who also forcibly dispersed demonstrations organized in its defence. This time, there were casualties among the left-of-centre demonstrators. Reports suggest that between three and 21 were killed. In the prevailing conditions of repression and apathy real support for the Assembly quickly melted away.

The Bolsheviks, however, could not leave the country without a formal constitution and began to move towards one by proclaiming their own Declaration of Rights in January 1918. This differed fundamentally from that of the French Revolution on which it was distantly modelled. In particular, instead of being rights for all, or more precisely "Rights of Man", the Soviet equivalent had the class principle deeply ingrained. Rights were for "the Working and Exploited People". Everyone had a duty to work, universal labour conscription being decreed (though, like much else at the time, not really practised). It also incorporated the basic demands of the popular movement, notably land to the people, workers' control and Soviet power. The constitution, as it was finally agreed in July, also divided citizens into active and passive categories. The former were those who "earn a living by productive and socially useful labour", the latter were people who "employ hired labour for profit . . . live on unearned income . . . Private traders and middlemen . . . Monks and ministers of religion" plus lunatics, major criminals and tsarist policemen.

By the beginning of 1918, the political conjuncture in Petrograd was complicated, to say the least. Many groups, ranging from remnants of the old elite, the civil service, the professional intelligentsia and many (though probably a minority) of workers were hostile to the Soviet Government. Many more were either neutral or apathetic. Opposition came to a head in March. The focus was the separate peace treaty signed with Germany at Brest-Litovsk.

189

Without doubt, this was the most draconian major treaty in modern history. As a result of it the old Russian Empire lost 32 per cent of its arable land; 26 per cent of its railway system; 33 per cent of its factories; 75 per cent of coal and iron ore mines and 62 million citizens. In addition, the Soviet Government was expected to pay a gold indemnity.

No one, even among those who had called for peace at any price, had envisaged such terms. Even the Bolshevik leadership was divided. Lenin was almost alone in his determination that it must be signed. He had two reasons, both of which turned out to be correct. First, there was no choice. No further resistance to the German army was possible, not least because he himself had greatly encouraged the disintegration of the Russian Imperial Army. Second, he predicted that the German war effort would collapse and the treaty become meaningless.

Even so, in the short term, the treaty greatly increased the unpopularity of the Bolshevik government. After all, what better evidence could there have been to fuel the still-existing rumours that they were in the pay of the Germans? Some Petrograd workers protested on ostensibly patriotic grounds, though there was a strong undercurrent of self-interest since many of them were munitions workers whose jobs were threatened by the winding down of hostilities.

March 1918 may well have marked the nadir of Bolshevik fortunes. Up to that time, many of the factors that had dominated the first year of revolution continued to apply. The popular movement still held to its basic principles and it was now the Bolshevik leaders' turn to have to make excuses for not implementing them as expected. The peace issue reached its crescendo in the debate over Brest-Litovsk which showed that, even by then, a substantial part of the population was not sufficiently war-weary to accept abject surrender rather than a just, negotiated peace as the price for ending the war.

However, the political map was in the course of being radically changed. The lack of a credible alternative to the new government demoralized and confused opposition on the left. The deepening of the economic crisis brought exhaustion. The continually diminishing hopes of an improvement in the general situation induced apathy. There was a radical shift in relations between capital and village in that the peasants, satisfied with the redistribution of the land, reverted to self-sufficiency and self-government, broken up only by intermittent raids on the village by the new authorities who were barely represented within it. In addition, the break-up of the army, the ending of hostilities with Germany and the consequent regrouping of the population that went on created a new set of conditions. The counter-revolutionaries began to form up where the Soviet Government's hold on power was at its weakest, at the periphery of the Empire in Finland, the Baltic States, the Western Ukraine, Poland, the Southern Ukraine and Siberia. On 11 March the Soviet of People's Commissars (*Sovnarkom*) moved to Moscow to protect itself from the growing band of external enemies. In its heartland, the soviets and factory committees, it was also under threat and frequently had to resort to grossly manipulative and even violent tactics to get its way.

We cannot know how far the situation might have degenerated of its own accord but two dramatic events – the rebellion on 25 May of the Czech legions returning home to Czechoslovakia from the front via Siberia and an attempted uprising by the Bolsheviks' coalition partners, the Left SRs, in July 1918 – transformed the conjuncture. Endemic and sporadic opposition flared up into renewed civil war. When the political question was posed in the acute form of White or Red, counter-revolution or revolution, the mass of the population could give only one response. At least the Reds stood for redistribution of the land, the establishment of workers' rights and, in theory at least, soviet democracy. The White generals could only offer landowners, employers, authoritarianism and foreign domination. Had the crisis not become so polarized there is no knowing what might have happened. As it was, no matter how reluctantly, what was left of Russia's revolutionary forces had to come into line behind the only realistic leadership, the Soviet Government.

The Russian revolutionary war

The October revolution was anything but a clean break. The final collapse of the unified state that followed was never fully reversed in that a number of major components, most notably Poland and Finland, became, and remained, independent states. Others were independent for up to four years, apart from the Baltic states which lasted until the Second World War. The very task of plotting precisely what power the new government exercised and where is a very complicated one as rival successors to the unified state were springing up like mushrooms. The new Soviet system soon proved itself to be by far the strongest single combatant but it was by no means able to cow the rest of the country into submission. The result is a very confused picture. The multitude of local struggles and regroupings of the early months eventually developed into a renewed civil war. For the ordinary population, it was after October that land and factory takeovers spread rapidly and the Imperial army disintegrated. In the course of the struggles the new Soviet system, that by 1921 had become the Soviet state, took on a form that had never been clearly foreseen. Its rule became more organized, and eventually quite undemocratic, even dictatorial. With so much happening it is best to think in terms not just of civil war but of a Russian revolutionary war, that is a complex process in which military and revolutionary developments went hand in hand.[17]

It was to be a tough fight. The war is one of the forgotten holocausts of modern history. No one knows the precise figure but it cost around ten million lives. Among the combatants, 350,000 died as a result of fighting, 450,000 from disease. Among the population as a whole, weakened by the privations of the world war and revolution, epidemics were rampant. Over a million people are thought to have died from typhoid and typhus in the peak year of 1920. In addition, there was cholera, dysentery and Russia's share of the massive post-war flu epidemic. Hunger stalked the streets, particularly of the northern cities that were far from the grain supply areas. In addition a further five million died in the famine of 1921–2.[18] The social costs were equally incalculable. By 1920, the entire old elite – landowners, large-scale property owners, capitalists, bankers, entrepreneurs, merchants, industrialists, people engaged in large-scale commerce – had all either disappeared or their power had been broken. A partial exception to this was certain necessary skilled groups, including some civil servants, army officers, a few managers and even former factory owners, who were taken on by the new regime, but they had no real power. The elite as a whole, including many of the talented, skilled and educated people associated with it, emigrated, died or were driven out. A figure of around two million émigrés–refugees had settled outside Russia by 1921. While the expulsion of the class enemy on a scale vastly greater than anything to have happened to a society of this size, either before or since, might be thought to have had advantages from the Bolshevik point of view, it also had grave disadvantages. In particular, the loss of educated and skilled personnel caused problems for decades. It also had less direct disadvantages, such as the links some of the émigrés built up in Central Europe with nascent fascist and Nazi groups whose virulent anti-socialism was greatly encouraged by their lurid stories.

The human losses were reflected in and partly caused by the collapse of the Russian economy. Terms like crisis and collapse are used frequently today, even to describe situations where economic growth falls below 2 per cent. There is no word of strong enough force to use when one comes to the situation of Russia in these years. Total industrial output fell to around 20 per cent of pre-war levels. Careful calculations by Alec Nove and Silvana Malle, produced similar results. Total output of finished products in 1921 was 16 per cent of 1912 levels. For unfinished products it was 12 per cent. Production in key sectors was down to around 29 per cent in mining; 36 per cent in oil; less than 10 per cent in the metal industries; 7 per cent in cotton textiles; 34 per cent in wool.[19] Transport (mainly rail and river) also collapsed to about 20 per cent of the pre-war level. Agricultural production was more robust but it became centred on the subsistence of the producers. Surpluses became smaller and smaller. People fled back to the countryside en masse, despite prohibitions by the authorities and armed guards patrolling the city boundaries. The most dramatic example of depopulation occurred in Petrograd, the cradle of Bolshevism, whose population fell from 2.5 million in February 1917 to less than 750,000 in August 1920.[20] While this was exceptionally high, the same thing was being repeated on a significant scale in many cities and towns, particularly in the grain deficit and rapidly de-industrializing areas of the northern and central regions. Mostly people were returning to the home villages with which they retained links in the hope that survival would be more likely, in terms of avoiding hunger and the growing spiral of violence. A peculiar consequence of the flight from the cities was the thinning out of the industrial working class. The world's first proletarian government had to watch the class on which it claimed to be based diminish from its already weak minority position. This paradox helps to explain the continuing suspicion between government and society and the siege mentality of the leadership that had increasing recourse to violence to fill the gap left by its missing supporters. Other major components of the urban population – bourgeois, professional, intelligentsia and white-collar strata – suffered from the same privations as everyone else but had the added problem of being considered "class-enemies". This meant that scarce food supplies were diverted away from them and towards more favoured groups. Failure to receive adequate rations was, for many, a long-drawn-out death sentence. Mortality, particularly among the distinguished and ageing intelligentsia elite of Petrograd, was very high. Only educated people whose practical skills were required by the new regime, plus a few select luminaries of cultural life, received a small measure of state protection from the worst of the conditions.[21]

The obstacles facing the Soviet government in summer 1918 seemed insurmountable. Counter-revolutionary armies were forming, the most important being in Siberia, the South-East Ukraine and in Estonia. Nationalist movements held effective control in Finland, the Baltic States, Poland, the Ukraine, Georgia, Armenia, Azerbaijan and parts of Central Asia. As if that were not enough, all the world's major powers, plus most of the Russian Empire's neighbours, had armed forces on former Russian territory. The most important of these were the Germans who, in pursuance of the Treaty of Brest-Litovsk, occupied the productive areas of southern Russia and the Ukraine. There were British armies in the northern ports of Archangel and Murmansk as well as a small force in the Caspian area. There were Americans and Japanese in the Far East. Turks, Finns, Poles and Romanians presented serious local military threats, particularly when the German and Austrian occupation collapsed in November 1918. French troops moved in to replace them on the Black Sea. The outside powers tended to manipulate politics in the areas that they controlled, protecting groups who shared compatible aims. In 1919, the situation looked especially bleak for the Soviet (Red) forces. There were major White advances. Kolchak advanced over the Urals as far as Ufa but was defeated in April having come within 75 miles of the Volga region. Denikin's Volunteer Army reached Orel, only 200 miles from Moscow, before falling back in October. Yudenich's forces reached the suburbs of Petrograd, also in October, before being beaten off.

In addition, non-aligned forces operated in areas that escaped firm Red or White control. They were often nationalists in the periphery or radical peasant-based movements like those of the anarchist Makhno in the Ukraine or the SR Antonov in Tambov Province.[22] At first the most extensive was the *Komuch*, the Committee of Members of the Constituent Assembly, that set up a Provisional Government in the Volga, with its capital in Samara. It was overthrown by a White-led coup in November 1918, although it was already on the retreat from the Reds who had taken over Samara.

At their lowest point, the Reds occupied only about one-fifth of the surface area of the Russian Empire as it was in 1913. According to one calculation, there were no less than 23 groups claiming to be governments on former Russian territory. While most were regional, they are, none the less, striking evidence of the extent of the disintegration of the old empire. The confusion continued into 1920 when Wrangel's troops broke out from the Crimea in June, were contained in September and liquidated by mid-October. A deep attack into the Ukraine was launched by the Polish army in April. This turned into a Red advance that was finally held before Warsaw and it was the Reds' turn to retreat until both sides were more or less back where they started. An armistice was signed on 12 October 1920 that marked the end of the main threat, though conflict elsewhere lingered on until 1922, when the Japanese finally withdrew from the Far East, allowing Vladivostok to be reincorporated into Russia.

Red victory was the result of many important factors. In the first place the Whites were not as formidable as they appeared. While they had one great advantage in that they controlled the areas that produced much of the grain surplus and this put the pressure of hunger on the Reds, their effort also suffered from serious limitations. The number of reliable forces that they could call on was fairly restricted. In his advance on Petrograd in September 1919, for example, Yudenich had only 14,400 men, a totally inadequate force to hold a large and potentially hostile city. The most reliable corps of the best White army, that of Denikin, comprised only 12,000 infantry and up to 1500 cavalry. At its peak, in any case, Denikin's combat troops consisted of only around 100,000 men. It was difficult for the Whites to recruit beyond these figures because they were heavily dependent on the limited pool of ex-tsarist officers and NCOs who were prepared to fight for them and were reluctant to include war veterans from the ranks in their armies because they were thought to have become infected with revolutionary sympathies as a result of their experiences in 1917. Fear of the population extended to the civilians in their areas of operation. As a result, they lacked secure base areas. Geopolitics made Denikin and Kolchak dependent on the good will of cossacks, whose support for the White intruders was lukewarm to say the least, particularly in the case of Denikin who made no effort to conceal his Great Russian nationalism and refused to make any concessions to the separatism of the cossacks or any other group. Most of the peoples of the periphery, among whom the Whites found themselves, were hostile to the notion of "Russia, One and Indivisible".

While the line-up of foreign interventionists also looked formidable, it too had limits. In the first place, most interventionist powers had specific, relatively narrow objectives. The Japanese were interested only in the Far Eastern territories, the British and the French, initially at least, only wanted to prop up the Eastern Front, prevent German forces from being transferred to the west

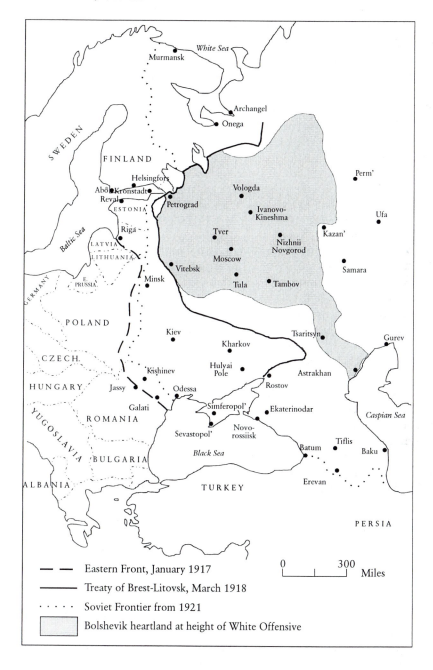

- – – Eastern Front, January 1917
- ——— Treaty of Brest-Litovsk, March 1918
- · · · · · Soviet Frontier from 1921
- Bolshevik heartland at height of White Offensive

0   300 Miles

and retrieve military stores before they fell into the wrong hands. Neighbouring powers were mostly only interested in slices of territory adjacent to their own, that were often populated by their ethnic brothers and sisters. There were also domestic and other political and practical constraints. The most menacing interventionist power, Germany, collapsed in late 1918 and took no further part in the conflict. War-weariness in Britain and France, plus a certain amount of pro-Bolshevik sympathy, undermined the efforts of those like Clemenceau and Churchill who wanted to set up a real anti-Bolshevik crusade. At no stage did intervention live up to such a description. The most influential interventionist group, the Czechs, were, in any case, only accidental combatants whose main aim was to extricate themselves and fight for Czech independence. They had no grand strategy for Russia's future, although they did tend to support SR-oriented politics. They were very few in number, about 40,000. In the early stages, when they were strung out along the Trans-Siberian railway, they were stretched very thin. As Mawdsley amusingly puts it "In terms of American geography the Volga group were 300 miles east of New York, the Vladivostok units were 1000 miles west of San Francisco; the Chelyabinsk group were in Pittsburgh and the Novonikolaevsk group in Salt Lake City".[23]

This reminds us of the difficulties of communication and co-ordination faced by the Whites. Political and diplomatic links between Denikin on the Black Sea and Kolchak in the Urals had to be maintained and co-ordinated via Paris, that itself could only be reached safely by circuitous telegraph and transport routes, one via Siberia, Japan and the United States, the other via the Mediterranean and Constantinople. Couriers taking short cuts through the Caspian risked interception and summary execution. Political and personal rivalries added to the Whites' difficulties as did a variety of conflicting pressures from the allies. They were chronically split. Even in their own Russian nationalist terms there were serious problems. The low prestige of Nicholas II and his abdication made it impossible for even the monarchists to see him as the unequivocal, legitimate claimant to the throne. The murder of the former tsar and many members not only of his immediate family but of other branches confused the situation further, particularly given the persistence of conflicting rumours about who was alive and who was dead. The alternatives to monarchism – republicanism and support for the Constituent Assembly – sat uneasily on the shoulders of the generals. As a result, the White movement was hopelessly divided over political tactics and competing nationalisms as well as broken up physically. All this prevented even a co-ordinated military strategy from emerging.

By contrast, the Reds enjoyed a number of intrinsic advantages. While they were limited in territory they always held the highly populated heartland, containing about 60 million people who provided a vast reservoir of human resources. In addition their territory included the remnants of industry and the majority of the military stockpiles from the world war. No matter how inefficiently such resources were used it was possible to build up manpower and firepower well beyond the capabilities of the Whites. Once efforts to organize the Red Army got under way it quickly built up to one and a half million men by the end of 1919 and 3.5 million by mid-1920. Moscow was also at the centre of the railway network, that greatly facilitated concentration of Red troops and enabled them to turn to each front as and when necessary. As Churchill memorably put it in 1929: "The ancient capital lay at the centre of a web of railroads . . . and in the midst a spider! Vain hope to crush the spider by the advance of lines of encircling flies!"[24] Red defeats, that pushed them back, concentrated their forces like a giant spring while it stretched out those of the Whites and drew them into treacherous, highly populated, urban and unsympathetic territory.

In a purely technical war, the above factors alone might well have been decisive, but war, particularly revolutionary war, is politics conducted by other means and it was in this vital dimension that Russia's fate was played out. In the first place, a notable feature of the conflict was the reluctance of the population at large to get involved on either side if they could avoid it. Both Reds and Whites had energetic and sometimes heroic activists but relatively small mass followings. This is no real surprise in the case of the Whites who essentially represented the old elite of Russian society, its property owners. What is surprising is that they, none the less, pinned their hopes on a popular upsurge in their favour and against the Reds. As Sakharov, one of Kolchak's generals, put it graphically, if only the rear would support them the road to Moscow would be open and "then the whole people would come over to us and stand openly under the Admiral's banner. The Bolsheviks and other socialist filth would be destroyed – from the roots up – by the burning rage of the popular masses".[25]

While this scenario tells us more about Sakharov's fantasies than it does about political realities it is, perhaps, surprising that the equivalent hopes of the Bolshevik leaders were equally unrealistic. They, too, had consistently put their faith in a popular upsurge that never materialized. Its absence accentuated their turn towards centralization and discipline. At the same time, the desperate methods of terror and grain requisitioning associated with this line made any such upsurge even more remote. Popular indifference was even reflected in the Red Army, whose discipline and training, particularly in the early stages, were very slack. Desertion rates were high, up to 70 per cent in Petrograd in 1919, and stern measures were taken to improve it. Despite complaints from the Commander-in-Chief, Vatsetis, that it would only lead to mechanical obedience, death sentences were passed on 2,000 troops of the Eighth Army, although only 150 were actually carried out. On one famous occasion, in the battle for Svyazhsk in 1918, Trotsky had 20 out of 200 members of a deserting regiment shot. Lenin wanted Cheka cordons behind the troops in order to bolster their fighting capabilities by demonstrating to them that while possible death lay ahead, certain death lay behind. All this indicates major reluctance of conscripts to get involved.

None the less, even though there was no massive upsurge in their favour, the Bolsheviks did have the trump cards in their hand when it came to popular support. As the war developed, it brought about a polarization that was favourable to them. Where the Whites could only offer the return of landlords and the essential elements of the old order, the Bolsheviks, despite grain requisitioning, still stood closer to the popular programme of property redistribution. Polarization also narrowed the area of operations of the non-Bolshevik left that had, as a result, nowhere else to go, not least because their militants had already been alienated by their own leaders' lack of revolutionary resolve in 1917. Efforts to set up a serious, united third force democratic left did not survive the first third of the civil war, although independent groups did continue to function in many localities. Even these, however, favoured Red over White and sometimes fought alongside Soviet forces. Only some of the cossacks fought with the Whites, and then often reluctantly and half-heartedly.

Compared to the Reds, the Whites were politically bankrupt. Given the divisions mentioned above, it is hardly surprising that they failed to evolve a serious political strategy. The slim hope the Bolsheviks' opponents had of building up popular support vanished when the generals overthrew the civilian politicians and took complete control themselves in the name of being "non-political" that meant, as it often does, being authoritarian and conservative. Sakharov was even proud to boast later, in exile in Munich nine months after Mussolini had come to power, that "the White movement was in essence the first manifestation of fascism ".[26] Unlike fascist movements which came to power, however, they were completely unable to build any popular base or evolve a political programme of any substance. This, above everything else, doomed them to failure. Only in desperate straits, with defeat staring them in the face, did they even toy with a democratic programme.

It was in the struggle against these multiple forces of disintegration that the real revolution was conducted and consolidated. From out of the conflict the new Soviet and socialist order emerged. It underwent further changes subsequently, but by 1921 its foundations had already been laid and a new framework rested upon them. Not surprisingly, given the advanced state of chaos, the main characteristic of the new order was centralization. Political and economic decision-making was inexorably concentrated in fewer and fewer hands. Spontaneity and genuine self-administration were being replaced by a more hierarchical and intrusive state than had existed prior to the revolution. The system that emerged by 1921 was nothing like that envisaged by Lenin, or anyone else, in 1917. How had it come about? How did the popular movement react?

CHAPTER NINE

The Bolshevik dictatorship

On 4 November – ten days after the October revolution and, therefore, the tenth of the days that shook the world – the following protest against Bolshevik policy was published:

> It is our view that a socialist government must be formed from all parties in the soviet . . . We believe that, apart from this, there is only one other path: the retention of a purely Bolshevik government by means of political terror.

The leadership would become cut off from the masses and the outcome would be "the establishment of an unaccountable regime and the destruction of the revolution and the country". The signatories to these prophetic words were not Mensheviks or SRs. Astonishingly they included Kamenev, Zinoviev, Rykov and Larin, four of the most senior figures in the Bolshevik party after Lenin himself.

Ominous signs had already begun to appear. Within days of coming to power the government decreed the closure of newspapers of the centre and right. Within weeks those of the left were also being shut down. Far from his mock magnanimity of September, Trotsky fully confirmed Sukhanov's fears of the concealed message within Bolshevik slogans. On 4 November he explained that he had demanded freedom of the press at a time when "we could demand only a minimum programme, but now we ask for a maximum" that, in this case, meant controlling the press. What other U-turns were in store in the transition from minimum to maximum?

The Central Committee's response to the dissidents within its ranks was itself unpromising. They were accused of "totally disregarding all the fundamental tenets of Bolshevism", "repeating deeply unMarxist phrases about a socialist revolution being impossible in Russia" and of having "a state of mind which reflects the exhausted (not the revolutionary) section of the population". To give in to the minority would, the resolution continued, mean "the complete renunciation not only of Soviet power but of democracy". The minority was accused of hampering revolutionary work, "criminal vacillations", "disruptive activity" and "sabotage". While the word "wrecking" had not yet been invented, the full panoply of "Stalinist" accusations was thrown at them. Stalinist sanctions, however, were not. Full compliance with party discipline was required and no further action was taken. Some of the protestors did, however, resign from the party in disgust.[1]

The leadership did not even pause to weigh up whether there was any truth in the accusations but pressed on regardless, convinced of their own correctness, even though, to many outsiders, the system was evolving in quite the opposite direction from that anticipated before October. The transition from minimum to maximum, it seemed, implied a reversal of many deeply held values of 1917. Above all it involved the emergence of a centralized state with important features resembling those of conventional states – a bureaucratic administration, a military and a political police force. This was far from the popular democracy and self-government envisaged by left-wing participants in the revolution, including Lenin. The proclamation of soviet power by the Second Congress of Soviets was the beginning of the rapid decline of soviets as institutions having any real power. Over the ensuing weeks and months they were transformed. They convened less frequently, they became dominated by their less and less representative executive committees that were themselves increasingly beholden to their Bolshevik fraction. Even executive committees met less frequently and decision-making authority tended to drift upwards. Regional and local soviets were rapidly transformed into transmission belts for decisions arrived at centrally. Indeed, according to Marc Ferro, the process can be observed even before the October revolution.[2] To some extent the problems are attributable to the inevitable decline of revolutionary enthusiasm and corresponding growth of apathy, but this in turn was caused in part by disillusion with the results of the revolution so there is something of a vicious circle here. Where interference in the functioning of soviets was less direct, at least for the first weeks and months, participation remained relatively high, a notable example being Kronstadt.

The rapid decline of the soviets under the new Bolshevik order was quite extraordinary, particularly in that it was accomplished with little organized resistance. Many factors help to explain this. In the first place, there was no serious counterweight on the left to Bolshevik power. The non-Bolshevik soviet leadership had marched out into oblivion at the Second Congress. Their poor record in supporting soviet power in 1917 made them ambiguous advocates of it in 1918 so, having walked the plank in October, it was almost impossible for them to climb back on board and put in a serious bid to retake command of the ship. Secondly, the steady attrition caused by declining living conditions and growing disillusion with the fruits of the revolution brought cynicism and apathy where formerly there had been hope. This made it more and more difficult to rouse people for a new struggle when the old one had brought dubious results. Thirdly, support for Bolshevism was widespread and, among activists at least, there was no other group to match them even though they may not have been a majority and may have passed their peak in terms of active backing in the population. As the revolutionary war developed the Soviet government became the only serious bulwark against counter-revolution. Even some right-wing nationalists began to support it by 1919 when it, rather than the Whites with their raggle-taggle parade of foreign backers, seemed to them to be the only real focus of Russian resistance against her traditional enemies.[3] However, an additional factor, coercion, particularly through the growing use of the political police force, the Cheka, has been the favourite explanation of many observers for Bolshevik survival.

The Cheka

In the early days the Cheka remained small, with only 120 employees by mid-March 1918.[4] None the less, a number of aspects of its existence are of interest. First, it was at the centre of the process of taking over the less organized institutions thrown up in the course of the revolution. Spontaneously organized militias, Red Guards and politically active military units, began to be brought under the control of the Cheka, the military revolutionary committees and, eventually, the Red Army, or to be disbanded. In many cases the personnel were divided up. Bolsheviks and close sympathizers were transferred to the new institutions. The less reliable members were dispersed. The significant difference between the old forms and the new is obvious. The new ones were based on nuclei of reliable Bolshevik supporters.

In the case of the Cheka, the Latvian rifle regiment was an early core. The need for a dependable security force was immediately apparent after October and built up from mundane tasks, like requiring a security guard for Smolny where the new government installed itself or the need to face early threats like strikes. According to one leading authority on its formation "it was to deal with a crippling strike of government employees that the Vecheka was specifically created".[5] As security problems developed, so a larger force was needed. The evolution of the government's own immediate guards was a microcosm of what was happening nationally. For the first week of Bolshevik power, Red Guards and Baltic sailors protected Smolny. In early November a more organized system was set up by the Polish-born Bolshevik and close comrade of Lenin, Felix Dzerzhinsky. He, and other future Cheka leaders like Peterson and Peters, initially shifted the duties from the irregulars to "a specially formed composite battalion . . . hand-picked from the eight Latvian rifle regiments serving in the Russian army", under the control of the Petrograd Military Revolutionary Committee. When the government moved to Moscow in mid-March 1918 there were 500 members in this battalion, more than half of whom were Bolshevik party members.[6] By this time the Latvian riflemen and their commanders had become associated with the Cheka.

The various *ad hoc* initiatives came together in early December 1917 when the Council of People's Commissars (*Sovnarkom*) set up the All-Russian Extraordinary Commission for Combating Counter-Revolution and Sabotage, known as the Cheka (or, sometimes, Vecheka) from its Russian initials. In the decree of 7 December that set it up, its main task was defined as searching out and liquidating all attempts at counter-revolutionary and sabotage activity in the whole of Russia, from any source.[7] More specifically the commission was enjoined to turn its attention in the first place to the press, then to sabotage, then to the Kadets, the Right SRs, saboteurs and strikers. It was permitted to confiscate, evict, deprive people of rations and to publish a list of enemies of the people. It was to take over such duties from the Liquidation Commission of the Military Revolutionary Committee.[8] Its head was Felix Dzerzhinsky. The key personnel were all party members going back at least to the 1905 revolution, and even to 1898, and were therefore deemed to be the loyalest of the loyal. The spirit with which the Cheka was supposed to be imbued was embodied in Dzerzhinsky. By origin an aristocratic Pole with a Catholic upbringing, he brought all the burning devotion of a medieval monk to the cause of revolution that he had served courageously since 1895, when he was 18. He was a pure, incorruptible, fanatical Savonarola of the new regime. A couple of famous quotations exemplify his values. "Life", he wrote in his prison diaries around the turn of the century, "is such that it rules out sentiment, and woe to the man who lacks the strength to overcome his feelings".[9] His best known words asserted that Chekists needed "cool heads, warm hearts and clean hands".[10] The phrase about warm hearts rather contradicts the stark, macho Nietzscheanism of the first quotation. However, in reality, the Cheka was built up of souls, many of whom scarcely embodied any high-minded ideals.

For the time being its operations remained small in scale. In its first significant action, on 22 December 1917, about 100 leaders of the strike of government employees were arrested, detained and, two months later, released.[11] Various minor speculators and swindlers were arrested. In February, two of them had the tragic distinction of being the first victims to be executed by the Cheka on its own authority.[12] The limited extent of its activities can be gauged from the fact that, in its first six months of existence, it had "only" executed 22 people, all deemed to be bandits and speculators.[13]

None the less, there were other portents in the wind. Already, although it was essentially a political police force, it was getting sucked into economic functions. Indeed, politics and economics were all but inseparable in the outlook of the Bolshevik leadership. After all, the chief political enemy was defined in crude class terms relating to income and employment. In addition, Lenin continued to believe in political solutions (arresting, shooting, setting up proletarian-led institutions) to economic problems (production, distribution). Shortages were not just accidental or economic (for example, resulting from the breakdown of transport). Many were seen to be the result of conspiracies by the ubiquitous speculators, hoarders, saboteurs and enemies of the people. The problem is graphically illustrated by a decree of 9–10 November signed by Lenin:

> The collapse of the supply system, brought about by the war and economic disintegration, is raised to the highest level by speculators, brigands and the like on the railways, steamships and in transport offices.
> In conditions of the greatest poverty of the masses criminal brigands were happily enriching themselves by playing with the lives of millions of soldiers and workers.

To solve the problem the Petrograd Military Revolution Committee was empowered to lock up in Kronstadt those guilty of "concealing stocks, maliciously holding back goods and so on".[14] While one might be sympathetic to the dilemma, the solution began to open up the floodgates to arbitrary coercion as a main means to solve problems caused by "economic disintegration". Similarly, in late November, in a letter to Shliapnikov and Dzerzhinsky, Lenin proposed solving an economic crisis in the Ural region by immediately arresting the management and confiscating all the factories in the Urals.[15] This put into practice Lenin's view that "a short term of imprisonment" would bring the capitalists to their senses. However, the administrative–coercive reflex did not bring the expected results, and dreams of "gradual, peaceful and smooth" transition faded fast. For the time being, however, such actions were the merest foretaste of the Bolshevik tendency to use massive political force to achieve economic ends.

A major question raised by looking at the Cheka in this period relates to the problem of law faced by the Bolsheviks. It was all very well setting up law-enforcement agencies, but what law were they supposed to enforce? Obviously, adopting tsarist law was out of the question. The new authorities had more immediate preoccupations than codifying a complete new set of laws. In any case, as the liberal writer and thinker Bogdan Kistiakovsky had pointed out in 1909 in a controversial article, the revolutionary intelligentsia did not give a high priority to law or to legal consciousness. Bolsheviks had barely even raised the problem before October. This is not especially surprising since the same was also true of the old regime. Despite liberal endeavours between 1906 and 1917 tsarist Russia was still far from being a law-governed state in the west European and American sense of the term. Laws were arbitrarily drafted, passed, enforced and adjudicated upon. Customary rather than statute law continued to be more familiar to the mass of the population. Lack of concern for legality was one more poisoned cultural legacy passed on by tsarism to its successor.

But what were the Bolsheviks to do? In the short term they attempted to rule through enforcing values rather than laws, in a sense introducing their own customary law. Instead of statutes, law-enforcement was associated with conscience and also with that nebulous but ever-present Leninist entity, socialist consciousness. It was to be found in many areas of the application of justice. The Party Programme, approved in March 1919, solved the problem by providing that "in cases of absence or incompleteness" of Soviet decrees judges were "to be guided by socialist conscience".[16] As a result, many early Soviet law enforcers were plenipotentiaries entrusted with making Solomon-like judgments on the spot, judgments that did not stop short of the power to execute with an absolute minimum of legal formalities. Unsurprisingly, once initiated, such processes evolved rapidly and extensively in the desperate conditions of revolutionary war.

In the early months justice in all its forms was subject to a restraint that was soon to disappear, the Bolsheviks' need to appease their coalition partners, the Left SRs. One of their leaders, I. Z. Steinberg, was People's Commissar for Justice. In his memoirs, Steinberg portrays, perhaps with some exaggeration, his struggle against the Frankenstein monster of Bolshevik justice in general and the Cheka in particular. He claims to have been "hostile to the entire machinery and 'spirit' of the Cheka".[17] He made efforts to restrain it and to bring it under the control of the Justice Ministry.[18] It may be that the deep repugnance of the Left SRs at the use of the death penalty helps to account for the relatively modest total of executions in this period. In the longer term, however, there was nothing Steinberg could do to restrict its special powers. Indeed, by mid-1918 he and his own party were the targets of Cheka repression.

Thus, in the field of justice, a pattern emerged similar to that elsewhere in the early days. Unforeseen real problems of law and security emerged and sometimes reasonable sounding stop-gap solutions were proposed in the forms of a special commission to co-ordinate action against counter-revolutionaries or the appointment of trustworthy individuals as revolutionary judges. The difficulties multiplied rapidly, however, as these solutions – that in any case could only have worked perfectly in an ideal world since they required individuals of angelic disposition to run them – began to be applied in an increasingly narrow, violent and, above all, fundamentalist, sectarian spirit. One cannot blame the pressures of civil war alone. Full civil war had not even begun.

When the conflict heated up, the Cheka soon transformed itself into a very extraordinary commission indeed. By mid-July 1918 its Special Corps consisted of 35 battalions.[19] By 1921 it had, according to one of its chiefs M. Ia. Latsis, 31,000 agents and commissars[20] and, in December 1921, 143,000 employees. The effect of the New Economic Policy of the period, requiring a stringent balancing of accounts, helped reduce this number to 105,000 by May 1922.[21] In its early days its budget had shown upward tendencies. Although the peculiar financial conditions of war communism make comparisons difficult, the growth in its budget is clear. The Cheka was allocated 53 million roubles for the second half of 1918, 348 million for the first six months of 1919 and 2.2 billion for the second half of 1919. Most of the money was spent on the upkeep of internal security troops.[22] As with most bureaucracies, it is hard to know the extent to which its budget expanded to meet its functions or its functions expanded to justify its budget. In any case, the ever growing number of Chekists had no difficulty in finding themselves something to do.

The Cheka was divided up into a number of sections. Some of them occupied themselves with regular activities of ensuring the security of government personnel and guarding borders. Of course, the early Soviet government also found itself in unusual conditions of extreme hostility from foreign powers and political émigrés. The Cheka was particularly effective in exposing agents and counteracting monarchist and other right-wing conspiracies. It achieved this by taking over and perfecting tsarist police tactics of infiltration, double agents and setting up dummy political and economic organizations, the very tactics that, until 1917, had been used very effectively against revolutionary organizations including the Bolsheviks themselves.

Its tasks, however, also included actions against workers, peasants and intellectuals. While much of its work in this field was small-scale surveillance and arrest of individuals and small groups there were a number of major landmark operations that demonstrate its ever broadening sweep through the remnants of the independent left and the popular movement.

The first such operation was an attack on the Moscow headquarters of the anarchist movement conducted on the night of 11–12 April 1918. The anarchists put up fierce armed resistance and it was reported that 12 Cheka personnel had been killed in the action. At the end of the month, the Petrograd anarchists were also broken up. The remnants went underground and carried out occasional bombings of Cheka and party targets. The White advance, however, brought some of them into uneasy alliance with the Bolsheviks. One or two anarchists even joined the Cheka.

It is interesting that the Bolshevik government should have started off by mopping up the extreme anarchist left, even though it had never had major appeal to the population. It may have been its very weakness that made it an exemplary preliminary target. On the other hand there were also vestigial fears in the minds of the leaders. In spring 1918 they had problems. Even within their own party there was a resurgence of the slogans of 1917 – especially workers' control, a militia, revolutionary war and stepping up class struggle – when the party leaders were turning towards one-person management, a regular state-controlled army, accommodation with specialists and a disastrous peace treaty with Germany. The left may have appeared potentially to be ready to pick up the revolutionary baton from Lenin and his allies just as Lenin had picked it up from the Right SRs and mainstream Mensheviks as they compromised their ideals when faced with the realities of power. It seems unlikely that a new radical surge based on local soviets and factory committees would have roused the apathetic workers but the extreme left were an uncomfortable prod to the Bolshevik conscience, a constant reminder that their promises of 1917 had been broken in the grim realities of the post-October world. It is clear that Lenin did not want to repeat the cardinal error of his Provisional Government predecessors and fail to close down the left from which a new Lenin might emerge, no matter how remote such a possibility might seem. After all, the prospect of the Bolsheviks taking power (and even more, holding on to it) had seemed equally remote, almost until it happened.

The next major Cheka action was much more serious but did, however, come out of the same mould. This time it was the Bolsheviks' coalition partners, the Left SRs, who tried to outmanoeuvre them from the left and steal their apparently abandoned revolutionary clothes.

On 6 July 1918 a group of Left SRs attempted a coup. They assassinated the German ambassador in an attempt to capitalize on anti-German sentiment that had been prominent since the Treaty of Brest-Litovsk. However, their ill-organized plot soon became a fiasco. Bolshevik reprisals hit out at the whole party. Many leaders were arrested. Some were given very light sentences and immediately amnestied, the apparent leniency perhaps being explained by the fact that those who benefited from it had not had anything to do with the uprising. For the rest of the year the party was officially tolerated but was also subjected to increasing surveillance and repression. Their remaining representation in the soviets fell to four non-voting delegates at the Sixth All-Russian Congress of Soviets (November 1918) and had been completely eliminated at the Seventh Congress held a year later. By the end of 1918 the leaders went into semi-underground. In the forefront of their clandestine activities was denunciation of increasing Cheka repression of workers and peasants and of the widening reign of terror.

Red terror had, in fact, taken a major leap forward in July and August 1918, not only because of the Left SR uprising but because of the serious wounding of Lenin after he was shot by a former populist terrorist on 30 August 1918. A Petrograd Cheka leader, Uritsky, was assassinated. Hundreds of Cheka prisoners are thought to have been summarily executed in the heightened paranoia that followed the assassination attempt and the build up of the White armies and their foreign backers. From August 1918 onwards the Cheka became a great deal more active in the internal political sphere, a development heightened by the first major anti-Bolshevik uprising, that broke out in Izhevsk, between the Volga and the Urals in which substantial numbers of workers participated. It began on 8 August and was not finally suppressed until 7 November.

The Cheka's hand also began to fall more directly on the popular movement. Official figures for the period tell their own story. According to Latsis the Cheka suppressed 245 uprisings in 1918 and 99 in the first seven months of 1919. In these incidents 1,150 were reported dead on the Red side and

3,057 among the insurrectionists. These figures are for only 20 provinces (less than half the European part of the former Russian Empire).[23] Most were rural protests against grain requisitioning and road blocks. In the same period 1,000 people were shot for embezzlement.[24] By the end of 1918 there had been 6,300 official executions including 2,431 for participation in revolts.[25] Given the slow start to 1918 when the Left SRs were in the government the later part must have been especially bloody. The pace continued in 1919 with 3,456 executions (excluding the Ukraine).[26]

While these figures alone are significant enough they represent only the tip of the iceberg of repression. Careful unofficial calculations have tried to go further. Some of the Cheka's victims calculated their own losses. There were some 200 Left SRs in jail on 10–11 February 1919, including prominent leaders like the former Minister of Justice, Steinberg, and Maria Spiridonova.[27] Some of the better known ones were released quickly but most were held indefinitely. A batch of 34 were released on 21 June 1920.[28] By 1922, 26 were thought to have been executed and four to have died in prison.[29] About 1000 people, mostly army officers and cadets, were arrested in a Cheka sweep on the night of 18/19 September 1919, undertaken as a pre-emptive strike against White sympathizers, the self-styled National Centre, in Petrograd and Moscow.[30] Many other less extensive right-wing conspiracies were dealt with in similar fashion, usually with subsequent executions of ringleaders. Patriarch Tikhon calculated that by 1920 a minimum of 322 bishops and priests of the Orthodox church had been executed during the revolution. Another estimate put the figures at 28 bishops and 1000 priests who had died by 1923.[31] The Cheka had also played a leading role in closing down first of all the right-wing and eventually the entire Menshevik, Left SR and anarchist press, leaving only official Soviet and party publications.

The figures are only a sample of the work of the Cheka and its associates. The full cost of the Red Terror cannot be calculated. In giving evidence to US Senate Judiciary Committee Hearings in 1971 one scholar, Robert Conquest, who is unlikely to have underestimated the numbers, gave a figure of 500,000 executions and deaths in custody in the Civil War years.[32] In any case, one cannot disagree with Gerson's conclusion that the Red Terror claimed far more victims than had all tsarist state security forces in the whole of the previous century.[33] Of course, the context was different and, if the White terror is anything to go by, the supporters of the old regime could be equally, perhaps even more, murderous. After all, they were the first to embark on mass antisemitic pogroms that, according to some accounts, cost the lives of 115,000 Jews in the Ukraine in 1919 alone.[34] Compared with indiscriminate murder on this scale by a much smaller force, the actions of the Red side, although cruel, excessive and unjustifiable, appear, at least, to have been subjected to some serious attempts at control.

Whatever its precise scope, it is clear that the Red terror had a major effect, not only in suppressing active counter-revolutionaries in Soviet Russia but also in crushing the popular movement itself. It continued to do so after the end of the civil war. As we shall see the Cheka was, perhaps, even more effective in wiping out the remnants of the popular movement in 1920 and 1921 than it had been during the civil war itself. After all, during the war, the Red cause in general and the Cheka in particular, was able to mobilize extensive worker, peasant and soldier support. For instance, when the well-to-do districts of Petrograd were searched for arms on June 14 1918, 20,000 workers are said to have joined in.[35] Even more astonishing, some of its most extreme opponents became Cheka operatives, like the anarchist Alexander Ge who died fighting the Whites in the Caucasus.[36] Such examples remind us, once again, that it was not repression alone but a potent combination of repression plus the power to mobilize key areas of support which explain Bolshevik survival.

A final reflection. The Cheka is one of the best illustrations of the gap between Lenin's dreams of 1917 and the realities of power. As we have seen, in the April Theses, *State and revolution* and the early months of the revolution, Lenin emphasized the traditional socialist policy of military and internal security being entrusted to ultra-democratic, self-governing, proletarian-based militias. Instead, the Red Army and, to an even greater extent the Cheka, had become centrally controlled agencies of the party. The Cheka, far from being immersed in the popular ethos, was already becoming an institution apart, whose members lived relatively privileged lives behind closed doors. By the mid-1920s, its much vaunted role in caring for civil war orphans and dealing with the hard cases of juvenile crime had left it in control of labour communes, numbering 35 by 1928, known as Dzerzhinsky's baby farms. Young people convicted of serious robbery, theft and murder were kept without guards. They were left to discipline and organize themselves into work groups. Many of them were said to have become police recruits. Their tough background, lack of conventional social ties and their gratitude to their ersatz Chekist "family" made them potentially ideal material for the growing Cheka caste.[37]

While evidence is unsystematic, it also appears that the Cheka was disproportionately staffed by some of the former Russian Empire's smallest nationalities with Latvians, Poles and Jews normally being considered particularly prominent. Clearly, such allegations lend themselves to crude anti-semitic and Russian nationalist propaganda along the lines that the revolution (and even the Bolsheviks) were non-Russian entities foisted on the unsuspecting and innocent Russian majority by malevolent minorities. While such conclusions are absurd there are, none the less, grounds for thinking that small nationalities were deeply involved in the Cheka. According to Leggett's survey of 20 leading Chekists about whom we have the most information, seven were Russian (including Ksenofontov whose name suggests a Greek background), four to six were Poles, three were Latvians, one an Armenian, one a Ukrainian and one a Russian Jew. At least one and possibly four of the Poles were Jews. It is also of interest that at least 12 were of bourgeois (mainly intelligentsia) origin, three were peasants and only two were from a working-class background.[38]

The same phenomena have also been noted by another leading western scholar, Lennard Gerson, who reported that 70 per cent of Kiev Chekists were said to be Jews. Given White pogroms in the area it would not be surprising if many Jews joined the most militant anti-White organization.[39]

Gerson also pointed out that, as a result of the hostility shown to them by a large segment of the population as well as the need to defend themselves against counter-revolutionaries, Chekists tended to live in increasing isolation. Cheka detachments began to live in their own compounds with their own shops, restaurants and recreational facilities. They sequestered "themselves behind barbed wire and machine-guns where they carried on like the fighting monks of an embattled order".[40] One Cheka leader, Kedrov, travelled the country in an armoured train to bolster resistance and to purge local Chekas of undesirable hangers-on.[41]

All in all, there can be no doubt that the Cheka was very far from enjoying the popular control and closeness to the people envisaged in 1917. It was not only the legitimate need to secure itself against determined enemies that had cut it off from the population, nor was it simply the naivety of the early vision. There was a deeper process at work. At the most abstract level the Cheka, like political commissars and party activists themselves, was a substitute for the missing "socialist consciousness" of the population. The weaker the consciousness, the less reliable was popular support for the Bolshevik vision. The weaker the support the more the regime had to turn to coercion. Speculatively, one might add that the greater the coercion, the less probable it was that the vision being enforced would win over willing converts. In this way, the Cheka was not just an instrument of dictatorship but a barometer of the presence or absence of Leninist "consciousness".

From militia to Red Army

In another key sphere revolutionary hopes were giving way to more conventional practices. It had been a central concept in the April Theses that the army should be abolished. In practice, the old tsarist army was destroyed by early 1918. The idea was that it would be replaced by a democratic militia, in which all would serve and thereby guarantee that it could not be used as a repressive instrument since the people would not, it was assumed, attack themselves. However, as the military threat to the new government began to build up, there was a rapid return to more conventional military thinking. The democratic gains of the revolution, such as the election of officers and the abolition of the death penalty (the issue on which the Bolsheviks had won their first majority in the Petrograd Soviet), were lost in a wave of restoration. As elsewhere, army committees were replaced by soviets that themselves became transmission belts of central priorities to the men rather than places for the expression of the opinions of the soldiers and sailors. Tsarist army officers were reinstated in the guise of "military specialists". There appears to have been a core of around 15,000 to 20,000 ex-tsarist officers constituting 75 per cent of the officer core in the Red Army in 1918 and 53 per cent in 1919.[42] Even in 1920, when dilution by conscripts was at its height, Trotsky asserted that 33.8 per cent of officers had served in the Imperial army.[43] In order to maintain political control, theoretically over the tsarist officers but increasingly over the troops as well, the institution of commissars was introduced. They were expected to be politically reliable people who oversaw all the activities of the military units to which they were attached. They were not, usually, qualified military personnel, but they exercised ultimate control over the actions of the military commanders. In the event of trouble, they had a hot line to the Cheka who would arrest anyone who disobeyed them.

The relationship is worth contemplating for a moment or two since it illuminates the processes going on in the rest of society. The main purpose of the commissar was to instil in the army that missing essential ingredient – the correct political consciousness. As such, the institution, like the Cheka and many others emerging, was clearly linked to Russia's political unpreparedness for the kind of revolution the Bolsheviks were conducting. It was necessary to use the limited "conscious" resources to oversee the rest. Concentration of resources in the party, among commissars and in the Cheka meant that a small number of adherents of the true ideology could impose it on the broader, supposedly hostile, society, a situation justified as democratic by the belief that "advanced", "conscious" ideas represented the true interests of the people that had been concealed from them by the old ruling class. These would now be revealed to them and mass support would be forthcoming. How limited those "conscious" resources were is highlighted by the fact that it was very difficult to find reliable commissars. If one could not even find a few thousand reliable adherents of the official ideology how was the new society supposed to function? In December 1918 there were around 6,400 commissars in the army.[44] The evidence suggests that not all of them were communists. At a conference of political commissars in Moscow in June 1918 only 271 out of 359 delegates were communists. In December 1918, 40 per cent of political workers were non-party, though this proportion had fallen to 11.2 per cent by May 1919.[45]

In March 1919 there were 60,000 communists in the army representing 20 per cent of the total membership. A year later there were 280,000 communists, 50 per cent of the total party membership but only about 8 per cent of the army.[46] The obvious corollary is that, outside the army, less than one person in 600 was in the party, yet the party was supposed to exercise decisive influence in all spheres. Even within the army, distribution of party members was very uneven. On the Southern Front, there were only 5,000 party members in March 1919 leading one historian to talk about "the scant presence and poor level of organization of the party in the detachments".[47]

There were extensive doubts within the party itself about such developments. The discussion, like a number of others, came to a head at the Eighth

Party Congress in March 1919. Opponents of the new line continued to call for a democratic militia army with universal conscription. They were completely rebuffed. The resolution adopted was uncompromising. In conditions of civil war, it stated, "the slogan 'people's militia' is deprived of its meaning ... and becomes a weapon of the reaction". "To preach the doctrine of guerrilla forces is tantamount to recommending a return from large-scale to cottage industry". "The requirement that the command staff be elected ... entirely loses its significance as a principle in the class-based workers' and peasants' Red Army". The use of military specialists and commissars was defended. As a sop to the opposition the existing arrangements were said to be "transitional" towards a militia, but one which was far from the traditional expectations of socialists.[48]

The resolution was a clear victory for the organizers of the Red Army, of whom Trotsky was the most prominent. But not all party members were convinced. Stalin, for example, did not believe it was necessary to give so much ground to the class enemy and defended the view that the workers' own resources were sufficient to ensure their victory. Later in 1919 he had a serious clash with Trotsky over the issue. Stalin tried to dismiss Sytin, the military specialist in command of his section of the front at Tsaritsyn. Trotsky, who had appointed Sytin, was outraged and successfully appealed to Lenin and the Defence Council to have him reinstated. It was Stalin who was recalled. The issue at stake here was one that dogged relations between Trotsky and Stalin for many years. Stalin's instinct for worker self-reliance was a constant feature of his career. This relatively minor incident is extremely revealing of the crucial differences that were to emerge between Stalin and Trotsky.

Power and the party: consciousness versus bureaucratism

The visions of 1917 about the nature of post-revolutionary power and the role of the party proved to be fantasy. The reassuring picture of the overwhelming majority of the population eagerly gathering round to learn and then implement Bolshevik truth did not materialize. By and large, the failure was not deemed to have revealed shortcomings in the model so much as in the population. There was, however, another aspect of the situation that was having profound consequences. Between 24 and 25 October 1917 the party had undergone a rude, overnight transition. It had totally changed its direction. Up to that point its focus had been exclusively on breaking down the existing order. Now it had to cope with the problems of creating a new one in the extremely unfavourable circumstances of the time. The acute tensions caused came out in the relationship between party and society and also in relations within the party itself. Unforeseen and, sometimes, unwelcome developments characterized both as dreams of an explosion of consciousness began to give way to a nightmare reality of ever expanding bureaucratization.

One aspect that the acquisition of power had not changed was the party leadership's view that the party was a supervisory, tutelary body rather than a representative one. The context in which this was applied was, however, vastly different from the one in which the idea had been born. It was one thing to see the party as the repository of working-class consciousness in the repressive conditions of tsarist Russia, it was another to maintain it while at the head of the physically largest and one of the most populous states in the world, especially when that state was fighting desperately for its life. To maintain its role it had, as we have seen, to exercise control in a multitude of areas. Every soviet, every factory, every school, every court room, every military unit was intended to have an effective party presence. At the top all decision-making apparatuses had to act in accordance with party principles. This applied to the state, the economy and cultural–educational life as well as the absolutely key areas of the military and the Cheka, that were the last line of defence of the new order. As well as being a revolutionary organization the party was becoming a managerial and administrative apparatus, a peculiar combination of roles it was to maintain throughout its existence, and one that put unimaginable pressure on the party's resources. Its pre-revolutionary membership of 25,000 was totally inadequate. Even its October membership of 200,000 was insufficient. It had to recruit on a large scale. Initially, membership peaked at around 400,000 shortly after October but by March 1919 it had fallen to 350,000. In successive years it rose to 611,000 and 732,000.[49]

In a conventional political party massive recruitment might have been acceptable, but in a vanguard party like the Bolsheviks it had unwanted implications. Lenin had insisted on a party of professional revolutionaries. Mass expansion ensured that the standard could not be maintained. Before the revolution, and to a lesser extent between February and October, joining the Bolshevik party was a momentous step in a person's life. The party was repressed. Members risked their careers, sacrificed their personal lives and faced imprisonment for their activities. Under such conditions the commitment of members could be guaranteed. By 1918 this was no longer the case. The party was recruiting wherever it could. People with specially needed experience or skills were particularly welcome. Some of the former tsarist army officers, for instance, not only fought for the Reds but became party members, rising to the top of the tree like Tukhachevsky. This was happening on a small scale in other sectors, as a few "class enemies" from the professions and senior state administration came over to support the party. The main bulk of the recruits, however, came from among the workers, peasants and white-collar groups, this last being particularly significant because of the type of tasks of control and supervision the party was taking on. They were people who had not been interested in joining the party before it came to power and, therefore, their commitment was more suspect. In effect, what had happened was that the membrane which had separated the party from society and acted as a filter keeping the less committed out, had ruptured. This brought about a great risk of diluting the consciousness characteristic of a Bolshevik, according to Lenin's theory. Its vanguard nature was under threat.

To make matters worse, the party suffered serious losses in the civil war among precisely the most committed cadres. In the first place, to join the party in 1918–20 was, for many, the equivalent of volunteering for war service because assignment to the front often followed. Once in the army, communists were expected to take the lead and suffered losses as a result. According to one calculation, of 500,000 party members who served in the Red Army at some point during the civil war, 200,000 were killed. In one unit, party cadres suffered 96 per cent losses compared to 38 per cent for the unit's conscripts.[50]

The party's new role was also giving rise to a persistent evil that afflicted the Soviet system, in varying degrees, forever after – bureaucratization, meaning a tendency to resolve problems by administrative means, according to rules laid down from above without reference to the people being administered. In this sense, it was the opposite of "democratization", or the handing over of responsibility to people to administer themselves.

The main difficulty for the party in dealing with the problems, however, was that mutually contradictory steps had to be taken to solve them, at least in the short and medium term. The dilution of the party by less reliable recruits was best combated by more centralization and discipline, including purges to weed out the least reliable. This inevitably brought about more bureaucratization and less democracy in the party. Very few in the party at the time (or since, in many cases) saw the relationship with real clarity, not surprisingly since to do so would have brought the very nature of the party into question and implied that the October revolution had been premature. The solution proposed in the long term was the usual, somewhat utopian one, of raising consciousness to the level at which the contradiction would disappear, that is there would be no conflict between the democratic will of the members and central authority.

The tensions were brought out into the open at the Eighth Party Congress in March 1919, which had also debated the military question. There was a second key resolution, on questions of party and state organization. The main problem was set out in the opening paragraph:

> Numerical growth of the party is progressive only to the extent that healthy proletarian elements are brought into the party . . . The party must follow with care the changes occurring in its social composition . . . Expansion of the numerical base of party organizations must in no case be conducted at the cost of worsening their qualitative composition. Great care must be exercised in admitting non-worker and non-peasant elements to the party.

In practice a worsening of quality was bound to follow from rapid quantitative expansion, but this was not recognized. The growing complexity of

relations between the party and society were also referred to. It was, the resolution continued, "natural" for the party, since it was in power and held "the
entire Soviet apparatus in its hands, to have assigned tens of thousands of its
best members to the task of running the country". It was even necessary to
expand this by enlisting thousands more of its "best people" in management
of "railroads, food, supervision, the army, the courts etc". However, this
"urgent task" brought about "a serious danger. Many members of the party
assigned to these state tasks are becoming cut off from the masses to a considerable extent and are becoming infected with bureaucratism". The resolution
even went so far as to associate the party with "unhealthy symptoms" of "red
tape, slipshod work, organizational diffuseness and narrow-minded local 'patriotism'" that were seen to be at work in soviet organizations. "There is", the
resolution continued, "an extensive influx into the party of elements that are
insufficiently communist and even of outright hangers-on. The Russian Communist Party is in power, and this inevitably attracts not just the best elements,
but also careerist elements, to its ranks".[51]

Various solutions were proposed. Party members were ordered to maintain
closer links with the membership of local soviets and trade unions. Party
organizations were required to submit more written reports to each other.
The mutual duties of party bodies at different levels were laid down and the
frequency of meeting was specified, though all this was within a framework of
"the strictest centralism and the most severe discipline" that were justifiably,
given the crisis of early 1919, said to be "an absolute necessity". "All decisions
of higher echelons are absolutely binding for those below. Every resolution
must first be carried out, and only then is it permissible to appeal the resolution to the appropriate party body. In this sense regular military discipline is
necessary for the party in the present era. All conflicts", the resolution continued, "are resolved by the appropriate higher party echelon". The Central
Committee was also given the power "to regularly re-assign party workers
from one sphere of work to another and from one area to another for maximum efficiency".[52] In addition "a thoroughgoing *purge*" of party and state
organizations was said to be necessary.[53]

The resolution also laid down rules for relations between party and soviets.
In essence, the party was to remain "the vanguard of the proletariat and the
poorer peasantry, i.e., the portion of these classes that is consciously striving
to make a communist programme a reality" while "the soviets unite tens of
millions of working people and must strive to unite within those ranks the
entire working class and all poor and middle peasants". The party's task was
to win "decisive influence" and "complete control" in all organizations of
working people such as unions, co-ops and rural communes and especially to
establish its "complete control" (the phrase being used for a second time) in
the soviets. To achieve this it was "absolutely necessary that a party fraction be
set up in all soviet organizations, and that such fractions be strictly subordi-
nated to party discipline". In this conception the party was the primary unit of

mobilization behind the goals of the leadership while the soviets were seen as transmission belts between the party and society as a whole. This is not what had been understood by "All Power to the Soviets" in October 1917.[54]

No clearer example of the insoluble contradiction facing the party could be found. Setting out from a diagnosis that blamed bureaucratism and associated problems for the party's ills it prescribed treatment – more writing of reports; more intervention from above, for example to reassign party members and even to post them elsewhere; more discipline; more centralization; more control over non-party bodies; purges; tighter registration of members – that stood a very good chance of making the disease worse. For instance, the provision about reassignment gave the central authorities extensive power over members, a power that was used to control troublemakers by the secretariat and organization bureaus of the party that were also formalized at this time to exist alongside the Politburo and the Central Committee. One of the major figures in this growing central bureaucracy was Stalin.

The counterweights seemed feeble by comparison. The declaration that the soviets, the state and the "dictatorship of the proletariat" which they exercised were transitional "until all state power of whatever sort withers away" lacked conviction. In addition to the provisions about maintaining links with the masses, reporting back to one's constituents and holding frequent meetings the resolution also proposed better party education and exhorted members not to "have recourse to petty tutelage over soviets", as well as reminding them that "membership of the Russian Communist Party accords no privileges whatsoever, but merely puts heavier responsibilities on them".[55] However, the mechanisms to enforce these pious exhortations, such as the Commissariat of State Control, set up in April 1919 and transformed into the Worker–Peasant Inspectorate in February 1920, reinforced the trend to bureaucratization rather than eliminated it. In any case, a number of the provisions, the stipulated frequency of meetings for example, were not even obeyed by the highest party organs, let alone the local ones.

The references to party education and to consciousness do, however, remind us of these crucial areas for the party. Here, too, steps were being taken to try to improve the situation.

In the realms of theory the party was still working within its utopian perspectives of, as the resolution on the organizational question confirmed, the withering away of the state. Alongside this the aim of unifying the proletariat, not only of Russia but of the entire world, on the basis of its own class consciousness was an explicit party objective. Raising class consciousness, it was thought, was the key question for the future of the revolution. But how could it be done? The backwardness of Russia in this respect was obvious to all. Deproletarianization made matters worse. The party's resources to achieve its grandiose objective were meagre. It could no longer even rely on party members to have the correct consciousness since committed members had been swamped by the influx of newcomers, who outnumbered pre-revolutionary

Bolsheviks by about 15 to one in March 1919. One of many vicious circles asserted itself. The low level of consciousness made it imperative to take steps to raise it, but this was almost impossible given the low level of the starting point. The few reliable cadres were being called on to do the most important work in every sphere – party and state management, law, the military, the Cheka and now education and propaganda. There were too few to go round. None the less, the task had to be undertaken. In the forefront of the party effort was the adoption by the Eighth Party Congress of a new programme that was published together with an explanatory gloss entitled the *ABC of Communism*, written by two leading party theoreticians, Nikolai Bukharin and Evgenii Preobrazhensky, who were both on its left wing at the time. The two documents provide an extensive encyclopaedia of party aspirations.

The programme opened with a thumbnail sketch of Marxism that emphasized Leninist themes such as the evolution of monopoly capitalism; the opportunity this opened up "for replacing the capitalist relations of production by communist relations"; the dictatorship of the proletariat, defined as "the political power which will enable (the proletariat) to crush all resistance of the exploiters"; the internationalism of the communist party "the aim of which is to make the proletariat capable of fulfilling its historic mission" and hostility to social democracy "that bourgeois perversion of socialism".[56]

It then moved into an account of the gains of the revolution, notably the establishment of "proletarian democracy". Where "bourgeois democracy" remained, despite its principles of freedom "an instrument for exploitation and oppression of the broad masses of workers by a small group of capitalists" because it allowed "the existence of private property in land and other means of production", proletarian democracy "instead of formally proclaiming these rights and freedoms, actually grants them first of all to those classes that have been oppressed by capitalism, i.e. to the proletariat and the peasantry".[57] Other gains followed on from this, including abolition of "all the laws of the overthrown government" which were replaced by decrees of the proletariat and "in the case of the absence or incompleteness of such decrees, ... by socialist conscience".[58] The use of "bourgeois specialists" was defended as part of the general theme of productionism.

> All possible increase in the productive forces of the country must be considered the fundamental and principal point upon which the whole economic policy of the Soviet government is based ... everything else must be subordinated to the practical aim of immediately and at all costs (increasing) the quantity of the most indispensable products required by the population. The successful functioning of every Soviet institution connected with the economy must be measured by the practical results in this direction.[59]

It was largely as an extension of this that strong centralization was recommended in many spheres. In agriculture it was recognized "that the small-scale system of agriculture will continue for a long time" although large-scale socialist institutions were to be promoted. The party, it was stated, "in all its work in the village, looks for support to the proletarian and semi-proletarian strata" and "organizes these into an independent force" in order to free them "from the rural bourgeoisie and the interests of small property-holders". With respect to the "kulaks, the rural bourgeoisie" the party aimed to carry on "a resolute struggle against their attempts at exploitation" and to suppress "their resistance to Soviet policy". In contrast with this, policy for the "middle peasantry consists in gradually and systematically attracting it to the work of socialist construction".[60] Other, less immediate issues were also included such as public education – where the aim was to transform "the school from an instrument of class rule of the bourgeoisie into an instrument for the abolition of class divisions in society, into an instrument for a communist regeneration of society" – and religion – where the aim of the party was "the complete destruction of the ties between the exploiting classes and the organization of religious propaganda" and "helping the toiling masses to liberate their minds from religious prejudices", by means of scientific education and anti-religious propaganda, without "offending the religious susceptibilities of believers, which leads only to the hardening of religious fanaticism".[61] In some cases, the positions defended did not hold up for long, notably with respect to trade unions that, the programme said, "must actually concentrate in their hands the entire administration of the whole public economy as a single economic unit".[62] This conflicted with the growing trend towards one-person management that was victorious at the next party congress the following year.

There was also no small element of out-and-out utopianism. Private trade was to be replaced "by a systematic distribution of products organized on a national scale".[63] The description in the *ABC of Communism* made socialism sound like a system of supermarkets without checkouts. "Under communism . . . products are not exchanged for one another; they are neither bought nor sold. They are simply stored in the communal warehouse, and are subsequently delivered to those who need them". The implication was, as the programme stipulated, that the party should "prepare the ground for the abolition of money". The *ABC of Communism* imagined that there might be objectors to this "'How can that be?' some of you will ask. 'In that case one person will get too much and another too little. What sense is there in such a system of distribution?'" The reassuring answer was that, although "perhaps for 20 or 30 years it will be necessary to have various regulations" subsequently "when communist society has been consolidated and fully developed" they would not be needed. Instead "there will be an ample quantity of all products, our present wounds will long since have been healed, and everyone will be able to get just as much as he needs".[64]

Another "of the most fundamental tasks" was the rather utopian one of "the consolidation of all economic activity in the country according to a general state plan: the greatest centralization of production", that would even be extended to establishing "a single economic plan" with other nations "which have already come over to the Soviet system".[65]

While propaganda and the problem of consciousness were not explicitly dealt with in the programme, they were important components of several of its sections. The "low cultural level of the masses" was seen to be a major reason for difficulties in evolving new, communist forms of administration and the raising of this level was seen to be a necessary prerequisite for "the abolition of state authority".[66] The school system was to be "the bearer of communist principles".[67] There was also to be "large-scale development of propaganda of communist ideas and employment of state resources and apparatus for that purpose".[68] Trade unions were also expected to engage in "systematic work directed to the re-education of the masses".[69] It was also proposed that workers should be helped to appreciate "all the art treasures which were created by the exploitation of their labour, and which have also been so far only at the exclusive disposal of the exploiters".[70] These two provisions, plus support for already existing measures "directed to the development of science and its closer contact with production" that included "the establishment of a number of new scientific institutions, laboratories, research institutes, and experimental production", allowed extensive collaboration with parts of the artistic and scientific intelligentsia who were prepared to work with the new Soviet system.[71] The Education Ministry, Narkompros, had extensive links with artists who were drawn into the work of producing propaganda – especially posters and films, both of which were thought to be relatively effective in a society where literacy was low – and educating a new generation of workers in artistic techniques and appreciation of painting, sculpture, music, literature and other arts.

The programme itself, however, was not so much a precise blueprint as an educational document intended to explain, first of all to party members themselves, what the chief theoretical and practical policies of the party were. This explains not only the nature of the programme with its potted history, justification of current practices and delineation of future goals, but also the decision to publish the *ABC of Communism* as a full-length book. They were used as primary teaching materials in party schools, discussion groups and so on, although it is difficult to say what influence they had since both were written in rather dense jargon (that even the above, brief extracts have, no doubt, revealed) that must have been impenetrable to the average worker or peasant. They are also of great value in bringing out the party's assumptions about itself at this critical moment in its history, when it was facing the most immediate threat to its very survival. In the light of this conjuncture some of its implications, notably the complete absence of any serious distinction between party and state spheres that are dealt with almost interchangeably, are particularly revealing.

The Soviet system

The governmental system that emerged by 1921 was very different from the one outlined in the April Theses. Soviet Russia had become a one party state. It had a conventional army of three and a half million men, making it the largest in the world at that time. An active political police force with extensive powers and a system of labour camps for opponents had emerged. Organizations independent of the state were infinitely fewer than before the war. This applied in the economic field – where the state had become the major industrial employer, owner and manager; in finance – where the state controlled the banking system; in politics – where no parties were permitted to mount serious competition to the Bolsheviks, although they had not yet been totally abolished; in cultural life – where independent intelligentsia institutions had diminished in number, or been brought under firmer state control although, surprisingly given party penetration elsewhere, the universities, the Academy of Sciences and literary and artistic life retained some real independence. At the head was a small and unchallengeable political leadership, motivated by boundless visions of the future. In short, a highly centralized, authoritarian system of government, that allowed less and less space for criticism of its actions and none at all for independent organizations, had come into existence. True, some features were still limited in effect because of the continued weakness of the government in many respects such as its lack of "conscious" personnel to carry out its policies and the need to conciliate "specialists" and the more productive peasants.

There were less tangible, cultural effects of the experience. Success bred self-confidence and a sometimes frightening certainty about the correctness of the party's methods. This was embodied in a new generation of party members many of whom were intoxicated by success in the civil war, as well they might have been since it appeared that the fledgling Soviet system had beaten off not only the massed weight of the old tsarist elite – Russia was now completely clear of generals, landowners, bankers, capitalists, aristocrats, royals and the conservative and liberal parts of its educated class – but also the massed weight of international capitalism in the form of the interventionists. To these people, it seemed that there was no force on earth capable of preventing the party from reaching its goals. They came back from the war talking of "fronts", "enemies", "battles", "battalions", "armies", "campaigns", "hit-squads" (*udarniki*) and "wars". They represented a militant force looking for new objectives to capture. Their prime targets were the remnants of internal class enemies such as former members of other political parties; former property owners, engineers and managers who had qualified under the old regime; the vast number of administrators and civil servants from the tsarist period who were still in post; university graduates and "bourgeois" intellectuals. They conducted a relentless campaign against them throughout the twenties. The peasantry, of course, were seen by the new generation as the main "enemy", but for the time being, they could do little about them.

Sometimes the militants embarrassed the leadership, particularly old Bolsheviks like Lenin and Bukharin who were members of the intelligentsia and had a rather more complex view of the world and were trying to be less confrontational. On the other hand, the militants' attitudes were reflected in an increasingly aggressive group within the leadership that came to focus more and more on Stalin, who had not come from an intelligentsia background. Stalin himself appears to have been influenced throughout his career by his experiences of the civil war. His closest friends were his comrades in arms of that period such as Budenny and Voroshilov. His own solutions to the revolution's problems, that he imposed at the end of the twenties, were marked by a revival of civil war sentiments, the main slogan of those days – "There is no fortress the Bolsheviks cannot storm" – perfectly expressing the militaristic mood of both periods. In his declining years he is said to have watched again and again the epic film *Unforgettable 1919*, that recreated the heroic times. Thus there is a strong case for seeing the civil war experience as an important source for the complex of policies and attitudes usually referred to as "Stalinism", though personalizing it with such a name can conceal the complexity of the phenomenon.

In recent interpretations the civil war has been considered a decisive influence shaping the Soviet system, that, until the mid-1980s retained a degree of productionism and "militarization", especially in terms of its attitude to centralization, to discipline and to mobilization of its citizens to achieve the leadership's proclaimed goals.[72] It would, however, be a mistake to see the war as the only, or even the main, source of the Soviet system's extreme authoritarianism.

It is important, first of all, to recall that tsarism was itself extremely authoritarian and did its best to strangle independent and oppositional movements. The revolutionaries who emerged in 1917 had felt its full force, even though, for most of them, the main objective of their programme was simply the setting up of a democratic, constitutional system based on "one person one vote". Repression bred repression so that hard-line revolutionaries, like Lenin, were themselves products of the tsarist environment. Beyond this, tsarism had done its best to keep the people ignorant. Mass education had been practically non-existent, literacy levels minimal. Even after 1905, politics was still hedged around with a multitude of restrictions and free popular political institutions were difficult to organize. The period of relative freedom was too short to make much impact. Political attitudes, political culture, perforce remained authoritarian at the national level though, at the local level, the commune created a quite different environment.

In the struggle to overcome the antiquated, repressive conditions, Lenin and many other intellectuals had turned to organizations that, since they were driven underground, had had no alternative but to use disciplined, conspiratorial methods. Lenin, as in so many other respects, was something of an extreme case though by no means the most extreme. Nothing in Lenin's career in the party between 1907 and 1917 suggested he had modified the basic stress on discipline and obedience to decisions from above. Even before the civil war proper got going one can find examples of it being carried over into government. The Seventh (Special) Party Congress declared in March 1918 that it recognized:

> as the primary and fundamental tasks of our party, of the entire vanguard of the conscious proletariat and of the Soviet government, the adoption of the most energetic, mercilessly resolute and draconian measures for the heightening of self-discipline and the discipline of the workers and peasants of Russia . . . [and] the creation everywhere of strongly united and iron-willed organizations of the masses.[73]

According to Evan Mawdsley, "This was, in theory at least, the charter of the totalitarian state" and had come, not in response to fighting the Whites, but as a result of the disastrous war against Germany that had led to the treaty of Brest-Litovsk.[74]

Such tendencies had not gone unnoticed even within the party. It was, after all, an influential minority of Central Committee members and commissars who had pointed out that the revolution had taken the road of repression. Although her German prison cell was not the best vantage point, the Polish revolutionary Rosa Luxemburg, close friend of the Soviet revolution and an ally and admirer of Lenin, had felt the need to warn the new government of the danger it was courting. "The whole mass of the people", she argued, "must take part . . . otherwise socialism will be decreed from behind a few official desks by a dozen intellectuals". Lenin, she continued, "is completely mistaken in the means he employs. Decree, dictatorial force of the factory overseer, draconic penalties, rule by terror". "It is", she wrote, "rule by terror which demoralizes".

> In place of the representative bodies created by general, popular elections, Lenin and Trotsky have laid down the soviets as the only true representation of the labouring masses. But with the repression of political life in the land as a whole, life in the soviets must also become more crippled. Without general elections, without unrestricted freedom of the press and assembly, without a free struggle of opinion, life dies out in every public institution, becomes a mere semblance of life, in which only the bureaucracy remains as the active element.[75]

In her words we hear not only a difference of opinion but a whole difference of culture, with Rosa Luxemburg representing a strain of radical Marxism that had evolved in the somewhat more democratic atmosphere of western Europe. For someone brought up under tsarist conditions, the point was not so obvious. In the prevailing circumstances it was hard to see why opposition should be tolerated when the Russian tradition was to eradicate it as heresy.

Once the war was over and the Whites and the Poles had been defeated, the trend to authoritarianism continued in party and society, as did the utopian economics of rapid transition to communism. Far from being abandoned as a war-time emergency, the pressure was stepped up. Militarization of labour was promoted. Measures were introduced in November 1920 to extend nationalization to small-scale enterprises and workshops even though the Party Programme of 1919, had envisaged them being used "to the widest extent", albeit subject to the condition that they should be encouraged to amalgamate into larger units. There were also plans to increase administrative interference in the countryside by means of "sowing committees" that would compel the peasants to produce more grain. The dream of replacing the market by direct administrative intervention over labour and over the peasants was being matched by equally ambitious aspirations to control the economy as a whole by means of a general economic plan. Such aims were equated with socialism and have been seen as such by more authoritarian inclined observers who found virtue in these methods. E. H. Carr, for example, claimed that the tendency towards compulsory labour service was "not merely a concession to the needs of civil war, but an authentic advance into a socialist order" because it saw "labour as a service to be rendered rather than as a commodity to be sold" and, as such, was representative "of everything that distinguished the loftier ideals of socialism from the base mechanics of the capitalist wage-system".[76] However, in all respects, Russia was totally unprepared for an all-out assault on the market and its replacement by administrative controls. The drive to do this, stepped up again by Stalin in 1928, has at least as much to do with Bolshevik aspirations to "complete control" as it did with "authentic advance into a socialist order".

The most important factor underlying Bolshevik initiatives was utopianism, the desire to transform the world. The leaders were not prepared to sit back and simply administer the country nor did they understand their task to be straightforward representation of the demands of workers and peasants – the despised vice of "tailism". Instead their ideological commitment demanded that they should construct weapons that would enable them to intervene decisively in the flow of events. Their initial powerlessness after October meant that they could only watch what was happening and go along with it – by means of the land decree; observing the liquidation of estates; abetting the inevitable decay of the Imperial army; surrendering abjectly to Germany; accepting the spontaneous initiatives of factory committees. But they gave the highest priority to fashioning the instruments they needed to impose their own values, their consciousness. Many of the mechanisms were original – the Cheka; political commissars; party fractions and cells; the Worker–Peasant Inspectorate; the Organization bureau of the party and the use of length of party service as an index of reliability. Civil war against the Whites or not, the Bolsheviks would have been totally committed to class struggle under one form or another. Their certainty of their own correctness; their nurturing of consciousness; their vanguard instincts; their sense of superiority over the masses; all pointed to an authoritarian, centralized, elitist, technocratic system.[77] Only if the vast majority of the population had gone along with the enterprise could it have been considered, in any sense of the term, a democratic project. The more mundane concerns of peasants and workers, however, put the remnants of much of the popular movement on a collision course with the new authorities.

CHAPTER TEN

The popular movement in the revolutionary war

Within the broad political framework created by the Bolshevik takeover and the disintegration of the unified state, the revolution developed with great speed at grass-roots level. Many of the supposed "causes" of the October revolution actually occurred after it had taken place. In particular, it is often said that the land was divided up between February and October 1917 and that this, in turn, provided an incentive for soldiers to desert in order to share the spoils. What actually happened was rather different. After October, the war, or at least the fighting, quickly ended and the Bolsheviks began to urge the six million soldiers still at the front to go home, taking their weapons with them. Thus it was only after October that the army crumbled away, leaving only the thinnest of screens to defend Russia. While this undoubtedly fulfilled the main specific aim of the soldiers' and sailors' movement it was, like other "gains" of the period, highly ambiguous. No one had wanted to dissolve the means of defence before agreeing armistice terms with Germany. Bolshevik haste to do so is explained by their frantic desire to deprive the old elite of the power to strike at the revolution. In fact, it would have been impossible for the officers to use the mass of the army for their own political purposes as the Kornilov affair had shown, but by dissolving the army in this over-hurried fashion the Bolsheviks left themselves at the mercy of Germany. At the same time, army committees and soviets briefly flourished. Kronstadt became virtually independent. But Bolshevik centralization was already beginning to make itself felt in this most vital of areas.

Similarly, workers' control of factories was only beginning in autumn of 1917. Far from leading to the October revolution, here too it was the October revolution that opened up the floodgates. In many ways, the first six months or so of the Soviet period constituted a "golden age" for parts of the popular movement. Private landowning was liquidated, factories were taken over, the armed forces were broken up. New local institutions – village and *volost'* committees, peasant communes, factory committees, soldiers' and sailors' committees and local soviets – had unprecedented power. More than at any other time, and more or less uniquely in modern history, the population of the Russian Empire became self-governing and self-administering. However, there can be no doubt that the new authorities were unhappy with the situation and, as soon as they had the power to do so, began to intervene in the grass-roots revolution to force it to conform to the leaders' blueprint.

Agrarian policies

There can be no doubt that the Bolsheviks were not prepared to leave the peasants to their own devices. In the first place they were increasingly concerned – just as their tsarist and Provisional Government predecessors had been – over the grain surplus needed to feed what remained of the urban population and the developing Red Army. Secondly, they were completely unprepared, intellectually and politically, to tolerate an independent, peasant-based rural revolution. Unlike Mao in China ten years later, no Soviet communist was ready to argue for the positive revolutionary role of the peasantry. After all, Russian Marxism had defined itself in opposition to populism on precisely this point for its entire 35 years of existence. It was unlikely to abandon its central assumption in the heat of struggle against, among others, the successors of the populists. For the Bolshevik leadership, it was workers, and only workers, who could exert leadership in the revolution. Even though part of the peasantry, it was thought, was capable of following the workers' lead they would only be in the second rank of the revolution and a large proportion of the peasantry would, in any case, remain incorrigibly petty bourgeois and hostile to the socialist revolution. Finally, other practical exigencies of the central state (which would have asserted themselves in one form or another no matter what its ideological complexion) put it on a collision course with the village. The peasants wanted to be left alone, the state began to demand conscripts and taxes. It could only raise them by forcible intervention in the countryside.

The first requirement, however, was grain. To get hold of it the government declared a food dictatorship in May 1918. It was prompted by the disappearance of the surplus that had grave consequences for the towns. (We could, perhaps, recall here that one of the key reasons behind Menshevik and Right SR opposition to October was precisely that it would have this effect.) The response proposed echoed the political solutions to economic problems characteristic of Lenin's approach. No economic measures were envisaged only the forcible extraction of supposedly concealed stocks from the hands of kulaks who had, it was said, been holding grain from the 1916 and 1917 harvests without even having threshed it. Clearly, the deeply held views of the party on class struggle had overcome the need for evidence. The stocks must be there because the ideology said they must be. Not unnaturally, there were some such stocks but nothing like enough to solve the crisis and, in any case, it was hard for the requisitioning squads to distinguish supposedly hoarded grain from the essential seed corn that the villages had also withheld.

While none of the Bolsheviks' successive approaches to the countryside was the pure realization of one single motive, pride of place has to be given to similar ideological and political considerations rather than pragmatism, in another associated venture. For 20 years Lenin had argued that the peasantry was divided into contradictory classes and that the poor peasants were, roughly, the rural equivalent of the proletariat and would follow the lead of the proletariat. As a consequence the leadership thought the best way to secure its position was to fan the flame of the supposed class war in the countryside. To this end, in June 1918, committees of poor peasants (*kombedy*) were set up. The problem was that Lenin's hypothesis was wrong. The committees were artificial from the beginning and did not correspond to real divisions of class within the rural community. Most working commune peasants appear to have recognized the committees for what they were – attempts by the state to interfere in rural life. Recent research has stressed that the rural division that the committees did exploit was not that between poor peasants and supposed kulaks but that between commune peasants as a whole and rural outsiders – migrants, refugees from the underfed cities, wandering soldiers with no homes to return to and other less settled elements of Russia's revolutionary countryside. The evidence is overwhelming that the commune peasants, if they had differences with one another, sank them in a much stronger common hostility to the outside world. The *kombedy* also added to the confused institutions of the countryside by not having functions clearly different from those of rural soviets. The result was catastrophic failure that made the pragmatic problems – the supply of food, taxes and recruits – much more acute because the committees gave precedence to the least active and least productive rural dwellers at the expense of the more productive, whose efforts were sorely needed to meet the crisis. While, in the short term, they may have helped by working with the increasing number of detachments sent to confiscate grain supposedly withheld in the villages, the cost was enormous in undermining whatever confidence the peasants had had earlier in the new authorities. In view of their extremely damaging influence, they were effectively abandoned in November 1918 and a Sovnarkom decree of 2 December called for them to be disbanded after the next round of local soviet elections. There seems little reason to disagree with E. H. Carr's judgement that "the creation of the committees of poor peasants in June 1918 had been mainly a political gesture designed to split the peasantry".[1] They were abandoned because they had succeeded too well in their task, not so much by splitting the commune peasantry as by setting peasants and outsiders at each other's throats. Lenin's explanation, that they had become "so well established that we found it possible to replace them with properly elected soviets"[2] was economical with the truth. In fact, the new government had seriously miscalculated. It had underestimated the key problem of the surplus. The result was that the rural economy had been flung into deeper crisis.

Taken together the agrarian initiatives of 1918 had been an unmitigated disaster. They had discouraged middle and wealthier peasants not only from producing a marketable surplus – since it was impossible to market it because of prohibitions on private trade, not to mention the lack of goods to buy with the profits and the unreliability of money as currency reform and massive inflation took hold – but also from producing more than a minimum amount of grain anyway since it was subject to arbitrary confiscation. This led very quickly to shortages and starvation in the cities – exacerbated by the Treaty of Brest-Litovsk and, later, the civil war, that cut the main grain-producing areas off from the grain-hungry cities of the centre and north – and precipitated the massive exodus from them in 1918 and 1919. As E. H. Carr put it, the "mass of industrial workers were converted peasants" so that crisis did not result in unemployment but in "mass flight of industrial workers from the towns and reversion to the status and occupation of peasants".[3] In the face of the new threat, the peasantry appear to have reverted to their deepest instincts of subsistence, self-reliance, solidarity and distrust of the authorities. In the circumstances, it is not surprising that one of the most quoted peasant slogans of the period was "Down with the Communists. Long live the Bolsheviks" since the government that had passed the land decree in October 1917 appeared totally divorced, in peasant eyes, from the one that had sent in requisition squads in the summer of 1918. It seems that peasants, too, had a lot to learn about the difference between the Bolsheviks' minimum and maximum programmes.

After disbanding the *kombedy*, party policy remained confused. At the same time as they were being merged with the soviets, the first national conference of *kombedy* was in session calling for radical policies of energetic, even forced, collectivization of agriculture from above.[4] There was even a decree passed by the Central Executive Committee of the Soviet (VTsIK) on 14 February 1919 that called for the rapid socialization of the rural economy.[5] It remained in force until the adoption of NEP, even though, only a few weeks later in March at the 8th Party Congress, Lenin announced the opposite policy – conciliation of the middle peasant – as the heart of the party's approach to the countryside, and the key to the success of the revolution. Ambiguities of policy at the centre were not, however, as important as they might seem in that the state still lacked the instruments fully to enforce any policy on the whole of the countryside and local factors, not least of which were the variable quality of party cadres and the chaotic system of communication, remained paramount when it came to implementation. As far as it could, the peasantry went its own way irrespective of government that, for the time being, could only watch developments and conduct intermittent and unsystematic raids against peasants. As a result, no further decisive initiatives were embarked upon in 1919–20 and requisitioning, repression of the market and fitful attempts to allocate centrally scarce goods in exchange for grain were what passed for policy. Without the illegal survival of the market many more would have perished.

Finally, one should not ignore the pragmatic impulses that provoked rural policies. According to E. H. Carr "only under the compulsion of impending hunger in the towns did they at length turn their active attention to the measures necessary to establish their power in the countryside".[6] Orlando Figes more or less agrees with this. For him the so-called food dictatorship of May, the establishment of the *kombedy* and the introduction of conscription for the Red Army on 12 June were the measures "which marked the beginning of the end for self-rule" in the Volga region which he studied.[7] In other words, like any state, the practical needs – grain, taxes and conscripts – lay behind their policies. However, the forms that the Bolsheviks' pragmatism took were heavily influenced by their ideological assumptions, that also played a major part in determining what was done with the resources raised.

The revolution in the villages

It took more than six months for the policies of the new government to be felt in the villages. From October 1917 to late spring of 1918 peasants followed their own agenda. As we have seen, many of them had been militant since spring but very few had done more than improve the position of the peasants at the expense of the landowners. In only a minority of cases had estates been completely broken up. After October they were almost all taken over within a few months. Figures published by Soviet historians show that most manors were confiscated or destroyed after October. In 1966, for instance, Pershin drew together the findings of four local studies of central *guberniias* that all told a similar story. Only 3 per cent of manors were confiscated in October 1917. The figure for November was about 20 per cent while December and January were each around 30 per cent. Thus, it was in these three months that 80 per cent of manors in the areas studied were confiscated.[8] While there were, as in everything else, important regional differences, the general picture was largely similar. For example, in a more recent study, a British historian, Orlando Figes, states that in Penza 20 per cent of manors that were burned were attacked in September, though he also concludes that, in general, the main period for extreme attacks of this sort was the autumn and winter.[9]

While all the evidence bears out Figes' judgement that October went by unnoticed in the villages[10] it has to be remembered that this only applies to the immediate events of the October revolution. The consequences of October had a far-reaching effect on the rural areas. It should be stressed that this was not because the peasants were Bolsheviks – most of them had probably never heard of the Bolsheviks and had no idea what they stood for – but because the October revolution threw the opponents of revolution into a fatal confusion from which they never, ultimately, recovered. Eventually, the peasants realized that the new authorities were encouraging them to act and that the fitful and increasing repression of the peasant movement by the state, that characterized the last few months of Provisional Government rule, was no more. In effect, there was, until at least the summer of 1918, a power vacuum in the rural areas that was quickly filled by the peasants themselves.

The peasants' first targets continued to be the separators who were finally pulled back into the commune. In 1916 they had held about 30 per cent of arable land. By 1922 they had only around 2 per cent, a figure that had been achieved almost entirely in 1917.[11] Many separators had rejoined the commune voluntarily in order to participate in the next stage of the revolution, the concerted attack on landowners that peaked in the autumn and winter of 1917–18. By spring of 1918 the landowners of most of the European Slavic regions of the Russian Empire had been dispossessed. Many of them fled, some tried to resist, others stayed on trying to eke out a living from the land allotments they were permitted to retain.[12] As a result, the revolution had a somewhat paradoxical effect, at least from the Bolshevik point of view. Where they had aimed, traditionally, to encourage large-scale socialist agriculture to replace the evolving capitalism of the landowners, in fact, as one Soviet historian put it, "in the course of the revolution the peasant commune revived".[13] In other words, the peasants reverted to their traditional organizational forms and extended their traditional, inefficient agricultural methods.

In effecting a massive social revolution and an unprecedented transfer of land from private to peasant ownership the best and worst features of the peasant movement came to the fore. First of all, and contrary not only to subsequent myth but also to the rumours and beliefs of the urban elite at the time, the change was not conducted by means of unrestrained violence. In fact, violent disturbances, in which landowners and their associates were seriously injured or killed, were few and far between. Serious damage to property was rarer than legend would have it. After all, peasants were practical people who preferred to take over and use resources rather than destroy them aimlessly. Where manor houses were burned it was, as we have seen, usually to ensure that the landowner would not have a "nest" in the area from which he or she could eventually reassert privileges. In Saratov, a province that had been among the most troubled in 1905 and had a reputation for the fierceness of its peasants, disturbances were recorded in only 1–3 per cent of villages in early 1918.[14] This does not mean that confiscation of estates was a gentle process, far from it. The peasants acted roughly and crudely but, as a rule, they were not wantonly destructive.

Other characteristics emerged that reinforce our knowledge of the "moral economy" of the peasant movement. The fundamental assumption of Orthodox, Slavic peasant communities was that labour was the basis of entitlement to land. Only those who worked the land themselves should have an allotment. Within the broad framework a variety of methods of applying the principle evolved in different villages. Weaker members of the community – for instance, elderly widows without sons and the disabled, a not inconsiderable category after the war, there being 4.4 million invalids in the 16–49 age group by 1922[15] – were protected. Orlando Figes has emphasized that, in the Saratov region, outsiders were excluded from the reapportionment of land but in many areas non-commune members were brought into the system. Most surprisingly, many landowners and their families were given allotments equivalent to those given to any commune family. There are cases of monks being allowed personal allotments when monastery land was divided up.[16] The Russian historian V. V. Kabanov has pointed out that what often concerned the peasants about outsiders was their lack of means to farm land they might be given – for instance the poorest refugees would lack equipment and funds to buy it, not to mention the knowledge and skills necessary. Where they had such means, or could reasonably show that they would acquire them, they were sometimes given land by the commune or the soviet.[17]

Everywhere, land was distributed to commune members according to need. This has caused a certain amount of difficulty for interpreters of the complex patchwork of landholding that resulted. Traditionally, Soviet historians tried to show that there was a war against the kulaks in this period. It appears to be the case that the number of large farms, that is those with eight *desiatinas* of land or more, fell from 9 per cent in 1917 to less than 4 per cent in 1919. Recent evidence has shown that the remaining larger farms in this category tended to belong to households with larger numbers of members. For example, figures from Kursk and Tula indicate that nearly all farms of more than eight *desiatinas* were farmed by families of seven or more and, in the case of Kursk, 66 per cent by families of 11 or more.[18]

By the end of 1918 a massive takeover of land had occurred. According to Kabanov, over 17 million *desiatinas* had been re-distributed. Ninety-five per cent of it had gone to peasant households, 1 per cent to peasant co-operatives and *artels*, 4 per cent to state farms and other state institutions such as factories, schools and hospitals.[19] Peasants increased their landholdings by 50 per cent per head in Samara and 100 per cent in Saratov.[20]

While peasants undoubtedly benefited in the short term from having more land per head, the outcome was by no means universally satisfactory. The biggest problem resulting from the land settlement was that the most productive sectors of Russian agriculture – the large estates and the farms of the separators – had been liquidated. The fragile marketed surplus, that fed the towns and the army and that, in peacetime, was the bedrock of Russia's balance of payments through exports, was seriously threatened. The peasants' main aim was to end the exploitation that had enabled the surplus to be extracted and thereby improve their own level of consumption and their working conditions. In order to maintain the surplus necessary to sustain Russia's non-peasant population the peasants would have had to double the amount of produce they marketed. In the conditions of the time, as Kabanov has pointed out, this was beyond their immediate possibilities.[21] The productive land taken over by the peasants was divided up and subjected to the less productive traditional farming methods of the peasant commune, that controlled 90 per cent or more of the land by 1922.[22] Much of it was divided up into small plots and, even though the evil of "parcelization" has perhaps been over-exaggerated[23] there were still plenty of examples of it. For instance, one household in Moscow *guberniia* had 7.6 *desiatinas* of land in 12 parcels. 4.6 *desiatinas* were the traditional commune allotment, 2.1 were added from the re-distribution of land-owners land, 176 square *sazhen'* (one *sazhen'* is equivalent to 2.13 metres) came from joint purchase and 0.6 *desiatinas* was *artel'* land individually farmed, probably as a family vegetable plot.[24] In most places, households held their land in six to 20 parcels, though in some areas one-third had 21 parcels or more. One household has been traced whose land was divided up into 65 parcels. In Viatka there were parcels 1.5 *sazhen'* wide and 20 *sazhen'* long. In some cases the parcels could be several kilometres apart. This traditional ailment was made worse by the division of the new land on top of the old.[25] In addition, there were many more redistributions than usual in the revolutionary period. One enquiry showed that by 1922, 66 per cent of villages had had at least one redistribution since 1917. Many had had three or four.[26] In some regions 80 per cent were partitioned by 1922. There are also reports of 66 per cent of communes repartitioning annually in some areas.[27] The problem was seen to be so serious that on 30 April 1920 a Sovnarkom decree attempted rather unsuccessfully to restrict repartitioning of land.[28]

When one also recalls that the basic problem of the Russian village was rising population it becomes clear that the revolutionary settlement, though it "satisfied" peasants in the short term could not stand the strains put upon it. In 1884 in Tambov *uezd*, Kursk *guberniia*, the average village had consisted of 92 households. In 1920 the number was 168. Although households gained land in 1917 their position, as indicated by the same *uezd*, had, none the less, dramatically deteriorated. In 1884 there had been 2.8 *desiatinas* per person. In 1920 there was 0.8.[29] 1920 was probably the worst point of overcrowding in villages because the shortages ensuing from war and revolution – that led, for instance, to a steady decline in the sown area of 17 per cent in 1919 and a further 11.3 per cent in 1920[30] – caused, as we have seen, a massive flight from the urban areas back to the villages. It is absolutely clear, however, that traditional village agriculture would be hard put to it to bear the burdens that would be placed on it if the Russian urban and industrial economy were ever to take off once again.

The problem had been foreseen by the Bolshevik leadership in October and special provisions of the land decree had attempted to preserve model farms – market gardens, breeding stations and so on – intact to serve as showpieces of socialist agriculture. They would demonstrate that full socialization of land would enable new methods and mechanization to enrich the whole community. In reality, at least in the conditions of civil war, such aims remained unfulfilled. A few genuine co-operatives, of a bewildering variety of types, were set up but they occupied only some 1 per cent of the land.[31] Their historian has suggested that they were indeed more productive but they did not catch on.[32] The state farms that were set up, occupying some 3 per cent of the land,[33] seem, ironically, to have been among the least efficient of all. The main reason was that most peasants wanted their own farms and only the least efficient found themselves without land and went into the state farm more from desperation and lack of any alternative rather than from conviction.[34] The labour problem was a constant one for many state farms in the early years. Even those who had been forced by circumstance to work on them often left at the first opportunity because of the poor conditions, compounded by the state's rapacious levies of their output and the inexperience of their managers who were often political appointees trusted by the party rather than expert farmers. Ironically, the most productive farms appear to have been the tiny number that were set up, separator style, as individual family farms. But even their productivity was below that of the engulfed landowner estates.[35]

There was little the government could do to influence the way the peasants were taking over estates. But even in these early moments we can discern signs of future bitter conflict. For example, Bolshevik policy statements invariably referred to class divisions within the peasantry and singled out the minority of landless, wage-earning peasants as the most reliable ally of the proletariat in the countryside. The majority of the peasantry was mistrusted and considered to be the bedrock of the petty-bourgeoisie. Most of the party also remained hostile to private, individual landholding, that was, within the traditional framework of the commune and the household, the form of landholding most favoured by the peasants. The Bolsheviks did not recognize the commune and persistently talked about authority being exercised by village committees and, increasingly, rural soviets. The government had also been consistently hostile to the break-up of large estates fearing, quite rightly, that their disappearance would threaten the food surplus essential for supplying the towns, cities and the army. Thus, Bolshevik support for the peasant revolution contained very significant areas of what remained, for the time being, small print. As yet, however, the government had no power to implement its deeper levels of policy.

It has always been known that there was peasant resistance to the government but it has only been with the work of Kabanov, Figes and Brovkin that we have more idea about its nature. There were scattered political uprisings but, in the nature of things these were sporadic and isolated though they could be significant for a region. According to the Cheka there were 108 large-scale peasant uprisings in European Russia between July and November 1918 and Soviet historians uncovered traces of a multitude of peasant disturbances. Orlando Figes also gives examples of various uprisings in Saratov in protest at the state grain monopoly and the *kombedy*. In a particularly serious example, villagers in Kuchek murdered 11 members of the *kombed* and a group of food brigade workers and set up their own military–political organization that issued leaflets calling on neighbouring villages to arm against the "alien food brigades, which have given power to hooligans calling themselves members of the 'rural poor'". As a result, a sizeable group of armed peasants fought off the food brigades before being quelled by Red Guards sent from Petrograd.[36] Figes concludes that such uprisings were "neither 'kulak' nor counter-revolutionary in character" and "they commanded the support of the whole peasantry" in areas where the *kombedy* had got out of hand. With the turn towards the middle peasant, Lenin himself came to blame the *kombedy's* "reckless destruction of the middle peasantry's interests" as the main cause of the revolts.[37] It has also long been known that there were "green" groups – so-called because they were neither White nor Red, not because they were precocious conservationists – who tried to resist both sides. But these were forms of resistance that only a small proportion of peasants turned to. There were less dramatic, but much more widespread forms that were more typical. The majority of peasants seem to have engaged in passive and economic resistance.

The most significant example of passive resistance was their response to conscription. Again according to Figes, whose work constitutes the most systematic survey of the question, barely 20 per cent of conscripts in the Volga region reported for duty in 1918. Three thousand peasants participated in an anti-conscription uprising. In some cases sophisticated arguments against war were put forward as the reason. One village gathering said "We refuse to have anything to do with war or human suffering, since this is against human rights and can only benefit the authorities" while another agreed to conscription only on condition that the Whites refused a negotiated peace.[38] Non-arrival at recruiting points was matched, in some cases, by desertion rates up to 80 per cent in some front-line units. In the second half of 1919 there were 1.5 million deserters and draft dodgers who frequently hid out in the forests and formed the core of green bands. According to Figes the majority were largely motivated by economic reasons, notably the need to work on the farm especially to get in the harvest. Weight is given to this suggestion by the fact that after August a million delayed draftees turned up at the recruiting points.[39] Figes argues that it was only in 1920 that desertion became more political but it seems likely that the peasants' anti-state instincts and even, perhaps, traces of Tolstoyanism helped shape their response in the earlier period also. Be that as it may, it is clear that the peasantry as a whole was reluctanct to join in what was, for the vast majority of them, a remote and perhaps illegitimate war in 1918. The improved recruitment of late summer 1919 might also be attributable to the the improved party infrastructure in the provinces but even more to peasants' growing sense of urgency as the Whites encroached on the Volga region and threatened the return of the landlords, an eventuality against which the peasants were prepared to fight.[40]

The civil war was also a period of massive economic resistance on the part of peasants. They resented the *chreznalog* (special tax), the grain monopoly and *prodrazverstka* (forced requisitioning). They especially resented the arbitrary means of implementing government policy. For instance, the *kombedy*, in which the peasants had no faith, decided who should hand over what in terms of tax and guided the requisition squads to peasants' grain stores.[41] In order to avoid such exactions the peasants took numerous steps. In the first place, they had a tradition of falsifying returns declaring the size of their landholding to such an extent that one Soviet statistician claimed in 1922 that some 15 per cent of arable land may have "disappeared" from official view in the census of 1917.[42] They might also simply stop cultivating part of their land, contributing to the catastrophic contraction of the sown area by 17 per cent in 1919 and 11.3 per cent in 1920.[43] When requisitioning was introduced on certain types of grain normally consumed in the city (like rye and wheat), the peasants switched to buckwheat which was largely consumed in the village.[44] As the scope of requisitioning broadened in 1919 to cover all main products they tried to avoid it by night harvesting as well as concealment of produce. The best known form of avoidance was the continuation of a suppressed market. Alongside the legal market for non-requisitioned produce that was never fully abolished, there was an illegal parallel economy of considerable proportions. Illegal traders, known as "bagmen", swarmed into the villages and overloaded the trains by carrying supplies into the cities. Lenin himself was aware that they were essential to the survival of the towns. He claimed that workers obtained half of their food from the state for 10 per cent of their outlay and half from the market for 90 per cent of their outlay. In addition to resisting requisitioning, peasants also concealed renting arrangements and wage labour from the authorities. Without such deals landless village "outsiders" – refugees and former urban dwellers – would have had no means of survival in the countryside.[45] Peasants also increased their economic self-sufficiency, not only by the traditional expedient of home-distilling of vodka, *samogon'* but, more seriously, by substituting urban industrial products – that were scarce and out of their price range – by a revival of rural artisanal and cottage production that further destabilized the economic relations of town and country.[46]

Through 1919 the exactions of the state had collapsed into chaos. In 1918, 76 per cent of taxes had been collected in money. By 1920 they represented only 0.2 per cent of the state budget.[47] For the peasants 99.3 per cent of taxes were natural, that is, in kind – 65.6 per cent forced requisitioning of produce, 25.5 per cent state labour and haulage duties and 8.1 per cent mobilization of horses. The tax burden on them appears to have at least doubled compared to pre-war.[48] The speed of introduction and replacement or modification of taxes and the arbitrary means of collection suggest that they were no more than an ill-thought-out series of arbitrary and desperate expedients. In any case, the collection system was haphazard. According to Figes the procurement campaigns of 1918–19 failed because of "the breakdown of the state infrastructure at every stage of the procurement process". In addition to obstacles, such as the destruction of bridges, caused by the war, there were many resulting from chronic inefficiency, arbitrariness and disorder. The wrong quantities were levied, central storage depots were inadequate, trains were stripped clean as they travelled. Soviets even set up road blocks to prevent grain from leaving the local area. Peasants received only 10–65 per cent of the promised industrial goods in exchange for their produce.[49]

The peasants' struggle against the government was like that of an oversized beetle caught in a web. Its ungainly writhings used up its strength while the smaller but more active and mobile spider continued to run round it, binding it with tighter and tighter threads, although without any certainty which of the two would become exhausted first. Characteristically, the government spider had begun to spin its web of political controls from the top down. In the free conditions between February and October 1917 the peasants voted overwhelmingly to be represented by SRs and continued to vote for them until they had no choice in the matter. The last such free vote was for the Constituent Assembly in which the SRs obtained half of the overall vote. In the rather confused conditions of October 1917 and January 1918, the SRs continued to dominate the Extraordinary, Second and Third All-Russian Congresses of Soviets of Peasants' Deputies. By then of course, the choice had become complicated by the split in the SR party and the fluctuating relationship between the Left SRs and the Bolsheviks. The hastily convened Extraordinary Congress, held in mid-November 1917, is thought to have had about 330 delegates of whom 260 were SRs, 195 from the Left and 65 from the Right of that party. Even though soldiers appear to have been disproportionately represented at the Congress the Bolsheviks still had only around 37 deputies. No other party had double figure representation. The continuing fluidity of party discipline is shown by the fact that when the Right SRs staged a walkout they took some 150 delegates with them – and must therefore have been joined by some of the Left SRs – leaving some 175 delegates in the Congress. The same complexity is shown by the fact, which alarmed the Bolsheviks, that the remaining delegates voted to refuse to hear a speech by Lenin and even proposed the election of the Right SR leader, Chernov, as honorary president.[50]

In the next few months a series of rival peasant congresses, elected unsystematically, produced a variety of results. At the Second Congress (26 November–11 December) there were 796 deputies, 511 of whom had voting rights. Three hundred and five were Right SRs, 350 Left SRs and 91 Bolsheviks.[51] However, in the last Peasant Congress which met in January 1918 the Bolsheviks had more delegates than the Left SRs.[52] Its only task was to wind up separate peasant representation and merge with the Congress of Soviets of Workers' and Soldiers' Deputies. The shifts represent centrally controlled political manoeuvring rather than changes in peasant thinking.

The composition of the most important peasant assemblies convened in 1918 show the results of the continuation of the process of central interference. Some 60 per cent of the 534 deputies to the All-Russian Congress of

Land Committees, that met in January 1918, supported the Soviet Government. However, 150 deputies were Left SRs. Only 81 were Bolsheviks.[53] Of the rest, 157 of the 534 delegates (about 30 per cent) walked out in response to a Right SR appeal for a boycott.[54] The equivalent meeting in December – of the All-Russian Congress of Land Departments, *kombedy* and Agricultural Communes – had 550 delegates. This time the overwhelming majority, 456, were Communists, 68 sympathizers, 14 non-party, seven Left SRs and five others.[55] Even though, by this time, the situation had changed radically in spring and summer 1918 in that the Left SRs had, as Pershin laconically expresses it, "left the scene" and the renewed civil war was getting under way, there can be no doubt that the figures were totally unrelated to the political preferences of the peasantry as a whole. They did, however, testify to the short-term political effectiveness of the *kombedy* in providing a political wedge for the party in the countryside. They had enabled it to establish a virtual one-party system in rural Russia even though the medium-term political and economic costs were incalculable.

None the less, there can be no doubt that, in reality, peasant communists were few and far between. In 1917 there were officially 203 peasant cells in the party and 2,304 in 1918. Between early 1918 and early 1919 the number of peasants in the party rose from 16,700 to 54,900.[56] This rise is probably accounted for by poor peasants joining the party when the *kombedy* were active. Although the number of rural party cells was 7,370 with 97,119 members in November 1918, the majority were probably workers in factories located in rural areas and party officials in the countryside.

In the face of the chronic weakness of the party among the peasants – a situation that persisted until collectivization in 1929 when the peasantry was, in effect, destroyed – the authorities asserted their control through heavy-handed means. While, as Lenin eventually came to realize, it was vital to win over the support of the middle peasantry, the government was forced to rely on a network of local dictatorships, focused on local and regional soviets, that were, as we have seen, thoroughly distrusted by the peasants. Thus, a vicious circle was created. Lack of peasant support forced authoritarian means on the party; the means alienated the peasants further; peasant alienation, expressed in rebellion and passive resistance, was interpreted by the authorities as "kulak sabotage",[57] in the face of which they felt justified in stepping up the pressure; this in turn caused more peasant resentment and so the circle turned.

The government confronted the problem by relying not only on soviets set up from above rather than the peasants' own committees and communes but also in dominating the soviets through executive committees dependent on the higher echelons of the state and party bureaucracy rather than on the peasants whom they were supposed to represent. While the general picture has long been known from the work of Russian historians, Figes' local study puts additional flesh on the bones. Only around 10 per cent of village soviets in the Simbirsk and neighbouring region had communist members and less than 1 per cent of the village electorate were registered Bolsheviks. However, as one moves up the soviet hierarchy, even at local level, the proportion of Bolsheviks rises dramatically. Some 14 per cent of village and 50 per cent of *volost'* executive committee members belonged to the party in 1919, even though many party members were posted away from the localities and thrown into the military front-line.[58] Data from 18 provinces collected in 1920 show that, at *uezd* level, where party domination was even stronger, the pre-revolutionary occupations of executive committee members were: workers 33 per cent, white-collar 25 per cent, peasants 21 per cent, teachers 8 per cent, other professions 8 per cent, students 1 per cent, technicians 1 per cent.[59] One can only concur with Figes' conclusion that:

> During the early period of the revolution the majority of the VIKs [*volost'* executive committees] comprised up to a dozen or more peasants, and perhaps one or two rural *intelligenty*, who met on an amateur and non-partisan basis to implement the resolutions of the *volost'* assembly. By the end of 1920, most of the VIKs had become bureaucratized state organs, run by three to five executive members, most of them in the Bolshevik party, and a team of salaried officials.[60]

The conclusion is all the more convincing in that precisely the same thing was happening to the rest of the state apparatus.

None the less, one also has to take into account the fact that the peasantry, in the final analysis, preferred the arbitrary and oppressive Soviet institutions to the return of the Whites. At least the Soviet government left them in control of their land. The peasant fear of restoration is testified to by the fact that they kept land confiscated from the landlords in a separate fund from the rest of the commune land in case they might be forced to return it.[61] Despite difficulties they did supply recruits. Seventy-seven per cent of the four million-strong Red Army was made up of peasant conscripts in 1920.[62] They did give large quantities of grain to supply the needs of the army and a proportion of what the city needed, although they received next to nothing in exchange.

Even more significantly, there was nowhere in the entire Empire where significant numbers of peasants supported the Whites. Even in cossack regions the villages refused to go along with the military chieftains. As a result, the Volunteer Army was only grudgingly tolerated on cossack territory not only because of its espousal of centralization that the cossacks opposed, but also because of the internal tensions their presence created within the cossack community. The White cause of Russian chauvinism, anti-semitism, restoration of landowners, return to the old class system and restoration of property had no appeal to the peasants. The Whites were, of course, forced to conscript peasants but, although evidence is not systematic, it seems that the degree of violence they had to use was greater and the desertion rates even more fearsome than with the Reds, suggesting they had more difficulty in getting peasant support. What is beyond doubt is that their complete failure to find a popular base doomed them to inevitable defeat.

However, it also follows that, when the defeat of the Whites finally came in 1920, the peasants' limited, conditional support for the Soviet government, was no longer to be relied upon. From being the lesser of two evils the Communist government became the single main evil in the eyes of the peasantry. As a result the barely contained rebelliousness of the peasants was to flare up into a last flame of popular resistance in 1920 and early 1921. Before turning to that, however, we need to look at the new government's policies for industry and, even more crucial, the response of workers to the self-proclaimed proletarian state.

Productionism: the highest stage of Bolshevism

The rural economy was the result of the destruction of the conventional Russian economy by corrosive revolutionary forces that were at the time themselves severely modified when the moment came to construct the new order. The industrial economy went through a similar process. Destruction of Russia's pre-revolutionary economy was hastened in 1917 by supporting the democratization of production. The new order, however, led to a major modification of principles. Experiments in genuine workers' control were short-lived. There was a rapid return to imposed discipline. This was achieved through the agencies of party, state, trade union and Cheka as well as the return to the principle of one-person management and the encouragement of former managers to stay on and work for high salaries (the equivalent of the tsarist officers who fought in the Red Army). As in other areas of the new system, there was rapid growth of centralization.

The economic system that emerged had little in common with the expectations of 1917. This is particularly true with respect to Lenin's assumptions. The vagueness of his views on the economy before October was ruthlessly exposed. As we have seen, Lenin, in the April Theses, saw the first step of the revolution not as one of "immediate introduction" of socialism but a transitional one of soviet "supervision" of production and distribution. This implied that, for a while, capitalism and the market would continue to operate alongside the new political order. It would be replaced bit by bit, though the timescale for this was never clear. True, more ambitious plans surfaced during Lenin's feverish drive for power in September, but the main theme was one of temporary cohabitation of capitalist industry, petty-bourgeois agriculture and socialist Soviet political structures. The proposed set of relationships collapsed like a house of cards. Capitalists and managers were not prepared to abandon their side of class war while it was being vigorously conducted against them. Rather than recognizing the impossibility of struggling against the overwhelming mass of the population, which is what Lenin had argued would happen, they fought energetically to protect their property and position. In the early months, capitalist co-operation with the new authorities was minimal, struggle against them widespread. There were few significant examples of management agreeing to work under conditions of workers' control (in the sense of supervision of management by workers, of a kind of joint management, in other words). The failure of such relations to evolve led to the withdrawal of managers and owners and exacerbated the collapse of factories, industries and whole economic sectors that, in turn, necessitated complete worker takeover and increasing state involvement as a last resort. Rather than stay on under the new conditions many, perhaps most, capitalists and managers preferred to abandon their factories and take refuge in White areas or try their luck abroad.

By early 1918 Lenin realized the risks for the revolution and began to make concessions to persuade managers to stay on and thereby salvage his vision of what he called "state capitalism" as the first stage of socialist transition. The new emphasis – that involved paying managers much higher salaries than workers and restoring authority to them at the expense of workers' soviets, factory committees and trade unions – outraged the left of the party.

Even in the early months of 1918 the principles of discipline and production emerged. They dominated Soviet economic life until the end, surviving many twists and turns. Prior to the October revolution, Lenin assumed that there would be a spontaneous releasing of resources as a result of freeing the population from oppression by capitalists and landowners. The Bolsheviks' opponents in the Soviet had, of course, based their opposition to the Bolsheviks precisely on the argument that such a scenario was nothing but a fantasy, hence the need for collaboration with the bourgeoisie. It was small consolation to them that the Bolsheviks themselves were now having to face up to the extreme difficulties caused by this cold douche of reality.

Lenin began to redefine the revolution in the light of these experiences. His post-revolutionary discourse quickly began to take into account the fact that correct consciousness was, as yet, insufficient. In place of arguing that the support of nine-tenths of the population would make the transition "gradual, peaceful and smooth" Lenin reverted to other themes. In particular, consciousness became linked with "iron discipline" and was backed up by an increasingly menacing discourse of "harmony" and the rediscovered "backwardness" of Russia, conveniently overlooked in the optimistic belief in a smooth transition. In April 1918 Lenin, in "The Immediate Tasks of the Soviet Government", started out from the assumption that the most important feature of the situation was "the ruthless struggle against chaos and disorganisation".[63] Of course, the Lenin of September 1917 had dismissed fears of chaos and disorganization and proposed the Soviet takeover as a way of avoiding them. Now, however, the reality, that had always been apparent to his critics, had become central to Lenin. He still argued that the revolution "can be successfully carried out only if the majority of the population, and primarily the

majority of the working people, engage in independent creative work as mak-
ers of history". [64] But this discourse of free creativity was bound in with another on class-consciousness and discipline. Discussion centred on "a big
word" – dictatorship that is "iron rule, government that is revolutionarily
bold, swift and ruthless in suppressing both exploiters and hooligans". [65]
Lenin then went on to argue that, since large-scale machine industry required
"absolute and strict unity of will" and that it was also "the foundation of socialism" [66], it followed that socialism also required "that the people unques-
tioningly obey the single will of the leaders of labour". [67]

He also began to discover new theoretical foundations for the developing
authoritarian system. "Socialism", he argued, "owes its origin to large-scale
machine industry. If the masses of working people, in introducing socialism,
prove incapable of adapting their institutions to the way that large-scale
industry should work, then there can be no question of introducing socialism".[68] In May, in an argument with the left communists, he stated that the
most up-to-date forms of capitalist economic organization should be combined with Soviet political organization to produce "the sum total of the conditions necessary for socialism. Socialism is inconceivable without large-scale
capitalist engineering based on the latest discoveries of modern science. It is
inconceivable without planned state organization, that keeps tens of millions
of people to the strictest observance of a unified standard in production and
distribution."[69] Even the most hated systems of mass production should be
adopted.

> We must raise the question of piece work and apply and test it in
> practice; we must raise the question of applying much of what is sci-
> entific and progressive in the Taylor system; we must make wages
> correspond to the total amount of goods turned out . . . The task that
> the Soviet Government must set the people in all its scope is – learn to
> work. The Taylor system, the last word of capitalism in this respect,
> like all capitalist progress, is a combination of the refined brutality of
> bourgeois exploitation and a number of the greatest scientific
> achievements in the field of analysing mechanical motions during
> work, the elimination of superfluous and awkward motions, the
> elaboration of correct methods of work, the introduction of the best
> system of accounting and control, etc . . . The possibility of building
> socialism depends exactly upon our success in combining the Soviet
> power and Soviet organization of administration [sic] with the up-to-
> date achievements of capitalism.[70]

Trotsky was even more emphatic:

> Under capitalism, the system of piece-work and of grading, the appli-
> cation of the Taylor system, etc., have as their object to increase the

exploitation of workers by the squeezing-out of surplus value. Under socialist production, piece-work, bonuses etc., have as their aim to increase the volume of social product and consequently to raise the general well-being.[71]

Lenin continued to believe that, somehow, the contradictory halves of his discourse – creative freedom/iron discipline – could be brought together. Can dictatorship be linked to creative freedom? "Given ideal class-consciousness and discipline on the part of those participating in the common work, this subordination would be something like the mild leadership of a conductor of an orchestra". But, Lenin went on, "It may assume the sharp forms of a dicta-torship if ideal discipline and class-consciousness are lacking".[72] Given the fact that the entire article was aimed at the indiscipline of the situation it fol-lows that, for Lenin, ideal conditions were absent. Thus, it becomes clear that Lenin attributed the ruthlessness of the dictatorship to the absence of "ideal class-consciousness and discipline", not simply to the ravages of war and class struggle. None the less, he still believed there was a way out. "We must", Lenin concluded, "learn to combine the 'public meeting' democracy of the working people – turbulent, surging, overflowing its banks like a spring flood – with iron discipline while at work, with *unquestioning obedience* to the will of a single person, the Soviet leader, while at work". Not surprisingly, Lenin wrote, "We have not yet learned to do this".[73] Indeed, earlier in the article he had commented that, far from being dictatorial "our government is exces-sively mild, very often it resembles jelly more than iron".[74]

In this way, subordination to a single will, supposedly limited to when a per-son was at work, although this was a purely artificial distinction, opened up a more "Stalinist" set of propositions. They were also being put forward before the civil war proper had begun. Nowhere in the article did Lenin argue that the deepening civil war is shaping the system. To the contrary he argued that "the nearer we approach the complete military suppression of the bourgeoisie, the more dangerous does the element of petty-bourgeois anarchy become"[75] im-plying that the nearer one is to victory the greater the need for discipline and dictatorship, a thought analogous to Stalin's view that the closer the state came to withering away the more it had to assert itself. Lenin did, however, revert to a quite different law of revolution from the one he had been promoting in autumn 1917. "[E]very great revolution, and a socialist revolution in particu-lar, even if there is no external war, is inconceivable without internal war, i.e. civil war, which is even more devastating than external war, and involves thou-sands and millions of cases of wavering and desertion from one side to another, implies a state of extreme indefiniteness, lack of equilibrium and chaos".[76] So much for gradual, peaceful and smooth transitions.

Naturally enough, given the collapse of the economy and the growing needs of the military, production was a genuine preoccupation. The Bolshevik gov-ernment had inherited a major industrial crisis that had, since October, become worse by several orders of magnitude. The new authorities tried to prop up as much of the industrial economy as could be salvaged. Initially, this meant trying to keep industries going as "normally" as possible (though with increased levels of worker participation in management) and, when that failed, resorting to the emergency measure of nationalization. From spring 1918 the number of nationalizations multiplied. There was little method to the process, its course being defined simply by the degree of collapse faced by a factory or sector. Power companies, workshops, the Putilov factory, the merchant navy, were all taken over in the early months. The first entire industry to be nationalized was sugar in May 1918, quickly followed by oil in June, though in both cases the main production centres, in the Ukraine and the Caspian respectively, were beyond the government's reach in the post-Brest-Litovsk and incipient civil war conditions then obtaining.[77]

In the language of the time, nationalizations were either "punitive" (that is to punish owners for "sabotage" or other misdemeanour) or "spontaneous" (that is, they collapsed into the hands of workers and Soviet authorities in the absence of anyone else to keep them going).[78] This was given political significance through Bolshevik sponsorship of the enticing slogan "Loot the looters" that, in the early months, substituted for an economic policy. Excessively literal interpretation by workers, who dismantled machines and engaged in massive pilfering of stocks and equipment, was a continual problem. Cases of workers cutting slices out of conveyor belts to make new soles for boots were typical of the way that the shortage of goods created a vicious circle. The shifts to which the population was put in order to survive cut across efforts to remedy the situation.

The haphazard takeover of industries meant it was a prime necessity for the state to try to run them. To co-ordinate their activities, particularly in view of the need for maximizing the use of resources as the civil war stepped up in intensity, a Supreme Council of the National Economy (*Vesenkha*) was set up in December 1917. It gradually took on the role of overall supervision while, at the same time, various departments (*glavki*) were set up to run the particular sectors of industry, over which they exerted an as yet imperfect and inefficient monopoly control. They relied heavily on non-Bolshevik specialists including SR and Menshevik economists. Through empirical experience as much as theory, the idea of co-ordination through a central economic plan began to gain ground. This eventually resulted, in April 1921, in the establishment of the State Planning Commission (*Gosplan*). In the conditions of the time the idea of a comprehensive plan was completely utopian but the example of the capitalist war economies, especially Germany, which had evolved forms of centralized state planning, had had considerable influence on Lenin and other party leaders. For the time being, however, hand-to-mouth allocation of increasingly scarce resources was more typical than anything resembling the emerging vision of a harmonious and expanding centrally planned industrial economy.

The corollary of the emphasis on production was a return to labour discipline. It was assumed, quite contrary to the expectations of 1917, that strong management rather than self-management would achieve higher output. The entire party and state apparatus was brought into line behind this goal. Since the one thing that might have smoothed the way – high real wages and something to buy with them – was completely out of the question, given the increasing chaos of Russia's economy in 1918 and 1919, exhortation by party and state activists, backed up by police action where necessary, were the only means available. Even labour conscription, which was proposed, notably by Trotsky, was eventually implemented. Labour armies, modelled on military units, were formed. By and large, apart from punitive actions against former "parasites", compulsory labour seems to have been confined, for the most part to calling up unskilled workers to break particular short-term bottlenecks in forestry, transport and so on. Cynics might see in this a peculiar "socialist" form of *corvée* (labour obligation). The peak of the revolutionary war in late 1919 and its winding down in 1920 brought the necessity and the opportunity of extending the system. As military units became disengaged, so they were transferred to labour tasks. This set the scene for the drive to "militarization" of labour. At the time of the Ninth Party Congress (March 1920) and the Third All-Russian Congress of Trade Unions (April 1920) party leaders, on left and right, brought forward rather ominous justifications for the practice. The most forthright came from Trotsky:

> We are now advancing towards a type of labour socially regulated on the basis of an economic plan which is obligatory for the whole country, i.e. compulsory for every worker. That is the foundation of socialism . . . And once we have recognized this, we thereby recognize fundamentally – not formally, but fundamentally – the right of the workers' state to send each working man and woman to the place where they are needed for the fulfilment of economic tasks. We thereby recognize the right of the state, of the workers' state, to punish the working man or woman who refuses to carry out the order of the state, who does not subordinate his will to the will of the working class and to its economic tasks.[79]

Trotsky's knowledge of Marxism seems to have failed him at this point. Instead of looking forward to unalienated, truly free labour under socialist conditions he defined all work as "socially compulsory labour. Man must work in order not to die. He does not want to work. But the social organization compels and whips him in that direction".[80] Others on the left echoed the theme. Radek appealed "to organized labour to overcome the bourgeois prejudice of 'freedom of labour' so dear to the hearts of Mensheviks and compromisers of every kind".[81] For Bukharin, compulsory labour was not "the enslavement of the working class" as it had been in capitalist conditions but was rather, under the dictatorship of the proletariat, "the self-organization of the working class".[82] On the right of the party, the same message came across. Rykov claimed it was "the waster and the blockhead" who "must be forced under fear of punishment to work for the workers and peasants in order to save them from hunger and penury".[83] Lenin remained more oblique in his comments arguing that "labour must be organized in a new way, new forms of incentives to work, of submission to labour discipline, must be created".[84] The central message of his speech was "let us get closer to one-person management, let us have more labour discipline, let us pull ourselves together and work with military determination, staunchness and loyalty, brushing aside all group and craft interests, sacrificing all private interests".[85] The resolution adopted called for the immediate introduction in all trade unions of "severe labour discipline from below upwards", whatever that meant.[86] Two weeks earlier Lenin had been a little more direct when he said "we must create by means of the trade unions such comradely discipline as we had in the Red Army".[87]

The various barks were, in fact, considerably worse than the associated bite. Universal labour conscription and the militarization of labour never became dominant, not least because of the resistance of workers themselves to such practices, a late victory of the popular movement over the Bolsheviks, and also because they were so directly contradictory to the ideals and policies of the revolution that serious minority opposition to them was mounted within the party itself.

The revolution in the factories

No Russian worker would have considered her or his experiences in the aftermath of the October revolution to constitute a "golden age". The economic crisis that had played a major part in stimulating the revolutionary activity of workers, continued and even worsened. In the early months of Soviet power the urban, industrial economy was in free fall. For three and a half years nothing was done that halted the process, let alone brought any upturn. Factory production collapsed. The growing disruption of transport broke the fragile interconnections between the supply of raw materials, production and distribution to markets. These last were themselves collapsing as a result of inflation and chaotic social reorganization. Workers abandoned hungry, ill-supplied cities, above all those like Petrograd that were situated in grain-importing areas, to seek survival back in their villages. Parts of the middle and upper classes fled Soviet-held territory for the greater security of the newly independent and White-held areas.

None the less, with the very important proviso that the industrial sector as a whole was in a state of continuing collapse until 1921, it is possible to distinguish two phases in the political and organizational life of industry that roughly correspond to the "golden age" and repressive phases observable in the countryside. In the first few months after October, important parts of the workers' institutional agenda were implemented. By late spring and early summer of 1918 this had given way to unrelenting pressure for centralization.

In the forefront of the achievements of workers in the early days were the overthrow of private ownership; the extension of workers' control and/or nationalization; widespread democratization of workplaces and the growth of organized working-class power in factory committees, trades unions, soviets and, to a more limited extent, in national institutions. On the face of it, this would appear to be a series of massive steps towards the attainment of the proletarian revolution which is what, after all, October was supposed to be, according to its leaders. Unfortunately, here, as elsewhere in Russian history before and since October, there was no silver lining without its accompanying cloud. Even the apparent gains of the early months prove, on closer examination, to be highly ambiguous in their impact on working-class life. They fell very far short of fulfilling the deepest aspirations of workers that had surfaced so forcefully in 1917.

An excellent example is provided by the most dramatic development of the post-October period – the rapid liquidation of private ownership of the industrial economy. Within a few months the impossible dream of nineteenth- and early-twentieth-century radical workers had come true. The bosses had been expelled. Surely, this must have been a major gain for workers? In fact, it did not bring the hoped-for benefits. In the first place, the whole process was conducted chaotically and further disrupted the running of factories. Many owners attempted to worsen the situation in their own enterprises in the hope that the militant workers would be brought to their knees and would beg the owners to return to sort out the mess on their own terms. But the owners had badly miscalculated. Nowhere did workers call for owners to come back.

More disruptive than the disappearance of the owners was the flight of managers, senior white-collar employees and engineers. Without them enterprises ground to a halt. Their skills and knowledge in organizing supplies to the factories, distributing finished products, organizing the work process, controlling the finances, repairing and maintaining ageing equipment and so on were absolutely essential. Without them, manual workers were helpless until such a time, far into the future, when they could acquire the skills for themselves. Even so, the workers did not want concessions to be made to managers and engineers. It was the Soviet authorities who attempted to keep managers in post through financial and other incentives. Highly paid "specialists" were very unpopular on the shop floor.

The rapid collapse of the factory hierarchy posed obvious and immediate problems. What would replace the old authorities? How would the discipline essential to the efficient running of a factory be restored and maintained? It was here that, in the short term, a "golden age" of worker self-administration briefly flourished.

Workers continued to press for a democratic order within the factories and a bewildering variety of organizational forms within industrial enterprises emerged very quickly to replace those of the old owners. These forms are usually referred to under the rather loose term "workers' control". As we have seen, the phrase is itself ambiguous. Its Russian meaning is closer to "workers' supervision", that is checking management, rather than outright control.

However, such niceties of definition were lost in the harsh conditions prevailing in 1917. The main impulse of workers after October continued to be the one that had increasingly gripped them before October and that had led them to support Soviet power – namely the urge to survive, to save their jobs in order to keep their increasingly meagre income alive. We still have to bear in mind that, above all, workers wanted to save their industries and restore the economy. Their political outlook continued to be the expression of more fundamental aspirations.

A kaleidoscopic variety of forms of workers' control emerged, often as emergency measures stitched together to meet an immediate crisis threatening the particular institution. Factory committees, shop committees in the larger enterprises, unions, enterprise general meetings took on key roles. The Bolshevik party had gained extensive support among workers before October by appearing to support such initiatives. It is no surprise then that, in the aftermath of October, it appears, from the fragments of information available, that they flourished as never before. Enterprise after enterprise was taken over.

Even by the time of the October revolution, 68.7 per cent of factories employing more than 200 (22 per cent of all factories) had factory committees. The more up-to-date the factory the more likely it was to have a committee. Nearly two-thirds of committees (79 per cent in the factories employing more than 200) were taking an active part in management.[88] Between November 1917 and March 1918, 836 enterprises were nationalized. In 75 per cent of cases the initiative came from the localities – trade union, soviet or factory committee. Only 5 per cent were nationalized on the initiative of the centre.[89]

There are also a number of examples of local workers' control organizations, including local and regional associations of factory committees, attempting to extend their powers. In the immediate aftermath of the October uprising, a delegate from the Petrograd Central Council of Factory Committees visited Lenin with proposals for industry to be run democratically by elected workers.[90] Regionalism also emerged with Ural and Volga workers calling for more control over their localities.[91]

The spread of worker self-administration was a major issue at the First All-Russian Congress of Trades Unions held in Petrograd in early January. A minority of anarcho-syndicalist speakers, not unnaturally, stressed its importance. One rank-and-file factory committee spokesperson said "the only way out remaining to workers is to take the factories into their own hands and manage them".[92] Another called for the working class "to organize in the localities and create a free, new Russia without a God, without a Tsar and without a boss in the trade union".[93] Cries of alarm from those at the conference who wanted to slow down the pace of development of factory committees only testify to their increasing importance. Lozovsky, a leading Bolshevik, said "the factory committees were so much the owners and masters that, three months after the revolution they were to a significant degree independent of the central controlling organs".[94] One Menshevik speaker said "it was not just some of the proletariat, but most of the proletariat, especially in Petrograd, who looked upon workers' control as if it were actually the emergence of the kingdom of socialism . . . The very idea of socialism is embodied in the concept of workers' control". Another Menshevik complained that "an anarchist wave in the shape of factory committees and workers' control was sweeping over our Russian labour movement".[95]

However accurate these comments are in matters of detail, it is clear that workers were energetically implementing part of their democratic agenda, but were finding there were no instant solutions to their deep-rooted problems. To make matters worse, the party began to try to take matters in hand.

From its very origin, the party had distrusted worker initiatives from below. For Lenin, the proper relationship was, as we have seen, always one in which, ultimately, the workers as a whole would follow the party since the latter was the embodiment of "advanced" class-consciousness to which the majority of the workers should aspire. In the party debates of the February and October period the tendency to subordinate the workers to the Bolshevik leadership was frequently expressed. At the Sixth Party Congress (26 July–3 August 1917), Miliutin said "we will ride on the crest of the economic wave of the workers' movement and will turn this spontaneous movement into a conscious political movement".[96] Lenin himself had tended to give a rather minimalist definition of workers' control. During the campaign for the October revolution he argued, in "Can the Bolsheviks retain state power", that:

> when we say workers' control, always juxtaposing this slogan to the dictatorship of the proletariat, and always putting it immediately after the latter, we thereby explain what kind of state we mean . . . [I]f we are speaking of a proletarian state that is, of proletarian dictatorship, then workers' control can become the country-wide, all-embracing, omnipresent, most precise and most conscientious accounting of the production and distribution of goods.[97]

It was also beginning to emerge that, at least in the early stages, the agent of renewed centralization would be party-dominated, national trades unions. When the First (and, as it turned out, only independent) All-Russian Conference of Factory Committees met (17–22 October 1917) Bolshevik speakers began to show this emphasis. Otto Shmidt, soon to be Commissar for Labour, said "At the moment when the factory committees were formed, the trade unions actually did not yet exist. The factory committees filled the vacuum".[98]

Even more explicitly another Bolshevik speaker pointed out that "the growth of the influence of the factory committees has naturally occurred at the expense of centralized economic organizations of the working class, such as the trades unions. This, of course, is a highly abnormal development which has in practice led to very undesirable results".[99]

After October, Bolshevik leaders became increasingly outspoken and the factory committee movement was repeatedly attacked. Lenin was quick to draft a decree on workers' control that was an attempt to limit the process rather than promote it. Its first points gave wide scope to workers in enterprises of five or more employees to intervene in all aspects of management. (It should be emphasized that, at this early stage, it was still assumed that enterprises would continue to be privately owned.) However, in its later clauses, significant qualifications were introduced. Point 5 said that decisions of workers and employees could be "annulled by trades unions and congresses". Point 6 said that in "all enterprises of state importance" those who exercised workers' control were "answerable to the state for the maintenance of the strictest order and discipline" and for the protection of property. Given that point 7 defined important enterprises as those "working for defence purposes, or in any way connected with the production of articles necessary for the existence of the masses of the population", one can see that the, at one level reasonable-sounding propositions, actually gave the central authorities enormous powers of intervention.[100] Such implications were even more obvious in mid-November when the draft became law in an extensively revised version that stressed the need for centralization and set up a party-dominated All-Russian Council for Workers' Control to supervise the process. The Council was used to contain workers' aspirations within acceptable channels and the party also put obstacles in the way of initiatives by decentralizers to set up regional and national meetings of factory committee delegates. As Maurice Brinton has pointed out, the party did not hesitate to claim that one of the problems with factory committees was their localism at the same time as they were suppressing initiatives aimed at linking them up on a wider basis.[101] It was increasingly implicit in these measures that trades unions, rather than factory committees, would be the chosen instruments of worker self-administration. It is this that explains the comment, by Bill Shatov at the First All-Russian Congress of Trades Unions, quoted earlier, that the new Russia would be liberated not only from God and the tsar but also from the boss in the trade union. While, in the early months, workers continued to enjoy greater democracy within the enterprise than they had done before or since, it is, none the less, clear that direct worker self-administration and their most democratic institutions, notably factory committees, were living on borrowed time.

The full story of worker reactions to the formation of the Soviet state and its evolving industrial, social and economic policies is only just beginning to be told in any detail. It was often claimed that the series of strikes, protests, demonstrations and even uprisings were isolated outbreaks caused by backward workers coming under the spell of class enemies such as Mensheviks, SRs, wily capitalists and even foreign agents. Clearly such interpretations are exaggerated. And what of the "average" worker who neither actively supported the Bolsheviks nor their opponents? What were their attitudes? While much needs to be done, we can, perhaps, establish a few preliminary contours of worker reaction to the growth of the centralized, one-party state, to war communism and to the use of centralized trades unions as agents for the transmission of Bolshevik values and policies to the workers.

In the first place, workers continued to be motivated by immediate, practical issues, as they had been throughout the revolutionary period. In the forefront were wages, working conditions, the threat of unemployment and, increasingly as conditions continued to deteriorate, the elemental question of food. It follows also that, since the situation varied from area to area, regional differences were accentuated. Workers tended to remain attached to the political means they had used since February. They continued to fight for independent institutions to defend their interests against the growing party and state monopoly. Factory committees, committees of elected factory representatives, factory mass meetings continued to exist against a background of increasing difficulties, including arrests and even shootings of protesting workers. In 1919, when conditions were at their worst, and even in 1920–21, these characteristics of the worker movement remained prominent. Workers remained attached to their mainly "labourist" agenda of defending their living standards and saw politics as the means to achieve such ends. Their aims continued to include an aspiration to the greatest amount of self-administration and direct self-government they could achieve, although it became increasingly obvious that, in the face of the one-party state, this was the aspect of their agenda that the Bolshevik government opposed most thoroughly.

It would, however, be wrong to see the workers' movement after October as no more than a continuation of pre-October. There were many absolutely vital differences, not least the massive decline in the number of workers. In Moscow the industrial proletariat fell from 190,000 workers in 1917 to 140,000 by August 1918 and 81,000 by January 1921.[102] Some leading Moscow factories were very hard hit. The Guzhon works employed 3,688 workers in 1919, 825 in 1921. Krasnyi Proletarii (Red Proletariat) fell from 2,394 in 1916 to 700 in 1919. The Dinamo factory lost two-thirds of its workers between 1918 and 1921. The Mikhel'son factory had employed 2,000 in 1913. It lost 80 per cent of them in 1918 and only 300 workers were left in 1921.[103] Petrograd's 412,000 workers of 1910 had become 148,000 by 1920.[104] In both cities the number of trained, skilled workers had fallen disproportionately and many of those who remained were yet another wave of new peasant migrants or the wives and children of workers who had left production.[105] In truth, the figures seem rather high given that – as a result of low skill levels, transport disruption, the fuel crisis and the constant search for food – hardly anything was produced. Only the Moscow textile industry expanded in this period, by 29 per cent in terms of the number of workers, comparing 1913 with 1920, a result of the demand for military uniforms.[106]

A second major difference was the existence of a "workers' state", that, far from banning trades unions or hedging them in, was encouraging a broad recruitment of workers into unions, which were, of course, intended to be controlled from the centre. How could workers respond to this unprecedented situation? Undoubtedly, the claims of the Bolshevik leadership caused hesitation, ambiguity and division among workers. The majority of activists in the Bolshevik party came from worker backgrounds, even though the émigré intelligentsia continued to dominate its leadership. Although hard to calculate, Bolshevik propaganda and promises must have had some effect in damping down opposition, not least through creaming off a sizeable proportion of the politically active and aware workers. It would, however, be unforgiveably romantic to overlook the impact of repression in backing up propaganda, a repression that, as we shall see, was used with surprising ruthlessness against protesting workers. But we should also recall the final factor, which may help to explain the ruthlessness and worker acquiescence in the last resort, the crisis of civil war and the threat of restoration. No worker wanted the owners back.

None the less, there can be no doubt that Bolshevik support among workers fell from its autumn 1917 peak. There are some spectacular examples of decline. In the textile town of Ivanovo-Voznesensk, for example, party membership fell from 7,200 to 700 by spring 1918.[107] Quite how representative this was is a matter of dispute. According to Vladimir Brovkin the Bolsheviks had lost so much support, especially in soviets, that they were already relying mainly on force by early 1918. There can be no doubt that, by 1919 and 1920, Bolshevik support among workers still at work was low and falling. It is also clear that nearly all workers who entered the party very quickly left proletarian occupations, not just to join the Red Army which would have been understandable in the circumstances, but to become managers, supervisors, propagandists, planners, party organizers and so on. In a word, most of them became part of the evolving state bureaucracy. Moscow provides a good example. According to figures gathered by William Chase, in March 1918 the Moscow party claimed 20,000 members. By March 1921 it claimed 40,000 members and candidates, of whom more than half were workers by social origin. However, only 6,000 worked in factories and more than half of these worked in administration. Factory party cells were often astonishingly small. The Dinamo factory party cell consisted of 32 people of whom only eight were involved in production.[108] In Petrograd the situation was very similar. In October 1917 the party had some 40,000 members. By August 1918 it may have been down to 7,000.[109] In 1920 it was still only 17,000.[110] One can only echo Chase's conclusion:

> The party that had risen to power in 1917 in large measure because of their influence in the factories and shops had lost its grassroots

organization and influence. Significantly, most of the party's members in factories were managers and administrators. Whereas in 1917 Communists actively participated in the assault on such personnel, by 1921 they were often the enforcers of unpopular policies not dissimilar from those enacted by their "bourgeois" predecessors.[111]

Throughout the civil war, party and workers, despite being bound together in a desperate struggle for mutual survival, none the less eyed each other mistrustfully. A whole series of worker protests are recorded for 1918–21 although in most cases the details remain sketchy and much disputed. A well known, controversial early example occurred in Petrograd in March 1918 at the time of the signing of the Brest-Litovsk Treaty. The Assembly of Petrograd Factory Delegates was formed and convened a meeting of factory committee representatives from some of the largest factories in the city on 13 March. The German advance that preceded the treaty had caused panic in Petrograd. Many workers left, including 10,000 from a single factory. The Soviet authorities were also planning to evacuate machinery and workers from key defence plants. All this highlighted the vulnerability of the workers in the new conditions. Serious accusations were made by the delegates against the new government. The preamble to the account of the meeting stated:

> The Soviets of Workers' and Soldiers' Deputies seem afraid of the workers: they are not allowing new elections, they have thrown up a wall of armor around themselves and turned into mere government organizations that no longer express the opinions of the working masses.[112]

A meeting of "socialist workers and unemployed persons" in the Narva district of the city was reported to have passed a resolution stating that "Trade Unions were involved in the organization of economic life and were losing their significance as bodies defending working-class interests . . . As for the Soviets of Deputies, they had been transformed into agencies of government power and lost their original character of class representatives of the proletariat. The workers were left without any organs of defence".[113] There were complaints that elections to factory committees were being continually postponed. Evacuation was being carried out without consultation with those involved. State orders for military output were drying up. The closure of newspapers and presses had caused severe unemployment among print workers who called for press freedom to remedy this. A follow-up meeting on 15 March adopted a resolution on the press stating that "from the very first moment of the October revolution the Bolsheviks made one of their most important goals the fight against the free word. All newspapers that criticized their activities were declared counter-revolutionary, confiscated and closed down". The authorities were, the resolution continued, "particularly assiduous in muzzling the socialist papers, the papers that are read by the workers and peasants".[114] There were protests against the massive increase in unemployment in many other areas of the city's industries. The final resolution, some four pages long, was a litany of protests against Bolshevik abuses. The October "seizure of power, accomplished in our name" was said to have been accepted by the workers of Petrograd even though it was carried out "without our knowledge and without our participation, on the eve of the Second Congress of Soviets which was to have voiced its own opinion on the question of power". Now, four months later, "we have seen our faith cruelly shattered and our hopes rudely trampled". Soviets were being by-passed in the decision making process. "The voices of workers and peasants are stifled" by delegates of an army that only exists on paper. "Soviets which do not agree with the government's policies are unceremoniously disbanded by armed force . . . [M]any times already the workers of Petrograd have heard representatives of the new regime threaten to use their machine guns or have been fired upon during their meetings and demonstrations". "They promised us immediate peace, democratic peace, peace concluded by the peoples over the heads of their governments. In fact they have given us a shameful capitulation to German imperialists . . . They promised us bread. In fact they have given us a famine of unparalleled dimensions. They have given us a civil war which is devastating the country and completely ruining its economy".[115]

While there is much dispute about how representative the criticisms were, it is undoubtedly striking that the fundamental objections of workers to the new order should have been formulated so rapidly. They were to be repeated frequently. Its resolutions are remarkable for echoing what had once appeared to be Bolshevik slogans but were now turned against them. Popular power, the Constituent Assembly, democratic institutions, economic restoration, independent workers' organizations and a general arming of the people were called for. In addition, the peace treaty was roundly denounced as were the "experiments of Soviet socialism".[116]

Throughout the country, similar protests were heard. In June 1918 workers in Tula protested against a cut in bread rations by boycotting the local soviet. Force was used to end strikes that followed on from the boycott. In Sormovo, 5,000 workers struck when a Menshevik–SR newspaper was closed. Violence was used here, too.[117] Through late spring and summer 1918 the Bolsheviks implemented drastic changes in the factories of Petrograd that fulfilled aims initially put forward by the Provisional Government, but went far beyond them in terms of means. Piecework was instituted.[118] It was not unusual for half the workers of an enterprise to be dismissed. New systems of discipline were introduced. The Soviet state even resorted to lockouts to enforce their plans.[119] Soviet power was well entrenched in Petrograd making it very difficult, since March, for workers to set up even vestigially independent organizations. The authorities were not going to make the same mistake twice. An attempted general strike called for 2 July failed because of the actions of loyal workers and Red Guards. The mass arrests that followed effectively ended the movement.[120]

Spectacular protests none the less continued into 1919. In Astrakhan, a cut in the bread ration brought on a serious mutiny in the garrison that was followed by sympathy strikes among workers, repeating the 1917 pattern of soldier protests backed up by worker action. A mass meeting was held that was surrounded without warning by loyal troops who opened fire. Two thousand were reported killed, another 2,000 taken prisoner and subsequently executed.[121] Even if the numbers are seriously exaggerated in the sources there can be no doubt of the ruthlessness of the action nor of the preparedness of the authorities to use force.

To get the measure of workers' activities in these years we can return to our example of the Putilov factory, remembering that it is not presented as typical, just a way of seeing how the developments were felt in one place. Like other factories, Putilov was under pressure to improve its miserable level of output in early 1918. The factory was accused of wasting fuel and raw materials. The authorities closed it for two weeks in July as punishment for the attempted general strike and to bring the declining workforce more securely under their thumb. Matters appeared to be coming to a head again in mid-August but, typically, it was the growing national political crisis following the Left–SR uprising and the attempted assassination of Lenin and the rising threat from the civil war which seem to have brought the workers back into line.[122]

However, during moments when the military threat receded the same old grievances came to the fore once again. In early spring 1919, Putilov workers demanded a more competent form of food distribution, the freeing of grain imports from the countryside and increases in wages and rations. Significantly, an official report concluded that the problems of Putilov arose from the influence of SRs.[123]

The example of Putilov suggests a strong element of continuity in labour protest throughout the revolutionary period. The central issues – wages and conditions – remained the same. The means – independent worker organizations, direct participation in management and democratic national institutions (notably soviets) – were also similar. Even the apparent affiliation of Putilov workers with the SRs seems to have survived from the February revolution through to 1919. This is not to say that there are not the important differences already noted – a workers' state, catastrophic working and living conditions and the civil war – but the continuities remain striking, particularly the fact that, under Bolshevik conditions as under tsarist ones, protest was so constrained that any economic protest quickly escalated into the political sphere. There is little reason to dissent from Thomas Remington's judgement that:

Workers were torn between resentment at the political regimentation of labour and loyalty to the cause of proletarian dictatorship. At various times groups of workers rebelled against Bolshevik rule. But for the most part, forced to choose between "their" regime and the unknown horrors of a White dictatorship, most willingly defended the Bolshevik cause. The effect of this dilemma may be seen in the periodic swings in the workers' political temper. When Soviet rule stood in peril, the war stimulated a spirit of solidarity and spared the regime the defection of its proletarian base. During lulls in the fighting, strikes and demonstrations broke out.[124]

It follows that the end of the civil war was a point of great danger for the Bolsheviks in their relationship with workers, and so it turned out to be. Remington's formulation also reminds us that there was worker support too for the Bolsheviks, some of which we have seen in the form of the recruitment of a minority of workers into the party. Large numbers of young, male workers also fought in the evolving Red Army. According to official figures for Moscow workers some 70 per cent of 20–24 year olds, 55 per cent in the 25–29 age group and 35 per cent of 30–35 year olds joined the Red Army.[125] Women workers plus men who were unable to fight often gave of their time and labour in voluntary extra work days, known as subbotniks, though the ratio of spontaneous enthusiasm to sullen acquiescence is hard to gauge.

However, the war alone, important though it is, cannot explain the survival of the Bolshevik government and the, at least partial, defeat of the popular movement. The Bolshevik leaders were prepared to be ruthless. The element of coercion was always present. However, it must be stressed that the success of Bolshevism lay, above all, in its ability, for the time being, to *combine* mobilization of support *with* repression of opposition, sometimes to an unbelievable degree. Yesterday's victims could well be tomorrow's activists. At crucial moments political prisoners were released to fight in defence of the Red cause and were returned to prison once the crisis was over. We must bear in mind the extraordinary capacity of Bolshevism to mobilize and to repress.[126]

Worker unrest and party discontent

In the eyes of the Bolsheviks the working class was the growing point of history, the locomotive that would pull humanity towards its bright future. The welfare of workers was its first priority. It is, therefore, not at all surprising that the unrest of many workers was reflected within the party itself. The factiousness of the Bolshevik party, which had been one of its notable features since its origin, did not miraculously melt away once power was taken. In the first four years of the revolution a succession of oppositions emerged, the Left Communists, the Democratic Centralists, the Workers' Opposition. While each was significantly different from the others they did, none the less, have important similarities. A major concern of all of them was the contrast between the programme and promises of 1917 and the realities of the civil war period. Far from being expendable luxuries, fundamental values of democracy and self-administration of workers were seen as being crucial to the survival of the revolution and to its spread abroad. The abandonment of pure working-class policies was excoriated by the oppositions. In their view, too many concessions were being made to capitalists, managers, tsarist army officers, the bourgeoisie and the petty-bourgeois elements of the peasantry. The workers were the ones who suffered as a result. Their gains were being lost. Their living standards were declining, their jobs were disappearing, externally imposed discipline was returning to the factories. The army was being reconstituted on conventional lines with regular officers, abolition of elections, the return of the death penalty and abandonment of the militia concept. Grass-roots institutions – local soviets, union branches, factory committees – were all seen as having lost their function as weapons of worker defence and had, instead become instruments of state control. There was a particularly fierce battle over trades unions.

The background to the discontent was the collapse, in 1918, of workers' control (extended by this time, of course, to include actual takeovers of factories as conventional management disappeared or refused to collaborate with the labour force). Exactly why this happened is difficult to say. Workers' control was criticized, particularly by Lenin, on grounds of its inefficiency which arose because the workers lacked the necessary skills to run their factories. But, in any case, the collapsing economy rendered all management methods, including conventional ones, powerless in the face of the storm. Arguably, the economic collapse caused the failure of workers' control at least as much as workers' control caused the economic collapse. In addition, the pell-mell way in which workers were forced to take over meant that there was very little preparation for such a momentous step. The failure of workers' control meant, none the less, that new forms of worker organization had to be found. As we have seen with the question of militarization of labour, the authorities' solution was to bring in the state with full force and authority, arguing that since it was, in the fullest sense, a workers' state, it could not be in conflict with the workers. In the conditions of the time, this formula was something of an Orwellian joke.

Given the twin drives for production and discipline – both of which the state deemed to be in the best interests of the workers – the outcome of the situation was the emergence of trade unions as a main means of labour management and as the disseminator of party–state objectives within the declining and "backward" parts of the working class. This brought the party leadership into conflict with a substantial proportion of its militants who wanted to see more direct worker expression and representation in the trades unions. Opposition came to a head at the Ninth Party Congress in March–April 1920. It was to this Congress that Trotsky brought his proposals for the militarization of labour and Lenin achieved final recognition by the party of the principle of one-person management. The opposition to the proposals was vociferous, but limited in terms of support. The final resolution on trades unions was accepted unanimously. It declared that "under the dictatorship of the proletariat the trades unions cease being organs which struggle against the capitalist ruling class as sellers of labour and are converted into the apparatus of working-class rulers". Their tasks were defined as "principally organizational – economic and educational". They were not to be "self-contained" or "isolated" but to be "one of the fundamental apparatuses of the Soviet state, guided by the Communist Party". Conflict between unions and state was declared to be impossible: "any opposition between the trades unions, as the economic organization of the working class, and the soviets, as its political organization, is completely absurd". Not surprisingly, any dissent was declared to be a "deviation from Marxism in the direction of bourgeois – specifically bourgeois-trade-unionist – prejudices". Unions were to be "a school of communism and a link between the vanguard of the proletariat, the Communist Party, and the most backward masses of the proletariat" whom the unions "must raise to the communist level and train for the role of creators of the communist order". Other provisions stated that the unions "must be gradually converted into auxiliary organs of the proletarian state, and not the other way around"; that they should "participate" in the organization of production although they were "in no way the complete and exclusive directors of the economy of the Soviet republic"; and that they should fulfil this task "without interfering in the administration of the enterprise". Other tasks included helping "to improve labour discipline"; taking part in the "intense and excessively difficult struggle for economic regeneration" and "explaining to broad working-class circles the full necessity of restructuring the apparatus of industrial administration, making it more elastic and businesslike" that meant giving "special prominence" to one-person management. A number of provisions stressed the importance of the leadership of "a disciplined and organized communist fraction" at each level of the process. The aim of the overall settlement was to "ensure the maximum stability of the whole system of proletarian dictatorship" as well as "maximum productivity".[127]

The resolution provides a clear model of the relationship existing between party and workers. There was not the slightest admission that there could be any genuine gap between the authorities and the class they claimed to represent. Only the failure of certain "backward" groups of workers to grasp the truth could account for the conflicts that existed. It was particularly useful, and increasingly frequent in polemics to play the "peasant background" card at this point to explain the roots of that backwardness. The solution was simply to expose the laggards to propaganda and they would join up with their vanguard. In addition, the philosophy of productionism was deeply embedded in the resolution. The number one task of the party, the state and the working class was to restore the industrial economy.

The opposition at the congress, having put its case and been defeated, went along with the majority and, in the words of Lutovinov, who had led the attack on the leadership's position, it was necessary to work loyally to implement one-man management and the new arrangements "not out of fear, but as a matter of conscience".[128] None the less, a year later the Tenth Party Congress brought a further sustained effort by the opposition to redress the balance in favour of actual workers and their grass-roots organizations. The ambiguous relationship between worker and state was to reveal further complexities.

By the end of the revolutionary war, the resources of the urban and rural *narod* were at a low ebb. Above all, economic exhaustion to the point of famine had wrought havoc on the popular movement. Although the glimmerings of its programme of peace, bread, land and genuine popular democracy in economic as well as state institutions could still be perceived through the gloom, the impressive unity of worker, peasant and soldier was under serious threat. In the first place, the collapse of the unified state into competing fiefdoms diversified the number of enemies and broke the political struggle into separate arenas for, let us say, Polish, Finnish, Ukrainian and Central Asian workers and peasants. Economic disintegration and the collapse of a unified rail network hastened the process. In addition, where SR-dominated soviets in 1917 had stressed the common cause of workers and peasants, there were no powerful equivalent agents able to foster unity after October. For their part the Bolshevik leadership, although they nurtured a kind of popular movement ideology linking workers, poor peasants and agricultural labourers, stressed class divisions within the peasantry and scorned the role of intellectuals (despite this being the class to which most of them belonged). As a result, they drove ideologically powered wedges into the popular solidarity of 1917 in their attempts to turn poor and middle peasants against kulaks. The ensuing conflicts often spilled over into straight worker versus peasant antagonisms since the lack of goods convinced peasants that workers were shirking their task in the civil war effort and were living as parasites off the products of peasant labour transferred at gunpoint by requisition squads often composed of urban worker volunteers. The resistance met by the squads could also be played upon by Bolshevik propagandists to turn workers against the apparently counter-revolutionary countryside. The real rural division, between the commune peasants and the "outsiders" who clung to the new institutions such as rural soviets and state farms, was never officially acknowledged. In the cities, too, trust between different groups of workers might also disappear given the life-or-death nature of the search for supplies to feed themselves and to keep their factories running. However, this was a much less significant solvent of solidarity than the ubiquitous Cheka which stamped heavily on all attempts to link workers up other than through officially approved party and trade union channnels.

In the grim circumstances it seems quite improbable that any real solidarity might have survived but the post-civil war period shows that a shadowy popular movement still retained some life and had by no means forgotten the causes dear to its heart.

CHAPTER ELEVEN

Anti-Bolshevik insurrections

The growth of the centralized Soviet state, the broadening scope of internal repression and the need for unity against the Whites had considerably reduced the impact of the popular movement in Soviet-held areas. Part of it had been absorbed into the party and state, part had been intermittently active against centralization. A third, and probably the largest part, had simply tried to get by in the worsening conditions. However, civil war against the Whites was virtually over by the end of 1919. The broader revolutionary war, on the other hand, still had major crises to negotiate. Expectations that the discipline imposed on the revolution by the White threat would break down once they were defeated were not disappointed.

The Makhno movement

Areas beyond Bolshevik control – the national peripheries of the former Russian Empire – provide interesting comparative examples of how events developed without significant Bolshevik influence. Only in the Caucasus and the southern Ukraine did left-wing forces emerge on top, notably the Mensheviks of Georgia and the independent peasant–anarchist movement of Nestor Makhno. Elsewhere, the property-owning classes – bourgeois and/or landowners – dominated. In Poland, Finland, the Baltic States and the western half of the Ukraine, nationalist parties usually tending to the right, took over government. In some places they did so only through extreme repression. The White terror in Finland cost tens of thousands of lives. Few of them, for obvious reasons, set up democratic governments in any real sense of the term. Various oligarchies moved in quickly to take control of the political process. In Siberia the Whites dominated. In Central Asia, traditionalists fought it out with modernizing bourgeois nationalists. The Bolsheviks' main claim to legitimacy rested on the argument that they were the only ones capable of preventing a similar disaster for the workers and peasants of Russia and that their harsh methods were necessary in the face of a ruthless and unrelenting enemy.

However, the Makhno movement in the Ukraine suggests that there was more than one way to fight against the counter-revolution. The most important feature of Makhno's movement, from this perspective, was that it was made up almost entirely of uneducated peasants with only the smallest leaven of theorists. The movement arose, whole and entire, from the depths of the ordinary population of the eastern Ukrainian lands around Hulyai Pole, that is between Kharkov, the Don and the Crimea. Arming themselves with the abundant stock of light weapons and ammunition left over from the world war, Makhno's followers and numerous other groups of peasants, set about conducting a spontaneous rural revolution. Landlords were dispossessed. Those who resisted were treated without mercy. Loose peasant organizations took over the self-administration of the land and local government functions. They armed and policed themselves. The remoteness of the region made it easy to institutionalize Makhno's antipathy to all political parties, which were deemed to be corrupted by authoritarianism no matter how much they claimed to support or represent the people, and they were duly banned. Soviets were set up everywhere but no central or executive committees were allowed to congeal.

Much of this was rather typical of rural revolution throughout European Russia and the Ukraine. The developing differences in the eastern Ukraine stemmed from one vital distinction. The Treaty of Brest-Litovsk had handed the area over to the Central Powers, who occupied it in 1918. In the east, it bordered the area of southern Russia in which Denikin's Volunteer Army began to form. Thus, in the crucial formative months of 1918, Hulyai Pole lay at, or even beyond, the edge of competing political powers. Apart from a few representatives in the towns, the Bolsheviks were totally absent. Petliura's nationalists in Kiev, the occupying Germans and Austrians and Denikin's army could only exert the most tenuous hold on the region. This gave Makhno's movement its opportunity. There was no other significant force in the area at the time to fight for the revolution against foreigners, landlords and the Ukrainian bourgeois and commercial classes grouped around the nationalist movement in Kiev.

Makhno was able to harness popular revolutionary energies. His major asset was the close relationship between his activists and the local population. In a well-known comment Mao Tse-tung described the guerrilla as a fish in water. Perhaps it would be truer to say a guerrilla was a fish in a shoal. This would certainly describe Makhno's greatest advantage more accurately. To all intents and purposes, his men and women activists were wholly indistinguishable from the rest of the peasant population. They could, however, detach themselves without warning from the rest of the shoal, strike, and then merge back into it. Short of destroying the whole shoal – that is, the entire peasantry of the locality – Makhno's opponents could do little.

There are many examples of Makhno's followers using their indistinguishability to make surprise attacks. On one occasion in 1918 they were able to take Ekaterinoslav from Petliura's nationalists by the simple expedient of concealing their weapons, boarding what appeared to be an ordinary passenger train, sending it across the river into the centre of the town, grouping in the station and attacking the enemy strong points without warning.[1] On this occasion they only held on for a few days but the principle was widespread. They were also able to infiltrate enemy positions by hiding under hay and produce in peasant carts and then springing out at a moment's notice to surprise and often rout the enemy. When they were in retreat they would abandon their weapons and merge with the local population. The fact that they were able to succeed shows how closely they were linked with the ordinary peasants because such tactics made Makhno's men very vulnerable to informers. There were very few examples of betrayal.

Makhno's Insurgent Army, as it called itself, was the quintessence of a self-administered, people's revolutionary army. It arose from the peasants, it was composed of peasants, it handed power to the peasants. It encouraged the growth of communes, co-operatives and soviets but distrusted all permanent elites attempting to take hold within them. It would be foolish to think that Makhno was supported by every peasant or that he and his followers could not, on occasions, direct their cruelty towards dissidents within their own ranks, but, on the whole, the movement perhaps erred on the side of being too self-effacing, of handing too much authority to the population at key moments.

Such criticism could be levelled especially at their attempts to deal with cities and the industrial economy, about which they knew comparatively little as compared with rural matters. Their principles, when confronted with a large town, were much less appropriate than in a village of small, household production units. In towns they banned parties, set up soviets, chased out owners, encouraged workers to set up co-ops and then urged them to sort things out for themselves. Lack of experience, the shortness of the time spent there and the harsh conditions of the period meant that their urban experiments tended to fail. Factories were much larger and less independent than farms. Raw materials, suppliers, markets, could be far away. There was more chance of internal conflict arising within factories about how to reorganize. The anarchists did not have enough time to find satisfactory solutions. In any case, Bolshevik factories fared little better at the time.

Makhno's ability to promote his movement between 1917 and 1920 was not just the result of the power vacuum in the region and its close integration with the local peasantry. In addition, Makhno showed considerable skill in balancing various external foes against one another. The conflict between Whites and Reds was essential to Makhno's survival. While there was a credible White threat in the region the Soviet government could do little more than tolerate his movement. They needed his support and Makhno's Insurgent Army was, for a time, incorporated as a senior irregular division of the Red Army. Nothing, however, is more revealing of Bolshevik aspirations to sole, unified power than their actions to liquidate Makhno's movement once the Whites were defeated.

Between the beginning of 1919 and 1921 the Bolsheviks conducted three separate campaigns against the Makhnovites. Two ended in uneasy agreements to join forces and fight the Whites. The third ended in the complete defeat of Makhno. The twists and turns of this peculiar relationship are worth dwelling on for a few moments.

After October 1917 Ukrainian politics, especially in the south-east around Hulyai Pole, became very confused. After Brest-Litovsk it was occupied by the Central Powers. Their defeat left four main foci of power – Ukrainian nationalists, Whites, anarchists and Bolsheviks. Divisions existed within all groupings but were particularly significant among the nationalists. A confused armed conflict continued until 1921. Some nationalists were prepared to ally with the occupying powers, others with the Whites. One of the leaders, Grigoriev, fought with the Reds against the occupiers and then approached the Whites and the anarchists for help against the Reds. The anarchists, though they sometimes negotiated with the Whites and Grigoriev, never contemplated a serious alliance. In fact, Makhno and one of his associates shot and killed Grigoriev at a public meeting called to mediate between the factions. On another occasion they executed an emissary sent by the White leader in the Crimea, Wrangel', who may have been misled by Bolshevik black propaganda into thinking that the anarchists were prepared to ally with the Whites against the Reds. The anarchists were, however, prepared to ally with the Reds. They had no illusions about the threat posed to them by Bolshevik authoritarianism and statism but, like so many left-wing opponents of the communists, they had to recognize that the Soviet government was the least bad option.

The first Bolshevik campaign in the region began after the collapse of the Central Powers in November 1918. Initially, the Bolsheviks allied with the Insurgent Army and Grigoriev's nationalists against the Whites. When Grigoriev switched sides the Bolsheviks became even more dependent on Makhno. There was, however, no belief in Moscow that this was more than a temporary conjuncture. In a telegram of 7 May 1919 to Kamenev, the highest ranking Bolshevik in the area who visited Makhno on the the day the telegram was sent, Lenin instructed that "For the time being, until Rostov is occupied, we must be diplomatic with Makhno's forces".[2] The cynical and temporary nature of the alliance was obvious to all. The critical situation caused the anarchists to call a new council to decide policy. This provoked a serious clash with the Bolsheviks who interpreted it as a pre-emptive and hostile act. Trotsky, in particular, threw himself into the campaign. With characteristic energy and disregard for the truth, he spearheaded a new round of propaganda fabrications against the anarchists. Above all he accused them of being a front for kulak power. The Soviet government hampered the anarchists in their fight against Grigoriev and Denikin. On 4 June, four days after the Insurgent Military Council at Hulyai Pole had called for democratic election of delegates to the congress to be held in its area of operations, Trotsky issued an order forbidding the congress and making it a treasonable offence to assist in its organization. On 6 June the Whites occupied Hulyai Pole. Despite increasing political tension, military co-operation between Reds and Insurgents continued. Makhno collaborated with Voroshilov who had, in his pocket, an order signed by Trotsky for the arrest of Makhno and all his associates. Makhno was warned. On 9 June he quit his official Soviet post, protested the order banning the congress and left Voroshilov's armoured train. His chief-of-staff, several members of the Insurgent Military Council and other leading Makhnovites who fell into Bolshevik hands, were summarily executed. The Red command remained in control of Makhno's troops. However, the inner conflict did nothing to strengthen defences against the Whites whose assault seems to have been seriously underestimated by the Bolsheviks. Denikin took Ekaterinoslav at the end of June and the main city of the region, Kharkov, in mid-July. The Bolsheviks hurriedly evacuated the Ukraine.

Makhno's supporters suspected that Red units had deliberately opened the front facing Denikin's Volunteer Army to allow him to ravage Makhno's base area. Indeed, the Whites did conduct a savage war against Jews, Ukrainian peasants and Makhnovites alike. It was only when all seemed lost that Makhno was able, on 26 September 1919, to hurl himself, with a handful of men, onto the advancing White forces at Peregonovka. The Whites suffered a terrible defeat and were subjected to a merciless pursuit. Exhausted survivors threw themselves into the River Siniukha only to find that Makhno had already forded it and was waiting on the bank to cut them down as they emerged from the water. The anarchists took no prisoners. Their regular policy towards defeated opponents was to release the ordinary soldiers, some of whom joined the Insurgent Army, and shoot all the officers and party representatives unless their men approached them asking for them to be spared. The Whites, however, consisted only of officers.

It may be that Insurgent operations in the area distracted Denikin in his crucial campaign against Moscow, which faltered at Orel in mid-November 1919, shortly after the disastrous encounter at Peregonovka. Whatever impact Makhno had on the course of the campaign, it was clear that Denikin's defeat opened the way for a new Bolshevik drive in the south-east. This, too, was halted by the unexpected strength of the Whites. This time it was Wrangel' in the Crimea who was causing trouble. Again an uneasy alliance was patched up between the Reds and the Insurgents. The final assault on Wrangel's positions, in which the Insurgents played an heroic part, was greeted realistically in Makhno's camp. In mid-November 1920, one of his aides, on hearing of the imminent fall of Wrangel's stronghold in Simferopol' said, "It's the end of the agreement. I'll bet you anything the Bolsheviks will be on us within the week."[3]

On 26 November, once again on the pretext that he was preparing an anti-Soviet kulak uprising, Makhno was outlawed by the Soviet authorities. Confident predictions that he would be arrested and his movement liquidated proved easier to proclaim than to fulfil. In a final tragic coda to his revolutionary career, Makhno and a small band of supporters eluded all the efforts of the Reds to subdue him for nine months. Hundreds of thousands of Red troops were engaged in the final pursuit. On several occasions Makhno extricated himself from apparently impossible situations. In individual engagements Makhno's 3,000 or so irregulars faced up to 10,000–20,000 Red troops and survived. On one occasion they escaped after a defeat and travelled 120 miles in 13 hours, a speed which far outpaced the pursuers.[4] Despite the difficulty of finally liquidating the remnants of the Insurgents, the end was inevitable. At the end of August Makhno, with probably around 100–150 men,[5] crossed the Dniester into Romania. He spent the rest of his life in exile. The Bolsheviks tried to extradite him from Romania, Poland and Germany. He finally died in poverty in Paris in 1934 and was buried, along with other revolutionary heroes, in the Père Lachaise cemetery. After his departure Soviet power, largely in the form of the Cheka, swept the south-eastern Ukraine for weapons and sympathizers. By the end of 1921, nothing more was heard of the movement.

Two of its features were particularly important. First, it was a clear case of the Bolsheviks clashing head on with popular revolution. Secondly, it brings into question the assumption that the authoritarian tactics chosen by the Bolsheviks were necessarily the most effective.

As far as the first point is concerned, there can be no question that the anarchists did everything they could to free the peasants and workers and give them the opportunity to develop their own forms of collective control over land and factories. Like the Bolsheviks of October the Ukrainian anarchists fought under the slogan of land to the peasants, factories to the workers and power to the soviets. Wherever they had influence they supported the setting up of communes and soviets. They introduced safeguards intended to protect direct self-government from organized interference. All parties were banned and permanent central committees were frowned upon. Their presence in towns and cities was too fleeting for their principles to take root but there can be no doubt that in the countryside they protected a revolution that corresponded closely with the wishes of the peasantry. They conducted relentless class war against landlords, officers, factory owners and the commercial classes who could expect short shrift from Makhno and his men, especially if they had taken up arms against the people or, like the Whites pitilessly massacred after Peregonovka, had been responsible for looting, pogroms and vicious reprisals against unarmed peasants on a colossal scale. Makhno actively opposed anti-semitism, on one occasion summarily executing an acquaintance from among his own supporters who had put up a poster saying "Beat the Jews! Save the Revolution! Long Live Bat'ko [Little Father] Makhno!"[6] Not surprisingly, many Jews held prominent positions in the Insurgent movement and Jewish farmers and villagers staunchly supported Makhno in the face of the unrestrained anti-semitism of Ukrainian nationalists like Grigoriev and of Great Russian chauvinists like the Whites. On one occasion in the early days of the insurgency a wealthy Jew is said to have paid a substantial ransom for Makhno's release from the Austro-Hungarians who had captured him in July 1918 when he was on his way back from a meeting with Lenin in Moscow.[7]

Anarchist principles were also applied to cultural life. Schooling was supervised by joint commissions of workers, peasants and teachers.[8] Rather than impose an overall solution to the knotty problem of language, schools were allowed to decide for themselves what the language of instruction should be.[9] The spirit of the movement is well illustrated by the policy statement dated 18 October 1919 of the Cultural–Educational Section of the Insurgent Army:

> In the interests of the greatest intellectual development of the people, the language of instruction should be that toward which the local population naturally lean and this is why the population, the students, the teachers and the parents, and not the authorities or the army, should freely and independently resolve this question.[10]

Schools were separated from the church and the anarchists opposed all religions, but it does not appear that Makhno engaged in systematic religious any more than ethnic persecution. Religion and nationality were left to the individual and collective conscience.

It is doubtful that the Insurgent Army ever numbered more than 30,000 members at its peak and probably averaged around 15,000. It was organized on a voluntary basis and respected the principle of election of commanders and staff. The regulations governing conduct were drawn up by commissions of soldiers and approved by general meetings of the units concerned.[11] In other words, it embodied the principles of the soldiers' movement of 1917, principles rejected by the Bolsheviks when they set up the Red Army, supposedly because of their harmful effect on fighting efficiency, a characteristic of them discovered by the Bolsheviks only after they had come to power on the basis of promoting them. But the Insurgent Army, given its size and equipment, was very effective. Some have even credited it with greater responsibility than the Red Army for the defeat of Denikin.[12] It took enormous efforts by the Bolsheviks, including the arrest or shooting of thousands of people,[13] in order to pacify the region. As we have seen, even after the Insurgent Army was militarily broken, it took six months to mop up the remnants and drive Makhno over the frontier. Within its area of operations, which consisted of only two to three per cent of the total population of European Russia, the

Insurgent Army was undoubtedly highly effective. While one can never know how history might have turned out had things been different, the Insurgent Army gives plenty of grounds for thinking that a people's revolutionary war of the kind it represented might have been at least as effective on a national scale with nationwide resources at its disposal as Trotsky and the Red Army's ruthless centralization. It would not, however, have been compatible with the imposition from above of the Bolshevik leadership's vision of revolution. When the Insurgent Army drove the enemy out of an area they encouraged the local population to solve their own problems. Where the Red Army took over, the Cheka quickly followed. The Bolsheviks themselves were energetically snuffing out the ideals of 1917.

Given such considerations it may be, though it cannot be logically proven one way or the other, that the Bolsheviks' deeply rooted authoritarianism rather than the civil war itself led to the construction of a highly centralized system that aimed at "complete control" over political and many other aspects of social life. It could even be argued, though it is equally unprovable, that the tendency to authoritarianism, far from ensuring victory, nearly led to catastrophe. For one thing, it helped alienate many workers who felt cheated by the outcome of the revolution, and support for the regime was, as we have seen, far from universal even in this core group. Even though opposition was more and more difficult to organize there were still a number of strikes, as well as more passive resistance through poor work discipline, pilfering, black market trading and desertion of the cities which showed that the working class was not fully at one with its ostensible leadership and it may, indeed, have been becoming more alienated as a result of Bolshevik measures depriving it of the means of expression of its growing catalogue of grievances. Certainly, as far as the peasantry is concerned, the harsh measures of grain requisitioning not only alienated the producers, they also failed to feed the cities and aggravated the problem. Vatsetis's complaint that harsh discipline enforced by terror would produce only a barren, mechanical obedience to orders did not apply solely to the army. Far from being "necessary" or even functional, the Bolshevik leadership's obsession with externally imposed discipline and authority might even have made the task of victory in the war more difficult and more costly. If the counter-example of Makhno is anything to go by then it certainly did.

Elsewhere protests began to reappear by 1920, particularly since the transition to peace had raised hopes that the political and economic situation would improve. The extension of state interference was the last thing much of the population wanted. It was more than symbolic that the final popular struggles of the revolution should have taken place in regions that had been the heartlands of rural and urban revolution of 1917 – Tambov province and Kronstadt.

The Tambov rebellion

By the late summer of 1920 one might have expected that the energies of the ordinary population of Soviet Russia would have been completely exhausted. On top of the privations of world war, revolution, civil war, foreign intervention and the partial dismemberment of the old empire had come the war with Poland. But the astonishing truth was that the dreams of 1917 had not been completely extinguished. In some measure, the very desperation of the country drove workers, peasants, soldiers and sailors to renewed revolutionary action. As had been the case three or four years earlier, self-defence against crisis had been a powerful motivation. As a result, a multitude of revolts and rebellions, great and small, occurred all across Russia. According to Cheka sources there were 118 separate risings throughout Soviet Russia in February 1921.[14] In particular, there was the Armenian revolt of 13 February that led to the seizure of the capital Erevan on the 18th. The Kronstadt mutiny began on 28 February. The West Siberian rising started up in late January and early February. An uprising took place in the left-bank Ukraine. In 1920, there had been a number of forerunners notably Sapozhkov's mutiny in Buzuluk *uezd* of Samara province that lasted from mid-July 1920 until January 1922. In December 1920 a mutiny led by Vakulin occurred in the Don region. But the best known and most widespread was the Tambov uprising that began in August 1920 and continued for almost a year or so until it was finally extinguished.

Today, most observers agree that the protests were triggered by the ending of the civil war. As well as being relieved that the Whites were no longer a threat, the population began to realize that they no longer had such pressing reasons to put up with Bolshevik bullying. In times of dire military emergency they could see the need for it. But now the crisis was over it was time for the Bolsheviks to fulfil their promises. In the eyes of the population it was time for them to show whether they were the real defenders of the popular revolution. Of course, the popular movement in 1920 was not that of 1917 but there was a surprising amount of continuity. An examination of the peasant uprising in Tambov clarifies what remained of the spirit of 1917.

The Tambov rebellion began in August 1920 and lasted until June 1921 when the main forces were broken up, after which only a few scattered bands continued some sporadic resistance. A year later the movement's leader, Antonov, was finally tracked down and shot, along with his brother, on 24 June 1922. At the height of the rebellion, large parts of the countryside of three *uezds* of Tambov province were no-go areas for Soviet power and there were patches of rebellion elsewhere in the province. The central government was only able to reassert its authority through massive concentration of military power led by some of the major figures of the developing Soviet military establishment – such as Tukhachevsky, Uborevich and Zhukov – who were under the overall political direction of the man who had led the "storming" of the Winter Palace, V. A. Antonov-Ovseenko. It was one of the most extensive revolts against Soviet power. How did it begin? Where did its strength come from? Was it doomed from the start?

It seems certain that, though there had been groups and individuals working towards armed uprising in the area, the actual outbreak was the result of spontaneous grass-roots resistance to what were seen as excessive demands on the peasants by the Soviet authorities. In separate incidents in mid-August 1920, two villages, Khitrova and Kamenka, had fought back against food-levy brigades that had begun their visitations immediately the harvest was in. In Kamenka seven members of a second brigade had been killed and the area braced itself for the inevitable punishment detachment. When 20,000 armed militia duly descended on Kamenka they, and succeeding detachments, were beaten off. The events at the two villages forced anti-Bolshevik conspirators, led by A. S. Antonov who had around 500 or so followers, to launch their armed struggle. The rebellion was on.

It had three main components: the armed conspiracy led by Antonov; the civilian political organizations that linked up in the STK (*Soiuz Trudovogo Krest'ianstva*, the Union of Labouring Peasantry or Peasant Union) and spontaneous grass-roots peasant activism.

Systematic information about the various components is hard to come by but memoirs, Soviet studies and western overviews, notably that by Oliver Radkey,[15] enable us to form a general picture of what happened. The network of arms and people to use them appears to have been built up by Antonov over a period of several years starting in 1918. Antonov himself was not a peasant but came from an urban artisan background. He was probably born in the second half of the 1880s. He soon marked himself out as a rebel, even while he was at school, from which he was duly expelled. He is conventionally considered to be an SR – as was almost every radical in Tambov province in which Bolshevism and Menshevism had been practically unknown in the pre-war period. Consequently, the label hid great varieties of attitude and strategy. Antonov was not a moderate party man or a political–cultural propagandist. Rather he was an adventurer–activist engaged in expropriations and, maybe, terrorist acts. He was, in essence, a "professional revolutionary" who considered violence to be an inevitable part of his strategy. He was eventually arrested and in 1907 or 1909 was sent to Siberia as a convict rather than a political exile. He was released following the February Revolution, taking up where he had left off on the radical wing of the peasant movement in his home territory. Characteristically, given his views on the need for violence, he became head of a district militia in Tambov *uezd*.[16] It appears to have been the Cheka crackdown against Left SRs and others and the Red terror of August 1918, during which some of his associates were captured and shot, that drove Antonov underground. A group of some 150 similar outcasts and hunted men gathered around him. It is most likely that, in 1919, with the outcome of the civil war still very much in doubt, Antonov and his band restricted their anti-communist activities though they were involved in small-scale terrorist acts. Once Denikin was defeated, however, Antonov was able to advance on a broader front. His principles and contacts as a legal militia chief in 1917 and 1918 had been maintained in the clandestine period. He had encouraged groups to retain their arms. Once the rebellions began, the *volost'* and *uezd* committees of the areas involved were called on to provide men, such weapons as they had and horses, wagons and supplies. The armed forces comprised volunteers and conscripts. Figures for the number of men under Antonov's command range from a few thousand to 50,000. The most careful analysis is that of Radkey[17] who concluded, along with Tukhachevsky, that a peak of around 20,000 is the most credible estimate. Hostile Soviet sources normally describe them as deserters and bandits. Undoubtedly there were plenty of the former who were hiding out in the forests of the Volga and Black Earth regions, but peasant rebels often come in this form. The bulk of the force was certainly composed of peasants, many of whom had joined the Antonov bands directly from the village, though we cannot say exactly what proportion.

This leads us on to the crucial question about Antonov's movement. What were the links between the armed bands and the rest of the population of the area? Did the bands represent ordinary peasants? Where did the local anti-Bolshevik political elite stand? A penumbra of doubt surrounds the answers we can give to such questions.

The formal political side of the movement is easier to deal with since it revolves around the STK, the local umbrella organization of anti-Bolshevik groups that consisted largely of SR and Left SR sympathizers. It published a formal programme in May 1920, three months before the outbreak of the armed insurrection which the STK had not specifically called for, not surprisingly since SR policy at the time opposed spontaneous rebellions and terroristic acts against the Soviet state. The most prominent demand in the programme was for a complete break with Communism and the Soviet regime with a new Constituent Assembly to be called to decide on a new political structure for the country. The model for the Assembly had, however, moved closer to the Bolshevik model by including a provision for recall of delegates, an essential element in establishing direct rather than representative democracy. Secondly, the October 1917 land settlement was supported. Other radical propositions were also prominent. Major industrial enterprises such as coalmining and metalworking would remain in state hands. Workers' control and government supervision of industry were also included. The difference from war communism came out more strongly in demands for legalization of domestic and craft industries, the restoration of normal relations with foreign countries and allowing private Russian and foreign capital investment. The state was also called on to provide credits to private individuals in order to support small-scale entrepreneurship and improvement of land. Finally, broad liberal and more socialist welfare provisions included recognition of basic civil liberties; eradication of illiteracy; free basic education and the retention of guerrilla and volunteer militias pending settlement of the question of a new structure for the army by the proposed Constituent Assembly. Implicit in the programme was the preservation of the *mir* and, probably *volost'* committees though it is not clear what the intermediate levels of local government would be. Also, as Radkey points out,[18] hiring of labour was not banned because there was no consensus on the issue. He also describes the programme as that of the SRs but, more importantly, it shows many similarities with the grass-roots peasant programme of 1917 and, as we shall see, with that of the later Kronstadt rebels. The programme is clear evidence of the persistence of the popular movement and of its post-civil war re-emergence. As Radkey says, the Tambov revolt stood for the February revolution minus the war and the October revolution minus the food levy, and against the communes (that is the large-scale *kommuny* not the traditional village commune which was defended) and the highly unpopular state farms.[19] These last were viewed by working peasants as state-subsidized outdoor relief for rural misfits, drunkards, loafers, agriculturally incompetent ex-soldiers and urban refugees who were given privileged conditions and wasted good land that the peasants considered to be theirs. One can only agree with Radkey's overall judgement that the STK programme, far from being counter-revolutionary as the Bolsheviks alleged, contained nothing that could "be construed as incompatible with the Russian Revolution in the true and broader sense".[20]

To what extent did the programme represent the aspirations of the people of Tambov province? Traditionally, Tambov as a whole – rebellious and non-rebellious *uezds* – had been a solid SR fiefdom. Chernov himself had been a party activist in the region in the 1890s. Eight hundred and thirty thousand of its mainly peasant population had voted for the SRs in November 1917, 240,000 for the Bolsheviks.[21] Consequently, communism had very weak roots in the area. The Tambov Communist party organization had only 1,500 members when it was set up in May 1918. By July 1919 it had around 12,000, some 5,000 of whom were purged. On 1 January 1920 it had 11,000 members, of whom 7,000 had joined in late 1919. Membership seems to have peaked at around 14,000 members (including candidates) in July and August when it had 285 urban cells (8,500 members) and 400 rural cells (5,000) members. By January 1921 membership was down to 9,000.[22] The figures graphically illustrate the weakness of the party particularly in the rural areas among the population of around 3.5m. If patterns elsewhere in European Russia hold true for Tambov then the party membership would have stretched very little beyond state and party officials, soldiers garrisoned in the area and youth organizations. Party weakness is confirmed by the outcome of elections to the soviets in 1921. In Borisoglebsk, one of the rebel *uezds*, only one in six of the population voted. *Volost'* soviet executive committees in the *uezd* were composed of 44 communists, three candidates and 125 non-party. Communist weakness was even more marked at village level – 46 communists to 1,915 non-party – but the organizational grip of the party over the population is shown by the city soviet which had 55 communists and 22 non-party.[23]

There can be no doubt about the widespread indifference, if not hostility, of the Tambov peasantry to the Soviet system as it existed between 1918 and 1921. In this way it is a microcosm of much of European Russia. The standard Soviet charge attributes opposition to kulaks but, as Figes showed for the neighbouring Volga provinces, the Bolsheviks were caught in a loop. They attributed almost all opposition to kulak influence on dogmatic grounds and proved kulak influence from the existence of opposition. As far as we can see from the case of Tambov, the picture was more complex than Bolshevik doctrine allowed.

The extensive peasant support for the STK and for the armed uprising had one major source, opposition to food requisitioning detachments such as those that had sparked conflict in Kamenka and Khitrova villages. Peasants were accustomed to levies of able-bodied young men as well as of food in wartime conditions and had put up with the system in 1917 and beyond, providing it did not conflict with their sense of social justice. By 1920, however, the Tambov peasantry had had enough. At the best of times, Tambov had been a favourite stamping-ground for requisitioning detachments since it was relatively close to food deficit areas like Moscow and points north. It was readily accessible because of its relatively good railway communications and it was fertile and therefore deemed to be near inexhaustible. In this light the fact that the most fertile areas of the province were the most rebellious begins to make sense, as does the proclivity of the rebels to attack and tear up railway lines, not just to hamper the arrival of Red Army reinforcements, which could switch to road and horseback fairly easily, but to prevent the grain trains from scouring the region.

In any case, by 1920 the Tambov peasants realized that the reasons behind the food levies had changed. Rather than supplying a legitimate war effort, which was now clearly dying down, the levies of August 1920 seemed to be designed to feed the parasitic (as the peasants saw them) cities which were no longer producing anything the peasants needed. The peasants, therefore, saw no need to support them for nothing from the sweat of their own brow. This was one way in which the end of the civil war contributed to the Bolsheviks' internal problems. The other was that the self-discipline and restraint necessitated by the approach of the Whites was replaced by growing opportunities to express pent-up resentments and grievances against the Soviet system itself. Some of these, notably legalizing small-scale domestic and craft production, were clearly represented in the STK programme. Consequently, all available evidence suggests that far from being a purely kulak cause, the roots of the revolt reached down deep into the middle and maybe even the poor peasantry, even though the last group was theoretically favoured by Bolshevik policies.

A few other features of the participants in the revolt can be sketched in. Despite the ethnic mix in Tambov, which included Mordvins and Tatars, the rebels were almost entirely Russian. As far as the non-peasant classes are concerned it seems likely that the liberal and conservative urban middle class and the intelligentsia sympathized with the rebels but gave them little active support, with the exception of a handful of radical intellectuals of various ideological hues including Mensheviks and anarchists. The sympathies of the rather small working class – about 25,000 in Tambov's plants and factories in 1918 and 17,500 in 1921[24] – are harder to gauge. It seems likely that a substantial number of workers, especially railwaymen, did take part since there are examples given of arrests and attempts to imprison and deport them, although it was hard to carry out the sentences because their skills were sorely needed to restore the severely depleted post-civil war rail network. Equally difficult to know is the number, if any, of Red Army men who went over to the rebels. Naturally enough, rebels who went over to the Soviet side were given great prominence in Soviet accounts.

In summary, then, one can say that the Tambov revolt was a genuine peasant movement, led by radical populists and supported by a broad band of the Russian working peasantry provoked especially by the continued armed requisitioning of August 1920. In most of these respects it reflected the series of peasant outbursts of the same period, most notably in western Siberia. It differed in having an embryonic armed resistance movement which could back up initially spontaneous outbursts. This is what enabled it to last longer than pure peasant outbreaks which were relatively easily suppressed. Only movements with significant organized armed elements – the Insurgent Army, the mutinies in Saratov and on the Don – were able to hold out for significant periods of time, although the example of Kronstadt shows that even a mutiny could be rapidly crushed if it occurred near the heartland, where communist forces were already concentrated, rather than at the periphery where Soviet authority was thin on the ground.

Does it then follow that military repression was the only reason for the movement's failure? For sure, the small Tambov garrison of 3,000 in 1920, while giving evidence that the authorities were not expecting trouble, was totally inadequate for the crisis about to hit it. Only in early 1921 did reinforcements begin to pour in. On 6 May Tukhachevsky took command of around 50,000 well-armed and often battle-hardened troops. By 3 June Antonov's main force was broken up, just within the month the Politburo had allotted to Tukhachevsky to complete the job. The suppression cost many thousands of dead and injured on both sides. Clearly, military repression is the main explanation. But other factors have considerable weight. In the first place, Antonov's horizons were local. The rebellion did not spread to a single town nor did it engulf more than a fraction of the province, or link up with other revolts taking place in nearby areas at the same time. This was in part due to structural differences, notably the absence of indigenous organizations in other places as well as differences of situation and geography. The inhabitants of the extensive forested regions of the area were not so troubled by requisitioning. Ethnic minorities were indifferent for reasons we can only guess at but which might include the calculation that their own developing ethnic agenda was only loosely related to quarrels among Russians. Topography favoured rebellion in some areas rather than others. Concentrations of Soviet power were also vital. Areas which still had loyal troops in place as the war wound down would find it less easy to rebel. In particular, the Cheka's grip on the towns made rebellions in them very difficult. In addition, tradition, (itself the result in part of some of the structural factors) played its part. Tambov had been one of the most turbulent provinces in 1905 and 1917. Kozlov *uezd* provided our most spectacular example of peasant uprising against the Provisional Government in August and September 1917 and the "Tambov formula" gained fleeting prominence as a possible solution to the land question. Perhaps it was the memory of recent failure or, most probable of all, the spread of the Volga famine into the area, which damped down the ardour of rebels in Kozlov. For whatever reason the area saw only sporadic participation though one of Antonov's bands, led by Karas, held out in the locality until mid-July when it was run to earth near the town of Kozlov. None of the sources mentions what was happening in Sychevka in 1920–21.

There is, however, one other major reason for the failure of the revolt to spread. In February 1921, the Soviet government made its most extensive concessions to the peasantry since the land decree of October 1917. It abandoned the policy of forced requisition and Lenin began to draft schemes to replace it with a tax in kind, which was implemented in March through the Tenth Party Congress. This ushered in the era of NEP, the New Economic Policy, which also made extensive concessions to the peasants over domestic and craft production and permitted the legalization of small-scale market activities. As the STK had proposed, only large-scale enterprises remained in state hands. In the light of this, to talk of the failure of the revolt (and of the other conflagrations) is incorrect. In economic matters the rebels were, for the time being, clearly victorious over the party. However, on other crucial matters, notably civil and democratic rights and the monopoly of the Communist Party, not only were no concessions forthcoming, the Communist political, cultural, ideological and intellectual stranglehold was tightened and formalized. The fate of the Kronstadt mutiny, in which protest against Communist political monopoly was paramount, shows Lenin's determination to preserve Communist political power beyond any shadow of doubt.

The Kronstadt rising

The Kronstadt revolt cooked in the same cauldron as Tambov. The privations of civil war had been equally hard both materially in declining living standards and politically in the imposition of centralization and dictatorship which were supposed to facilitate victory. Also, despite being cut off from the countryside, most Kronstadters, especially among the sailors, were from the village and, through home leave, letters and reports from travellers, they were well-informed about rural conditions. The Kronstadters were incensed by the continuation of the food levy and the armed detachments sent out to collect it; by continued restraints on free peasant production and exchange and by the heavy-handedness of the Soviet authorities in much of rural Russia. In Kronstadt a multitude of complaints were recorded about corruption, gangsterism, selfishness and relatively luxurious living on the part of rural Soviet cadres. The enormous gulf between the peasants and the regime exerted its baneful effects in Kronstadt as much as elsewhere, perhaps more, since egalitarian instincts may have been more finely tuned there.

While they might be prepared to maintain restraint about these deformations of the revolution while the Whites continued to threaten, once the war began to fade away the Kronstadters, like many others, no longer saw the need to suffer in silence. The expectations which had been repressed since early 1918 began to re-emerge. The freedoms of 1917 had not been forgotten. The increasing imposition of party control over Kronstadt, and the corresponding decline, even complete destruction, of the vibrant soviet democracy of 1917, had left many resentments.

Even so, Kronstadt had become a Communist stronghold by the end of 1919. In March 1920 the military section of the party comprised 5,630 members[25] out of a population, according to the August 1920 census, of around 27,000 sailors, soldiers, officers and commissars.[26] The civilian population of around 30,000 in August 1920, included 1,000 party members in March.[27] Incidentally, the disparity between party membership among soldiers and sailors on the one hand and civilian workers on the other is a clear reminder that the military remained the leading revolutionary "class" even in 1920.

It seems likely that these peak figures for party membership do not show that communist principles had conquered in Kronstadt. More likely, Kronstadters had rallied to the party not so much to defend Communism as to support the revolution as the White onslaught threatened Petrograd in the late summer and early autumn of 1919. Two pieces of evidence suggest that this is the case. First, the tide of party membership ebbed as the White threat receded. By the end of 1920 the military membership of the party had fallen from 5,630 to 2,228 members and the civilian membership from 1,000 to 802 including candidates. Secondly, analysis of those remaining in the party at the end of 1920 shows that, among the military, only 87 or 88 (3.9 per cent) were pre-1917 Bolsheviks. One hundred and eighty (8.1 per cent) joined between October 1917 and January 1919. This meant that 88.1 per cent had joined since October 1919 including 64 per cent who had joined in the party's intensive recruitment drives of October 1919 to January 1920 when they tried to capitalize on their prestige following the defeat of Yudenich. The picture among civilian party members was very similar. Only three members predated the February revolution, 61 had joined between the two revolutions in 1917 and 140 had joined in the first two years of Soviet power. That left 449 (70 per cent) recruited in the party weeks of late 1919.[28]

The rapidly declining prestige of communism in Kronstadt in 1920 and the proportional rise of the old democratic instincts is confirmed by all the evidence. Complaints about provisions began to increase. Voices were raised protesting the food levies. Corrupt, even criminal, Soviet officials in the countryside were denounced. The supposedly luxurious lifestyle of Kronstadt's newly appointed commissar, Fyodor Raskol'nikov, and his partner Larissa Reisner attracted unfavourable comment. Resentment at the new "commissarocracy" was on the rise.[29] In addition, the leading historian on the rebellion, Israel Getzler, points out the crucial division in the leadership of the party in the Petrograd and Kronstadt region which ended, in February 1921, with the departure of Raskol'nikov after a profound battle with the Petrograd party chief, Zinoviev and the political commissar of the Baltic Fleet N. N. Kuzmin who both saw Raskol'nikov as a protégé of Zinoviev's rival, Trotsky. The confusion precipitated by Raskol'nikov's departure at such a crucial moment, enabled unauthorized meetings of ships' crews to take place "behind the backs of their commissars, there being too few loyal rank-and-file party members left to nip them in the bud".[30] In Getzler's words "In the very thick of the general crisis of War Communism and on the eve of large-scale workers' unrest in Petrograd, Kronstadt had shed party control".[31]

In the neighbouring city of Petrograd the situation had reached its lowest point for the workers and their families who remained there. In the first place, food supplies had dwindled to next to nothing. On 22 January, the already inadequate food ration for the city was reduced by a third. Workers responded by calling meetings to denounce the prevailing conditions and call for a restoration of basic freedoms. A similar crisis had broken out in Moscow but, as Paul Avrich, Mary McCauley and others argue, the situation in Petrograd was far more serious because the food and fuel crises were deeper. Food reserves were at only 20 per cent of 1914 levels. In early February 60 Petrograd factories had had to close because of fuel shortages. By 25 February isolated protest meetings had spread to more than half-a-dozen of the city's major enterprises. The authorities, fearful of the equally dangerous situation in Kronstadt, resorted to the tactics of the former employers and the Provisional Government and shut down some of the factories. By the 28th, however, the Putilov workers joined in the protests which centred on the food shortages but also began to reach into the territory of demands for lost (or, in theory, suspended) rights to be restored and democratic norms – which, as in 1917, the workers saw as the only guarantee of their material demands – to be returned to. The escalating threat, reminiscent of the February crisis only four years previously which had brought down the autocracy, triggered off the Bolsheviks' instinct to use overwhelming force. Regular troops were confined to barracks, some were even disarmed, while elite squads were called in to patrol the streets. Party members were put on alert. Hundreds of workers were arrested. More factories closed. The remnants of Menshevik and SR organizations were made scapegoats for the unrest. Their influence, plus that of White

Guards and foreign powers were blown up out of all proportion by an intensive propaganda barrage. Finally, rations were increased by rapidly depleting
the available supplies and scouring the country for replacements. The party
chief, Zinoviev, also made lavish promises of fuel purchases from abroad to
alleviate the heating and energy crisis. He also pointed to the approaching
decision to abandon forced food requisitioning and replace it with a more orderly tax in kind. On 1 March the hated roadblocks (used to prevent private
traders and direct exchange between rural and city dwellers) were suspended
in the Petrograd region. As a result, by 2 and 3 March the movement had
reached its peak and forced significant concessions out of the Soviet government.[32] It had also provided the final spark to ignite the Kronstadt tinder box.

When the workers of Petrograd began to strike the Kronstadt sailors were
already strong enough to hold emergency meetings against the wishes of their
commissars and elected a fact-finding delegation of 32 to go to the city. They
found the workers sullen and demoralized and so cowed by the Cheka and
party authorities that hardly any dared speak openly. Returning on the 28th
the delegation reported its findings and, in response to the sailors' representatives gathered on the dreadnought *Petropavlovsk*, passed a resolution which
severely criticized the Bolshevik regime.

The authorities responded to this dangerous turn of events by calling a general meeting in Anchor Square for 1 March. The meeting, attended by 15,000
to 16,000 military personnel and civilians showed how far the Communist
authorities had misjudged the situation. They had, no doubt, expected to isolate a presumed tiny minority of troublemakers by drowning them in a flood
of loyal party members. The mood of the meeting was, however, unequivocally critical of the authorities and favourable to the basic propositions of the
Petropavlovsk resolution. Many party members must have voted for it because
the meeting approved it almost unanimously. The Kronstadt revolt was under
way.

Unlike the rebellions in the countryside which might last for months or even
years, the Kronstadt revolt was short. It lasted only 16 days. None the less, its
meaning shines with an unambiguous clarity. Its fundamental motivation was
to revive the democratic conditions prevailing before the Communist stranglehold had gripped Kronstadt. Far from being counter-revolutionary the sailors
called for a return to the revolutionary principles of 1917 which, they argued,
had been trampled on by the "commissarocracy". The unambiguous theme at
the heart of the *Petropavlovsk* resolution and other programmatic statements
was that true soviet democracy should be restored at once. By that, they meant
free elections in which no party should have any privileges. In particular this
implied that the Communist party should be disestablished, that is it should
not be allowed to wrap the resources of the state around itself in order to
monopolize channels of information, to set up a state police to carry out its
political demands and to use the state-supported party commissars and soviet
executives to control the military and the factories. The Kronstadt rebels did

not abandon or oppose the class principles of the communists. They actually called for them to be implemented in the form of genuine democratic rights for workers and peasants and the freeing of all workers and peasants and their supporters from the political prisons of the Cheka. They did not base their protest on universal human rights. They showed no sympathy with the old bourgeois and landowning classes and were not interested in a liberal Constituent Assembly. Direct soviet democracy freely participated in by all toilers and the restoration of democratic army and navy committees – the system promised by the Bolsheviks themselves – was the political goal for which the rebels fought. Besides this, their demands for an end to forced requisitioning and for legalizing of peasant production and exchange, though important, were very much secondary.

The Soviet authorities were quick to perceive the deadly threat posed by the principles of Kronstadt. They cut the base off from the rest of Russia, set up a massive barrage of lies about the revolt being led by White Guards and their sympathizers, and prepared elite, volunteer squads for the rapid military suppression of the revolt. The rebels may have played into the government's hands by refusing to take any active offensive action. Instead, they waited for the Bolshevik strike force to descend on them. The first assault, on 8 March, failed, partly because the troops were reluctant to face the rebels and partly because they were hesitant to cross open expanses of ice under constant machine-gun and artillery fire from Kronstadt and its outlying chain of forts. A week later a more reliable force of around 50,000 was ready. It was made up of the most trusted cadres. No less than a quarter of the delegates to the Tenth Party Congress, taking place at the same time in Moscow, took part. In ordinary units the percentage of party members averaged 15–30 per cent and in spearhead units between 60–70 per cent.[33] Clearly the party was throwing the cream of its membership into the fray.

The attack began on 17 March. Inevitably it prevailed. The fighting was very bitter. There were thousands of dead and wounded on both sides. As the attacking force gained the upper hand thousands of Kronstadters fled to Finland. In the aftermath thousands of others were dispersed among other military units. It is impossible to say exactly how many executions there were but no one doubts there were hundreds. All trace of the revolt was extinguished. Even the names of the battleships involved were changed. Clearly, on the crucial issue of political power, the Communists were not prepared for the slightest dialogue with their critics.

The revolt had, and still has, an obvious symbolic dimension. Above all it represents the poignant end of the popular revolution. The vibrant force of grass-roots democracy had been finally destroyed by one of its products – Bolshevism. The irony of the occasion was not lost on contemporaries such as the anarchist Alexander Berkman. He wrote in his diary for 17 March: "Kronstadt has fallen today. Thousands of sailors and workers lie dead in its streets". For 18 March he wrote that the Bolsheviks were celebrating the 50th anniversary of the Paris Commune. "Trotsky and Zinov'ev denounce Thiers and Gallifet for the slaughter of the Paris rebels".[34] In a final irony the *Sevastopol'* was renamed *The Paris Commune*.[35]

The symbolic dimension was not lost on the repressors. Trotsky tried to belittle its significance by recourse to what Getzler calls "facile sociology".[36] According to Trotsky the reliable revolutionary elements had been swamped by backward peasant and ethnic minority recruits. Unfortunately for Trotsky all the evidence points the other way. Evan Mawdsley has shown that by late 1920 "only 1,317 of a planned total of 10,384 recruits had arrived".[37] Furthermore, Getzler has convincingly argued for continuity of personnel at all levels. Data relating to the crews of the *Petropavlovsk* and the *Sevastopol'* show that of 2,028 sailors whose year of enlistment is known, 1,904 (93.9 per cent) were recruited into the navy before the 1917 revolution. Only 137 (6.8 per cent) had been recruited in the years 1918–21.[38] According to Getzler, at least 75.5 per cent of Baltic Fleet sailors serving on 1 January 1921 were likely to have been drafted before 1918. Eighty per cent of them were Russian, 10 per cent Ukrainian and only 9 per cent from the Baltic States including Russian Poland and Finland.[39] The majority of the Revolutionary Committee spearheading the revolt had also been participants in the 1917 revolution.[40] So much for Trotsky's handy theory.

Lenin himself was aware of the real significance of the events. Kronstadt, he told delegates to the Tenth Party Congress, did "not want either the white guards or our movement".[41] None the less, he had no doubt that the rising had to be crushed, not because it was counter-revolutionary but because he believed that any weakening of Communist power would only be advantageous to the White Guards. In his most famous comment he said of Kronstadt "this was the flash which lit up reality better than anything else".[42] The tragic reality it lit up was that Bolshevism was not interested in listening to the political arguments of the ordinary people of Russia and had, irony of ironies, become the executioner of genuine soviet democracy. While much of the country had hoped for better once the civil war had ended, the Bolsheviks gave unconditional notice that they would continue to maintain political control on no other terms than their own.

CHAPTER TWELVE

The end of the revolution

The Kronstadt rising was all the more poignant in that it was occurring at the same time as the Tenth Party Congress was meeting in Moscow. More than anything else, this conjuncture marked the end of the revolution. However, something had to be done about the reality that the revolts had lit up. In addition, 1921 was a moment in which the Bolsheviks were faced with a relatively unconstrained choice. The revolution as a whole, Bolshevik and popular, had routed its enemies. Rather than hiding behind the excuse that they had to militarize and centralize to win the war, the Bolsheviks were now free to decide which way they wanted to go. The Tenth Party Congress set out the route.

The Tenth Party Congress

The Tenth Party Congress set the scene for a, supposedly, more realistic, though no less authoritarian, advance towards socialism. The tone of the congress was set by Lenin. In his opening address he made it clear that there could be no relaxation, no euphoria as a result of victory. Indeed, it was necessary to continue the fight to win everything that was necessary, particularly "real freedom from imperialist invasion and intervention. On the contrary", Lenin continued, "their warfare against us has taken a form that is less military but is in some respects more severe and more dangerous" though he did not specify what he meant by this. The implications, however, were made clear. Incredibly, Lenin asserted that the party had passed "through an exceptional year" in that "we have allowed ourselves the luxury of discussions and disputes". In case anyone had missed the point, he repeated even more emphatically that this was "an amazing luxury". He then went on to describe the "hostile world" taking comfort because "all our enemies – and their name is legion" would argue that "discussion means disputes; disputes mean discord; discord

278

means that the Communists have become weak; press hard, seize the opportunity, take advantage of their weakening". For the third time he described discussion as a "luxury". In the face of the problems, he concluded, "formal cohesion is far from enough . . . Our efforts should be more united and harmonious than ever before".[1]

In reality, it was Lenin and the leadership as much as the outside world that equated discussion with weakness. A wide gulf separated Lenin's approach from that of Rosa Luxemburg for whom the absence of democratic life was the greater danger. It was as though Lenin could not abandon the oppositional outlook which he had nurtured all his life. Even in government he acted as though he were still in opposition, though no longer to the internal enemy which had been so thoroughly routed, but to the even more threatening monster of international imperialism. While sensible vigilance was certainly called for, the paranoid vision of "capitalist encirclement" characteristic of the Stalin period was only one step away. The Marxist view that capitalism was always divided by a multitude of internal contradictions (which even led capitalists to go to war with one another) was less useful to the leadership than the idea of it as a threatening, monolithic block. Even in 1917, however, Lenin had argued that, faced with the Soviet revolution, the British and French capitalists would patch up their differences with their German counterparts and they would all set out together to invade Russia.

Whether Lenin really believed in this view of capitalism or was simply exaggerating in order to get his way within the party we do not know. It was, however, the prelude to an important tightening up of party discipline. In his opening speech his call for greater harmony was coupled with the assertion that "there should not be the slightest trace of factionalism". This was ensured by a resolution "On party unity" which made it impermissible for party members to form factions. These were defined as "groups with platforms of their own and with a will to close ranks to a certain extent and create their own discipline". In essence, they were what today would be called pressure groups.[2]

The reason for concern was the continuation of the "Democratic Centralist" group and the emergence of the "Workers' Opposition", the latest form of the series of oppositions which had protested against the erosion of workers' rights since 1917. Its programme contained the familiar themes that the party had begun "to deviate from its programme" and that the revolution needed "purely class organs" rather than "the Soviet machine" to "develop creative powers in the sphere of economic reconstruction".[3] "Bureaucracy", it was argued, "binds the wings of the self-activity and creativeness of the working class; . . . deadens thought, hinders initiative and experimentation in the sphere of finding new approaches to production: in a word . . . it hinders the development of new forms for production and life".[4] In particular, they called for trades unions to have real independent powers to run the economy. Ironically for a movement devoted to democracy – but realistically given the situation as it was – it concluded with an imaginary worker saying that Lenin "will ponder, he will think it over, he will listen to us. And then he will decide to turn the party rudder towards the Opposition. Il'ich will be with us yet".

Lenin did turn the rudder towards the opposition, but only to run it down. A decree "On the anarchist and syndicalist deviation in our party" left no room for doubt. "The deviation in question" was said to have been "caused in part by the entrance into the party of elements that have not yet fully assimilated the communist world view" and "in major part . . . by the influence on the proletariat and the Russian Communist Party of the petty bourgeois elements that are exceptionally strong in our country" and "inevitably" cause "waverings in the direction of anarchism".[5] "One of the most complete and best formulated expressions of this deviation", the resolution continued, "are the theses and other printed works of the group known as the so-called 'Workers' Opposition.'"[6] It concluded that the party should conduct a "determined and systematic struggle against these ideas" and "consider the propagation of these ideas as incompatible with membership of the Russian Communist Party". As was frequently the case, the resolution ended with a sop to the defeated group this time in the form of a stipulation that while the Central Committee should "implement these decisions in the strictest fashion" space should be provided "in special editions, anthologies etc. for a more detailed exchange of opinions among party members on all the above questions".[7]

It was also, perhaps, significant that the Congress in general and these two resolutions in particular, had been surrounded by increasing political manipulation. Both had been left off the agenda and were only raised on the last day when numerous delegates had already left to join in the fight over Kronstadt. The leading figure in the Democratic Centralists, Rafailov, complained that the Central Committee and Organization Bureau of the party had intervened to invalidate the election of oppositionists and had substituted candidates of their own. Behind the manoeuvres Rafailov claimed to detect the hand of Stalin acting to pack the congress with supporters of Lenin.[8] The establishment by the Congress of party Control Commissions at all levels "to strengthen the unity and authority of the party" and the appointment of Stalin as General Secretary of the party the following year, could not have been very reassuring.

Lenin's other major initiative at the Congress was the rather uncharismatic sounding resolution "On the replacement of the requisitions with a tax in kind". The intention was that, instead of arbitrarily taking produce from the peasants by force, a regular system of taking a per centage of output, rising to higher levels for larger output, should be set up. While this sounded like a sensible concession to reality it had even more profound implications, notably that the peasants should be allowed to dispose of part of their produce openly. In other words, a space was to be opened up for genuine market relations which had been theoretically, though never actually, suppressed. This also led to a series of related measures allowing limited market relations in industry and a return to taxation of enterprises and institutions, which would be expected to become profit-making. These would replace administrative controls and the moneyless economy.

The adoption of NEP by the party was the greatest victory achieved by the post-October popular movement, but it was also its greatest defeat. Taken together with the other Congress resolutions and the actions against the risings in Tambov and Kronstadt it was clear that Lenin believed that a new balance between the utopian elements of the civil war period – what came to be called "war communism" once it had been superseded – and the popular movement had been reached. In particular, the peasants had gained an important victory. While they would still be urged towards socialism, they were to be left in relative peace. Lenin argued, particularly in his testament to the party, that they should not be subject to any more coercion as this would once again endanger the revolution itself. From the peasants' point of view, of course, the situation that prevailed in the 1920s was the revolution. The landowners had gone, the commune was unchallenged and enjoyed a brief "golden age" characterized by steady increases in output, but punctuated periodically by worrying refusals to sell when the state grain price fell too low.

However, enforced "retreat" on the economic front was accompanied by a further tightening of discipline within the party and greater systematization of control over society at large. After the congress, censorship was regularized. The GPU was established as a permanent political police force to replace the "temporary" Cheka on 8 February 1922. Political prisons became permanent and expanded their intakes. There was a political show trial of SRs. As yet partially autonomous institutions like the universities, were fully incorporated into the Soviet system. The remnants of the popular movement were disarmed and politically broken and, although traces of the movement remained until the end of the decade, it was, by then, unable to resist the renewed Bolshevik onslaught in the form of collectivization and the "second revolution" of 1928–31.

For the time being, however, the new balance of forces constituted an equilibrium which marked the end of the revolution in the sense that victory over counter-revolution had been won and the independent energies of the popular movement had been incorporated, satisfied or tamed. Bolshevik power was unchallenged. The new set of relations was intended by Lenin to last for a significant amount of time. In his last writings of 1922 and 1923 – his reflections on the revolution from his sick bed after a series of strokes had forced him to withdraw from the front line – he eulogized NEP as the ideal series of relationships that would enable socialism to be built in the unfavourable conditions of Russia, particularly in a period when it seemed likely that it would not be joined in this endeavour by any other socialist states. He did not live long enough to see the unravelling of NEP, politically and economically, which led to the abandonment of the alliance with the peasantry, and the return to utopianism and direct administrative intervention in the economy on an unprecedentedly massive scale in the form of the first Five Year Plan, adopted in 1928. We cannot know what he would have thought of these develop-ments, but we do know that the fragile stability represented by NEP was itself a long way from the ideals of either the party or the various components of the popular movement. The revolution was over. As is the way with history, no one was really satisfied.

CHAPTER THIRTEEN

Conclusion: revolutions in collision

No one can doubt that the Russian revolution was a seismic convulsion along deep fault lines in Russian society inherited from its recent, and not so recent, past. We can start to draw the main force fields of this cataclysm together by looking at the structural tensions and then conclude with some broad speculations.

Multiple revolutions

National and regional variations

It is vital to remember that the "Russian" revolution was not one revolution but many, conducted by various nationalities and classes in a kaleidoscope of combinations and with a whole series of outcomes. Although we have borne them in mind, we have not had the opportunity to dwell on regional variations. These are much easier to appreciate in the post-communist era of Russian and East European history, since national and regional problems have forced themselves back into prominence. The years 1917–21 were not only decisive years for the Slavic heartlands of the Russian Empire but also for its minority nationalities.

Even the areas closest to Petrograd underwent very different experiences. Lenin had argued that the October revolution might even have begun in Finland, but subsequent history showed a vastly different outcome there compared to Petrograd. A strong revolutionary working class in Finland was eventually overcome by White forces led by a former Imperial army commander, Mannerheim, who ruthlessly drowned the Finnish left in the blood of a terror which took many thousands of lives. The propertied classes enjoyed a security which was rapidly abolished for their Russian neighbours and Finnish and Russian history began to run in different channels. The rest of the Baltic area showed a similar evolution. The imperial provinces of Lifland, Kurland and Estland became the bourgeois enclaves of Lithuania, Latvia and Estonia, which lived relatively untroubled lives in the interwar period until they were trampled on in the deadly dance of the Nazi and Soviet elephants in the late 1930s and 1940s. The strongest national group of the region and one of the most vehemently anti-Russian for centuries, the Poles, not only established their independence but the increasingly right-wing dictatorial government even began to think it could take advantage of Russia's apparent weakness and enforce its claims for disputed border territories. The Russo-Polish war of 1920 was a turning point. At first the Poles enjoyed success and briefly dominated the western Ukraine, even taking Kiev, but concerted Bolshevik efforts drove them back to the point where Warsaw itself was threatened and fevered visions of Communist advance into Germany began to develop in Moscow where the founding congress of the Communist International was being held. The opportunity was, however, lost and a peace was made which restored the essentials of the status quo that had existed before the war. It did, however, provide a framework for peaceful relations between the two countries for nearly 20 years and enabled the Polish landowners to secure their military-clerical system. In Moscow, the outcome encouraged more sober reflections on the possibility of spreading the revolution to the west.

Elsewhere, despite a great variety of experiences in the revolutionary period, the rest of the former empire was reincorporated into the Soviet Union, as the new country called itself in 1923 once the process of redrawing the boundaries was complete. The losers in terms of national independence were the Ukraine, Georgia, Armenia and the various Muslim khanates of the Transcaucasus and Central Asia. At some point in the revolutionary wars all had enjoyed a period, however fleeting, of independence. The Ukraine required great efforts to subdue and Georgia and Armenia were independent for some years. Unlike the Baltic, moderate left- rather than right-wing groups took control. That made no difference to the Bolsheviks who imposed themselves by force and trickery regardless of political circumstances.

The evolution of Bolshevik nationality policy to deal with the diversity of the new country is beyond our scope. The tensions caused, not least within the party, lasted at least throughout the 1920s and they were submerged rather than eased by full-blown Stalinism. From our present point of view, however, it suffices to remember that the course of the "Russian" revolution was not neatly replicated in the periphery where social structures, culture and tradition were quite different from the Orthodox Slavic heartlands and created an additional dimension to the wider revolution.

The struggles were not those of united nationalities fighting for life but a series of internal battles, civil wars of greater or lesser intensity, compounded by outside interference. In each case, the balance of class forces (including outside links) was vital in determining the outcome. It follows that, enfolded within the "national" struggles, there were a series of attempted revolutions and partial counter-revolutions. The main actors – peasants; smallholders; agricultural labourers; migrant workers; established proletarians; free-floating soldiers and sailors (and, to an extent, their officers); radical intellectuals; clerks and office-workers; members of the professions; the commercial, financial and industrial middle class; the gentry and the great landowners – generally shared some of the same characteristics despite significant variations, for instance in the relative weight of each in different regions and, most obviously, the enormous cultural distinctions stemming from Muslim, Orthodox, Roman Catholic and Protestant religious backgrounds. As we have seen, each group, with the exception of the landowners and the gentry, had its own revolutionary agenda, within which there were additional conflicts based on, for instance, age – younger members of each group being, by and large more assertive than the more circumspect elders – and gender – women increasingly asserting their own rights within the various social groups to which they belonged without, in any way, coming together as a cross-class women's movement. It should also be remembered that the situation was not quite as chaotic as this series of divisions and subdivisions would suggest since a degree of order was introduced by the overarching self-identification of the great majority as part of the *narod*.

Class conflict

While the actual outcome of the series of struggles varied from one part of the Empire to another we can make some general conclusions about the result in the Slavic heartland by the early 1920s.

First and foremost, Russia had undoubtedly undergone the most profound social revolution experienced by any European country in modern times. In the space of four brief years not only had the antiquated political institutions of autocracy been swept away but also the classes on which the system had rested. It is hard to conceive of the extent of the change and it has, perhaps, been greatly underestimated in many interpretations of the revolution and its subsequent history. In the only comparable revolution, in France, the monarchy, aristocracy and church had, for a while, borne the weight of the revolution's fury but, in the end, the victorious middle class came to live alongside its defeated rivals, to some extent sharing their values of land, property, even royalism and apeing their social customs and intermarrying with them. No such *modus vivendi* emerged in Russia. The struggle was to the death. By 1921 the main institutions of the *ancien régime* – monarchy, administration, the legal system, police force, army, navy, State Council, Duma, civil service – were in shreds. But that was only part of the story. All the landowners had been dispossessed and either reduced to the average level or had gone into exile or died in the struggle to defend their property. The middle classes had undergone the same fate. All the factories, banks, commercial and financial enterprises, mines, transport and so on had been expropriated, nationalized or ruined. The skills of managers and trained professionals had been scattered to the four winds. Academic institutions, oddly, maintained a somewhat higher degree of continuity but even here the old professoriate was on the retreat and many went into voluntary or forced exile. But this was not all. The very foundations of the old and rising bourgeois systems – money and the right to property – had been profoundly transformed. In short, the entire old elite, and its most profoundly held values, had been completely eliminated from Russian life. The numerically small but socially decisive tip of the social pyramid had been wiped away. Russia became a country of small-scale entre-preneurs, peasants and a working class, ironically much reduced in size, which still had at least one foot in the village.

Conditions, as we have seen, were far from idyllic. Apart from the ravages of the First World War (wrought on a country which was already economi-cally in the second rank), the costs of the revolutionary gains were very high. In addition to their stranglehold on property the old elite had also more or less monopolized capital, expertise and intellectual power. Although the new Soviet authorities had quickly realized the need to preserve the last two, there was little they could do. The result of the multiple setbacks was the collapse of the economy. Industry was almost wiped out. The interconnections of the market were completely broken by the collapse of the railway system. The relatively resilient agrarian economy recovered sufficiently quickly to avoid further major famines after the disaster of 1921–2, although local famines occurred in most years of the decade preceding the new holocaust of collec-tivization. Even the slow restoration of industry did not bring radical improvement. Workers became increasingly subject to growing managerial control and their unions were less and less effective in promoting their inter-ests. Unemployment was endemic. Social security and medical care remained at a very low level (though by world standards they were by no means negli-gible). Living standards recovered from the low points of the civil war but that is not saying much. In rough terms one can say that it was only in the latter half of the decade that the economy returned to its 1913 levels. Nearly a dec-ade and a half of economic progress had been lost in the cataclysm. Even then, as we now know, Russia's suffering was far from over.

The cultural balance sheet of the revolution is even harder to determine. Given the overwhelming predominance, in the new Russia, of the peasantry, and its reversion to traditional forms, it is hard to conclude anything other than that traditional values – small-scale private property; petty enterprise; folk customs, wisdom and lore; rural religion – provided tough resistance to the revolution's rational, scientific and modernizing ideas, concentrated in its urban centres. Despite a massive expansion of utilitarian popular education after 1920 and the eventual nurturing of a massive scientific, technical and managerial intelligentsia, it would take decades to begin to overcome the legacy of Russia's cultural backwardness. In certain respects, the process has not yet been completed, since Stalinist isolation from the mainstream of world cultural evolution has only recently begun to break down on all fronts. Hitherto, it existed as a form of cultural protectionism.

While the social, economic and cultural effects of the revolution have often been underestimated, its political consequences have never been far from the centre of attention. Everyone knows that, presiding over the country was a single political party. What is less frequently given due weight is the fact that, in its formative years, its leaders and opinion formers were almost exclusively drawn from the radical intelligentsia. How this came about and the special problems raised need careful attention. Let us look, first of all, at the empirical reasons and then turn to the broader issues. This will lead us, in turn, to our final speculative reflections on the revolution.

One can only begin to understand the political foundation of the multiple revolutions if one gives full weight to the fact that the fall of the autocratic state preceded the explosion of the social revolution. As we have seen, it was the fatal blow dealt to tsarism in February which led to the inexorable welling up of revolutionary forces throughout the Empire. The widespread image of a hated tsarism succumbing to waves of popular revolt, like the French monarchy between 1789 and 1792, has to be returned to the realm of myth, or at least, to the screen of the propagandist film. In the final analysis, the immediate reason behind the autocracy's demise was the fear, on the part of crucial elements of the elite, that Nicholas II was no longer capable of holding back the tide of a possible future social revolution now that failure in war had brought that prospect considerably nearer. The less tangible, but by no means less important long-term reasons stemmed from the completely anachronistic nature of tsarism and Nicholas's personal stubbornness in refusing to open-heartedly reform the autocracy, even along the relatively modest, quasi-democratic lines of the German Empire. The inept blunderings of the February plotters brought to life the very dragon of social revolution that they were trying to slay. The central state was fatally weakened and its life blood ebbed steadily away. The question we then have to ask is, why, of all the competing forces, was it the Bolsheviks who were able to impose themselves on this chaos and act as history's instrument in reconstituting the central state?

One aspect, above all, explains their initial success between February and October – their refusal to have anything to do with the Provisional Government. Whatever Lenin meant by forcing this principle on his party in April (and we can speculate endlessly about it), there can be no doubt that it reaped handsome dividends. After the initial months of honeymoon the Provisional Government became more and more despised by the ordinary population, largely because it was not delivering the rewards that the people felt they deserved and was even, it seemed, allowing the democratic gains of February to become eroded. As its prestige declined, so all the major parties hustled to get on board the sinking ship, irretrievably tarnishing their own reputations, at least in the short term. By October, only the Bolsheviks (plus important minority splinter groups from the SRs and Mensheviks, and an influential sprinkling of independent leftists) stood unambiguously in support of the popular revolution. They became, at the crucial moment, the focus of popular aspirations for land redistribution, workers' rights, the democratization of the armed forces, peace, better living standards and, underlying all the rest, self-administration by means of soviets.

This is all well and good and would, no doubt, have been unexceptionable were it not for the fact that the Bolshevik party, in the words it liked to use to describe itself in the Stalinist era, was "a party of a new type". It did not really see itself as the servant of the popular movement, devoted to implementing the popular programme, the popular movement's greatest weakness being its inability – unsurprising given its lack of culture, inexperience and the brevity of the moment of revolution from February to October – to produce a national leadership of its own or to find a trustworthy one from the radical political intelligentsia. Instead, fatefully and ultimately tragically, the Bolshevik party saw itself as leader, teacher and guide of the popular movement, knowing what the people wanted more precisely and deeply than the people did themselves. It was also obsessed with numerous other principles, notably hostility to the peasantry and an almost magical belief in the historical potency of the, in Russia's case, almost non-existent proletariat, that led it, and the country, into many painful and unnecessary adventures. Before drawing out some of the implications of this "fundamentalist" dimension of Bolshevism we have to complete our empirical summary of its capture of power, because October was, as we have seen, not the end of the process but only its first step. Retaining power and forming a new state and new system were much more demanding.

Kadets, SRs and Mensheviks had found, to their cost, that power and popularity were incompatible. The early months of Bolshevik rule were not that different. The growing awareness of the Bolsheviks' "hidden agenda" and the continuing deterioration of the situation eroded at least part of their popularity. They evaded the fate of their predecessors through a number of factors which we have looked at in detail. In particular, they had no serious rivals since the other parties were burnt out and only showed fitful signs of revival in 1918; the very intensity of their convictions and self-righteousness meant they had no "liberal" scruples about imposing their programme on the country, by force if necessary; they had greater ability to mobilize crucial (albeit minority and, in the early months, armed) support than anyone else and, finally, the crude simplification of politics wrought by the civil war – in which, despite the reluctance of the mass of the population to get deeply involved, "Red" was, in the final analysis, preferable to "White" – worked to their decisive advantage. As unchallenged leaders of resistance to foreign intervention and to a counter-revolution which, unlike its more successful counterparts elsewhere, found no way to reach the hearts of a significant mass of the population, the Bolsheviks were able to build up a state embodying many of their principles. As yet, there were compromises. One-person management, petty peasant proprietorship and, in 1921, the market had been accepted. There had also been costs. Real grass-roots democracy had died out and/or been suppressed. Central control was increasing over party, trades unions, culture and education. A political police force and a large conventional army had become institutionalized. Effective opposition from outside the party had been suppressed and that inside the party was increasingly constrained. In short, by 1921–2 the Soviet government was firmly established although it only attracted the active support of a, probably tiny, minority of the population. Its claim to rule did not lie in a democratic, popular mandate but in its belief that, as tutor to the people, it had the right to lead and "enlighten" them (or "raise the consciousness of the masses" in the jargon phrase). Already, however, the contradictions were becoming apparent. Not only "class enemies" but even many workers and even more so peasants, were reluctant to accept the well-intentioned tutelage of an inexperienced and, in many respects incompetent, party. Where consent was lacking, force, in varying degrees, filled the gap. The problem was that, while force in its more extreme manifestations, could ensure compliance, it was only likely to weaken the active consent necessary to the whole enterprise. While there were yet many leaders in the party, including Lenin, who remained painfully aware of the dilemma, the "proto-Stalinist" elements, which saw force as a shortcut to achieving their firmly held goals, were already present. While there was no reason for events to move irreversibly in the "proto-Stalinist" direction, for the time being the tide was mainly flowing towards centralization and dictatorship and away from democracy. In trying to understand why this was so we will have to move into the broader realms of theory and speculation.

The Russian Revolution in historical context: "in my beginning is my end"

The Russian Revolution was the last of the great anti-"feudal", "modernizing" revolutions to occur in Europe. Subsequently, the tide has swept into Asia, Latin America and Africa where complex anti-imperialist and anti-traditional coalitions have produced a wide variety of outcomes. Where, in broad terms, the English, American and French revolutions laid the foundations for modern capitalist liberal democracy, the twentieth-century revolutions have been more ambiguous. Intellectual and cultural modernization – the adaptation of traditional customs and values to scientific and rational ideas derived from the Enlightenment – have been characteristic of all of them, at least until the Islamic fundamentalist backlash against precisely this. However, the social and economic bases have been much more varied. Peasants, migrant workers, intellectuals, entrepreneurs have all played leading roles in socialist, and nationalist revolutionary movements. Rarely has any one of these groups emerged with as clear an hegemony as the English, American and French bourgeoisie. It is not the purpose of the present exercise to examine the entire global revolutionary wave of the twentieth century but to reflect back on the core Russian Revolution in this broader context.

From this perspective, the most striking feature is that twentieth-century "communism" – meaning Bolshevism and its numerous progeny – has been characterized above all by two absolutely fundamental, related contradictions. While universally based on a "proletarian" ideology it has, where it has come to power, relied heavily on peasants and peasant-based revolutions. (This has also been true in areas where it has not come to power, including industrially more developed countries like France, Italy and Spain where communist peasant organizations were an influential component of communist movements.) Secondly, though endowed with a vision of post-capitalist socialism derived from Marx, communism was, almost everywhere, faced with pre-capitalist problems of cultural, political and economic "backwardness", with the problems of the "third world".

The existence of deep contradictions at the heart of communism has been all the more surprising given that ideology, of a quasi-religious intensity, has been a vital characteristic of all communist movements, especially in their "heroic" phases of coming to power and immediate post-revolutionary reconstruction. All major communist leaders, not only Lenin but Mao, Ho Chi Minh, Fidel Castro and many others, have been acutely aware of these contradictions. Indeed, in Russia's case, it was arguments about them which fractured the social democratic movement into Bolshevik and Menshevik wings, the latter arguing that Marxists had no business to be dealing with pre-capitalist problems and so adjusted their strategy accordingly. Lenin made very significant adaptations to Marxism to make it fit in better with Russian reality. In the forefront were his idea that the peasants themselves were divided along class lines and therefore contained a semi-proletarian stratum that would ally with the conventional industrial proletariat, and, the more celebrated idea of "world revolution" according to which capitalism was a seamless international system which could be initially attacked in any of its peripheral component parts (Bukharin optimistically terming them its "weakest links") from where the revolution would spread to the capitalist heartlands. The latter point, an important sub-text of Lenin's pamphlet *Imperialism*, was especially influential in turning communism in parts of the colonial world into a powerful anti-imperialist and anti-capitalist movement, more often than not also suffused with a form of left-wing nationalism. It was, of course, from such movements that communism enjoyed its greatest successes.

In Russia itself, ideology remained a potent driving force into the Stalin period. By the early 1920s, the initial belief of 1917 that "world revolution" would solve the contradictions in the Russian case and that the western European proletariat would restore history to its "proper" course, had faded and given way to a realization that the Russian Revolution might remain "isolated" for an indefinite period. Belief in world revolution never died out altogether but more pressing problems had to be dealt with. Within the communist movement the "Stalinist" response prevailed. Apart from reconciling the movement to the reality of "socialism in one country", there was a fundamental assumption that the Russian Revolution could pull itself out of the swamp by its own bootstraps. Its task was to hasten the destruction of the "historically condemned", mainly peasant, classes who had played no small part in bringing the party to power, and consciously to nurture, even create, the class – the advanced proletariat – that should have brought it to power. The energetic pursuit of this strategy between 1928 and 1938 in Soviet Russia brought about such catastrophes that no other Bolshevik-inspired movement followed quite the same path – although Mao and Pol Pot's variants created original disasters enough. An underlying assumption of all forms of "Stalinism" was that it was possible to smash through "objective" reality and cut history's corners by "consciously" applied ruthless violence which, while regrettable, was historically "inevitable". Although there were hot and cold periods Stalin and many of his world-wide progeny returned to this reflex despite great setbacks resulting from it because they believed, not only that it was "necessary" but also that it had produced results – Russian industrialization, victory in the Second World War, a global wave of revolution from 1949 to 1979 and so on.

However, despite the obvious importance of ideology, or, more accurately, because of its importance, it has also acted like a matador's cape, waving ostentatiously to draw the eye away from the crucial area and direct attack into thin air. This is not to say that, in the case of communism, there was a matador consciously manipulating the cape. Ideology has not only misled analysts – sympathetic to the revolution as well as hostile – but also leaders and participants, diverting attention away from real social and historical forces and giving excessive prominence to less tangible ones more in conformity with the precepts of ideology. As we have seen, one central example has been the minute search for the advanced revolutionary proletariat and emphasis on its role at the expense of studying, for instance, the migrant nature of much of the working class and its peasant links or the role of soldiers and sailors.

It would, therefore, seem desirable to downgrade the ideological perspective, particularly its role in setting the agenda for historical enquiry into the revolution. It is natural for historians to begin to take this step, after all it is no more than has been done in connection with the English, American and French revolutions. For long after the event the ideological components, the explicit values of freedom of conscience, democracy, liberty and so on proclaimed by the leaders of these revolutions were given undue prominence. (They still are in "official" histories of great national traditions they supposedly exemplify.) Today, however, while not denying the importance of anticatholicism, republicanism and jacobinism respectively as vital components, few historians would see the events solely, or even mainly, through the prism of their ostensible ideals. The ideologies themselves have been deconstructed into their component parts and clashing social and material interests have been brought more firmly into the picture.

In the preceding chapters we have been trying to do something similar for the Russian Revolution. Most fundamentally, distancing ourselves from a crude class interpretation of the revolution led us to see that it was not one but many revolutions intertwined. It was peasant, worker and bourgeois. It was anti-"feudal", in part pro-capitalist but, in even greater part, anti-capitalist. In national terms it was the simultaneous explosion of Russian, Ukrainian, Jewish, Baltic, Caucasian and Central Asian revolutions of various kinds. There was scarcely an individual whose life was not affected – usually very extensively – by the tumult of events. Many took part in carrying out their own revolutions in the microcosm of village, factory, regiment or battleship. As we saw, it followed that, although the inital spark came from the political sphere in the form of the collapse of the repressive tsarist state apparatus, which had kept these pressures in check at the expense of allowing them to build up to critical levels, the main force of the revolution in 1917 was social. In this way, after February it was not a primarily political revolution with social consequences but a social revolution with political consequences. Primarily political and ideological interpretations – whether it be the Soviet emphasis on the leading role of Lenin and the party or its obverse, the "proto-totalitarian" view which identifies these same actors as decisive Machiavellian manipulators – cannot explain the full depth, impact or outcome of the revolution.

In this light the "ideal", "natural" outcome of the mass revolution of 1917 "should" have been the establishment of a "populist", self-governing, self-administered, soviet-based society implemented by a broad coalition of organized socialist groups. Proclamation after proclamation, statement after statement, resolution after resolution show that, in autumn 1917 this was what the popular movement yearned for and, indeed, thought it had achieved in October. In more recent terms, the outcome "should" have resembled Allende's Popular Unity government in Chile or the Sandinista coalition at its height in the early stages of the Nicaraguan revolution, that is extensive peasant, worker and intellectual mobilization around a programme centred on immediate popular needs, not distant fantasies of utopian communism. Prominent reasons for the failure of such a solution to emerge include, as we have seen, the pusillanimity of the SR and Menshevik leadership who had no confidence in the popular revolution and the critical and constantly degenerating economic, social and political situation. Also, it should not be forgotten that Russia was the first test bed for what has become standard western (that is initially British and French, later in the century, American) counter-revolutionary tactics based on direct armed intervention where feasible, ample funding of contras if not and "low-intensity" (providing one is not on the receiving end) economic warfare in any case.

However, one can no longer use considerations of this kind to relieve Bolshevism of its own share of reponsibility for the outcome. Ironically, a, possibly *the*, key reason for the failure of the "dream scenario" did not lie with the revolution's enemies on the right – who were marginalized with surprising ease and never looked really likely to muster the power to roll back the social revolution – but from its Bolshevik "friends". While all political leaders see themselves to some extent as the avant-garde of their various movements there are very few who have taken this to the extremes shown by the Bolsheviks. Their tendency to "substitute" the action of the party for that of the revolutionary class has long been remarked on. Taken together, the role of ideology and Bolshevik elitism had the serious effect of creating a Bolshevik leadership that was mainly interested in the popular programme only as a first stage, as a means to the end of its millenarian goals of utopian communism, on a world-wide scale no less, on which its ideologically conditioned gaze was constantly fixed. In this way, the popular movement fell into alliance with a party which was not committed to fulfilling the popular movement's aims in a whole-hearted fashion but which was only interested in their pseudo-fulfilment in that, usually, the forms rather than the content were adopted and many of them were even ultimately reversed. It was, after all, the Bolsheviks not the counter-revolution who suppressed the popular movement – during the civil war, at the time of Tambov and Kronstadt and, eventually, through collectivization and the Great Terror which seemed to have extirpated it for good.

One does not have to assume that this outcome was consciously sought by the Bolsheviks. It came about by stages and under conditions which were not of the Bolsheviks' own making. It may well be that the times called for the kind of revolutionary ruthlessness and determination which have been such a constant, ambiguous feature of communism. Bolshevism was undoubtedly a particularly potent combination of toughness, self-confidence, unflinching support of the interests of the oppressed part of the population (albeit as they rather than the oppressed themselves understood them), resolute opposition to capitalism and imperialism. Many of its leading aspects represented an adaptation of Marxism to the peculiar conditions of Russia where a religious matrix for ideas was still prominent; where populist intellectuals had claimed a "leading role" in bringing about the liberation of the people for 50 years before 1917; where it was less surprising that the party should "substitute" itself for the class since that class was weak to the point of non-existence (at least as a fully developed advanced proletariat) and so on. In this way, Bolshevism itself appears not simply as an agent of history, as its apologists and detractors tend to exaggerate, but as an object itself conditioned by history. But at the same time there was no inevitably determined course being followed here. Many leading, and not so leading, Bolsheviks protested about the way the party seemed to be abandoning its ideals of 1917. Others pointed out from very early on that minority status could only be sustained by terror. Even in 1921 various "futures" remained open. "Proto-Stalinism" had certainly gained ground but its further evolution was by no means inevitable although Lenin did appear to be pushing an uncompromisingly fundamentalist line at the Tenth Party Congress in that year.

The long-term results of the revolution, were, however, quite different from those foreseen by Lenin or anyone else at that time. When the full extent of Stalin's crimes became known the hope of many non-Stalinist Bolsheviks (notably Trotskyists), as well as many non-Bolshevik and non-Marxist socialists and radicals was that the gains of the revolution – higher living standards; a strong stable state; powerful armed forces and, above all, mass education and cultural modernization – would eventually outweigh the tremendous human costs imposed in the Stalin years. In many ways, this is precisely what the best aspects of Gorbachev and *perestroika* represented – the healthy heart of Russia's post-revolutionary experiences bursting through the dilapidated and thoroughly discredited remnants of Stalinist dictatorship. Setting the political–ideological arguments to one side, the role of communism in Russian history has been to transform the feudal–autocratic system, to install the institutions of a pseudo-democracy (constitution, legal system, parliaments, soviets) where none had existed before for the majority of the population and to expand education and pursue economic growth to the extent that the population matured beyond the tutelage of secret police, informers, censorship and millenarian ideology and sought to pursue "normal", "modern" lives. If Russia's Bolshevik experience "shows" anything, it is not the "failure of Marxism", still less the "failure of socialism" but the impossibility of achieving fervently, religiously, held ideals without the support of the overwhelming majority of the population subjected to the implementation of those ideals. In learning this lesson the Bolsheviks are not alone in the twentieth century. Many other movements – fascism, Islamic fundamentalism, the "new" right, social democracy, nationalism – all have to face a similar test. The "awakening" of the masses in modern society complicates the task of any potential ideologue or dictator.

Chronology

1855		Alexander II succeeds to the throne
1856		Crimean war ends
1861	February	Manifesto proclaims emancipation of the serfs
1880		Pobedonostsev appointed as Procurator of the Holy Synod
1881	February	Alexander II assassinated by populist terrorists. Alexander III accedes to the throne
	August	Emergency regulations give government additional repressive powers
1891–2		Famine in Central Russia
1892	August	Witte appointed as Minister of Finance
1894		Nicholas II succeeds Alexander III
1898		Social Democratic Party founded
1901		Strikes, rural disturbances and populist terrorism begin. Socialist Revolutionary Party founded
1902		Union of Liberation set up. Develops into Constitutional Democratic Party in 1906
1903	August	Witte sacked as Minister of Finance
1904	February	War with Japan
1905	2 January	Fall of Port Arthur
	9 January	Bloody Sunday in St. Petersburg begins revolution of 1905
	February–March	Battle of Mukden
	August	Peace conference opens in Portsmouth, New Hampshire
	October	Wave of strikes leads to proclamation of October Manifesto
		Pobedonostsev resigns as Procurator of the Holy Synod
1906		Fundamental Laws promulgated
	27 April	First Duma inaugurated
	9 July	First Duma dissolved

295

1907	20 February	Second Duma inaugurated
	3 June	Stolypin's "coup d'état" dissolves Second Duma and leads to restricted franchise for Third and Fourth Dumas
1912	4 April	Lena massacre
1914	August	Outbreak of war with the Central Powers
1915	August crisis	Tsar becomes Commander-in-Chief, ministers beg him to desist
		Progressive Bloc formed in Duma
1916	June	Brusilov offensive
	16/17 December	Murder of Rasputin
1917	23 February	Workers demonstrate in Petrograd
	26 February	Pavlovsky Guards mutiny
	27 February	Petrograd Soviet set up
	28 February	Duma sets up Provisional Committee. Moscow Soviet set up
	1 March	Army Order Number One of the Petrograd Soviet issued
	2 March	Provisional Government formed
		Tsar abdicates
	3 April	Lenin arrives in Petrograd
	4 April	Lenin promulgates his April Theses
	18 April	Note of Foreign Minister Miliukov to Allied Governments, confirming Russia's loyalty
	20–21 April	Demonstrations of soldiers and workers against Miliukov and the Provisional Government
	2 May	Resignation of Miliukov
	4 May	Trotsky returns to Russia
	4–28 May	First All-Russian Congress of Peasants' Deputies
	5 May	First Coalition Government. Mensheviks and Socialist Revolutionaries join new Cabinet
	3–24 June	First Congress of Workers' and Soldiers' Soviets meets in Petrograd
	10 June	Bolsheviks call off planned demonstration in Petrograd
	18 June	Beginning of Russian offensive
		Huge Soviet demonstration against war in Petrograd. Bolshevik slogans and placards predominate
	2 July	Provisional Government grants autonomy to Ukraine. Kadet ministers resign in protest
	3–4 July	July Days in Petrograd
	5 July	Bolshevik press shut down and offices attacked. Government declares Lenin to be a German agent. Lenin goes into hiding
	8 July	Kerensky becomes Prime Minister. New (Second) Coalition Government formed
	18 July	General Kornilov appointed Commander-in-Chief
	23 July	Trotsky arrested (freed 4 September)
	26 July–3 August	Sixth Congress of Bolshevik Party held in Petrograd

12–15 August	State Conference in Moscow
21 August	Germans occupy Riga
26–30 August	General Kornilov moves troops on Petrograd, with aim of destroying the Soviet and reorganizing the Provisional Government
1 September	Russia proclaimed a republic
	Five-man Directory, headed by Kerensky, as temporary government pending solution of political crisis caused by a new withdrawal by Kadets
	Petrograd and Moscow Soviets pass first Bolshevik resolutions (31 August–5 September)
8–9 September	Bolsheviks take control of presidium of Petrograd Soviet
14–22 September	Democratic Conference held in Petrograd as platform for Soviet and trade union support for Provisional Government
25 September	Third Coalition Government formed
7 October	Lenin returns to Petrograd but remains in hiding
10 October	Bolshevik Central Committee meeting votes to put armed uprising "on the agenda"
12 October	Petrograd Soviet sets up Military Revolutionary Committee
16 October	Bolshevik Central Committee confirms decision of 10th over continued objections of Kamenev and Zinoviev
24 October	Provisional Government attempts to control streets and bridges of Petrograd
24–25 October	Lenin comes out of hiding. Petrograd Soviet takes over the city. The Military Revolutionary Committee proclaims Soviet power. The Second All-Russian Congress of Soviets convenes. Kerensky leaves city to find loyal troops.
26 October	Winter Palace "stormed". Provisional Government ministers arrested. Soviet Government of People's Commissars (*Sovnarkom*) set up with Lenin as chair.
27 October	Kerensky starts to move on Petrograd with General Krasnov and a small force of cossacks
30 October	Krasnov's force defeated at Pulkovo on outskirts of Petrograd
1 November	Kerensky goes into hiding
2 November	Victory of the Bolsheviks in Moscow
	General Alekseev arrives in the Don cossack capital, Novocherkassk, and begins forming the Volunteer Army
7 November	Ukrainian Rada proclaims its Third Universal declaring the Ukraine to be independent
12 November	Constituent Assembly elections begin
14 November	Armistice agreed with Central Powers. Negotiations start at Brest-Litovsk (19 November)
19 November	Kornilov, Denikin and other Generals imprisoned for participation in the Kornilov revolt escape and join Alekseev's Volunteer Army
20 November	Bolsheviks take over *Stavka* (General Staff Headquarters)

	7 December	Cheka set up
	12 December	Left SRs join the Soviet Government
1918	5 January	The Constituent Assembly opens
	6 January	Constituent Assembly dispersed
	10–18 January	Third Congress of Soviets
	15 January	Red Army founded from amalgamation of Red Guard and other independent soviet and factory militia
	15–16 January	Abortive Bolshevik uprising in Kiev
	3 March	Treaty of Brest-Litovsk signed
	8 March	The Bolsheviks adopt the name "Communists" at Seventh Party Congress (6–8 March)
	12 March	Government moves from Petrograd to Moscow
	15 March	Left SRs leave government in protest at Treaty of Brest-Litovsk
	16 March	Trotsky appointed Commissar for War
	13 April	Kornilov killed in action
	28–29 April	Central Powers proclaim Skoropadsky Hetman of Ukraine
	14 May	Beginning of open hostilities between the Soviets and the Czechoslovaks who occupy Chelyabinsk (26 May)
	8 June	SR government proclaimed in Samara. White Government created in Omsk, Siberia
	11 June	Committees of Poor Peasants (*kombedy*) set up
	17–19 June	Unsuccessful rebellion against the Soviet regime in Tambov
	20 June	Assassination of leading Petrograd Communist, Volodarsky, by an SR
	28 June	Nationalization of certain large industries
	6 July	German Ambassador, Count Mirbach, assassinated by Left SRs in Moscow as signal for rebellion (suppressed 8 July)
	8 July	City of Yaroslavl' seized by insurgents acting under the direction of Boris Savinkov
	16 July	Nicholas II and members of his family shot in Ekaterinburg
	21 July	Yaroslavl' captured by Soviet troops
	6 August	Czechoslovaks and anti-Bolshevik Russians capture Kazan, the furthest point of their advance
	14 August	Small British force occupies Baku
	15 August	Volunteer Army captures the capital of the Kuban Territory, Ekaterinodar
	26 August	Volunteer Army occupies Novorossiisk, gains access to the sea
	30 August	SR terrorist wounds Lenin. Uritsky, prominent Petrograd chekist, killed by SR
	6 September	"Red terror" proclaimed
	8–23 September	Representatives of anti-Bolshevik Governments of Siberia and Eastern Russia meet in State Conference at Ufa. Set up Directory with five members
	10 September	Red Army captures Kazan

	8 October	Red Army captures Samara
	9 October	Directorate retreats to Omsk
	9 November	Revolution in Germany
	11 November	Armistice ends First World War. Central Powers begin withdrawal from occupied territories of western Russia and the Ukraine, leaving a power vacuum behind
	13 November	Soviet Government annuls Treaty of Brest-Litovsk
		Ukrainian nationalists under leadership of Petliura rebel against Hetman Skoropadsky
	18 November	Admiral Alexander Kolchak proclaimed Supreme Ruler after coup d'état in Omsk and arrest of SR members of Directory
	21 November	Soviet Government nationalizes internal trade
	27 November	Provisional Soviet Government of Ukraine proclaimed
	14 December	Ukrainian nationalist troops under Petliura occupy Kiev; Hetman Skoropadsky flees. Red Army occupies Minsk
	17 December	French land at Odessa
1919	3 January	Soviet troops take Riga in Latvia, and Kharkov in the Eastern Ukraine
	6 February	Red Army takes Kiev
	15 February	General Krasnov, Ataman of the Don Territory, resigns leaving General Denikin as Supreme Commander of White forces in south-eastern Russia
	2–7 March	First Congress of the Communist International in Moscow
	13 March	Kolchak's army captures Ufa
	18–23 March	Eighth Congress of the Communist Party. Adopts more conciliatory line toward middle peasants
	6 April	Red Army enters Odessa after its evacuation by French
	10 April	Soviet troops occupy Simferopol in the Crimea
	26 April	Kolchak's offensive stopped after defeats
	7 May	Ataman Grigoriev changes sides and issues anti-Bolshevik and anti-Semitic manifesto
	15–17 May	Grigoriev's troops conduct savage pogrom in town of Elizavetgrad
	19 May	Denikin begins offensive
	4 June	Makhno breaks with Red Army command
	9 June	Ufa retaken by Red troops
	25 June	Denikin captures Kharkov
	30 June	Denikin captures Tsaritsyn and Ekaterinoslav
	1 July	Soviet troops in Urals take Perm
	25 July	Red Army occupies Chelyabinsk
	27 July	Grigoriev killed by Makhno
	23 August	Denikin captures Odessa
	30 August	Red Army abandons Kiev; Petliurists take over
	31 August	Denikin occupies Kiev
	11 October	Yudenich advances on Petrograd

	14 October	Denikin occupies Orel
	20 October	Red Army retakes Orel
	22 October	Yudenich defeated in suburbs of Petrograd
	9 November	Makhno captures Ekaterinoslav from Denikin's forces
	14 November	Red Army takes Kolchak's capital, Omsk
	17 November	Soviet troops occupy Kursk. Denikin's army begins to collapse
	12 December	Red Army captures Kharkov
	16 December	Red Army retakes Kiev
	30 December	Red Army takes Ekaterinoslav
1920	3 January	Red Army occupies Tsaritsyn
	4 January	Kolchak abdicates as Supreme Ruler in favour of Denikin
	8 January	Red Army captures Rostov, seat of Denikin's Government
	16 January	Allied Supreme Council raises blockade of Soviet Russia
	2 February	Peace agreement with Estonia
	7 February	Kolchak shot by order of the Revolutionary Committee in Irkutsk
	17 March	Red Army occupies Ekaterinodar
	27 March	Red Army takes Novorossiisk
	4 April	Denikin resigns command of armed forces of South Russia, nominating General Baron Wrangel' as his successor
	24 April	Russo-Polish war begins
	27 April	Red Army captures Baku; Azerbaijan Soviet Government instituted
	6 May	Poles take Kiev
	7 May	Soviet Government recognizes independence of Georgia
	6 June	Wrangel' breaks out from the Crimea
	12 June	Red Army retakes Kiev
	11 July	Red Army captures Minsk
	14 July	Red troops occupy Vilnius
	1 August	Red Army takes Brest-Litovsk
	15 August	Polish forces south of Warsaw launch counter-offensive
	21 August	Poles recapture Brest-Litovsk and Red Army retreats from the Vistula
	2 September	Congress of Peoples of the East opens in Baku
	12 October	Signature of peace treaty with Poland
	20 October	Red offensive against Wrangel'
	14 November	Wrangel' evacuates the Crimea
	26 November	Red Army attacks Makhno
1921	27 February	Soviet regime proclaimed in Georgia, after invasion by Red Army
	1–17 March	Kronstadt rebellion
	8–16 March	Tenth Party Congress

Notes

Introduction

1. "Living history: wiring the revolution", *Soviet Weekly* (23 December 1989).
2. This account is based on that of his daughter published, together with extracts from her father's letters, in Zenaide Bashkiroff, *The sickle and the harvest* (London, 1960). Spellings have been brought into conformity with the rules applying to the rest of the current book. This reference p. 8.
3. *Ibid.*, p. 32.
4. *Ibid.*, p. 54.
5. *Ibid.*, p. 53.
6. *Ibid.*, p. 218.
7. S. Jones, "The non-Russian nationalities", in *Society and politics in the Russian revolution*, R. Service (ed.) (Basingstoke and London, 1992), p. 38.

Chapter One

1. A. Yarmolinsky, *Road to revolution: a century of Russian radicalism* (New York, 1962), p. 200.
2. H. Seton-Watson, *The Russian empire 1801–1917* (Oxford, 1967), p. 657.
3. A. G. Rashin, *Naselenie Rossii za 100 let (1811–1913gg.)* (Moscow, 1956), p. 21. Excludes Poland and Finland.
4. S. L. Hoch, "On good numbers and bad: Malthus, population trends and peasant standard of living in late imperial Russia", *Slavic Review* 53(1), Spring 1994, pp. 41–75.
5. See, for example, S. J. Seregny, *Russian teachers and peasant revolution: the politics of education in 1905* (Bloomington, Indianapolis, 1989).
6. J. Brooks, *When Russia learned to read: literacy and popular literature, 1861–1917* (Princeton, 1985).
7. Discussed in the next chapter.
8. For further discussion see B. Eklof & S. P. Frank (eds), *The world of the Russian peasant: post emancipation culture and society* (Boston, London, Sydney, Wellington, 1990) and appropriate sections of J. Neuberger, *Hooliganism: crime, culture and*

power in St. Petersburg, 1900–1914 (Berkeley, 1993); L. Engelstein, The keys to happiness: sex and the search for modernity in fin-de-siècle Russia (Ithaca, New York, 1992); C. Worobec, Peasant Russia: family and community in the post-emancipation period (Princeton, 1991); S. P. Frank & M. D. Steinberg (eds), Cultures in flux: lower-class values, practices, and resistance in late imperial Russia (Princeton, 1994).

9. J. Blum, "Russia", in European landed elites in the nineteenth century, D. Spring (ed.) (Baltimore, London, 1977), p. 86.

10. P. Gattrell, The tsarist economy 1815–1917 (London, 1986), p. 34.

Chapter Two

1. H. Seton-Watson, The Russian empire 1801–1917 (Oxford, 1967), p. 627.
2. L. Wolf, Notes on the diplomatic history of the Jewish question (London, 1919), p. 59.
3. Ibid., p. 62.
4. It had been 1.26 million in 1897. S. Smith, Red Petrograd: revolution in the factories 1917–18 (Cambridge, 1983), p. 5 and M. McCauley, Bread and justice: state and society in Petrograd 1917–22 (Oxford, 1991), p. 264.
5. Sir G. Buchanan, My mission to Russia and other diplomatic memoirs, [2 vols, vol. 2] (New York, 1970), pp. 48–9.
6. N. Farson, The way of a transgressor (London, 1940), especially pp. 126–50.
7. G. Vernadsky & S. Pushkarev, A source book for Russian history from early times to 1917 (New Haven, London, 1972), vol. 3, pp. 865–8.
8. A. Shliapnikov, On the eve of 1917: reminiscences from the revolutionary underground (London, New York, 1982), p. 83, which claims to be an "almost verbatim" account.
9. Vernadsky & Pushkarev, A source book for Russian history (New Haven, London, 1972), vol. 3, pp. 865–8.
10. W. H. Chamberlin, The Russian revolution (New York, 1965), vol. 1, p. 73.
11. E. H. Carr, The Bolshevik revolution (Harmondsworth, 1966), vol. 1, p. 81.

Chapter Three

1. R. P. Browder & A. F. Kerensky (eds), The Russian Provisional Government 1917 – documents (Stanford, 1961), vol. I, pp. 135–6.
2. Ibid., vol. II, pp. 851–2.
3. Ibid., p. 1536.
4. For a record of proceedings see Gosudarstvennoe soveshchanie (s predisloviem Ia. A. Iakovleva) (Moscow, Leningrad, 1930).
5. Lenin's campaign for an insurrection and the October revolution are discussed in more detail in Chapter 7.

Chapter Four

1. N. N. Sukhanov, The Russian revolution: an eyewitness account (New York, 1962), vol. I, pp. 40–41.
2. P. Miliukov, Political memoirs 1905–1917 (Ann Arbor, 1967), p. 393.
3. Ibid.
4. F. A. Golder (ed.), Documents of Russian history 1914–17 (Gloucester MA, 1927), p. 261.

5. *Ibid.*, p. 263.

6. B. Pares, *The fall of the Russian monarchy: a study of the evidence* (London, 1939), p. 438.

7. W. H. Chamberlin, *The Russian revolution* (New York, 1965), vol. I, p. 73.

8. J. Neumann, "A note on the winter of the Kronstadt sailors' uprising in 1921", *Soviet Studies* 44(1), 1992, p. 153. January and March were also unusually cold.

9. O. Anweiler, *The soviets: the Russian workers', peasants' and soldiers' councils 1905–1921* (New York, 1974), p. 113.

10. S. A. Smith, *Red Petrograd: revolution in the factories 1917–18* (Cambridge, 1983), pp. 105–6.

11. *Ibid.*, p. 80.

12. See G. Swain, *Russian social democracy and the legal labour movement 1906–14* (London, 1983).

13. I. I. Gaza, *Putilovets v trekh revoliutsiakh* (Leningrad, 1933), pp. 370–71.

14. *Ibid.*, pp. 386–400.

15. V. L. Meller & A. M. Pankratova, *Rabochee dvizhenie v 1917 goda* (Moscow, Leningrad, 1926), pp. 224–38.

16. *Ibid.*, pp. 171–7.

17. D. Koenker, *Moscow workers and the 1917 revolution* (Princeton, 1981), p. 304.

18. Smith, *Red Petrograd*, p.145.

19. Leading items of the revisionist school include: D. Koenker, *Moscow workers and the 1917 revolution* (Princeton, 1981); D. Koenker & W. Rosenberg, *Strikes and revolution in Russia, 1917* (Princeton, 1989); D. Mandel, *The Petrograd workers and the fall of the old regime* (London, 1983); D. Mandel, *The Petrograd workers and the soviet seizure of power* (London, 1984) and Smith, *Red Petrograd*. R. Kaiser (ed.), *The workers' revolution in Russia: the view from below* (Cambridge, 1987) includes summary articles by leading proponents of the school. The "peasant–worker" school is led by R. Johnson, *Peasant and proletarian: the working class of Moscow in the late nineteenth century* (Leicester, 1979) and J. Bradley, *Muzhik and Muscovite: urbanization in late imperial Russia* (Berkeley, 1985). B. Bonwetsch, "Rußland, Oktober 1917: Hegemonie des Proletariats oder Volksrevolution? Bemerkung zur sowjetischen Historiographie seit Anfang siebziger Jahre", *Osteuropa* 39, 1990, pp. 733–47 summarizes some late Soviet contributions to the debate. A recent statistical examination of the issues, which, according to its authors is inconclusive but adds weight to the revisionist argument, can be found in R. Brym & E. Economakis, "Peasant or proletarian? Militant Pskov workers in St. Petersburg, 1913", *Slavic Review* 53(1), Spring 1994, pp. 120–39.

20. Mark Steinberg, *Moral communities; the culture of class relations in the Russian printing industry 1867-1907* (Berkeley, Los Angeles, Oxford, 1992), pp. 82–3.

21. *Ibid.*, p. 233.

22. *Ibid.*, p. 244–5.

23. *Ibid.*, p. 244.

24. *Ibid.*, p. 134.

25. For a more prolonged discussion of factors predisposing Russian workers to revolutionary activity see Christopher Read, "Labour and socialism in tsarist Russia", in *Labour and socialist movements in Europe before 1914*, D. Geary (ed.) (Oxford, New York, Munich, 1983).

26. A. Blok, "The twelve", in *Selected poems* (trans. by Jon Stallworthy and Peter France) (Harmondsworth, 1974), p. 118.

27. Gaza, *Putilovets*, pp. 320–22.

28. *Ibid.*, p. 404.
29. Smith, *Red Petrograd*, pp. 10, 23.
30. E. M. Dune, *Notes of a Red Guard* (trans and ed. by Diane P. Koenker and S. A. Smith) (Urbana and Chicago, 1993), p. 34.
31. Gaza, *Putilovets*, pp. 361–2.
32. A. Blok, "The twelve", in *Selected poems*, p. 117.
33. Meller & Pankratova, *Rabochee dvizhenie*, p. 317.

Chapter Five

1. see N. Stone, *The eastern front 1914–17* (London, 1975), p. 296.
2. A. D. Maliavskii, *Krest'ianskoe dvizhenie v Rossii v 1917g. mart–oktiabr'* (Moscow, 1981), pp. 169–70.
3. *Ibid.*, p. 134.
4. see J. Channon, "The landowners", in *Society and politics in the Russian revolution*, R. Service (ed.) (Basingstoke and London, 1992), pp. 120–46.
5. Maliavskii, *Krest'ianskoe dvizhenie*, p. 248.
6. *Ibid.*, p. 286.
7. see J. Channon, "The Bolsheviks and the peasantry: the land question during the first eight months of soviet rule", *Slavonic and East European Review* 66(4), October 1988, pp. 593–624.
8. M. Perrie, "The peasants", in *Society and politics in the Russian revolution*, R. Service (ed.) p. 29.
9. *Ibid.*, p. 105.
10. C. E. Vulliamy & A. L. Hynes, *The Red archives: Russian state papers and other documents relating to the years 1915–18* (London, 1929), p. 250.
11. See, for example, the discussion in J. Channon, "The peasantry in the revolutions of 1917", in *Revolution in Russia: reassessments of 1917*, E. R. Frankel, J. Frankel and B. Knei-Paz (eds) (Cambridge, 1992), pp. 121–4.
12. R. Stites, "Iconoclastic currents in the Russian revolution: destroying and preserving the past", in *Bolshevik culture: experiment and order in the Russian revolution*, A. Gleason *et al.* (eds) (Bloomington, Indianapolis, 1985), pp. 1–24.
13. Maliavskii, *Krest'ianskoe dvizhenie*, p. 10.

Chapter Six

1. A. Wildman, *The end of the Russian imperial army*, vol. 1 (Princeton, 1980), and vol. 2 (Princeton, 1987).
2. See P. Kenez, "Changes in the social composition of the officer corps during World War I", *Russian Review* 31, pp. 369–75 and D. Longley, "Officers and men: a study of the development of political attitudes among the sailors of the Baltic Fleet in 1917", *Soviet Studies* 25, pp. 28–50.
3. L. S. Gaponenko (ed.), *Revoliutsionnoe dvizhenie v Russkoi armii 27 fevralia–24 oktiabria 1917 goda: sbornik dokumentov* (Moscow, 1968), p. 30.
4. *Ibid.*, p. 36.
5. *Ibid.*, p. 37.
6. *Ibid.*, p. 40.
7. *Ibid.*, p. 53.
8. *Ibid.*, p. 48.

9. M. Frenkin, *Russkaia armiia i revoliutsiia 1917–18* (Munich, 1978), p. 70.
10. E. Mawdsley, *The Russian revolution and the Baltic fleet, war and politics February 1917–April 1918* (London, 1978), p. 157.
11. Frenkin, *Russkaia armiia*, p. 104.
12. *Ibid.*, p. 105.
13. Gaponenko, *Revoliutsionnoe dvizhenie*, p. 53.
14. *Ibid.*, p. 116.
15. Frenkin, *Russkaia armiia*, pp. 111–12; Gaponenko, *Revoliutsionnoe dvizhenie*, p. 116.
16. Frenkin, *Russkaia armiia*, p. 118–19.
17. *Ibid.*, pp. 131–8.
18. *Ibid.*, pp. 251–2.
19. *Ibid.*, pp. 126–30.
20. *Ibid.*, p. 146.
21. *Ibid.*, pp. 141–6.
22. *Ibid.*, p. 143.
23. *Ibid.*, p. 99.
24. *Ibid.*, pp. 79–80, 100, 121.
25. Gaponenko, *Revoliutsionnoe dvizhenie*, p. 83.
26. Frenkin, *Russkaia armiia*, pp. 148–9.
27. *Ibid.*, p. 705.
28. *Ibid.*, p. 153.
29. *Ibid.*, p. 217.
30. *Ibid.*, p. 179.
31. Gaponenko, *Revoliutsionnoe dvizhenie*, p. 100.
32. Frenkin, *Russkaia armiia*, pp. 284, 287–8.
33. *Ibid.*, p. 292.
34. *Ibid.*, p. 297.
35. *Ibid.*, p. 301.
36. *Ibid.*, pp. 449–54, 469–72, 477, 480–82, 485, 497.
37. Gaponenko, *Revoliutsionnoe dvizhenie*, p. 221.
38. *Ibid.*, p. 142.
39. Frenkin, *Russkaia armiia*, pp. 380–91; A. M. Zaionchkovskii, *Kampaniia 1917 goda* (Moscow, 1923), pp. 151–88; *Krasnaia letopis'* 6, 1923; Gaponenko, *Revoliutsionnoe dvizhenie*, pp. 223–4.
40. Gaponenko, *Revoliutsionnoe dvizhenie*, pp. 340–50.
41. *Ibid.*, p. 403.
42. *Ibid.*, p. 406.
43. *Ibid.*, pp. 412–13.
44. *Ibid.*, pp. 424–5.
45. *Ibid.*, p. 334.
46. *Ibid.*, pp. 358–9.
47. *Ibid.*, p. 364.
48. *Ibid.*, pp. 450, 452.
49. *Ibid.*, p. 423.
50. *Ibid.*, pp. 453–4.
51. *Ibid.*, pp. 528, 539.
52. *Ibid.*, pp. 547, 549.
53. *Ibid.*, pp. 539, 551.

Chapter Seven

1. W. Rosenberg, "Russian labor and Bolshevik power: social dimensions of protest in Petrograd after October", in *The workers' revolution in Russia in 1917: the view from below*, D. Kaiser (ed.) (Cambridge, 1987), p. 129.

2. F. F. Raskolnikov, *Kronstadt and Petrograd in 1917* (London, 1982), p. 281.

3. *Ibid.*, p. 271.

4. *Ibid.*, p. 272.

5. L. S. Gaponenko (ed.), *Revoliutsionnoe dvizhenie v Russkoi armii 27 fevralia–24 oktiabria 1917 goda: sbornik dokumentov* (Moscow, 1968), p. 595, f. 228.

6. M. Frenkin, *Zakhvat vlasti Bol'shevikami v Rossii i rol' tylovykh garnizonov armii: podgotovka i provedenie oktiabr'skogo miatezha 1917–1918gg* (Jerusalem, 1982), p. 203.

7. *Ibid.*, p. 310.

8. N. N. Sukhanov, *The Russian revolution: an eyewitness account* (New York, 1962), vol. 2, p. 529.

9. *Ibid.*, p. 524.

10. *Ibid.*, p. 529.

11. *Ibid.*, p. 530.

12. V. I. Lenin, "War and social-democracy", *Selected works* (Moscow, 1967), vol. 1, p. 663.

13. V. I. Lenin, *State and revolution*, Ch. V, Pt iv. See also Ch. III, Pt iii. All emphases in this and all other quotes from Lenin are taken from the original.

14. V. I. Lenin, "One of the fundamental questions of the revolution", in V. I. Lenin, *Between the two revolutions*, p. 379.

15. "The tasks of the revolution", in *ibid.*, p. 388.

16. "Marxism and insurrection", in *ibid.*, p. 396.

17. *Ibid.*

18. "Letters on tactics", in *ibid.*, pp. 73–4.

19. Speech on the Land decree at the Second All-Russian Congress of Soviets, in *The Bolshevik revolution, 1917–18: documents and materials*, J. Bunyan & H. H. Fisher (eds). (Stanford, 1934), p. 132.

20. "To workers, peasants and soldiers", in Lenin *Between the two revolutions*, p. 418.

21. "Marxism and insurrection", in *ibid.*, p. 396.

22. S. T. Possony, *Lenin: the compulsive revolutionary* (Chicago, 1964, rev. edn London, 1966).

23. D. Volkogonov, *Lenin: life and legacy* (trans. and ed. by H. Shukman) (London, 1994).

24. D. Volkogonov, *Stalin: triumph and tragedy* (London, 1991).

25. "To the Central Committe of the RSDLP", in Lenin, *Between the two revolutions*, pp. 482, 363.

26. *Ibid.*, p. 366. Written 1–3 September.

27. "The tasks of the revolution", in *ibid.*, p. 381.

28. "The Bolsheviks must assume power", in *ibid.*, p. 390. Written 12–14 September.

29. "Marxism and insurrection", in *ibid.*, p. 393. Written 13–14 September.

30. "From a publicist's diary: the mistakes of our party", in *ibid.*, p. 405.

31. "The crisis has matured", in *ibid.*, pp. 412–14.

32. "Letter to the Central Committee, the Moscow and Petrograd committees and the Bolshevik members of the Petrograd and Moscow Soviets", in *ibid.*, p. 469.

33. "Advice of an onlooker", in *ibid.*, pp. 474–5.

34. "Letter to the Bolshevik comrades", in *ibid.*, p. 482.

35. *The Bolsheviks and the October Revolution: minutes of the Central Committee of the Russian Social–Democratic Labour Party (Bolsheviks) August 1917–February 1918* (trans. A. Bone) (London, 1974), p. 88.

36. "Letter to Central Committee members", in Lenin, *Between the two revolutions*, pp. 505–6.

37. A. Rabinowitch, *The Bolsheviks come to power* (New York, 1976), p. 292.

Chapter Eight

1. N. N. Sukhanov, *The Russian revolution: an eyewitness account* (New York, 1962), vol. 2, p. 630.

2. A. Ia. Grunt, *Moskva 1917-i: revoliutsiia i kontrrevoliutsiia* (Moscow, 1976), pp. 220–21.

3. *Ibid.*, pp. 250, 327.

4. *Ibid.*, pp. 359–60.

5. *Ibid.*, p. 294.

6. *Ibid.*, p. 295.

7. *Ibid.*, p. 161.

8. see Chapter 3.

9. W. H. Chamberlin, *The Russian revolution* (New York, 1965), vol. I, pp. 387–8.

10. In many respects the situation bears no little similarity to that of the former Soviet Union after its collapse in 1991. Each area offers a complex history of its own reflecting its unique political, social and cultural mix. In the end, only Finland, Poland and the Baltic States were able to sustain their independence. Fascinating though they are, these cases and the more ephemeral independence movements are beyond the scope of the present study which focuses primarily on Russia.

11. M. Frenkin, *Russkaia armiia i revoliutsiia 1917–1918* (Munich, 1978), pp. 602–3.

12. *Ibid.*, p. 606.

13. *Ibid.*, pp. 625–32.

14. A. A. Bogdanov, "Fortunes of the workers' party in the present revolution", *Novaia zhizn'*, 19 (26 January) and 20 (27 January) 1918, unpublished translation by J. Biggart for The Study Group on the Russian Revolution, January 1984. Similar themes can be found in Bogdanov's volume *Voprosy sotsializma*, in particular the chapter "Voennyi kommunizm i gosudarstvennyi kapitalizm" written around the same time. It has been reprinted in A. A. Bogdanov, *Voprosy sotsializma: raboty raznykh let* (Moscow, 1990), pp. 295–351.

15. M. Frenkin, *Zakhvat vlasti Bol'shevikami v Rossii i rol' tylovykh garnizonov armii: podgotovka i provedenie oktiabr'skogo miatezha 1917–1918gg* (Jerusalem, 1982), pp. 356, 373. See also Part IV of J. L. H. Keep, *The Russian revolution: a study in mass mobilization* (London, 1976).

16. For the fullest analysis of the Constituent Assembly election see O. H. Radkey, *Russia goes to the polls: the election to the All-Russian Constituent Assembly, 1917* (Ithaca, 1989).

17. Evan Mawdsley suggests this in the conclusion of his book *The Russian civil war* (London, Sydney, Wellington, 1987), p. 289.

18. *Ibid.*, pp. 285–8.

19. Simplified from S. Malle, *The economic organization of war communism, 1918–21* (Cambridge, 1985), pp. 508–11.

20. M. McCauley, *Bread and justice: state and society in Petrograd 1917–22* (Oxford,

1991), p. 264.

21. On the white-collar intelligentsia see D. Orlovsky, "State building in the civil war era: the role of the lower-middle strata", in *Party, state and society in the Russian civil war: explorations in social history*, D. P. Koenker *et al.* (eds) (Bloomington, 1989), pp. 180–209. On the creative intelligentsia see C. Read, *Culture and power in revolutionary Russia: the intelligentsia and the transition from tsarism to communism* (London, 1990).

22. The Makhno movement and the Tambov uprising are discussed below in Chapter 10.

23. Mawdsley, *The Russian civil war*, p. 100.

24. *Ibid.*, p. 275.

25. *Ibid.*, p. 280.

26. *Ibid.*

Chapter Nine

1. *The Bolsheviks and the October revolution: minutes of the Central Committee of the Russian Social–Democratic Labour Party (Bolsheviks) August 1917–February 1918* (trans. A. Bone) (London, 1974), pp. 136–40.

2. M. Ferro, "The birth of the Soviet bureaucratic system", in *Reconsiderations on the Russian revolution*, R. C. Elwood (ed.) (Columbus, 1976), pp. 100–132.

3. See H. Hardeman, *Coming to terms with the Soviet regime: the "Changing Signposts" movement among Russian émigrés in the early 1920s* (DeKalb, 1994).

4. L. D. Gerson, *The secret police in Lenin's Russia* (Philadelphia, 1976), p. 38.

5. G. Leggett, *The Cheka: Lenin's political police, the All-Russian Extraordinary Commission for Combating Counter-revolution and Sabotage (December 1917 to February 1922)* (Oxford, 1981), p. 323.

6. *Ibid.*, p. 9.

7. *V. I. Lenin i VChK: sbornik dokumentov (1917–1922 gg.)* (Moscow, 1987), p. 23.

8. *Ibid.*, p. 24.

9. Gerson, *The secret police*, p. 14.

10. *Ibid.*, p. 68.

11. *Ibid.*, p. 30.

12. *Ibid.*, p. 31.

13. *Ibid.*, pp. 31–2.

14. *V. I. Lenin i VChK*, pp. 10–11.

15. *Ibid.*, pp. 17–18.

16. R. H. McNeal (ed.), *Resolutions and decisions of the Communist Party of the Soviet Union* (Toronto, Buffalo, 1974), p. 63.

17. Gerson, *The secret police*, p. 29.

18. *Ibid.*, pp. 27–9.

19. *Ibid.*, p. 80.

20. *Ibid.*, p. 77.

21. *Ibid.*, p. 77.

22. *Ibid.*, p. 38.

23. *Ibid.*, p. 83; Leggett, *The Cheka*, p. 279 and p. 329.

24. Gerson, *The secret police*, p. 295, f. 97.

25. *Ibid.*, p. 145.

26. *Ibid.*, p. 159.

27. Leggett, *The Cheka*, p. 312.

28. *Ibid.*, p. 314.

29. *Ibid.*
30. *Ibid.*, p. 286.
31. *Ibid.*, p. 309.
32. Gerson, *The secret police*, p. 188.
33. *Ibid.*, p. 130.
34. E. Heifetz, *The slaughter of Jews in the Ukraine* (New York, 1921), pp. 175–81, quoted in W. B. Lincoln, *Red victory* (London, 1991), p. 319. Estimates for the number of victims vary widely. R. Pipes, *The Bolsheviks in power* (London, 1993), p. 112, quotes 50,000–200,000 as the range.
35. Leggett, *The Cheka*, p. 285.
36. *Ibid.*, p. 310.
37. Gerson, *The secret police*, p. 128.
38. Leggett, *The Cheka*, p. 257 and table pp. 258–9.
39. Gerson, *The secret police*, p. 60.
40. *Ibid.*, pp. 59–60.
41. *Ibid.*, p. 68.
42. S. S. Khromov (ed.), *Grazhdanskaia voina i voennaia interventsiia v SSSR: entsiklopediia* (Moscow, 1987), p. 107.
43. F. Benvenuti, *The Bolsheviks and the Red Army, 1918–22* (Cambridge, 1988), p. 256, f. 63.
44. Khromov, *Grazhdanskaia voina*, p. 106.
45. M. von Hagen, *School of the revolution: Bolsheviks and peasants in the Red Army 1918–1928* (unpubl. diss. Stanford 1984, UMI), p. 57.
46. T. H. Rigby, *Communist party membership in the USSR, 1917–1967* (Princeton, 1968), p. 241.
47. Benvenuti, *The Bolsheviks and the Red Army*, p. 230, f. 109. Benvenuti says there were only 30,000 party members in the army in March 1919.
48. McNeal, *Resolutions and decisions*, pp. 73–83.
49. Rigby, *Communist party*, p. 52. Incidentally, it fell steadily to 472,000 in 1924 indicating, perhaps, post-civil war indifference to the party.
50. von Hagen, *School of the revolution*, p. 29.
51. McNeal, *Resolutions and decisions*, pp. 83–4.
52. *Ibid.*, p. 86.
53. *Ibid.*, p. 89. Emphasis in the original.
54. *Ibid.*, p. 88.
55. *Ibid.*, p. 89.
56. *Ibid.*, pp. 55–7.
57. *Ibid.*, pp. 58–9.
58. *Ibid.*, p. 63.
59. *Ibid.*, p. 65.
60. *Ibid.*, pp. 68–9.
61. *Ibid.*, pp. 63–5.
62. *Ibid.*, p. 66.
63. *Ibid.*, p. 69.
64. N. Bukharin & E. Preobrazhensky, *ABC of Communism* (Harmondsworth, 1969), p. 116.
65. McNeal, *Resolutions and decisions*, pp. 65–6.
66. *Ibid.*, pp. 40–41.
67. *Ibid.*, p. 64.
68. *Ibid.*, p. 65.

69. *Ibid.*, p. 67.
70. *Ibid.*, p. 64.
71. *Ibid.*, p. 68.
72. "Militarization", meaning following a military-type model of organization, should be carefully distinguished from "militarism" in the sense of a glorification of military violence, which has never figured highly in Soviet ideology.
73. *Ibid.*, p. 48.
74. E. Mawdsley, *The Russian civil war* (London, 1987), p. 37.
75. R. Luxemburg, "The Russian Revolution", in *The Russian Revolution and Leninism or Marxism* (Ann Arbor, 1961), p. 71.
76. Carr, *The Bolshevik revolution*, p. 209.
77. C. Read, "Values, substitutes and institutions: the cultural dimension of the Bolshevik dictatorship", in *Prelude to catastrophe: civil wars and the new order in the Russian Empire*, R. Pipes & V. Brovkin, eds. (Cambridge, Mass., 1996).

Chapter Ten

1. Carr, *The Bolshevik revolution* (Harmonsworth, 1968), vol. 2, p. 161.
2. *Ibid.*, p. 163.
3. *Ibid.*, p. 193.
4. V. V. Kabanov, *Krest'ianskoe khoziastvo v usloviakh "voennogo kommunizma"* (Moscow, 1988), p. 25.
5. *Ibid.*, p. 26.
6. Carr, *The Bolshevik revolution*, vol. 2, p. 57.
7. O. Figes, *Peasant Russia, civil war: the Volga countryside in revolution, 1917–21* (Oxford, 1989), p.71.
8. P. N. Pershin, *Agrarnaia revoliutsiia v Rossii: kniga 2. Agrarnye preobrazovaniia velikoi oktiabr'skoi sotsialisticheskoi revoliutsii (1917–1918 gg.)* (Moscow, 1966), p. 200.
9. Figes, *Peasant Russia*, p. 54.
10. *Ibid.*, pp. 61–2.
11. *Ibid.*, p. 56.
12. See John Channon, "The landowners", in *Society and politics in the Russian revolution*, R. Service (ed.) (Basingstoke, London, 1992), pp. 120–46.
13. V. V. Kabanov, *Krest'ianskoe khoziastvo*, p. 48.
14. Figes, *Peasant Russia*, pp. 155–6.
15. Kabanov, *Krest'ianskoe khoziastvo*, p. 32.
16. Pershin, *Agrarnaia revoliutsiia*, p. 231.
17. Kabanov, *Krest'ianskoe khoziastvo*, p. 144.
18. *Ibid.*, p. 235.
19. *Ibid.*, p. 47. Exactly what kind of land (e.g. arable, pasture or forest) was involved is not clear.
20. Figes, *Peasant Russia*, p. 127.
21. Kabanov, *Krest'ianskoe khoziastvo*, p. 111.
22. *Ibid.*, p. 90.
23. According to Figes, *Peasant Russia*, p. 276.
24. Kabanov, *Krest'ianskoe khoziastvo*, p. 50.
25. *Ibid.*, pp. 52–3.
26. *Ibid.*, pp. 61–2.
27. Figes, *Peasant Russia*, p. 103.
28. Kabanov, *Krest'ianskoe khoziastvo*, p. 67.

29. *Ibid.*, p. 57.
30. *Ibid.*, p. 112.
31. *Ibid.*, p. 47.
32. V. V. Kabanov, *Oktiabr'skaia revoliutsiia i kooperatsiia (1917 g.–mart 1919 g.)* (Moscow, 1973).
33. Kabanov, *Krest'ianskoe khoziastvo*, p. 47.
34. Figes, *Peasant Russia*, pp. 302–7.
35. Kabanov, *Krest'ianskoe khoziastvo*, pp. 77–8.
36. Figes, *Peasant Russia*, p. 198.
37. Quoted in *ibid.*, p. 198.
38. *Ibid.*, p. 312.
39. *Ibid.*, pp. 312–20.
40. O. Figes, "The Red Army and mass mobilization during the Russian civil war 1918–20", *Past and Present* **129**, pp. 168–211.
41. Figes, *Peasant Russia*, p. 196.
42. Quoted in *ibid.*, p. 122.
43. Kabanov, *Krest'ianskoe khoziastvo*, p. 112.
44. *Ibid.*, p. 116.
45. *Ibid.*, pp. 139–57.
46. Figes, *Peasant Russia*, p. 260.
47. Kabanov, *Krest'ianskoe khoziastvo*, p. 174.
48. *Ibid.*, p. 202.
49. Figes, *Peasant Russia*, pp. 254–9.
50. J. L. H. Keep, *The Russian revolution: a study in mass mobilization* (London, 1976), pp. 439–40.
51. *Ibid.*, p. 441.
52. *Ibid.*, p. 444.
53. *Ibid.*, p. 550, f. 25.
54. Pershin, *Agrarnaia revoliutsiia*, p. 127.
55. *Ibid.*, p. 154.
56. *Ibid.*, p. 405.
57. Figes, *Peasant Russia*, p. 248.
58. *Ibid.*, p. 210.
59. *Ibid.*, p. 245.
60. *Ibid.*, p. 220.
61. *Ibid.*, pp. 104–5.
62. Kabanov, *Krest'ianskoe khoziastvo*, p. 32.
63. V. I. Lenin, "The immediate tasks of the Soviet Government", in *Selected works* (Moscow, 1967), vol. 2, p. 645.
64. *Ibid.*, p. 646. Note, once again, the reversion to the "populist" category "working-people".
65. *Ibid.*, p. 670.
66. *Ibid.*, p. 672.
67. *Ibid.*, p. 673.
68. V. I. Lenin, *Collected works* (Moscow, 1964), vol. 27, p. 212.
69. V. I. Lenin, "'Left-wing' childishness and the petty-bourgeois mentality", in *Selected works* (Moscow, 1967), vol. 3, p. 697.
70. Lenin, "The immediate tasks of the Soviet Government", *ibid.*, vol.2, p. 664.
71. L. Trotsky, *Terrorism and Communism* (London, 1975), p. 149. C. Claudin-Urondo, *Lenin and the cultural revolution*(trans. B. Pearce) (Sussex, NJ, 1977), p. 112, f. 41.

72. Lenin, "Immediate tasks", p. 664.
73. *Ibid.*, p. 675.
74. *Ibid.*, p. 670.
75. *Ibid.*, p. 670.
76. *Ibid.*, p. 669. Lenin had a very complex attitude to civil war which would take us beyond our present scope. In this period he consistently believed it was unavoidable, proclaiming in September 1914 that the world war should be transformed into a European civil war. At various points in 1917 he found it expedient to divert attention away from the prospect and expressed changing opinions about how deep and serious such a conflict might be.
77. E. H. Carr, *The Bolshevik revolution* (Harmondsworth, 1966), vol. 2, p. 89.
78. *Ibid.*, pp. 87–8.
79. *Ibid.*, p. 217.
80. *Ibid.*
81. *Ibid.*, p. 215.
82. *Ibid.*, p. 218.
83. *Ibid.*, p. 217.
84. *Ibid.*, p. 216.
85. G. & H. Weber, *Lenin: life and works* (London, 1980), p. 168.
86. Carr, *The Bolshevik revolution*, vol. 2, pp. 216–17.
87. *Ibid.*, p. 216.
88. T. F. Remington, *Building socialism in Lenin's Russia: ideology and industrial organization, 1917–21* (Pittsburgh, 1984), p. 37.
89. *Ibid.*, p. 39.
90. *Ibid.*, p. 38.
91. *Ibid.*, p. 39.
92. M. Brinton, *The Bolsheviks and workers' control, 1917 to 1921: the state and counter-revolution* (London, 1970), p. 31.
93. *Ibid.*, p. 31.
94. *Ibid.*, p. 29.
95. *Ibid.*, pp. 29–30.
96. *Ibid.*, p. 8.
97. V. I. Lenin, *Between the two revolutions: articles and speeches of 1917* (Moscow, 1971), p. 435.
98. Brinton, *The Bolsheviks and workers' control*, p. 14.
99. *Ibid.*, p. 14.
100. *Ibid.*, pp. 15–16.
101. *Ibid.*, p. 19.
102. W. J. Chase, *Workers, society and the Soviet state: labor and life in Moscow, 1918–29* (Urbana and Chicago, 1987), p. 33.
103. *Ibid.*, pp. 33–4.
104. M. McCauley, *Bread and justice: state and society in Petrograd, 1917–22* (Oxford, 1991), p. 398.
105. Chase, *Workers, society and the Soviet state*, p. 34.
106. *Ibid.*, p. 34.
107. Remington, *Building socialism*, pp. 104–5.
108. Chase, *Workers, society and the Soviet state*, p. 50.
109. McCauley, *Bread and justice*, pp. 27–8, 162.
110. *Ibid.*, p. 416.
111. Chase, *Workers, society and the Soviet state*, p. 51.

112. M. S. Bernshtam, *Nezavisimoe rabochee dvizhenie v 1918 godu: dokumenty i materialy* (Paris, 1981), pp. 65–6.
113. *Ibid.*, p. 68.
114. *Ibid.*, p. 79.
115. *Ibid.*, pp. 87–90.
116. Remington, *Building socialism*, p. 103.
117. *Ibid.*, p. 105.
118. *Ibid.*, p. 105.
119. *Ibid.*, p. 107.
120. *Ibid.*, p. 108.
121. *Ibid.*, p. 109.
122. *Ibid.*, pp. 106–7.
123. L. D. Gerson, *The secret police in Lenin's Russia* (Philadelphia, 1976), p. 158; McCauley, *Bread and justice*, pp. 251–2.
124. Remington, *Building socialism*, p. 101.
125. Chase, *Workers, society and the Soviet state*, p. 32.
126. For an extensive account, mainly of the repressive element, see V. N. Brovkin, *Behind the front lines of the civil war: political parties and social movements in Russia, 1918–22* (Princeton, 1994).
127. R. H. McNeal (ed.), *Resolutions and decisions of the Communist Party of the Soviet Union* (Toronto, Buffalo, 1974), pp. 100–104.
128. L. B. Schapiro, *The origins of the Communist autocracy: political opposition in the Soviet state: first phase, 1917–22* (London, 1955), p. 231.

Chapter Eleven

1. P. Arshinov, *History of the Makhnovist movement* (Detroit, Chicago, 1974), p. 84. Some versions say there were two trains. M. Malet, *Nestor Makhno in the Russian civil war* (London, 1982), p. 23.
2. Malet, *Nestor Makhno*, p. 36.
3. *Ibid.*, p. 70.
4. *Ibid.*, p. 76.
5. *Ibid.*, p. 80.
6. Arshinov, *History of the Makhnovist movement*, p. 214.
7. Voline, *The unknown revolution 1917–21* (Detroit and Chicago), p. 557. Arshinov, *History of the Makhnovist movement*, p. 55.
8. Arshinov, *History of the Makhnovist movement*, p. 183.
9. *Ibid.*, pp. 210–11.
10. *Ibid.*, p. 211.
11. *Ibid.*, p. 96.
12. See W. B. Lincoln, *Red victory: a history of the Russian civil war* (London, 1991), p. 327.
13. Arshinov, *History of the Makhnovist movement*, pp. 207–9.
14. G. Leggett, *The Cheka: Lenin's political police* (Oxford, 1981), p. 325.
15. O. H. Radkey, *The unknown civil war in Soviet Russia, a study of the Green movement in the Tambov region, 1920–1* (Stanford, 1976).
16. Note: there is a Tambov *uezd* – the area surrounding the provincial capital, the city of Tambov – as well as Tambov province.
17. *Ibid.*, pp. 150–54.
18. *Ibid.*, p. 73.

19. *Ibid.*, p. 75.
20. *Ibid.*, p. 94.
21. O. H. Radkey, *Russia goes to the polls: the election to the All-Russian Constituent Assembly* (Ithaca and London, 1990), p. 148.
22. Radkey, *The unknown civil war*, pp. 38–9. Figures rounded off.
23. *Ibid.*, pp. 367–8.
24. *Ibid.*, p. 15.
25. I. Getzler, *Kronstadt 1917–21: the fate of a Soviet democracy* (Cambridge, 1983), p. 211.
26. *Ibid.*, p. 282.
27. *Ibid.*, pp. 211, 282.
28. All quoted in *ibid.*, p. 211.
29. *Ibid.*, pp. 209–12.
30. *Ibid.*, p. 212.
31. *Ibid.*
32. P. Avrich, *Kronstadt, 1921* (Princeton, 1970), pp. 35–51 and M. McCauley, *Bread and justice: state and society in Petrograd 1917–22* (Oxford, 1991), pp. 397–411.
33. Getzler, *Kronstadt 1917–21*, p. 243.
34. A. Berkman, *The Bolshevik myth* (London, 1989), p. 303.
35. Getzler, *Kronstadt 1917–21*, p. 244.
36. *Ibid.*, p. 257.
37. E. Mawdsley, "The Baltic fleet and the Kronstadt mutiny", *Soviet Studies* 24(4), April 1973, p. 509 and E. Mawdsley, *The Russian revolution and the Baltic fleet*, (London, 1978).
38. Getzler, *Kronstadt 1917–21*, p. 207.
39. *Ibid.*, p. 208.
40. *Ibid.*, p. 226.
41. V. I. Lenin, *Selected works* (Moscow, 1967), vol. 3, p. 574.
42. Quoted from Lenin, *Polnoe sobranie sochinenii* (Moscow, 1962–65), 5th. ed, XLIII, p. 138; in Avrich, *Kronstadt 1921*, p. 3.

Chapter Twelve

1. Lenin, *Selected works* (Moscow, 1967), vol. 3, pp. 559–61.
2. R. H. McNeal (ed.), *Resolutions and decisions of the Communist Party of the Soviet Union* (Toronto, Buffalo, 1974), vol. 2, p. 119.
3. A. Kollontai, *Selected writings* (Westport, 1977), p. 162.
4. *Ibid.*, pp. 199–200, slightly adapted.
5. McNeal, *Resolutions and decisions*, p. 121.
6. *Ibid.*, p. 122.
7. *Ibid.*, p. 124.
8. *Ibid.*, p. 115.

Select bibliography

Abraham, R. *Alexander Kerensky: the first love of the revolution*. London, 1987.

Acton, E. *Rethinking the Russian Revolution*. London, New York, Melbourne, Auckland, 1990.

Akhapkin, Iu. (ed.). *First decrees of soviet power*. London, 1970.

Anweiler, O. *The soviets: the Russian workers', peasants' and soldiers' councils 1905–1921*. New York, 1974.

Arshinov, P. *History of the Makhnovist movement*. Detroit and Chicago, n.d.

Atkinson, D. *The end of the Russian land commune 1905–1930*. Stanford, 1983.

Avrich, P. *Kronstadt, 1921*. Princeton, 1970.

Bashkiroff, Z. *The sickle and the harvest*. London, 1960.

Benvenuti, F., *The Bolsheviks and the Red Army, 1918–22*. Cambridge, 1988.

Berkman, A. *The Bolshevik myth*. London, 1989.

Bernshtam, M. S. *Nezavisimoe rabochee dvizhenie v 1918 godu: dokumenty i materialy*. Paris, 1981.

Blok, A. "The twelve", in *Selected poems* (trans. by Jon Stallworthy and Peter France). Harmondsworth, 1974.

Bogdanov, A. A. Fortunes of the workers' party in the present revolution. *Novaia zhizn'* **19** (26 January) and **20** (27 January) 1918, unpublished translation by J. Biggart for The Study Group on the Russian Revolution, January 1984.

—*Voprosy sotsializma: raboty raznykh let*. Moscow, 1990.

Bonnell, V. *Roots of rebellion: workers' politics and organizations in St. Petersburg and Moscow 1900–1914*. Berkeley, 1983.

—*The Russian worker: life and labor under the tsarist regime*. Berkeley, 1983.

Bonwetsch, B. Rußland, Oktober 1917: Hegemonie des Proletariats oder Volksrevolution? Bemerkung zur sowjetischen Historiographie seit Anfang siebziger Jahre. *Osteuropa* **39**, pp. 733–47, 1990.

Bradley, J. *Muzhik and Muscovite: urbanization in late imperial Russia*. Berkeley, 1985.

Brinton, M. *The Bolsheviks and workers' control, 1917 to 1921: the state and counter-revolution*. London, 1970.

Brooks, J. *When Russia learned to read: literacy and popular literature, 1861–1917*. Princeton, 1985.

Brovkin, V. N. *Behind the front lines of the civil war: political parties and social movements in Russia, 1918–22.* Princeton, 1994.

Brovkin, V. N. *The Mensheviks after October: socialist opposition and the rise of the Bolshevik dictatorship.* Ithaca and London, 1987.

Browder, R. P. & A. F. Kerensky (eds). *The Russian Provisional Government 1917 – documents,* [3 vols]. Stanford, 1961.

Brown, S. Communists and the Red cavalry: political education of the *Konarmiia* in the Russian civil war. *Slavonic and East European Review* 73(1), pp. 82–99, 1995.

Brym, R. & E. Economakis. Peasant or proletarian? Militant Pskov workers in St. Petersburg, 1913. *Slavic Review* 53(1), pp. 120–39, 1994.

Bukharin, N. & E. Preobrazhensky. *ABC of Communism.* Harmondsworth, 1969.

Bunyan, J. & H. H. Fisher (eds). *The Bolshevik revolution 1917–18: documents and materials.* Stanford, 1934.

Bushnell, J. *Mutiny amid repression. Russian soldiers in the revolution of 1905–1906.* Bloomington, 1985.

Carr, E. H. *The bolshevik revolution,* [3 vols]. Harmondsworth, 1968.

Carrère d'Encausse, H. *Lenin: revolution and power.* London, 1982.

Chamberlin, W. H. *The Russian revolution,* [2 vols]. New York, 1965.

Channon, J. The Bolsheviks and the peasantry: the land question during the first eight months of Soviet rule. *Slavonic and East European Review* 66(4), pp. 593–624, 1988.

—The landowners. In *Society and politics in the Russian revolution,* R. Service (ed.) Basingstoke, London, 1992, pp. 120–146.

—The peasantry in the revolutions of 1917. In *Revolution in Russia: reassessments of 1917,* E. R. Frankel *et al.* (eds). Cambridge, 1992.

Chase, W. J. *Workers, society and the Soviet state: labor and life in Moscow, 1918–29.* Urbana and Chicago, 1987.

Claudin-Urondo, C. *Lenin and the cultural revolution* (trans. by B. Pearce). Sussex, NJ, 1977.

Cohen, S. *Bukharin and the Bolshevik revolution: a political biography (1888–1938).* New York, 1973.

Coquin, F-X. & C. Gervais-Francelle (eds). *1905: la première révolution Russe.* Paris, 1986.

Crisp, O. *Studies in the Russian economy before 1914.* London, 1976.

Crisp, O. & L. Edmondson (eds). *Civil rights in Imperial Russia.* Oxford, 1989.

—*The conscience of the revolution.* Cambridge, MA, 1960.

—*Red October: the Bolshevik revolution of 1917.* London, 1968.

Daniels, R. V. (ed.). *A documentary history of communism,* [2 vols]. Vermont, 1984.

Danilov, V. P. *Rural russia under the new regime.* Bloomington, 1988.

Davies, R. W. *et al.* (eds). *The economic transformation of the Soviet Union 1913–1945.* Cambridge, 1994.

Davies, R. W. (ed.). *From tsarism to the new economic policy: continuity and change in the economy of the* USSR. London, 1990.

Diakin, V. S. *Samoderzhavie, burzhuaziia i dvorianstvo v 1907–1911gg.* Leningrad, 1978.

Dune, E. M. *Notes of a Red Guard* (trans. and ed. by Diane P. Koenker and S. A. Smith). Urbana and Chicago, 1993.

Edmondson, L. & P. Waldron (eds). *Economy and society in Russia and the Soviet Union 1860–1930.* New York, 1992.

Eklof, B. & S. P. Frank (eds). *The world of the Russian peasant: post emancipation culture and society.* Boston, London, Sydney, Wellington, 1990.

Elwood, R. C. (ed.). *Reconsiderations on the Russian revolution.* Columbus, 1976.

Engelstein, L. *The keys to happiness: sex and the search for modernity in fin-de-siècle Rus-*

sia. Ithaca, New York, 1992.

Ezergailis, A. *The 1917 revolution in Latvia*. Boulder, 1974.

Ferro, M. The birth of the Soviet bureaucratic system. In *Reconsiderations on the Russian revolution*. R. C. Elwood (ed.). Columbus, 1976, pp. 100–132.

—*October 1917. A social history of the Russian Revolution*. London, 1980.

—*The Russian Revolution of February 1917*. London, 1972.

Figes, O. *Peasant Russia, civil war: the Volga countryside in revolution, 1917–21*. Oxford, 1989.

—The Red Army and mass mobilization during the Russian civil war 1918–20. *Past and Present* **129**, pp. 168–211, 1990.

Fitzpatrick, S. *The Russian Revolution*. Oxford, 1982.

Frank, S. P. & M. D. Steinberg (eds). *Cultures in flux: lower-class values, practices, and resistance in late imperial Russia*. Princeton, 1994.

Frankel, E. R. *et al*. (eds). *Revolution in Russia: reassessments of 1917*. Cambridge, 1992.

Frenkin, M. *Russkaia armiia i revoliutsiia 1917–1918*. Munich, 1978.

—*Zakhvat vlasti Bol'shevikami v Rossii i rol' tylovykh garnizonov armii: podgotovka i provedenie oktiabr'skogo miatezha 1917–1918gg*. Jerusalem, 1982.

Galili, Z. *The Menshevik leaders in the Russian Revolution: social realities and political strategies*. Princeton, 1989.

Gaponenko, L. S. (ed.). *Revoliutsionnoe dvizhenie v Russkoi armii 27 fevralia–24 oktiabria 1917 goda: sbornik dokumentov*. Moscow, 1968.

Gattrell, P. *The tsarist economy 1815–1917*. London, 1986.

Gaza, I. I. *Putilovets v trekh revoliutsiakh*. Leningrad, 1933.

Geary, D. (ed.). *Labour and socialist movements in Europe before 1914*. Oxford, New York, Munich, 1983.

von Geldern, J. *Bolshevik festivals 1917–1920*. Berkeley, Los Angeles, London, 1993.

Gerson, L. D. *The secret police in Lenin's Russia*. Philadelphia, 1976.

Getzler, I. *Kronstadt 1917–21: the fate of a Soviet democracy*. Cambridge, 1983.

—*Martov: a political biography of a Russian social democrat*. London, 1967.

Gill, G. *Peasants and government in the Russian Revolution*. London, 1979.

Gleason, A. *et al*. (eds). *Bolshevik culture: experiment and order in the Russian revolution*. Bloomington, Indianapolis, 1985.

Golder, F. A. (ed.). *Documents of Russian history 1914–17*. Gloucester MA, 1927.

Goldman, E. *My disillusionment in Russia*. New York, 1923.

Golub, P. A. *et al*. (eds). *Istoricheskii opyt trekh rossiisskikh revoliutsii*, [3 vols]. Moscow, 1986–1987.

Gorky, M. *Untimely thoughts: essays on revolution, culture and the Bolsheviks 1917–1918*. London, 1968.

Gosudarstvennoe soveshchanie (s predisloviem Ia. A. Iakovleva). Moscow–Leningrad, 1930.

Got'e, I. V. *Time of troubles: the diary of Iury Vladimirovich Got'e* (trans. and ed. by T. Emmons). London, 1988.

Gregory, P. *Russian national income, 1885–1913*. Cambridge, 1982.

Grif sekretnosti sniat. Poteri vooruzhenykh sil SSSR *v voinakh, boevykh deistviiakh i voennykh konfliktakh; statisticheskoe issledovanie*. Moscow, 1993.

Grunt, A. Ia. *Moskva 1917-i: revoliutsiia i kontrrevoliutsiia*. Moscow, 1976.

von Hagen, M. *School of the revolution: Bolsheviks and peasants in the Red Army 1918–1928*. (Unpublished dissertation. Stanford, December 1984. UMI)

—*Soldiers in the proletarian dictatorship: the Red Army and the Soviet Socialist state 1917–1930*. Ithaca and London, 1990.

Hamm, M. F. (ed.). *The city in late imperial Russia*. Bloomington, 1986.

Hardeman, H. *Coming to terms with the Soviet regime: the "Changing Signposts" movement among Russian émigrés in the early 1920s*. DeKalb, 1994.

Hasegawa, T. *The February Revolution*. Seattle and London, 1981.

Heifetz, E. *The slaughter of Jews in the Ukraine*. New York, 1921.

Hoch, S. L. On good numbers and bad: Malthus, population trends and peasant standard of living in late imperial Russia. *Slavic Review*, 53(1), pp. 41–75, 1994.

Holmes, L. *The Kremlin and the schoolhouse: reforming education in Soviet Russia 1917–1931*. Bloomington and Indianapolis, 1991.

Hosking, G. *The Russian constitutional experiment: government and Duma, 1907–1914*. London, 1985.

Ignat'ev, G. S. *Moskva v pervyi god proletarskoi diktatury*. Moscow, 1975.

Ioffe, G. Z. *Krakh rossiiskoi monarkhicheskoi kontrrevoliutsii*. Moscow, 1977.

Johnson, R. *Peasant and proletarian: the working class of Moscow in the late nineteenth century*. Leicester, 1979.

Jones, S. The non-Russian nationalities. In *Society and politics in the Russian revolution*, R. Service (ed.). Basingstoke and London, 1992.

Kabanov, V. V. *Krest'ianskoe khoziastvo v usloviakh "voennogo kommunizma"*. Moscow, 1988.

—*Oktiabr'skaia revoliutsiia i kooperatsiia (1917 g.–mart 1919 g.)*. Moscow, 1973.

Kaiser, D. (ed.). *The workers' revolution in Russia: the view from below*. Cambridge, 1987.

Kakurin, N. E. *Kak srazhalas' revoliutsiia*, [2 vols]. (2nd edn.) Moscow–Leningrad, 1926. Reprinted Moscow, 1990.

Katkov, G. *Russia 1917: the February revolution*. London, 1967.

—*The Kornilov affair*. London, 1980.

Keep, J. L. H. (trans. and ed.). *The debate on soviet power: minutes of the All-Russian Central Executive Committee Second Convocation, October 1917–January 1918*. Oxford, 1979.

Keep, J. L. H. *The Russian revolution: a study in mass mobilization*. London, 1976.

Kenez, P. Changes in the social composition of the officer corps during World War I. *Russian Review* **31**, pp. 369–75, 1972.

Kerensky, A. *The prelude to Bolshevism: the Kornilov rebellion*. London, 1919.

—*The catastrophe*. New York, 1927.

—*Russia and history's turning point*. New York, 1965.

Khromov, S.S. (ed.). *Grazhdanskaia voina i voennaia interventsiia v SSSR: entsiklopediia*. Moscow, 1987.

Koenker, D. *Moscow workers and the 1917 revolution*. Princeton, 1981.

Koenker, D. & W. Rosenberg. *Strikes and revolution in Russia, 1917*. Princeton, 1989.

Koenker, D. *et al*. (eds). *Party, state and society in the Russian civil war*. Bloomington, Indianapolis, 1989.

Kollontai, A. *Selected writings*. Westport, 1977.

Kotel'nikov, K. G. & V. L. Meller. *Krest'ianskoe dvizhenie v gody voiny i pered Oktiabrem 1917 g*. Leningrad, 1927.

Kruchkovskaia, V. M. *Tsentral'naia gorodskaia duma v Petrograde v 1917 g*. Leningrad, 1986.

Leggett, G. *The Cheka: Lenin's political police, the All-Russian Extraordinary Commission for Combating Counter-revolution and Sabotage (December 1917 to February 1922)*. Oxford, 1981.

Lenin, V. I. *Between the two revolutions: articles and speeches of 1917*. Moscow, 1971.

—*Collected works*, [45 vols]. Moscow, 1960–1970.

—*State and revolution*. Petrograd, 1918.

—*Selected works*, [3 vols]. Moscow, 1967,

V. I. Lenin i VChK: sbornik dokumentov (1917–1922 gg.) Moscow, 1987.

Lih, L. *Bread and authority in Russia*. Berkeley, 1990.

Lincoln, W. B. *Red victory: a history of the Russian civil war*. London, 1991.

Living history: wiring the revolution. *Soviet Weekly* (23 December 1989).

Longley, D. Officers and men: a study of the development of political attitudes among the sailors of the Baltic Fleet in 1917. *Soviet Studies* 25, pp. 28–50, 1973.

Luxemburg, R. The Russian Revolution. In *The Russian Revolution and Leninism or Marxism*. Ann Arbor, 1961.

Malet, M. *Nestor Makhno in the Russian civil war*. London, 1982.

Maliavskii, A. D. *Krest'ianskoe dvizhenie v Rossii v 1917g. mart–oktiabr'*. Moscow, 1981.

Malle, S. *The economic organization of war communism 1918–21*. Cambridge, 1985.

Mandel, D. *The Petrograd workers and the fall of the old regime*. London, 1983.

—*The Petrograd workers and the soviet seizure of power*. London, 1984.

Manning, R. *The crisis of the old order in Russia: gentry and government*. Princeton, 1982.

Mawdsley, E. The Baltic fleet and the Kronstadt mutiny. *Soviet Studies* 24(4), April 1973.

—*The Russian civil war*. London, Sydney, Wellington, 1987.

—*The Russian revolution and the Baltic fleet, war and politics February 1917–April 1918*. London, 1978.

McCauley, M. *Bread and justice: state and society in Petrograd 1917–22*. Oxford, 1991.

McKean, R. *St. Petersburg between the revolutions*. New Haven, 1990.

McNeal, R. H. (ed.). *Resolutions and decisions of the Communist Party of the Soviet Union*. Toronto, Buffalo, 1974.

Meller, V. L. & A. M. Pankratova. *Rabochee dvizhenie v 1917 goda*. Moscow, Leningrad, 1926.

Miliukov, P. *Political memoirs 1905–1917*. Ann Arbor, 1967.

—*The Russian revolution*, [3 vols]. Gulf Breeze, 1978–1987.

Munck, J. L. *The Kornilov revolt: a critical examination of the sources and research*. Aarhus, 1987.

Neuberger, J. *Hooliganism: crime, culture and power in St. Petersburg, 1900–1914*. Berkeley, 1993.

Neumann, J. A note on the winter of the Kronstadt sailors' uprising in 1921. *Soviet Studies* 44(1), 1992.

Nove, A. *An economic history of the* USSR *1917–1993*. Harmondsworth, 1992.

Orlovsky, D. State building in the civil war era: the role of the lower-middle strata. In *Party, state and society in the Russian civil war: explorations in social history*, D. P. Koenker *et al.* (eds). Bloomington, 1989, pp. 180–209.

Pares, B. *The fall of the Russian monarchy: a study of the evidence*. London, 1939.

Perrie, M. The peasants. In *Society and politics in the Russian revolution*, R. Service (ed.). London, 1992.

Pershin, P. N. *Agrarnaia revoliutsiia v Rossii: kniga 2. Agrarnye preobrazovaniia velikoi oktiabr'skoi sotsialisticheskoi revoliutsii (1917–1918 gg.)*. Moscow, 1966.

Pethybridge, R. *The spread of the Russian Revolution. Essays on 1917*. London, 1972.

Pipes, R. *The Bolsheviks in power*. London, 1993.

—*The formation of the Soviet Union: communism and nationalism 1917–1923*. Cambridge, 1964.

—*The Russian Revolution 1899–1919*. London, 1990.

Pipes, R. (ed.) *Revolutionary Russia: a symposium*. Cambridge MA, 1968.

Possony, S. T. *Lenin: the compulsive revolutionary*. Chicago 1964, rev. edn, London, 1966.

Rabinowitch, A. *The Bolsheviks come to power*. London, 1979.
—*Prelude to revolution*. Bloomington, 1968.
Radkey, O. H. *The agrarian foes of Bolshevism*. New York, 1958.
—*Russia goes to the polls: the election to the All-Russian Constituent Assembly, 1917*. Ithaca, 1989.
—*The unknown civil war in Soviet Russia, a study of the Green movement in the Tambov region, 1920–1*. Stanford, 1976.
Raleigh, D. J. *Revolution on the Volga: 1917 in Saratov*. Ithaca, 1985.
Rashin, A. G. *Naselenie Rossii za 100 let (1811–1913gg.)*. Moscow, 1956.
Raskolnikov, F. F. *Kronstadt and Petrograd in 1917*. London, 1982.
Read, C. *Culture and power in revolutionary Russia: the intelligentsia and the transition from tsarism to communism*. London, 1990.
—Values, substitutes and institutions: the cultural dimension of the Bolshevik dictatorship. In *Prelude to catastrophe: revolution, civil wars and the new order in the Russian Empire*, R. Pipes & V. Brovkin (eds). New Haven & London, 1996.
—Labour and socialism in tsarist Russia. In *Labour and socialist movements in Europe before 1914*, D. Geary (ed.). Oxford, New York, Munich, 1983.
Reed, John. *Ten days that shook the world*. New York, 1919.
Remington, T. F. *Building socialism in Lenin's Russia: ideology and industrial organization, 1917–21*. Pittsburgh, 1984.
Revoliutsionnoe dvizhenie v Rossii. Dokumenty i materialy, [5 vols]. Moscow 1958–63.
Rigby, T. H. *Communist party membership in the* USSR, *1917–1967*. Princeton, 1968.
—*Lenin's government: Sovnarkom (1917–1922)*. Cambridge, 1979.
Rogger, Hans. *Russia in the age of modernization and revolution 1881–1917*. London, New York, 1983.
Roobol, W. H. *Tsereteli: a democrat in the Russian Revolution*. The Hague, 1976.
Rosenberg, W. *The liberals in the Russian Revolution: the Constitutional Democratic Party, 1917–1921*. Princeton, 1974.
—Russian labor and Bolshevik power: social dimensions of protest in Petrograd after October. In *The workers' revolution in Russia in 1917: the view from below*, D. Kaiser (ed.). Cambridge, 1987.
Rumiantsev, E. D. *Rabochii klass povolzh'ia v gody pervoi mirovoi voiny i fevral'skoi revoliutsii 1914–1917gg*. Kazan', 1989.
Russell, Bertrand. *The practice and theory of Bolshevism*. London, 1920.
Sakwa, R. *Soviet communists in power: a study of Moscow during the civil war 1918–1921*. London, 1988.
Schapiro, L. B. *The Communist Party of the Soviet Union*. London, 1963.
—*The origins of the Communist autocracy: political opposition in the Soviet state: first phase, 1917–22*. London, 1955.
—*1917: the Russian Revolutions and the origin of present-day communism*. London, 1984.
Seregny, Scott J. *Russian teachers and peasant revolution: the politics of education in 1905*. Bloomington, Indianapolis, 1989.
Serge, Victor. *Memoirs of a revolutionary* (trans. and ed. by P. Sedgwick). Oxford, 1963.
Service, R. *The Bolshevik Party in revolution 1917–1923*. London, 1979.
—*Lenin: a political life*, [3 vols]. London, 1985, 1991, 1994.
—*The Russian Revolution 1900–1927*. London, 1986.
Service, R. (ed.). *Society and politics in the Russian revolution*. London, 1992.
Seton-Watson, H. *The Russian empire 1801–1917*. Oxford, 1967.
Shanin, T. *The roots of otherness: Russia's turn of century*, [2 vols]. London, 1985, 1986.
Shepelev, L. E. *Tsarizm i burzhuaziia v 1904–1914gg. Problemy torgovo–promyshlennoi*

politiki. Leningrad, 1987.

Shliapnikov, A. *On the eve of 1917*. London, 1982.

Shukman, H. (ed.). *The Blackwell encyclopaedia of the Russian Revolution*. Oxford, 1988.

Sirianni, C. *Workers' control and socialist democracy*. London, 1982.

Slusser, R. *Stalin in October: the man who missed the revolution*. Baltimore, 1987.

Smirnov, N. N. *Tretii vserossiiskii s"ezd sovetov: istoriia sozyva, sostav, rabota*. Leningrad, 1988.

Smith, S. A. *Red Petrograd: revolution in the factories 1917–18*. Cambridge, 1983.

Solov'ev, Iu. V. *Samoderzhavie i dvorianstvo v kontse XIX veka*. Leningrad, 1973.

Spring, D. (ed.). *European landed elites in the nineteenth century*. Baltimore, London, 1977.

Startsev, V. I. *Krakh Kerenshchiny*. Leningrad, 1982.

—*Russkaia burzhuaziia i samoderzhavie v 1905–1917gg. Bor'ba vokrug "otvetsvennogo ministerstva" i "pravitel'stva doveriia"*. Leningrad, 1977.

Steinberg, Mark. *Moral communities; the culture of class relations in the Russian printing industry 1867-1907*. Berkeley, Los Angeles, Oxford, 1992.

Stites, R. Iconoclastic currents in the Russian revolution: destroying and preserving the past. In *Bolshevik culture: experiment and order in the Russian revolution*, A. Gleason *et al.* (eds). Bloomington, Indianapolis, 1985.

Stone, N. *The eastern front 1914–17*. London, 1975.

Sukhanov, N. N. *The Russian revolution: an eyewitness account* (trans. and ed. by J. Carmichael), [2 vols]. New York, 1962.

Suny, R. *The Baku commune 1917–1918*. Princeton, 1972.

—*The revenge of the past: nationalism, revolution and the collapse of the Soviet Union*. Princeton, 1994.

—Toward a social history of the October Revolution. *American Historical Review* 88, pp. 31–52, 1993.

Swain, G. *Russian social democracy and the legal labour movement 1906–14*. London, 1983.

—*The origins of the Russian civil war*. London, New York, 1996.

The Bolsheviks and the October revolution: minutes of the Central Committee of the Russian Social–Democratic Labour Party (Bolsheviks) August 1917–February 1918 (trans. by A. Bone). London, 1974.

Trotsky, L. *History of the Russian Revolution*, [3 vols]. New York, 1932.

—*How the revolution armed: military writings and speeches*, [5 vols] (trans. by B. Pearce). London, 1979–1981.

—*Terrorism and Communism*. London, 1975.

Velidov, A. S. *Krasnaia kniga VChK*, [2 vols]. Moscow, 1920. Reprinted Moscow, 1990.

Velikaia oktiabr'skaia sotsialisticheskaia revoliutsiia: khronika sobytii v chetyrekh tomakh. Moscow, 1959.

Vernadsky, G. & S. Pushkarev. *A source book for Russian history from early times to 1917*, vol. 3. New Haven, London 1972.

Voline, *The unknown revolution 1917–21*. Detroit and Chicago, n.d.

Volkogonov, D. *Lenin: life and legacy* (trans. and ed. by H. Shukman). London, 1994.

—*Stalin: triumph and tragedy*. London, 1991.

Vulliamy, C. E. & A. L. Hynes. *The Red archives: Russian state papers and other documents relating to the years 1915–18*. London, 1929.

Wade, R. *Red Guards and workers' militia in the Russian Revolution*. Stanford, 1984.

—*The Russian search for peace: February–October 1917*. Stanford, 1969.

Weber, G. & H. Weber. *Lenin: life and works*. London, 1980.

White, H. 1917 in the rear garrisons. In *Economy and society in Russia and the Soviet Union, 1860–1930*, L. Edmondson & P. Watson, (eds). New York, 1992, pp. 152–68.

White, J. *The Russian Revolution 1917–1921: a short history*. London, New York, Melbourne, Auckland, 1994.

Wildman, A. *The end of the Russian imperial army*, vol. 1, Princeton, 1980, and vol. 2, Princeton, 1987.

Williams, B. *The Russian Revolution (1917–1921)*. Oxford, 1987.

Worobec, C. *Peasant Russia: family and community in the post-emancipation period*. Princeton, 1991.

Yaney, G. L. *The urge to mobilize: agrarian reform in Russia, 1861–1930*. Chicago, Urbana, 1982.

Yarmolinsky, A. *Road to revolution: a century of Russian radicalism*. New York, 1962.

Zhilin, A. P. *Poslednee nastuplenie; (iyun' 1917 godu)*. Moscow, 1983.

Index

INDEX